X Marks the Spot

New Perspectives on Maritime History and Nautical Archaeology

Florida A&M University, Tallahassee
Florida Atlantic University, Boca Raton
Florida Gulf Coast University, Ft. Myers
Florida International University, Miami
Florida State University, Tallahassee
University of Central Florida, Orlando
University of Florida, Gainesville
University of North Florida, Jacksonville
University of South Florida, Tampa
University of West Florida, Pensacola

New Perspectives on Maritime History and Nautical Archaeology
James C. Bradford and Gene A. Smith, Series Editors

James C. Bradford
Department of History
Texas A&M University
College Station, TX 77843-4236
979-845-7165
jcbradford@tamu.edu

Gene A. Smith
Department of History
TCU Box 297260
Texas Christian University
Fort Worth, TX 76129
817-257-6295
gsmith@tcu.edu

This series is devoted to providing lively and important books that cover the spectrum of maritime history and nautical archaeology broadly defined. It includes works that focus on the role of canals, rivers, lakes, and oceans in history; on the economic, military, and political use of those waters; and upon the people, communities, and industries that support maritime endeavors. Limited neither by geography nor time, volumes in the series contribute to the overall understanding of maritime history and can be read with profit by both general readers and specialists.

Maritime Heritage of the Cayman Islands, by Roger C. Smith (1999; first paperback edition, 2000)

The Three German Navies: Dissolution, Transition, and New Beginnings, 1945–1960, by Douglas C. Peifer (2002)

The Rescue of the Gale Runner: Death, Heroism, and the U.S. Coast Guard, by Dennis L. Noble (2002)

Brown Water Warfare: The U.S. Navy in Riverine Warfare and the Emergence of a Tactical Doctrine, 1775–1970, by R. Blake Dunnavent (2003)

Sea Power in the Medieval Mediterranean: The Catalan-Aragonese Fleet in the War of the Sicilian Vespers, by Lawrence V. Mott (2003)

An Admiral for America: Sir Peter Warren, Vice-Admiral of the Red, 1703–1752, by Julian Gwyn (2004)

Maritime History as World History, edited by Daniel Finamore (2004)

Counterpoint to Trafalgar: The Anglo-Russian Invasion of Naples, 1805–1806, by William Henry Flayhart III (first paperback edition, 2004)

Life and Death on the Greenland Patrol, 1942, by Thaddeus D. Novak, edited by P. J. Capelotti (2005)

X Marks the Spot: The Archaeology of Piracy, edited by Russell K. Skowronek and Charles R. Ewen (2006; first paperback edition. 2007)

Industrializing American Shipbuilding: The Transformation of Ship Design and Construction, 1820–1920, by William H. Thiesen (2006)

Admiral Lord Keith and the Naval War Against Napoleon, by Kevin D. McCranie (2006)

Commodore John Rodgers: Paragon of the Early American Navy, by John H. Schroeder (2006)

Borderland Smuggling: Patriots, Loyalists, and Illicit Trade in the Northeast, 1783–1820, by Joshua M. Smith (2006)

Brutality on Trial: "Hellfire" Pedersen, "Fighting" Hansen, and The Seamen's Act of 1915, by E. Kay Gibson (2006)

Uriah Levy: Reformer of the Antebellum, by Ira Dye (2006)

Crisis at Sea: The United States Navy in European Waters in World War I, by William Still (2006)

Chinese Junks on the Pacific: Views from a Different Deck, by Hans K. Van Tilburg (2007)

X
Marks the Spot

The Archaeology of Piracy

Edited by Russell K. Skowronek
and Charles R. Ewen

Foreword by James C. Bradford and Gene A. Smith, Series Editors

University Press of Florida
Gainesville/Tallahassee/Tampa/Boca Raton
Pensacola/Orlando/Miami/Jacksonville/Ft. Myers

12 11 10 09 08 07   6 5 4 3 2 1

A record of cataloging-in-publication data is available from the Library of Congress
ISBN 978-0-8130-3079-1

The University Press of Florida is the scholarly publishing agency for the State Univer-
sity System of Florida, comprising Florida A&M University, Florida Atlantic Univer-
sity, Florida Gulf Coast University, Florida International University, Florida State Uni-
versity, University of Central Florida, University of Florida, University of North
Florida, University of South Florida, and University of West Florida.

University Press of Florida
15 Northwest 15th Street
Gainesville, FL 32611-2079
http://www.upf.com

This book is dedicated to
our pirate wenches
Gretchen and Peg "Leg"
. . . for indulging us.

And to our pirate whelps
Kate, Madeline, and Olga
. . . for gamely following us through this adventure.

Contents

Figures

Tables

Foreword

Water is unquestionably the most important natural feature on earth. By volume the world's oceans constitute 99 percent of the planet's living space; in fact, the surface of the Pacific Ocean alone is larger than the total of all the land surfaces. Water is as vital to life as air. Indeed, to test whether the moon or other planets can sustain life, NASA looks for signs of water. The story of human development is inextricably linked to the oceans, seas, lakes, and rivers that dominate the earth's surface. The University Press of Florida's series *New Perspectives on Maritime History and Nautical Archaeology* is devoted to exploring the significance of the earth's water while providing lively and important books that cover the spectrum of maritime history and nautical archaeology broadly defined. The series includes works that focus on the role of canals, rivers, lakes, and oceans in history; the economic, military, and political use of those waters; and the people, communities, and industries that support maritime endeavors. Limited by neither geography nor time, volumes in the series contribute to the overall understanding of maritime history and can be read with profit by both general readers and specialists.

Piracy, the unlawful taking of ships, cargoes, sailors, and passengers for profit, has been the scourge of maritime trade and travel since man first ventured to sea. Though almost universally condemned, piracy in its various forms has flourished in all parts of the world for thousands of years and continues today, especially in and around the East Indies and the west coast of South America. In no place and at no time was piracy as prevalent as it was in the West Indies and eastern North America during "The Golden Age of Piracy"—a period broadly spanning the years 1650 to 1750. During the same era pirates of European origin also plied their trade in the Indian Ocean where islands such as Madagascar and Mauritius served as haunts in much the same way as Jamaica and Honduras did in the Caribbean. Piracy generally retreats before the forces of strong government and did so in both locales. Yet the unrest of the Latin American wars for independence and the relative weakness of the United States government along the Mississippi River allowed pirates to ply their trade in those areas well into the nineteenth century.

Given the often gruesome nature of their activities, its is surprising that the pirates of these regions have become the attention of so much romantic folklore and acquired so much glamour. Perhaps the lure of wealth that led individuals to become pirates and the independent lives they are depicted as living coincides with the dreams of many people of becoming rich. Perhaps the pirate's rebellious streak attracts those who desire to escape the ordinary or to defy authority. The tropical locales habituated by pirates also appear attractive to people living in cooler climes. Whatever the reason, pirates have been the subject of every form of media, and historians and writers have eagerly sought information of all sorts concerning pirates, their vessels, their lives, and their treasures.

When nautical or underwater archaeology emerged as a new scientific discipline during the later half of the twentieth century, its practitioners soon offered new insights into the world of the pirates. The discovering, excavation, and documenting of pirate vessels and their contents—such as Blackbeard's *Queen Anne's Revenge*, Christopher Condent's *Fiery Dragon*, Samuel Bellamy's *Whydah*, and John Bowen's *Speaker*—have led to significant information about both the ships and the pirates who employed the vessels in the commission of their crimes. Both underwater and land excavations of sites at Port Royal, Jamaica, the mouth of the Belize River on the Bay of Honduras, Jean Lafitte's base on Barataria Bay, Louisiana, and the English logwood settlement at Roatan in the Bay Islands, Honduras, have cast additional light on the lives of the pirates who frequented the sites or used them as bases for their operations. In the following chapters the archaeologists who explored these sites assess their contents, offer solid conclusions, and draw interesting inferences concerning the lives of pirates and the objects, including the ships they possessed and employed. Others discuss the history of piracy on the Ohio and the Mississippi rivers and speculate about the characteristics of the remains of vessels captured by pirates; assess the role that archaeology can play in determining the effects of piracy on law-abiding residents of the Caribbean during the Spanish colonial period; and analyze the difficulties encountered when interpreting the archaeological record and relating it to pirates and piracy. A concluding essay traces the evolution of the image of pirates in modern America. Taken together the chapters provide a status report on the contributions of archaeology to the history of piracy, an assessment of the problems of linking archaeological information to the study of piracy, as well as insights into the image of pirates in popular culture. Through these contributions we learn that "X" rarely, if ever, marks the spot.

James C. Bradford and Gene A. Smith
Series Editors

Preface

Pirates and piracy have been a particular fascination of ours since we were small boys. The fascination for us (unlike many boys) never waned. After eating at the Pirates' House in Savannah, Georgia, as children, we were convinced that this was the greatest restaurant in the world. Twenty years later at an archaeological conference in Savannah we discovered that it was just as great (possibly even better, since we had not noticed the bar upstairs on our first visit!) (figure P.1). While researching this book we found that many adults still loved the images of pirates from their childhoods. How pirates came to be such cherished memories began to intrigue us almost as much as the archaeology associated with their sites.

Horatio Alger stories about little guys making it big in spite of the odds or government interference are a cornerstone of this world view. In the era before the passage of the Abandoned Shipwreck Act, Mel Fisher, an Indiana-born chicken rancher, stood up against the governments of Florida and the United States and won the rights to the *Atocha*. For archaeologists this was an act of piracy of the archaeological record, but the public lionized Fisher for gaining the upper hand on the ivory tower academics and big government. A decade later Gerald Klein lost his case against the United States government to salvage HMS *Fowey* in the waters of Biscayne National Park. This was seen as a landmark case protecting shipwrecks for the "little guys," the people of the United States who visit and enjoy the national parks (Skowronek et al. 1987). Are treasure salvors the "good guys" or are they the thugs that take advantage of the "little guys"? And what of pirates in the past? Was Jean Lafitte a smuggler and ne'er-do-well or was he closer to Yul Brynner's 1958 depiction in *The Buccaneer*: the great ally of the United States who turned the tide at the Battle of New Orleans?

Similarly, what of the infamous Blackbeard (Edward Teach)? In 1837 Charles Ellms (1996:209) described his "life, atrocities, and bloody death"; yet, less than a century later, Ben Dixon MacNeill (1958:58–64) recorded a very different image of the man that survived on the nearby Outer Banks of North Carolina. Two hundred years after his death, there was "a very lively belief that Captain Teach was a right considerable fellow." He was said to maintain a respectable house in Bath and to make gifts to the church and to the first library in North Carolina. Perhaps most importantly, "he preferred the hospitality of the simple folk across the Inlet from Portsmouth to the brawling thieves who built their warehouses and defrauded" the local Hatterasmen. "And, anyhow, what if he was a pirate? He was a respectable pirate and a good neighbor when he was around the community" (MacNeill 1958:61). Oral histories collected by MacNeill detail Teach's bravery and the unfair advantage of Lieutenant Robert Maynard's surprise attack. Teach died in the battle, and it is reported that his head hung from the

Figure P.1. Souvenir mug from the Pirates' House restaurant, Savannah, Georgia. Photo by Russell K. Skowronek.

bowsprit of Maynard's ship on its return to Virginia (Rankin 1960:58–59). The accounts suggest that following the battle Maynard fled the region for fear of reprisals at the hands of the local inhabitants.

"'He slunk out of here,' an Islander would say, near two and a half centuries afterward, and he says it as if it happened no longer ago than last week" (MacNeill 1958:63). MacNeill (1958:63) goes on to relate that many have wondered what happened to Teach's head and that he still reportedly haunts Teach's Hole, where the battle took place. Thirty-eight years after these accounts were published, the wreck that was alleged to be Blackbeard's *Queen Anne's Revenge* was found off Beaufort Inlet, North Carolina. Two years later the story of Teach's ghost materialized again, along with a story that his head had been converted into a silver-sided punch bowl that eventually disappeared. It was said that he could not enter Hell until he found his head (Blackman 1998:119–23). How did these myths come into being?

Pirates in Popular Culture

During the late nineteenth and early twentieth centuries most of the classics of pirate fiction were penned, each with the dichotomy of good and bad. They included William Gilbert and Arthur Sullivan's spoof of young women fantasizing about dashing pirates in the *Pirates of Penzance* (1879); James Barrie's *Peter Pan*, with the evil Captain Hook and the comical Mr. Smee (1904); Rafael Sabatini's *The Sea Hawk* (1915), *Captain Blood* (1922), and the *Black Swan* (1932); Howard Pyle's magnificently illustrated and written *The Book of Pirates* (1921); and the all-time great *Treasure Island* by Robert Louis Stevenson (1883). Stevenson's story is a perennial favorite that has appeared in its original form and in abridged form, including a comic book version in the Classics Illustrated series (Boyette 1991). Since 1918 more than ten versions of the story have made it to film, including 1996's *Muppet Treasure Island* from Jim Henson Productions; Disney's 2002 "update" *Treasure Planet*; and an episode of the PBS *Wishbone* television series titled *Salty Dog* (Rocca 1995) and the later book of the same title by Brad Strickland (1997), which cast a Jack Russell terrier in the role of Jim Hawkins. Each version depicts the epitome of scary pirates—Blind Pew, Black Dog, and Israel Hands—and the rough-hewn pirates with a heart of gold—the Captain or Billy Bones and the legendary Long John Silver.

In the first sixty years of the twentieth century no fewer than 100 movies and television programs were made on the topic of pirates (Parish 1995). John Ford's 1963 epic *How the West Was Won* and Disney's *Davy Crockett and the River Pirates* (see Wagner and McCorvie, this volume) depict the depredations of pirates on the weak westward-bound pioneers, yet the overall image of pirates is not in the least tarnished. Mass production and the shared experience of having little choice in television viewing meant that children across the country grew up with similar toys, birthday parties, and images of "cowboys and Indians" and pirates. For a few dollars children could play with American-made, realistically modeled rubber pirates (figure P.2) and a plastic pirate ship named the *Jolly Roger* (Ideal Toys 1-3974), complete with shooting cannon and a plank for mis-

Figure P.2. Toys in the 1950s and 1960s were realistic and evoked the movies. Figures by Ideal Toys. Photo by Russell K. Skowronek.

Figure P.3. Forerunner of the action figure (3½ inches tall). Photo by
Stephan Skowronek.

creants to walk. The ship would roll on the floor or float in the bath. There were
forerunners of today's action figures. Fearsome rubber pirates 3½ inches tall
came equipped with removable cutlasses, pistols, telescopes, and tricorn hats
(figure P.3). Board games such as the *Sunken Treasure Game* (1948), *Pirate and
Traveler: A World Geography Game* (1953), and *Trade Winds* (1960), to name
but a few (figure P.4), reinforced the images of television and film by bringing
identifiable pirate ships, recoverable lost treasure, and world geography with
pirate lairs into the kitchens and living rooms of America. Well-told stories could
make a profit even for the recording industry. United Artists Records created a
series of long-play albums titled *Tale Spinners for Children* that included
Robinson Crusoe and *Treasure Island*, while others enlisted famous radio and
television actors such as William Bendix (1959) to sing and tell *Famous Pirate
Stories* about Henry Morgan, Captain Kidd, Blackbeard, and Jean Lafitte—all
for less than a dollar.

Pirates are also part of America's sporting scene. In Major League Baseball the
Pittsburgh Pirates have been in the National League for more than a century.
Founded at the beginning of the twentieth century, East Carolina University
(North Carolina) sporting teams are known as the Pirates. Two professional
football teams, the Tampa Bay Buccaneers and the Oakland Raiders, have
adopted pirate images as part of their names and logos. The "Raider Nation" is
omnipresent in the San Francisco Bay Area, where seemingly every other mini-
van, pickup truck, and automobile sports a large silver and gray decal of a football player with an eye patch superimposed on crossed swords.

Figure P.4. Board games in the late 1940s, 1950s, and 1960s often had a pirate or treasure theme. Photo by Leslie J. Skowronek.

Finally, there was the print industry. The Gilberton Company of New York found an important market niche in its Classics Illustrated series of comic books, with the catch line "Endorsed by Educators." Children could purchase for fifteen cents a comic-book version of Stevenson's *Treasure Island* or Cecil B. DeMille's 1958 film *The Buccaneer* (figure P.5).

For the "Boomers" *The Buccaneer* would leave an indelible mark. The rampant nationalism of the early Cold War years had Americans celebrating past triumphs over seemingly overwhelming odds, such as the Battle of New Orleans in 1815. The role of Lafitte and his pirate compatriots is celebrated by Bendix and in Yul Brynner's interpretation in the 1958 film. The "democratic" way of the pirates is amplified as the reason they came to the aid of the democratic United States. This is another watershed in the perception of what being a

Figure P.5. Classics Illustrated brought pirate stories to life in a comic book format. Photo by Russell K. Skowronek.

pirate signified. A harbinger of that transformation was played out by the Boy Scouts of America. In 1954 the BSA published for younger scouts the *Bear Cub Scout Book*. In it the boys learned about flag history, bike and swimming safety, a variety of craft activities, nature, and wildlife conservation. This version was used through 1966. In 1967 the book was significantly revised, perhaps to reflect the deepening of the Cold War, to include sections on "American Freedom," "Religious Activities," and "American Folklore." Scouts learned that folklore tells us about "the life and spirit of our forefathers" (Boy Scouts of America 1967:62). The same page where Molly Pitcher, Johnny Appleseed, John Henry, and Daniel Boone are mentioned as "some of the heroes in your state" also included Blackbeard for North Carolina. Beyond a handful of Hatterasmen, it is difficult to imagine Blackbeard as a "hero" worthy of emulation by young boys.

Pirates have continued to be a part of the lives of the Boomers' children and grandchildren, although the caricatures may be further caricatured. Aspects of the "pirate experience" remain largely unchanged from the 1950s. Children still have pirate-theme birthday parties, dress up as pirates for Halloween, pretend to be pirates, and read about pirates (for example, Bulloch and James 1997; Thompson and Macintosh 1996). Although they are no longer as realistic and will not float in the bathtub, there are still plastic pirate ships and pirates (made in Denmark by Lego and in China by Fisher-Price, Inc.) (figure P.6), in addition

Figure P.6. At the turn of the twenty-first century children's toys had become less realistic and more caricatured. Pirate ship and crew by Fisher-Price. Photo by Russell K. Skowronek.

to pop-up paper pirate ships and crews (Hawkins 1994), sticker picture pirate adventures (Petruccio 1995), and maze books to find treasure (Moreau 1999). Children can have a stuffed bear sporting a three-cornered hat adorned with a skull and cross bones, with an embroidery of Blackbeard and a pirate ship on its chest. The owners of such stuffed animals living in the San Francisco Bay Area might spend their summer attending the "Stanford Pirates Camp." For $395 children fence, hunt for treasure, and play "pirate games."

One of the most popular cartoons of the new millennium, *Spongebob Square-pants*, often incorporates pirate themes into its episodes. "Who lives in a pine-apple under the sea?" has replaced "Away hey blow the man down" as the most recognizable sea chantey. The images in the show (such as the sinister Flying Dutchman and the pirate-talking Mr. Krabs) have changed little from those of a century ago. Many more of their images come from Walt Disney Productions. Disney's re-release of the 1953 animation of *Peter Pan* in theaters and later on videotape and DVD has meant that two new generations have been part of the experience.

Another aspect of the Disney phenomenon may be traceable to a creation that premiered at the 1964 New York World's Fair. Dubbed "Audio-Animatronics," it was a way to bring manikins to life. Four years later the Pirates of the Caribbean attraction opened between Adventureland and Frontierland in Disneyland. It had everything: skeletons, treasure, fierce pirates, comical pirates, pirates being chased by women, pirates chasing women, and a drunken debauch (Disney 1968). Clearly, this was an attraction with grown-ups in mind. It can only be rivaled by the Treasure Island Casino and Resort in Las Vegas, where visitors on the strip can watch a pirate and a Royal Navy ship fight it out several times a day. True to the spirit of Las Vegas, the pirates always win.

Thirty-five years after the opening of the Disneyland adventure, Walt Disney Pictures brought the "ride" to the movie theaters with its *Pirates of the Caribbean: The Curse of the Black Pearl*. It showed simultaneously in more than 3,200 theaters and earned $13.5 million on its opening day in July 2003 (Hernandez 2003). By the end of October that same year, it had grossed in excess of $300 million.

The literacy that helped create the fictional pirate has come full-circle. Pirates, the thieves and murderers of the past, are now seen as "cool" (Tudor 2003). On September 19 the United States observes "National Talk-Like-a-Pirate Day" (Barry 2002), and Barnes and Noble Bookstores across the country had displays of pirate books with a green and cream sign boldly proclaiming, "Ahoy, Matey! September 19th is National Talk-Like-a-Pirate Day." In nearly every exchange with the authors of this book, whether via email or in person, someone would inevitably insert an "Aaargh!" or an "Avast matey!" into the conversation. Indeed, it would seem that even the serious pirate scholar cannot completely rise above popular culture.

In our archaeological theory courses today we teach that our interpretations of the past are heavily influenced by the present. It is in the milieu just discussed that our live archaeologists will spin their yarns. We will attempt to defy the pirate lore that "dead men tell no tales," however, and use archaeology to present a glimpse of what it really meant to be a pirate.

Acknowledgments

The editors of this book are indebted to the authors and many other people who helped make it a reality. In a project such as this someone will always be overlooked; for all such omissions we plead *mea culpa* and beg your forgiveness for the oversight.

Specifically, we wish to thank Meredith Morris-Babb of the University Press of Florida for proposing this volume and divining the ideal title. We further wish to thank John Byram, associate director and editor-in-chief of the University Press of Florida, for guiding us through the process and giving us insightful comments on earlier versions of the volume. In that same vein we wish to thank the two anonymous reviewers of the manuscript for their careful readings and comments. If we have learned one thing through all our professional years, it is that there has never been a manuscript that has not benefited from revisions and editing. This leads us to Michele Fiyak-Burkley. As project editor, she smoothed the edges and brought this book together—thank you. We also thank our good friend Anita Cohen-Williams—archaeologist and librarian—for her masterful indexing of this book.

This volume did not leap fully formed from the minds of the editors. When charged with this admittedly interesting project, we were faced with the dilemma of finding researchers who are or have been involved in such endeavors. Some were easy to find because of their reputations (Donny Hamilton, Lawrence Babits); their location in one of our home states, North Carolina (Wayne Lusardi, Mark Wilde-Ramsing); or old graduate school connections and war stories told through the years at multiple Society for Historical Archaeology meetings (Christopher Hamilton, David McBride). Our old friend and classmate Stephen McBride suggested Mark J. Wagner and Mary R. McCorvie as *the* people to contact for the topic of "River Pirates." Patrick Lizé, Joan Exnicios, and John de Bry were found the old-fashioned way—through sleuthing.

In 2001 *National Geographic* published a map with information on pirates. It was there that we first learned about the *Speaker*. An email query to Mary R. Lamberton of the National Geographic Society provided us with the reference to Lizé's article in the *International Journal of Nautical Archaeology*. An Internet search helped us find Patrick in Portugal.

If there was one guiding framework for this volume it was William Bendix's 1959 recording of *Famous Pirate Stories* about Blackbeard, Henry Morgan, Captain Kidd, and Jean Lafitte. How could we have a book without at least two of the most famous pirates! The adage about it being a small world was never so true as in our search for a Lafitte scholar. In the fall of 2001 we wrote to the National Park Service. Terry Childs of the NPS's Archeology and Ethnography Program suggested that we contact Bennie Keel at the Southeast Archeological Center in Tallahassee. Simultaneously David P. Muth, chief of the Division of Resource Stewardship and Planning at Jean Lafitte National Historical Park and Preserve, suggested that we contact Edwin Lyon of the Army Corps of Engineers,

New Orleans District, regarding its work at Grand Terre Island. An e-mail to Dr. Lyon put us in touch with Joan Exnicios. We had met Joan twenty years earlier in Tallahassee. Indeed, it was a small world: we had a Lafitte scholar.

The final piece of the puzzle came in January 2003 at the Society for Historical Archaeology meetings in Providence, Rhode Island. We strongly believe in the power of visiting sites when the opportunity presents itself. Cape Cod and the *Whydah* museum were two hours from the conference site. Through subfreezing temperature and a blowing snowstorm we drove the length of the cape to Provincetown. There on a pier was the Whydah Museum and our host, Ken Kinkor. Ken opened the museum and gave us an insider's tour. We were amazed and pleased that we had made the journey. At the end of the museum there was a discussion of the search for Captain Kidd's *Adventure Galley*. As we left the warmth of the museum and faced the icy roads back to Providence, all of our synapses were firing. By the time we returned to our respective universities we had decided to contact Ken about the Kidd project. He put us in touch with John de Bry.

Many other people have helped us through this project. James P. Delgado graciously provided us with many insights regarding the effect of pirate attacks on communities such as Panama Vieja and victims, including evidence from CSS *Alabama*, *Florida*, and *Shenandoah* and the World War I Imperial German Navy ship *Dresden*. Jim has always been a font of information whenever we have asked for his help.

Our research on piracy in the Pacific was greatly aided by Eusebio Z. (Bong) Dizon of the Philippine National Museum, S. Henry Totanes of Ateneo de Manila University, and Miriam Stark of the University of Hawaii. The topic of modern piracy could not have been tackled without the support of Jayant Abhyankar, deputy director of the International Chamber of Commerce International Maritime Bureau, who graciously supplied us with summary statistics for global piracy. We are further indebted to the International Chamber of Commerce Commercial Crime Services "Weekly Piracy Report" for its complete coverage of this matter.

We were also aided by a number of other individuals who provided us with information, including George R. Fischer of Tallahassee, Florida, and J. Barto Arnold of Texas A&M University and Tom Oertling of Galveston, Texas, for their help tracking down Lafitte's "Campechy." Special thanks are due to Jeff Modzelewski, president of the Lafitte Society of Galveston, Texas, and Sheldon Kindall of Galveston for information on Lafitte in Texas.

Thanks to Demetra Kalogrides and Jessica Crewse of Santa Clara University for typing and formatting a number of the chapters, Patricia Whittier of East Lansing, Michigan, for reading and commenting on part of the manuscript, and Laura Seifert of East Carolina University for compiling the references into a single coherent whole.

Finally, we wish to thank Rob Ewen of Pisgah Forest, North Carolina, and Lester, Helen, and Leslie Skowronek of Hendersonville, North Carolina, for their hospitality during the revision of the book. Extra thanks are extended to Leslie Skowronek for proofreading the text for the second printing of this book.

I

Introduction

Charles R. Ewen

Archaeology is the search for fact. Not truth. If it's truth you're interested in, Dr. Tyree's philosophy class is right down the hall. So forget any ideas you've got about lost cities, exotic travel, and digging up the world. We do not follow maps to buried treasure and "X" never, ever, marks the spot!
—Indiana Jones

Sometimes it does.
—The authors of this book

Pirate! The word conjures images that were formed during childhood: bad men who are somewhat scary but not real enough or scary enough to cause most children to lose sleep at night. Everyone who writes about "real" pirates agrees that this does not portray the truth about pirates. But what is the "truth" about pirates, and will we ever know?

As we will read in several of the following chapters (especially the chapter by Babits, Howard, and Brenckle), most people in this country get their first exposure to piracy in children's literature such as *Peter Pan* and *Treasure Island*. Those first impressions never seem to leave us, despite what we learn later. It is curious that this image is so pervasive, given the relative lack of good recent pirate literature and movies. Although pirates are a staple in historical romances and children's books, they are rare in serious fiction. When they do appear, they are largely derivative of the literature and artwork of Robert Louis Stevenson and Howard Pyle.

Pirates in the cinema are even more stereotypical. It is all down hill after *Captain Blood*, to the point where the viewing public has lost interest and quit watching. This is not just personal opinion but box office fact. Only the recently released *Pirates of the Caribbean* appears to have made any money. Perhaps, since we already know the stories, we do not need to see them repeated on the big screen. And yet we continue to be fascinated by these historical icons.

In addition to romance novels and children's books, there is a third category of literature that deals with pirates: nonfiction historical studies. Dozens, perhaps hundreds, of books that purport to reveal who the pirates really were have been published, with more on the way (including this one!). Even the fictional works on pirates often have addenda that discuss the "true" nature of piracy. The Disney DVD of *Treasure Planet* (an animated loose adaptation of Stevenson's *Treasure Island*) includes bonus material that offers to teach the viewer about historical pirates and their ways.

The problem with trying to characterize historical pirates, though, is that piracy has existed for as long as humans have sailed the seas, wherever there were vessels to be robbed. How do you characterize piracy through time and space? Surely not all of them had eye patches and peg legs. That is the basic question that this book investigates. As archaeologists, we try to dispel popular misconceptions about the past by examining the material record that people have left behind. But is it even possible to recognize a pirate in the archaeological record?

A Pirate's Life for Me!

To look for a pirate, a pirate ship, a pirate hideout, or even evidence of piratical activity, you must first know what you are looking for. What is a pirate? As you progress through this volume, you will notice that there are many terms for pirate (for example, buccaneer, corsair, privateer) that are often used interchangeably when, technically, there are some not-so-subtle differences between them.

A pirate, as defined by Webster's dictionary, is one who commits robbery on the high seas or makes unauthorized use of another's idea or invention. The first definition is most pertinent to this book. A more colorful definition comes from the nineteenth-century *Pirate's Own Book*: "Piracy is an offence against the universal law of society. . . . As, therefore, he has renounced all the benefits of society and government, and has reduced himself to the savage state of nature, by declaring war against all mankind, all mankind must declare war against him" (Maritime Research Society 1924:x). So, in a nutshell, pirates were bad people who robbed ships. Not all those who robbed ships were bad, however—at least not in their country's eyes.

A privateer is an individual licensed to attack enemy shipping. These mariners had a contract with a specific government (a letter of marque), which permitted the bearer to prey upon the shipping of an enemy country and split the prize with the authorizing government. This makes the difference between privateers and pirates a matter of perspective (though I suspect that they would look similar in the archaeological record). Sir Francis Drake was knighted by his government as a hero of the realm, while at the same time he was viewed as a despicable pirate by the Spaniards living in the Caribbean upon whom he preyed. The term "corsair" refers to sea robbers and can apparently be applied to either pirate or privateer. I'm not sure whether this lessens or deepens the confusion.

"Buccaneer" is a corruption of the French *boucanier* and refers to a sort of proto-pirate. When the Spanish abandoned the western third of Hispaniola in the latter half of the sixteenth century, French smugglers filled the vacuum by squatting on the uninhabited area. They made a living by hunting the wild cattle that were plentiful in the region. The meat from these cattle was smoked over grills called *boucans* and sold to passing ships. It was not long before these *boucaniers* supplemented their income by preying upon some of the passing ships. The term later became anglicized into "buccaneer." Tortuga Island, off the northern coast of Haiti, became one of the early pirate lairs in the Caribbean.

A Brief History of Piracy

Given the scope of the topic and the extensive literature available, any synopsis of piracy is bound to leave out certain aspects and even whole arenas of piracy. In this book, for instance, pirates in antiquity, the Barbary pirates, and piracy in the Pacific are not discussed. The archaeology of piracy is not as widespread as piracy itself. The sites that we have been able to glean from the archaeological literature, with the exception of the Kyrenia vessel, which may have been sunk by pirates in the ancient Mediterranean (Katsev 1980, 1987), are primarily products of the "Golden Age of Piracy" and have been excavated by North American or European archaeologists. Therefore the focus of the background history is on the Caribbean, North America, and the Indian Ocean, relying primarily on Angus Konstam's excellent *The History of Pirates* for general historical facts.

The riches that the Spaniards were hauling out of the New World proved an irresistible draw to the masterless men of many nations. The French buccaneers were among the first who systematically harassed Spanish shipping. Early in the seventeenth century they established a stronghold on Tortuga Island off the north coast of Haiti. By the middle of the seventeenth century the ranks of these freebooters included many nationalities and numbered in the thousands.

The seizing of Jamaica by the British in 1655 prompted many of the pirates to relocate their base of operations to Port Royal. The story of this notorious pirate port is discussed in Donny Hamilton's chapter. It was during this time that the likes of Jean L'Olonnais, Sir Henry Morgan, and Sir Francis Drake terrified the Spanish Main. The depredations by these pirates extended to the land as well as the sea, causing the Spaniards to fortify their ports with imposing stone "castles" and sail their treasure fleets in armed convoys (see Skowronek and Ewen, this volume). Even these measures were not entirely successful, however, as evidenced by the sack of Panama Viejo by Henry Morgan in 1671 (Mendizábal 1999).

The end of the seventeenth century ushered in what has come to be known as the Golden Age of Piracy. Though officially discouraged by the European powers, piracy actually increased its scope during the period between 1690 and 1730. The notorious Edward Teach (aka Blackbeard) and Samuel Bellamy spread the terror up the east coast of North America and beyond. Their exploits are described by Mark Wilde-Ramsing, Wayne Lusardi, and Chris Hamilton in this volume. This infamous era drew to a close as the colonial governments in the New World became stronger, with increased peacetime trade.

At the same time when pirates were seeking new plunder up the Atlantic coast of North America, several discovered the rich booty to be had in the Indian Ocean. Captains William Kidd and Christopher Condent (see John de Bry and Patrick Lizé, this volume) preyed upon the treasure-laden ships of the Moghul Empire from their base off the coast of Madagascar. Ironically, it was the pirates' toll on the shipping of the East India Company that brought down the wrath of corporate Britain and essentially ended this pirate reign, or at least that colorful era portrayed in literature. But the scourge of piracy has never really ended; it continues as the bane of honest seafarers to this day (see Skowronek, this volume).

With the distance of history and the softening by children's literature, the atrocities committed by pirates seem less terrible than they actually were. They are more the stuff of scary bedtime stories than actual horrific events. This is no doubt due to the imprinting of the stereotypical image promulgated by childhood stories (see Babits et al. and Skowronek and Ewen, this volume). Terms like "scoundrel," "scalawag," "rogue," and even "cutthroat" do not truly portray the criminal nature of the pirate. Indeed, in today's romance literature, these are regarded as positive characterizations of the leading male characters. Of the pirate books I have recently read, only Peter Benchley's novel *Island* really captured the terror that these men must have inspired. Yet clearly the people of the seventeenth and eighteenth centuries were terrified. That is why an instant death sentence was pronounced on anyone choosing to pursue piracy. Perhaps using the term "terrorist" would equate them more with the murdering thieves that most of them were.

The Archaeology of Piracy

In conducting the research for this book two things became abundantly clear: (1) there is no shortage of historical works about pirates; and (2) there is very little in the archaeological literature about piracy. This was somewhat surprising, in that the recent discovery of what is being touted as the wreck of Blackbeard's flagship has dominated the recent archaeological discussions in North Carolina. When looking beyond this site, however, only a couple of other pirate-related sites came readily to mind. It took some searching to find the few other examples of archaeology being performed on pirate-related sites and still more effort to get their investigators to commit to this volume. Why is this?

History is replete with people trying to find pirate buried treasure. Even though there is virtually no historical record of pirates burying their gold (the historical literature suggests that pirates most often stole commercial cargoes, which they then sold for gold that they promptly spent as fast they could), this has not stopped folks from looking for it.

The Money Pit on Oak Island off Nova Scotia is a good example of a great deal of effort being spent looking for pirate treasure that may not exist. Captain William Kidd, the only pirate who is actually recorded to have buried some treasure, allegedly careened his ships in the area. Couple this with a mysterious booby-trapped pit on the north end of the island and voilà!: millions of dollars and at least ten deaths attributed to treasure-seekers attempting to find pirate booty.

I personally was involved in another, albeit less costly, attempt to locate pirate treasure. A homeowner in coastal Bertie County, North Carolina, contacted me about doing some archaeology at his family's eighteenth-century ancestral home. After an extensive tour of the house and grounds, I asked what the owner had in mind for an archaeological project. I was treated to a somewhat long-winded story about the owner's grandparents, who were "very sober and conservative people, not given to wild tales." To make a long story short, during his grandparents' residence at the house at the turn of the twentieth century, they were periodically visited by gusts of wind and an eerie rattling sound, which traveled through the house and ended at a hollow sycamore tree in the front yard. The homeowner finished his tale with a dramatic pause and then showed me the sycamore in the story. When I appeared nonplussed by this story, he added that it was well known that Blackbeard and other pirates frequented the Albemarle Sound during the early eighteenth century. He believed that the sounds were related to their ghostly visitations. He concluded this thought by looking meaningfully at the sycamore tree. With dawning comprehension I asked if I had been brought in so that I could look for pirate treasure. I must have appeared skeptical (it was all I could do to hide my amusement/outrage), because the owner sheepishly nodded and said that when I put it that way it sounded foolish. I could not disagree; after assuring him that I possessed no technology that would allow me to see any farther beneath the soil than he had dug already, I departed. I have no doubt that my skepticism did not diminish his pirate gold fever one whit.

Any archaeologist who has worked on historic sites has heard these tales of treasure. Sometimes the treasure takes the form of gold-coin–filled mason jars. Sometimes it is buried in secret tunnels beneath historic structures that lead to a nearby river. In the past thirty years of digging on historic sites, however, I have yet to find an actual tunnel or to hear of anyone who has, let alone recovered a jar full of coins more valuable than pennies. Is it because they don't exist or are we "serious archaeologists" not wasting our time looking for them?

Is the hunt for treasure, and by association pirate sites, too popular to interest the professional archaeologist? Even the recent work by Texas A&M at Port Royal has downplayed the popular pirate angle. I had to promise Donny Hamilton that he could write the "rest of the story" of Port Royal, sans pirates, before he would consent to contribute to this volume.

Curiously, the popular appeal of archaeology has been a problem for archaeologists. Until recently, any academic who wrote for the popular press was seen as having "sold out" and seeking media attention. Perhaps more importantly, publishing in the popular press (and I include *Archaeology* magazine and *National Geographic* here) did nothing to further the academic archaeologist's pursuit of tenure and promotion, so there was little incentive for the academic archaeologist to pursue sensational sites like pirate shipwrecks. Cultural resource management (CRM) archaeologists did not dig pirate sites either, unless they happened to be in the right-of-way of a planned highway project or likewise threatened with destruction by a government agency (which considerably narrows the opportunities for CRM pirate archaeology—though it does happen; see Exnicios, this volume).

A more serious reason why archaeologists have shied away from investigating pirate sites is that they are seen as the domain of treasure hunters. Many archaeologists feel that there is something inherently wrong with digging on a site that might contain artifacts of intrinsic value. It makes us feel "dirty" somehow—and not the good kind of dirty that comes from laboring with a shovel for days on end with only a handful of potsherds to show for it.

Archaeologists may not be anxious to work on treasure sites, but they are even less anxious to surrender them to treasure hunters. The legal licensing of treasure hunters by some states is anathema to most archaeologists. The aversion to treasure hunters is so strong that even collaborating with them in a required legal setting has been called a "Faustian bargain" (Elia 1992) and has threatened the careers of well-meaning archaeologists who were trying to salvage the data that would otherwise have been lost. Thus, any respectable archaeologist who was looking for a pirate site was also looking for trouble.

The ethics of collaborating with treasure salvors or pothunters are not trivial; in fact, that is a favorite question on comprehensive exams for students pursuing a graduate degree in archaeology. The conundrum is this: should the archaeologist work with the commercial collector to salvage as much information as possible before the artifact collection is sold and dispersed or does collaboration tacitly endorse and legitimize the activities of the collector and encourage them to mine even more sites? The ethical tenets of the Society of American Archaeologists are ambiguous enough so that both sides can be argued (which is why this makes such a great exam question!). Because of the censure in the profession concerning looted data, however, usually only senior archaeologists above reproach attempt their use (for example, Kathy Deagan's use of artifacts recovered by Mel Fisher from the *Atocha*—see Deagan 1987).

The *Whydah* project is an excellent case in point (see Hamilton, this volume). This unequivocally identified pirate vessel was salvaged, under permit, by Barry Clifford intermittently between 1982 and 1989. The project, troubled by turnover of archaeological personnel, eventually came under the direction of Christopher Hamilton, who completed reports on the previous work at the site (Hamilton et al. 1988, 1990). Although all the archaeologists entered into the project with the best of intent, the working relationship with the treasure salvors proved troublesome for all of them, and the accompanying controversy further exacerbated the situation. However, it should be noted that, contrary to professional fears, the collections from the *Whydah* are intact and currently curated in Provincetown, Massachusetts.

The issue of the ethics of using data associated with commercial ventures is contentious and complicated and is not addressed in this book, as it is better discussed elsewhere. We acknowledge the controversy surrounding some of the data presented in this volume. The authors do not condone the looting of sites and have only included data that were lawfully recovered.

The reasons above for the seeming aversion to pirate archaeology by most archaeologists may be more rationalization than reality. Perhaps the real reason that more pirate sites have not been reported in the literature is that they are so hard to find—or, more to the point, they are so hard to recognize in the archaeological record. The contributions in this book demonstrate that the identification of the site with piracy was the foremost research question of each project and that the identification of those sites was not always certain (see Wilde-Ramsing and Lusardi, this volume). In fact, without the historical documentation, most of these sites would probably not have been associated with piracy by their investigators. This book explores the question of identifying pirate sites, both on the land and under the sea.

Organization

The organization of this book is based on two different approaches: method and theory. The first approach—method—has to do with how pirate sites were found and identified. This part has been broken down into Pirate Lairs (terrestrial sites) and Pirate Ships and Their Prey (underwater sites).

Pirate Lairs ("land bases" might be more descriptive, but how often does one get the chance to use the word "lair" legitimately in an academic context?) begins with one of the best-investigated and best-known terrestrial pirate sites: Port Royal, Jamaica, once known as the "wickedest city in the world." Archaeologists, primarily from Texas A&M University (http://nautarch.tamu.edu/portroyal/), have uncovered a great deal of information concerning late seventeenth century life in the British Caribbean. Donny Hamilton recaps the work that has been done through the past several decades at the site and discusses the role that piracy did and did not play in the site's history.

Port Royal was the home port of such notable pirates as Henry Morgan. The next contribution discusses the notorious Jean Lafitte, who was not a sea-going pirate himself but rather dealt in the stolen booty that the brethren brought to him. Joan Exnicios explains how CRM laws provided for the investigation of the remains of Lafitte's smuggling base and settlement. The investigation included magnetometer, side-scan sonar, and fathometer survey of the bay behind Grande Terre Island and prompted a reassessment of Lafitte's activities in south Louisiana, based on primary documentation not previously examined by scholars.

These relatively well-known pirate settlements are followed by a discussion of more historically obscure pirate bases in the Gulf of Honduras. In these chapters David McBride and Daniel Finamore describe the history and archaeology of the seventeenth- and eighteenth-century British logwood/freebooter sites on Roatan, Honduras, and Barcadares, Belize. Roatan was first used by pirates in the sixteenth century for rendezvous, careening, and resupplying. It was briefly settled by Puritans in 1639, only to have the Spanish force them out in 1642. The island returned to its piratical ways and was a thorn in the Spanish colonies' side for decades thereafter. McBride uses his survey of the island as a focus for a discussion of the power struggles between England and Spain throughout the eighteenth century. Daniel Finamore discusses the similar site of Barcadares, Belize, where the freebooters left tantalizing traces of their lives but no buried treasure. He uses these data to address the question of whether this Bay Settlement was a kind of utopia or merely a last stop for debauched sailors.

The second section of the book begins with a wreck that is not well known to English-speaking audiences. The *Speaker* sank off the coast of Mauritius in 1702, although John Bowen survived the wreck and continued his career in piracy in the Indian Ocean. Patrick Lizé was part of a French team that studied the site, which has the distinction of being the first pirate ship ever excavated archaeologically. The report has been translated into English, and the author takes the opportunity to reflect on the project and how historical archaeology can illuminate the life of the pirate.

A more recent discovery in the Indian Ocean is the wreck of the *Fiery Dragon*. The wreck was first thought to be the *Adventure Galley*, associated with Captain William Kidd. Initial excavations turned up materials inconsistent with Kidd's vessel, however, and caused John de Bry to consider alternatives. De Bry also examines the lives of the pirates in the Indian Ocean and connects them with the pirates that formerly plied the waters of the Caribbean.

The second section of the book continues with one of the more notorious archaeological projects, the excavation of the pirate ship *Whydah*. The *Whydah* was a slave transport captured by the pirate Samuel Bellamy. Bellamy sailed with Blackbeard along the coast of North America until he lost his vessel in a storm off Cape Cod, Massachusetts. The wreck site was discovered by Barry Clifford, leading a team from Maritime Explorations, Inc., in the early 1980s, and was subsequently excavated under a permit from the U.S. Army Corps of Engineers and the Massachusetts Historical Commission. Chris Hamilton discusses the fieldwork and some of the discoveries made at the site through the end of 1992. The chapter goes on to discuss the archaeological issue of site formation processes and some of the anthropological implications of studying social systems, ship architecture, and trading systems, using a limited selection of analyses and results presented in the data recovery report (Hamilton et al. 1992). This project (as mentioned above) is also noteworthy in that it brought to a head the ethical arguments concerning archaeologists collaborating with treasure seekers. The popular versions of the *Whydah* project have been widely disseminated (Clifford and Perry 1999a, 1999b). The scholarly side has had only limited circulation until this volume.

The next two chapters in this section concern the recently discovered wreck off Beaufort Inlet, North Carolina. The popular press and even the state legislature immediately identified the wreck as Blackbeard's flagship, the *Queen Anne's Revenge*. The archaeologists involved were less quick to make a positive identification, insisting that more data were needed though mindful that the pirate cachet was a powerful fundraising tool to continue the investigation. Mark Wilde-Ramsing, the project's director, looks at the historical and archaeological evidence and makes the case that it is consistent with what one would expect of the famous pirate's ship. Wayne Lusardi, the project's former conservator, examines the recovered artifacts and sees room for doubt. Readers can weigh the evidence then reach their own conclusions and will be prepared to evaluate each new bit of evidence that is recovered in the future.

Mark Wagner and Mary McCorvie continue this section with an investigation of an alleged victim of a different kind of pirate, the river pirate. The Ohio River Valley of the late eighteenth and early nineteenth century is renowned in American lore as the abode of pirates who operated from hideouts such as Cave-in-Rock, plundering flatboats, killing the crews, and selling the cargoes. The authors have found that these tales are indeed larger than life. An early 1800s flatboat wreck discovered along the Ohio River shoreline in 2001 was popularly believed to be the remains of a boat plundered by a river pirate. The authors believe that there is another explanation for the wreck, but it is an uphill battle to convince the local populace to discard cherished beliefs concerning local history despite evidence to the contrary.

The editors conclude the section by looking at the response to pirates by their potential victims in the Caribbean. You could make a valid argument that the face of settlement and commerce was shaped by the presence of pirates in the area. Ironically, it is the responses to piracy rather than the pirates themselves that are most visible in the archaeological record.

Who Were the Pirates?

The book concludes with a reappraisal of what it meant to be a pirate and how the popular perception of piracy today has influenced our interpretations of piracy's past. It also addresses the question of how you might recognize a pirate site in the archaeological record. In fact, that thread runs through all of the contributions and is made explicit in the chapter by Babits, Howard, and Brenckle on recognizing pirate sites. Are there any archaeological markers that give away a pirate site? If the archaeologist did not have the documentary record to draw from, could a site be positively identified as a pirate shipwreck? In every contribution to this volume, the identification is only successful when there is good historical documentation. When the documentation is ambiguous or somewhat sketchy, as in the case of the *Queen Anne's Revenge*, then the identification is open to question.

This is not an uncommon situation in historical archaeology. Archaeologists working on plantation sites have been searching in vain for the marker artifacts that definitely denote the presence of African-American slaves. A single blue bead or cowrie shell does not a slave site make. But blue beads or cowrie shells in a historical context where slaves are historically recorded to have lived lend credence to such an association. This is also the case with pirate sites.

Archaeologists are not so much interested in individual artifacts as in patterns in the archaeological record. Each pirate site that is identified, explored, and published takes the archaeologist one step closer to defining such a pattern. Perhaps the pirate ship is characterized by a pattern of armaments, reconfigured mast placement, and a variety of cargo that differs from the cargo of a merchant ship or naval vessel. If such a pattern can be discerned, then it would be possible to identify a pirate ship for which no historical record exists. In fact, two of the chapters in this book (see Wagner and McCorvie, Finamore) explicitly look for such a pattern at the sites they investigated. The value of bringing these chapters together is that it makes comparisons and hence identification of pirate sites possible. Until we can be sure of our identifications we will not be able to recognize patterns or address questions relating to the lives of pirates and their impact on the larger societies in which they lived.

Part I

Pirate Lairs

2

Pirates and Merchants

Port Royal, Jamaica

Donny L. Hamilton

The mere mention of Port Royal, Jamaica, conjures up images of wanton lust, debauchery, greed, and notorious pirates of the high seas who roamed the streets of the port town in the mid- to late seventeenth century to dispose of their plundered loot. The historic accounts are replete with the tales of their episodes, but is this the true story of Port Royal? The fact that the famous port had the misfortune of being largely destroyed in an earthquake on June 7 in 1692 (corresponding to May 26 in the current Gregorian calendar) only served to exacerbate its reputation as the "wickedest city in the world." In that day, such a destructive act could only be the just retribution of God for the lifestyle of the people of the town, which was compared to the biblical city of Sodom.

A number of historic events and circumstances interacted to make Port Royal the boom town of the late seventeenth century. The first significant event was the influence of the Puritan merchants of London on Oliver Cromwell, Lord Protector of the Realm, leading him to send out an English force to capture Hispaniola so that the English could have a trading base in the middle of the Spanish New World. Failing miserably in this attempt, the English forces under the command of General William Penn and Admirable Robert Venables chose to take Jamaica as a consolation to ward off the wrath of Lord Cromwell. Soon after the capture of Jamaica in 1655, the English navy ships returned to England, leaving the island largely undefended against any reconquest attempt by the Spanish. The solution to the dilemma was for Governor Edward D'Oley to invite the "Brethren of the Coast" to make Port Royal their home port in 1657 (Dunn 1973:153). The pirates who made up the Brethren were the descendants of cattle-hunting buccaneers who had taken to a life of piracy as a result of depredations by the Spanish. Most of the brotherhood's activities were aimed at the hated Spaniards, who ran them out of Hispaniola. During the time when the pirates were invited to Port Royal, they were centered on the small island of Tortuga off the northeast coast of Hispaniola.

Coinciding with the arrival of the pirates, who became legal English-sanctioned privateers with letters of marque from the governor of Jamaica, a campaign was initiated against Spanish shipping and coastal towns. It can safely be said that the presence of the pirate/privateer ships and the constant attack on Spanish ships and coastal towns kept Spain on a defensive footing, preventing the organization of a successful offensive to retake the island. Now England had a large land mass in the center of the Spanish New World from which it could either attack Spanish ships and towns or carry on entrepôt trade with any of the many Spanish colonial towns desperately in need of manufactured goods.

Port Royal prospered with privateers present alongside the merchants who provided the outlet for their plunder. The combination of the two groups led to unprecedented growth in size, population, and economic status. It is clear that the merchants held the upper hand, however, and were the guiding factor. Preceding the capture of Jamaica, the relocation of the Brethren of the Coast, and the establishment of the Port Royal merchants, the annual Spanish fleets became much more erratic; Spain was no longer able to provide the New World Spanish colonies with the required manufactured goods. This fact is basic to understanding the growth of Port Royal. The Port Royal merchants stepped in and played dual roles. The merchants financed trading ventures with the Spanish on the one hand and financed privateers to raid Spanish ships and loot coastal towns on the other. In addition, the privateers acted independently but still needed the merchants to dispose of their ill-gotten gains. The combination was lethal, and Port Royal flourished as no other New World English town did.

Recent investigations by economists and historians have provided new insight on the economy of Port Royal: "Both opponents and advocates of so-called 'forced trade' declared that the town's fortune had the dubious distinction of being founded entirely on the servicing of the privateers' needs and highly lucrative trade in prize commodities" (Zahedieh 1986b:216).

This forced trade was so pervasive that it has been claimed that "one way or the other nearly all the propertied inhabitants of Port Royal seem to have an interest in privateering" (Pawson and Buisseret 2000:39); these pursuits made Port Royal the richest merchant community in English North America (Zahedieh 1986a:588). For instance, it is noted that Henry Morgan's raid on Portobello in June 1688 produced £75,000 in plunder, which was more than seven times the £10,000 in sugar production that year (Zahedieh 1986b:216). By 1690, just two years before the 1692 earthquake, it is estimated that £100,000 in bullion from contraband Spanish trade was shipped from Port Royal, in comparison to £88,000 in sugar (Zahedieh 1986b:216). In fact, most of the gold and silver going to England at this time was coming through Port Royal.

While the privateering activities were significant, the citizens of Port Royal came to "merchandize, and it was through all forms of clandestine trade with the Spanish and the asiento that were the lifeblood of Port Royal and made it so prosperous" (Zahedieh 1986a:592–93). The *asiento* was the system whereby a

Spanish representative was stationed in Port Royal to purchase slaves and ship them where they were needed in the Spanish colonies. In the late seventeenth century most of the slaves for Spanish America were secured from the Royal African Company's slave market in Port Royal, which regularly sold 25 to 50 percent of its slaves to the Spanish (Zahedieh 1986a:590). The *asiento* system was very profitable; the English ships delivering the slaves were able to enter Spanish ports, receive a significant shipping bonus, and under this cover engage in other lucrative trade.

The clandestine trade and combination of piracy and privateering made Port Royal the richest merchant town in English North America, with coins of different nationalities in circulation for daily trade transactions and set exchange rates (Zahedieh 1986a:583). By seventeenth-century standards, Port Royal's citizenry was affluent and noted as living above the standard of comparable social groups in England. By and large, the Port Royal citizens purchased what they needed and bought the latest in fashions and manufactured goods. As a result of this affluence, it might even be argued that at Port Royal, a town with currency in circulation, one sees the beginning of conspicuous consumption that becomes much more evident elsewhere, starting in the 1730s of the next century.

Throughout this time, Port Royal was the only legal port of entry into Jamaica; and the merchants of Port Royal were the economic and political powers on the island (Claypole 1972). Starting with the signing of the second Treaty of Madrid in 1670, which obligated England to stop issuing letters of marque to privateers against Spain, privateering was suppressed. Henry Morgan, who had been sent to London and held prisoner for his notorious raid on Panama City in 1671, was knighted as Sir Henry Morgan by King Charles II and returned as the lieutenant-governor of Jamaica, tasked with ending piracy there (Black 1983:46–48). Both the privateers and pirates were expendable, but the undercover trade with the Spanish colonies was not.

More realistically, Port Royal should be considered a mercantile center first and a pirate port second. In addition, it can be looked upon as a redistribution center. All the manufactured goods and other materials being shipped in from England and other European ports were by law supposed to pass through Port Royal as the only legal port of entry, which meant that many of them passed through the hand of the town's merchants. From there they were distributed to the rest of Jamaica. Likewise, much of the booty from the privateering and piracy operations passed through the same merchants' hands: they were the fences, so to speak. The Port Royal merchants likewise controlled the flow of manufactured goods to the Spanish colonies through an elaborate system of clandestine trade. It was an efficient and richly rewarding system, which the merchants controlled. Much of the development of Jamaica's huge sugar plantations of the eighteenth century was financed through them, and many became planters in their own right. This increase in plantations led to a shift of political and economical power from the merchants to the planters in the eighteenth century.

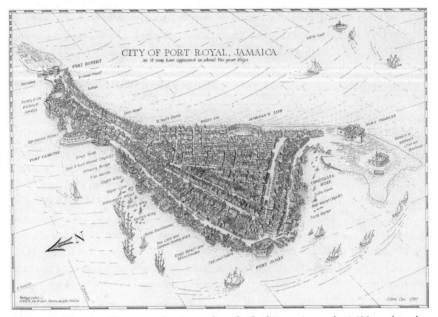

Figure 2.1. The city of Port Royal as it may have looked just prior to the 1692 earthquake. Drawing by Oliver Cox.

Anyone visiting Port Royal just prior to the 1692 earthquake would have been struck by the prevalence of multistoried brick buildings, the high population density, and the general appearance of wealth compared to the other English colonial towns in the New World. With an estimated population of over 7,000–8,000, Port Royal was rivaled in size and economic importance only by Boston, with 6,000 or so citizens (Black 1983:49; Hamilton 1992:40; Pawson and Buisseret 2000:136). The town was laid out with broad unpaved streets named after familiar streets in London, each lined with buildings one to four stories in height, with brick sidewalks along the front of many (figure 2.1).

In 1692 the density of structures was comparable to that of London, and the rent was described as being as high as in Cheapside, a high-rent district of London (Taylor 1688:252). All the amenities and vices of any seventeenth-century port town were present. During its heyday the town covered some 52 acres; but following the earthquake in 1692, when 33 acres of the town sank into the harbor, it was commonly referred to as "the wickedest city in the world."

Nothing remotely analogous to the seventeenth-century Port Royal remains today. All that is left is a small fishing town with approximately 2,000 citizens, along with an abandoned nineteenth-century British naval base and the headquarters of the Jamaican Coast Guard. Very little exists above the ground or the water to indicate the past glory of Port Royal. Archaeological work quickly reveals the affluence of the old town, however, as evidenced by the prevalence of

Figure 2.2. Array of material culture from an archaeological excavation. *From left to right*: Staffordshire slipware posset pot, coarse earthenware pot, Borderware porringer, hafted hammer, copper pot, delftware cup, brass strainer, pewter plate, crystal glass, hafted ax, stoneware juglet, slipware bowl, hafted cleaver, brass mortar, silver nutmeg grinder, silver spoon, Italian slipware jar, storage jar, Staffordshire mottled slipware bowl, and silver fork.

brick buildings, the density of construction, and the vast array of material culture in the latest styles of the period (figure 2.2).

As described earlier, this affluence was the result of trade with the Spanish colonies, Jamaican agricultural products, and various combinations of privateering and piracy. Despite the amount of material culture remaining, little archaeological evidence exists for the pirates and privateers who frequented Port Royal and were pivotal in establishing the roguish reputation of the town that still exists today.

Over the past four decades, three major underwater archaeological excavations in the areas of the old town submerged in Kingston Harbor have been undertaken; and various excavations have been conducted on land (figure 2.3).

The first excavation was conducted by Edwin Link in cooperation with the National Geographic Society and the Smithsonian Institution (Link 1960). The Link excavations concentrated around Fort James, Littleton's Tavern, and the King's Warehouse. The second and largest excavation was conducted along Fisher's Row by Robert Marx (1973) in 1965–67 in association with the Institute of Jamaican Culture (figure 2.4).

The third and longest-running excavation was directed by me (Hamilton 1991, 1992; Hamilton and Woodward 1984) in conjunction with the Institute of Nautical Archaeology, Texas A&M University (INA/TAMU), and the Jamaican National Heritage Trust. The excavation took place along Lime Street at the

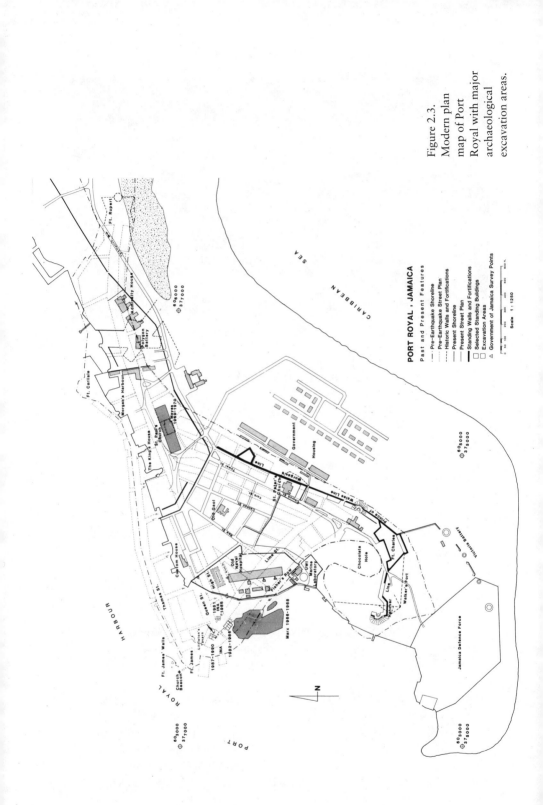

Figure 2.3. Modern plan map of Port Royal with major archaeological excavation areas.

PORT ROYAL, JAMAICA

Past and Present Features

- - - Pre-Earthquake Shoreline
 ·-· Pre-Earthquake Street Plan
- - - Historic Walls and Fortifications
 —— Present Shoreline
 —— Present Street Plan
 ■ Standing Walls and Fortifications
 □ Selected Standing Buildings
 □ Excavation Areas
 △ Government of Jamaica Survey Points

Scale 1 : 1250

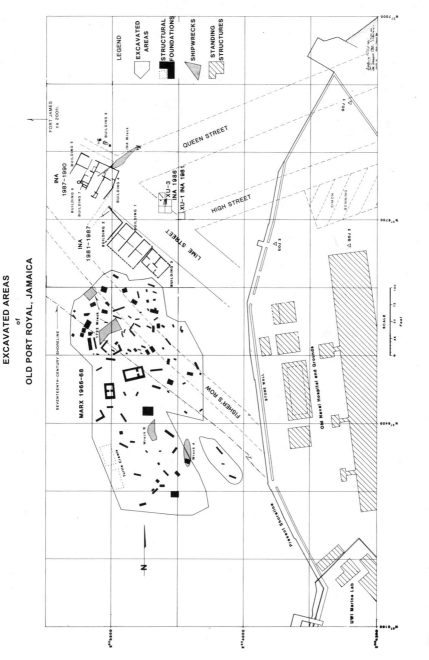

Figure 2.4. Underwater archaeology excavation areas of Port Royal along Lime Street. Courtesy of the Nautical Archaeology Program, Texas A&M University.

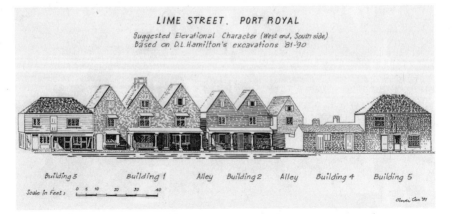

Figure 2.5. Proposed front view of excavated houses along Lime Street. Drawing by Oliver Cox.

intersections of High and Queen Street and resulted in the recording of the best-preserved structures and in situ artifacts (figure 2.5).

In addition to the major underwater excavations, there have been numerous small land excavations but only two major ones. The largest land excavation, conducted by Philip Mayes (1972), was located in the center of the nineteenth-century naval base. His work is noted for the partial excavation of St. Paul's Church, which was destroyed in the 1692 earthquake. Finally, Antony Priddy (1975) excavated a complicated, densely packed building block facing onto New Street (figure 2.3).

The main archaeological evidence that can be unequivocally equated to piracy and privateering is found in the form of shipwrecks. During Marx's excavation, he located and tentatively identified three shipwrecks, labeled A, B, and 1722 Wreck (figure 2.4). Along the southeast side of the excavation area, Wreck A was identified as the HMS *Swan*. Just west of this ship was Wreck B, identified as the French prize; and at the north end of the excavated area was a ship separated in two localities that Marx identified and labeled as the 1722 Wreck on the basis of a 1721 French coin (Marx 1973:202). Historic accounts describe how Port Royal was overwhelmed by the sea during the disastrous August 28, 1722, hurricane and 26 merchant vessels along with 400 persons perished in the harbor (Millás 1968:178). Another observer mentions that only four men-of-war and two merchant ships survived the storm out of fifty sails in the harbor (Millás 1968:178). The 1722 ship was one of the vessels that sank in this hurricane that demolished much of the town and destroyed once and for all Port Royal's chance to revive its former prominence.

After establishing the 1692 boundary of the harbor side of Port Royal on the excavation maps (figures 2.3 and 2.4), it is clear that the shipwreck that Marx identified as the HMS *Swan* lies in the old harbor, not in the streets of the town. Because the ship lies outside the town boundary it cannot be the HMS *Swan*, which is described as being careened at the time of the earthquake and washed into town, landing on top of the house of Lord Pike (Oldmixon 1969:324). A more likely candidate for the HMS *Swan*, a fifth-rate warship known to have engaged pirate ships, is the shipwreck that rammed through the front wall of Building 4 and lies at the ends of Lime and Queen Streets in the INA/TAMU excavation (figures 2.4 and 2.6) (Clifford 1991:82). It is impossible to state con-clusively that this wreck is the *Swan*, but it does fit the description of the ship: there is no ballast (which suggests that the ship was being careened), the ship is definitely lying on top of a building, and the keel has the same 74-foot length as the *Swan* (Clifford 1991, 1993). The wood was identified as slippery elm, also fitting the historic description of the *Swan*. In any case, this is the first archaeo-logical evidence of a ship that literally rammed through the front door of an occupied house during the earthquake. That in itself is an exciting discovery, which justified to my colleagues that I was finally doing shipwreck archaeology and not just excavating buildings.

The most likely scenario is that the *Swan* was being careened at one of the wharves along Thames Street. Because the ballast had been removed, the large wave generated by the earthquake carried the ship over or through the buildings along Thames. Once the ship reached Queen Street, the water was funneled west-ward down that street, where the ship rammed into Building 4, which lies along a narrow extension of Lime Street and juts out into Queen Street (figures 2.4, 2.5, and 2.6). Notice in figure 2.6 how the front of Building 4 was destroyed and the back wall has been pushed forward out of alignment with the in situ section of the wall to the east (right). The *Swan* started off as a Dutch ship that was captured by the English in 1672. At the time of the earthquake the ship was at least twenty years old and had served as a fire ship that was converted to a fifth-rate man-of-war (S. Clifford 1993:145–46). During its long service in the Caribbean the ship was sent on numerous patrols to engage pirate ships.

If the ship lying on top of Building 4 is a more likely candidate for the *Swan*, the question of the most likely identification for the three ships in Marx's excava-tion arises. In an attempt to identify these wrecks, a number of historic docu-ments and maps of Port Royal were consulted. The most significant find was a map titled "An Exact Plan of Chocolata Hole and the South End of the Town of Port Royal in Jamaica," surveyed in 1724 by James Cascoigne (figure 2.7). The key to the map reads:

A Charles Fort, *B* The Magazine, *C* The Captain of the Forts Apartment, *D* The Guard Room, *EF* The Lieutenants their apartments, *G* The Hanover Line, *gg* The Brafshire joined to the Wall of the Town (since the hurricane 28th Aug. 1722), *H* the Wall of the Town, *I* A Store Platform, *K* A Boarded Platform, *L* Barracks for the Soldiers, *M* The ruins of a pitch house which

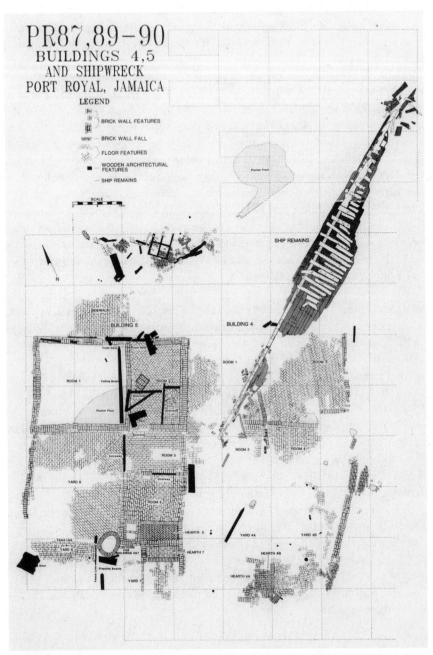

Figure 2.6. Plan view of Buildings 4 and 5 with ship remains, possibly the HMS *Swan*, lying on top of Building 4. Courtesy of the Nautical Archaeology Program, Texas A&M University.

belong'd to the King, *mm* Embrasures of the old Fortifications ruin'd by the earthquake 7th June 1692, *N* The wreck of the Lewis hulk, *O* the Wreck of a Galeon taken by James Littleton Esq (Since a Flagg Officer), *P* The Wreck of the Ranger a Pirate ship taken by Capt Chaloner Ogle (since Knighted) *Q* Mathews's Wharf, *R* Clarks & Sandys's Wharf, *S* Morgan's Wharf, *T* Lodderdale's Wharf, *U* Prudge's Wharf, *W* A Smith's Shop, *X* A Nine Pin Alley, *Y* The Kitchen belonging to the Fort, *Z* The Market House, *a* The Cage Pillory & Stocks, *b* The Exchange.

☐ Cranes   ⌐ ⌐ Tortoise Crawls

N.B 1. The parts drawn colour'd with Red are built with Brick & Stone

2. " " " Black " " " Wood or Earth

3. Where the foundations are Speck'd the houses were demolished in the huricane 28th Aug 1722.

Latitude 17.51 N

Longitude from London 16.00 W

Variation (anno 1724) 6.15 E

ddd A Wharf proposed by Sr Jacob Ackworth Knt. Surveyor of his Majesty's Navy, The Kings Ships, *eee* An Enclosure of Pahng, propos'd to keep the Seamen from stragling, *fff* A line of loose stone for a breakwater.

The map locates and identifies three ships labeled N, O, and P in exactly the same locations as the three ships recorded by Marx. All the vessels appear to have been ships that sank in the 1722 hurricane that struck Port Royal. The ship identified as the *Swan* by Marx corresponds to the ship labeled "N" on the 1724 map and is identified as "N the wreck of the Lewis hulk." Marx's "French Prize" corre-lates with "O the wreck of a Galeon taken by James Littleton, Esq. (Since a Flag Officer)." The ship identified by Marx as the 1722 Wreck is identified as "P the wreck of the Ranger a pirate ship taken by Capt Chalenor Ogle (since Knighted)." Thus the ships have been identified as a hulk, a captured galleon, and a pirate ship called the *Ranger*.

Significantly, the *Ranger* was a ship used by Bartholomew Roberts, who has been described as the most successful pirate of the early eighteenth century. This shipwreck is the only conclusive archaeological evidence that can be associated with piracy activities at Port Royal. But how did the *Ranger* come to be riding at anchor in Port Royal just before the 1722 hurricane?

Bartholomew Roberts is considered to be the greatest of the last of the Golden Age pirates (Marx 1992:256). A Welshman, like the famous Henry Morgan who helped establish Port Royal's reputation, Roberts was active throughout the West

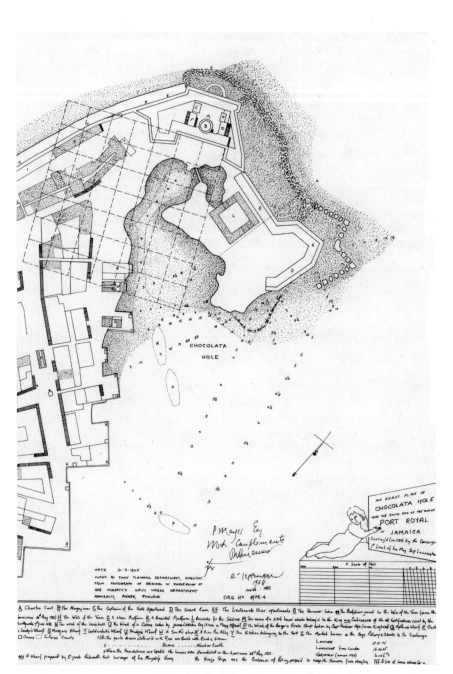

Figure 2.7. "An Exact Plan of Chocolata Hole and the South End of the Town of Port Royal in Jamaica, survey'd (in 1724) by J'm Cascoigne 1st Lieut. of his Maj. Ship *Launcestone.*" Lime Street is located on the left side of the figure with the stocks and market in the middle of the street.

Indies and eastern coast of America as far north as Newfoundland, south to Brazil, and along the eastern coast of Africa. In the spring of 1721 Roberts was running out of vessels to plunder in the West Indies, so he took his booty-laden ship to the Guinea coast of Africa (Marx 1992:260; Defoe 1999:104–287). Just off the Senegal River in present-day Senegal, the French sent out two warships to engage his sloop, not realizing it was a heavily armed pirate ship. Roberts raised the black pirate flag and captured both French ships, one with sixty-five men and ten cannon and the other with seventy-five men and sixteen cannon (Defoe 1999:225). One of the captured French ships was renamed the *Ranger* and became the consort of the *Royal Fortune*, Roberts' flagship (Black 1989:68; Defoe 1999:226). The other ship was used as a store ship. Despite the *Ranger*'s short career as a pirate ship, it participated in the capture of numerous ships of various nationalities—English, Dutch, Portuguese, and French.

Meanwhile, two Royal Navy ships, the *Weymont* and the *Swallow* (under the command of Captain Chalenor Ogle), returned to the area to engage any pirate ship attacking British ships or interrupting the lucrative British trade in slaves, gold, and products. Despite severe hardships and the death of many of his crew, Captain Ogle continued his search for Roberts along the Guinea coast. When Roberts saw the *Swallow* sailing toward him, he did not recognize the ship for what it was and sent the recently captured *Ranger* to take it. Out of sight of the *Royal Fortune*, the *Swallow* turned and fired a broadside. A crew was placed on the *Ranger* to keep it from sinking and sail it to port. Five days later, the *Swallow* sailed back to Cape Lopez on February 10, 1722, to engage Roberts, who was commanding the *Royal Fortune* (Black 1989:70; Marx 1992:261). In the course of the battle, Roberts was killed, and 254 pirates were captured and taken to the Cape Coast for trial in April of 1722 (Marx 1992:261). Many of the captured pirates were hanged or died in prison; however, a few were acquitted. Thus ended the career of the acknowledged greatest pirate of the era.

How the *Ranger* ended up in Port Royal is not known at this time, but it did sink on August 28, 1722, during a particularly destructive hurricane that largely destroyed the town of Port Royal as well. The ship identified by Robert Marx as the 1722 Wreck is now known to be a French ship of either ten or sixteen cannon captured off the Senegal River in West Africa by Roberts and renamed the *Ranger*. This short-lived pirate ship sits on the bottom of Port Royal Harbor in Jamaica, heavily ballasted with 150-pound cannonballs, 9 inches in diameter. With a little research, it should be possible to identify the French ship that became the *Ranger* and the details of how it came to be at Port Royal.

There are other pirates whose names are much more closely related to Port Royal, such as Henry Morgan, Calico Jack Rackham, Anne Bonny, and Mary Read; but nothing appears archaeologically at Port Royal that can be attributed to them. Somewhere in the mangrove swamp northeast of Port Royal, Henry Morgan, the best known of the Port Royal privateers, was buried in the old cemetery. During the great earthquake of 1692 the burial grounds were de-

stroyed; Morgan's lead coffin and headstone probably lie undiscovered somewhere in the adjacent mangrove swamps. Other than his grave and the ruins of
his plantation house on the east end of the island, what we know about Morgan
comes from written records and folklore. For instance, the probate inventory of
Henry Morgan survives in the Jamaica Public Archives and provides us with
good insight into the range and variety of material used in this period. In addition, it gives us a good indication of the wealth that could be obtained by a select
few of the privateers. With an inventory value of £5,263, 1 shilling, 3 pence,
Morgan was a very wealthy person by 1688 standards. However, very few privateers died still in possession of the wealth they received from privateering.

Just outside the entrance to Kingston Harbor lies a small cay named for Calico
Jack Rackham, where his body was caged after he was hanged at Gallows Point
as a warning to all who might be considering crossing the line (Black 1989:116).
A short distance north across the part of Kingston Harbor called Port Royal
Harbor, a low-lying piece of land juts out from the mangroves. This is Gallows
Point, where the pirates were hanged and their bodies allowed to swing as a
warning to all who sailed into the harbor. Gallows Point is largely submerged in
a mangrove swamp, and no archaeological work has ever been conducted there.
All things considered, the archaeological record provides us with very tenuous
evidence for a segment of society that contributed substantial wealth to the thriv-
ing economy of Port Royal.

While the pirates and privateers played an important and by today's standards
even romantic role in Port Royal's history, it clearly was in no way as significant
as the role played by merchants and trade in establishing Port Royal as an economic powerhouse. By and large, the wealth accumulated by the pirates and
privateers was transitory, quickly ending up in the pockets of the Port Royal
merchants, tavern owners, and brothel establishments: easy come, easy go. The
money accumulated by the merchants was used to finance the establishment of
plantations in Jamaica, which were to create even greater fortunes in the eighteenth century. Some of the merchants became plantation owners. Eventually
some of the money even made it back to the merchants of London, who backed
many of the merchants of Port Royal.

Archaeologically speaking, little has been found that can be attributed exclusively to privateers or pirates. The best archaeological evidence comes from shipwrecks, and even here good historic documentation is essential to identify the
ship. Without the written wills, inventories, deeds, and grantor's records that
often record partial ownership of vessels used in privateering or trade, there
would be little to equate Port Royal with its privateering citizenry.

Henry Morgan's Probate Inventory (Inventories, vol. 3, folios 258–61)

Morgan died during the reign of James II (1684–89), who was deposed in 1689
and died in 1701. Morgan was buried in the cemetery on the spit on August 25,

1688. The original spelling and syntax of the inventory in the archives are maintained.

Sir Henry Morgan Port Royall (Jamaica Public Archives 1689)
19th February 1688 [this would be 1689 in the Gregorian calendar now in use]
Jamaica Ss.
James the second by the Grace of God of England Scotland France and Ireland King and
    of Jamaica Lord Defender of the faith etc. To all to whome these Persons shall come
    greeting Know Yea that Constituted authorized and apoynted and by these Persons
    doe Constitute authorize and apoynt Our Freely and well beloved Nathaniell Ferry
    and Robert Needler Esqs or officer of them to administer an Oath unto Peter
    Heywood and John Moone Esqs that they shall well and honestly and according to
    the best of their Judgments & Consciences Inventory and Chattells Rights and
    Creditts of Sr Henry Morgan late of this Island Knt decd as they shall be shown unto
    them by Dame Mary Elizabeth Morgan his Relick and Executive and thereof the said
    Nathaniel Ferry and Robert Needler or offices of them are to make a true returne
    unto our Governor of our said Island under their own offices of their hands and
    seales together with this present Power annexed so that the said inventory and
    apraysement may be recorded in the Secrys office of this our island witness Sir
    Francis Watson Knt President of the Council and Governor of our said Island of Ja-
    maica and the Territories thereon depending and Chansellor of the same the Thirtieth
    day of October 1688.

Hickman, Secry F. Watson

According to the Power to me by the within written writt given I did on the within
    named Peter Heywood and John Moone Esqs administor the oath to them that by
    the said writt is directed witness my hand and shall this Eleaventh day of February in
    the fifth year of his Majesties reign.

                                                            Robt Needler

Jamaica
An Inventory and Appraisment of the Goods and Chattels Rights and Creditts of the
    Honble Sir Henry Morgan Knt as shewn unto us this 19th February 1688
Sir Hen Morgan's Inventory

wrought plate 4961 § at 5s2d p §	128 02 08
one silver watch	03 00 00
Two gold rings wth ord stones	02 00 00
Two plaine gold rings	00 10 00
2 pr white buttons & 3 pr shoe buckells	00 05 00
a sett of gold buckells and buttons sett wth stones	04 10 00
some Emerauld dropps and a lump of pomander	00 07 00
one ounce of small p ashe	01 00 00
one ounce & 18 _____ wrought gold	07 10 00
nine small Coker nutts tippt with silver	00 09 00
a parcell of glasses	01 10 00

A parcell of china tea cupps and Earthen waire	01 10 00
a parcell of agatt hafted and other old knives	01 00 00
Two brass horozontal dyall & small compass	00 10 00
three dozen of woven chaine chaires	10 00 00
sixteene old chaires	01 00 00
a pcoll old tables	06 00 00
one silke mohaire suite of curtins lynd wth Persian with bedd coverlidd &c	30 00 00
four feather bedds wth boulsters	30 00 00
forteene Hamakoes	14 00 00
a musketo nett	01 00 00
one flock bedd & c	00 10 00
six purple bayes gowns	03 00 00
five looking glasses	05 00 00
Two Inlaid Scriptores	20 00 00
one plaine scriptore	01 00 00
One Inlaid chest Drawers table stand &c	10 00 00
One cedar chest drawers	02 00 00
One dressing box cabinet & c	02 10 00
One hundred twenty three bound books	50 00 00
a prcell of old charts mapps & c	05 00 00
a prcell of sermons playes and phampletts	01 00 00
a prcell of sheets and pillow boors	28 00 00
a prcell of Diaper Table cloths and napkins	12 00 00
a prcell of damask ditto	05 00 00
a prcell of Ozenbrigg napkins	03 00 00
a pcell of damask diapers & Oz towells	01 10 00
six side board cloathes	01 00 00
six old cushions	00 06 00
Three remnts of Holland	10 10 03
Several remnts of course linen	02 00 00
Thre yds & ½ of Cambrich	00 10 00
Sir Henry's wareing linnen	50 00 00
Two silk night gowns	09 00 00
Three Old Beaver hatts	05 00 00
Two pr of laced gloves	01 00 00
A Barber's & tweezer cases & Instruments	01 05 00
Two prospect glasses & other old things	03 00 00
a prcell of Chests Trunks and a Press	05 00 00
a velvet saddle & c?	02 01 00
a wast belt	00 05 00
twenty seaven gunns & 19 cartoush boxes	55 00 00
three pr pistolls and three swords	16 00 00
five powder horns & two lances	01 00 00
nine pictures	35 00 00
a clock	10 00 00

foure sconces	01 10 00
a pr of old tables wth a box of troy weights	01 00 00
three close stooles and panns	02 10 00
one cold still	02 00 00
a pair of And Irons	01 10 03
a Jack 5 Iron Potts 5 spitts two frying panns & cookeroom utensills	15 00 00
a parcell of tinn ware	02 10 00
five brass kettles and other brass and copper ware belonging to the cookeroom	30 00 00
36—oz of Pewter	10 05 00
a pcoll of beeze wax	02 00 00
A pair of stillyards	01 10 00
Twenty five pounds of candles	00 12 06
a parcell of soape	02 10 00
a parcell of spices	02 12 06
a parcell of fruite	00 11 03
Half a barrell of flower	02 01 09
A Dantswirk case of bottles wth a parcell of bottles & jarrs	03 10 00
a Cassadar Iron	00 10 00
a Casting nett	00 10 00
a parcell of basketts & brushes	00 10 00
a prcell of wooden ware	01 10 00
three doz & 3 pr shoos	11 14 00
eleaven barrells of beefe	13 15 00
a parcell of salt	01 10 00
a parcell of old Carpenters tooles	00 10 00
fourty four negroe men at 20£	880 00 00
fourty two negro women at 17£	165 00 00
thirteen negro boys at 8£	104 00 00
twenty negro girls at 7£	140 00 00
To Indians at 17£	34 00 00
eleven white servants from one to seven years time to serve	88 00 00
Thirty five working steers at 7£	252 00 00
foure Bulls and 4 Bulkings	28 00 00
Twenty one cows and 6 yearlings	93 00 00
five hefers	15 00 00
twenty mules	240 00 00
eight horses	64 00 00
a mare fillee and horse colt	08 00 00
a parcell of hoggs	35 00 00
a prcell of goates	12 00 00
a parrel of dunghill fowls turkeys 5 Ducks & geese	20 00 00
a gang of dogg	05 00 00
sixty five thousand weight of mustavado sugar at 2s6d p £	406 05 00
six hundred and forty Gall. Rumm	26 13 04
One thousand Gall. Molasses	12 10 00

One thousand wooden potts	75 00 00
Two rumm butts two pipes & 2 Iron bound Puncheons	02 00 00
Two mills six wth cases gudgeon stopps & c	120 00 00
Two spare gudgeons	05 00 00
six spare brasses	10 00 00
Eight capooses & 6 stopps	04 00 00
Two Iron crowes and 6 splitting wedges	01 00 00
Six Copper string	65 00 00
One new copper	23—06
foure ladles and eight skimmers	03 10 00
Two Potting basons	02 10 00
Six lamps and two scrapers	00 05 00
a receiver and six wooden coolers	02 00 00
three stills wormes & tubbs hung	50 00 00
Eight Dripps	00 04 00
six Barricoes	00 10 00
a parcell of nailes	00 05 00
a parcell of plantation tooles	15 00 00
eight yoakes fixed with chaines	05 00 00
a paire of steadd wheels	08 00 00
a paire of plaine wheeles	04 00 00
a hempen rope & 2 single blockes	02 10 00
foure old coppors	12 00 00
a parcell of old copper old iron tooles & severall other old things about the house & Sir Henry's Plantation	03 00 00
a parcell of Horses and mares running at Coleburry and Ivy's savannas	25 00 00
Debts due to the estate are	
Imp from Coll. Geo Woodham a bond of Three Hundred Pounds	150 00 00
From the Executer of his Grace the Duke of Albermarle	344 12 00
From Mr. Thomas Pinatbrase	35 00 00
From Sir Richard Doreham	60 16 00
From Mr. Thomas Byndleys	290 00 00
	£5263 01 03

In Obedience to the Comands from the Right Hon[ble] Governor wee have according to the best of Our Skills and Judgments appraised the fouregoing Inventory amounting to five Thousand Two Hundred Sixty Three pounds One Shilling and Three pence as witness our hands & Seales

Peter Heywood
John Moone

3

On the Trail of Jean Lafitte

Joan M. Exnicios

Jean Lafitte, hero of the Battle of New Orleans or ruthless privateer of the Gulf Coast and Caribbean (figure 3.1)? What do we really know about this legendary figure, and can we separate the fact from the fiction? Who was this "gentleman pirate"? He is so famous in Louisiana and Gulf Coast history that a town is named after him, books have been written and movies made of his exploits, and even a National Park (Jean Lafitte National Historical Park and Preserve) is named after him (figures 3.2, 3.3, and 3.4). Yet until recently, beyond a few documents, there has been absolutely nothing tangible associated with the real person. Curiously, it was the quest to save the coastal marshes and barrier islands of south Louisiana that led to a better understanding of the legendary figure of Jean Lafitte and the Barataria marshes that he ruled.

Today the real story of Jean Lafitte is being rediscovered where the Mississippi River meets the Gulf of Mexico by the U.S. Army Corps of Engineers. West of the mouth of the river on the southern edge of Barataria Bay stands Grand Terre (figures 3.5 and 3.6). At the beginning of the nineteenth century, Grand Terre was a single island (figure 3.7). Over the past century and a half, three-quarters of the island has been lost (figures 3.5, 3.8, 3.9, 3.10, and 3.11). A combination of cultural and natural processes, including the dredging of canals and storm surges, has caused rapid erosion of this area into the Gulf of Mexico. Currently Grand Terre consists of two separate low-lying islands of salt marsh, mangrove swamp, and open beaches and sand dunes. It is predicted that the islands will be awash before 2050 (Godzinski et al. 2001:1-1).

Before erosion jeopardized its existence, the island was home to a horse and cattle ranch (1795), a sugar plantation (1821), Fort Livingston (1840), and the Grand Terre lighthouse (1857). The most famous or infamous occupation of the island was short-lived (1808 to 1814) and very illegal (Godzinski et al. 2001).

Smuggling

As early as 1722, the sixty-mile route from New Orleans along Bayou Barataria through Barataria Bay and out Grand or Barataria Pass to the Gulf was well

Figure 3.1. Popular sketch of Jean Lafitte.

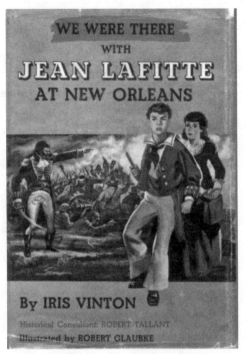

Figure 3.2. One of many books written on Jean Lafitte.

Figure 3.3. Yul Brynner played Jean Lafitte in the 1958 movie *The Buccaneer.*

Figure 3.4. A national park and preserve in Barataria was named after Jean Lafitte. Material courtesy of the National Park Service.

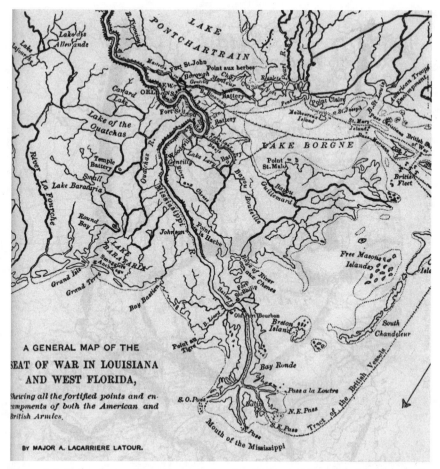

Figure 3.5. Early nineteenth-century map showing the famous "smuggler's anchorage."

known to local miscreants (Evans et al. 1979:14). Smuggling was a common activity in Louisiana throughout the eighteenth century during both the French and Spanish regimes (Godzinski et al. 2001:4-3–4-4). In order to avoid import duties, vessels would enter the shallow waters of Barataria Bay and anchor in the protected bay north of Grand Terre Island. There the ships would be met by pirogues (dugout canoes) or bateaux (flat-bottomed boats). These lighters would then carry the cargoes over four routes through the bayous to New Orleans (Vogel 1990:72–73). The raising of the Stars and Stripes in 1803 did not signal an end to these illicit activities. As far as the "merchants" were concerned, it was still business as usual.

In 1808, five years after the Louisiana Purchase, the United States was at peace with a Europe in the throes of the Napoleonic Wars. To ensure its neutrality the United States outlawed the outfitting of privateers within its territorial boundaries. Furthermore, the Embargo Act of 1807 forbade all international trade to

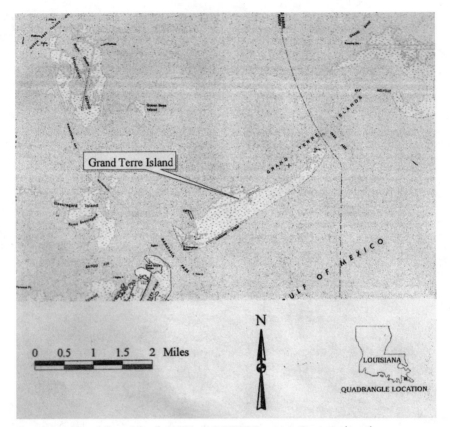

Figure 3.6. Grand Terre Islands, 1993. 7.5' USGS Barataria Pass quadrangle.

and from American ports. Although nominally enforced by the U.S. Navy, the act resulted in wide-scale smuggling. On the Gulf Coast, the result was the effective closing of the Mississippi. To circumvent the embargo, the "back door" to New Orleans continued to be used. The threshold to that door was Grand Terre Island.

Enter Lafitte

Who was the real Jean Lafitte? He was viewed by some as the hero of the Battle of New Orleans, by others as a cutthroat pirate who dealt in slaves, and by himself as a privateer. The early years of Lafitte are shrouded in mystery. For instance, it is unclear when and where he was born, and even where he lived during his early years. We do not know for sure, but it is believed that Jean Lafitte was born in France, possibly Bayonne, sometime around 1780.

At the turn of the nineteenth century Napoleon Bonaparte had just been named first consul and Spanish Louisiana was returned to France. About that

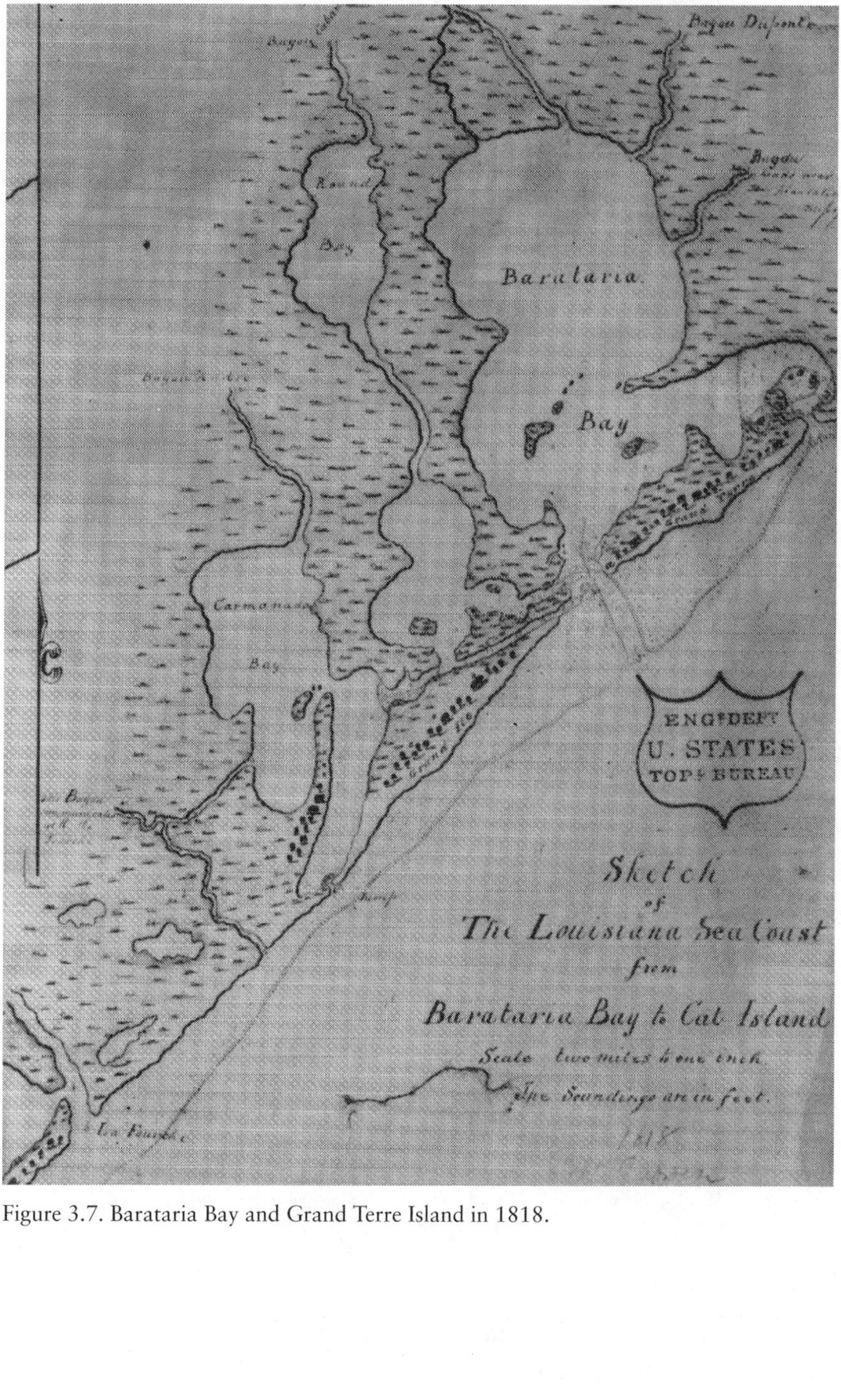

Figure 3.7. Barataria Bay and Grand Terre Island in 1818.

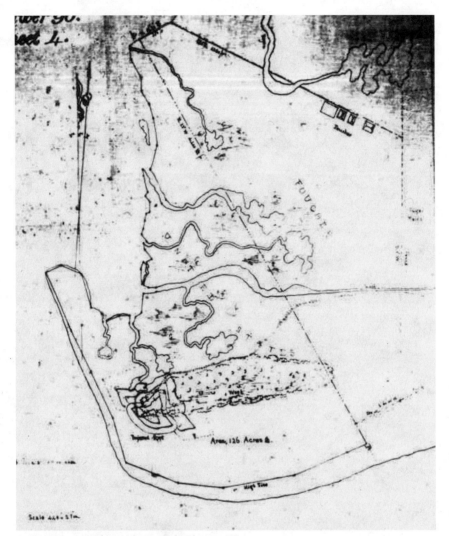

Figure 3.8. Part of Grand Terre Island in 1833.

time, the French-born brothers Pierre and Jean Lafitte arrived in New Orleans and shortly afterward married. Accounts vary as to the brothers' occupation. Some, including the owners of the "watering-hole" at 941 Bourbon Street called "Lafitte's Blacksmith Shop" (figure 3.12), have stated that the brothers were smiths and tool makers (Faye 1940:745; Saxon 1930:6; Vogel 1990). Others have suggested they were seafarers. Their legitimate jobs, if indeed they had any, are unknown to historians, but they were quickly up to no good.

Slave labor was important throughout the territory. Plantations and businesses relied on it. The smuggling of slaves and goods into the colony was a

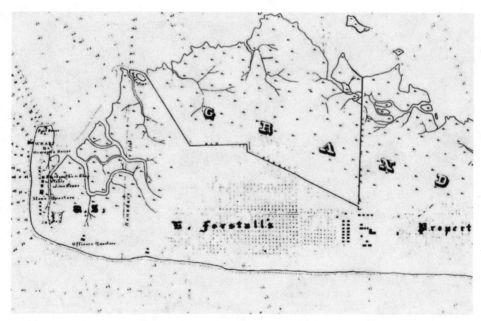

Figure 3.9. Barnard's 1841 map of Grand Terre Island.

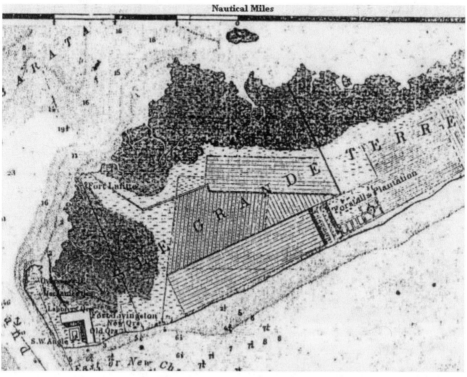

Figure 3.10. Map of Grand Terre Island, 1853, showing the location of Lafitte's old settlement, Fort Livingston, and the Forstall Plantation.

Figure 3.11. Grand Terre as it appears today. Overlay of Barnard's 1841 map with the 1999 aerial photograph (NA RG 77 FF Dr. 90 Sht. 12).

Figure 3.12. E. Olga Skowronek in front of "Lafitte's Blacksmith Shop" in New Orleans at 941 Bourbon Street. Photo by Russell K. Skowronek.

lucrative business, which had been going on since the establishment of the Louisiana colony by the French. The Lafitte brothers realized that smuggling could be a profitable business. A community of smugglers and privateers already existed on Grand Isle, a barrier island off the coast in Barataria Bay. Barataria was an isolated area that for years had provided shelter to escaped slaves, criminals, and smugglers. It was also home to fishers, hunters, and trappers who lived off the rich natural resources of the area. The Lafitte brothers began to engage in the smuggling trade. Initially, smuggling was a free-for-all activity that periodically resulted in clashes between various groups of privateers and smugglers in Barataria. Jean Lafitte was an enterprising man and soon rose to become leader of the smugglers and pirates living in Barataria.

In 1808 it is reported that Pierre Lafitte set up a small "establishment" on "Barataria Island," as Grande Terre was historically known. Lafitte served as an agent or "fence" for the vessels using the Barataria Bay route to avoid American customs and revenue inspectors at the mouth of the Mississippi River (Faye 1940). To this illicit entrepôt, merchant vessels brought enslaved Africans, foodstuffs, and dry goods for the growing number of plantations in Louisiana (Saxon 1930). They would then smuggle the slaves and cargoes past the customs agents at the mouth of the Mississippi River and sell them at isolated locations in the upper Barataria such as the Temple, a large Indian shell mound that loomed above the surrounding marshes.

Many of the privateers living on Grand Isle had received letters of marque from the French Republic. When the war between France and Spain ended, they continued under a letter of marque from the republic of Cartagena (Colombia), which gave them authority to seize Spanish vessels. The operation of French- and Cartagenian-flagged privateers out of Grand Terre was in violation of the neutrality of the United States. Nonetheless, captured vessels were brought to Grand Terre, stripped of their cargoes and fittings, and burnt. As a result, the citizens of the Louisiana territory carried on a contraband trade with the Baratarians in captured goods and slaves.

Records are scarce, and it has never been proven, but it is believed that the Lafitte brothers and their fellow privateers did not restrict their attacks to Spanish vessels but preyed on vessels flying flags of other countries as well. These commerce raiders, though armed with letters of marque, fell not only upon "legitimate" targets but also upon neutrals. This made them pirates (Godzinski et al. 2001: 4-19–4-26).

The Lair at Grand Terre

Little is known about Lafitte's small "establishment" on Grand Terre Island. Since the community did not officially exist, there are few primary accounts, associated either with intelligence gathered by the Spanish consul of New Orleans in 1812 or with the destruction of the establishment by U.S. forces in September of 1814. Anyone familiar with the inflated "body counts" of the Vietnam era must realize that the reports that were penned were meant for Madrid and Washington-bound bureaucrats.

According to the Spanish consul, Grand Terre boasted a fortification mounting fourteen guns and a community of 200–250 people (Faye 1940:748). While such a fortification apparently never existed, this "intelligence" was reiterated in the British *Naval Chronicle* in 1814 (Sugden 1979:160).

On September 16, 1814, a flotilla of eight U.S. vessels attacked Grand Terre. They captured some twenty vessels, and the landing party "took possession of their establishment upon the shore, consisting of about 40 houses of different sizes, badly constructed, and thatched with palmetto leaves" (Godzinski et al. 2001:4-34, 4-40–4-42). Commodore Daniel Patterson, author of this dispatch, indicated that the island had a population of 800–1,000 and that large-caliber guns were only to be found on the vessels. The materials seized during the raid included such mundane articles as a variety of cloths, window and table glass, paper, soap, salt, coffee, cocoa, rope, and bar iron (Works Progress Administration of Louisiana 1940:#746).

Exit Lafitte

Four months after the capture of Grand Terre, the Battle of New Orleans (later made famous in song by Johnny Horton) was fought at Chalmette battlefield on January 8, 1815. Lafitte and many of his cohort joined General Andrew Jackson in the defeat of the British. The role the Baratarians played in winning the Battle of New Orleans is debatable. The general consensus among historians was that, while Lafitte and his Baratarians contributed to the American victory, they were not a decisive factor in winning the battle. There are those, however, who believe that the Lafitte brothers and the Baratarians played a pivotal role in the battle and that if they had not contributed their services General Jackson and his forces would not have won the campaign for New Orleans. Historian Jane Lucas De-Grummond (1961) published a book titled *The Baratarians and the Battle of New Orleans*. She based much of her book on a journal that was believed to belong to Jean Lafitte. DeGrummond states that the arms, men, and intelligence provided by Lafitte and his followers gave General Jackson a tactical advantage over the British forces. Wilbert S. Brown (1969:31) believes that General Jackson and the Americans might have defeated the British without the Baratarians, but probably not if the Baratarians had aided the British.

Rehabilitated with a pardon from President James Madison, Lafitte attempted, but failed, to reclaim the vessels and goods taken at Grand Terre. He went to Washington and Philadelphia in the winter of 1815–16 to plead his case before the president but returned to New Orleans when he did not succeed.

A year later, the Lafitte brothers left New Orleans and relocated to Galveston on the coast of Texas. They renamed the settlement Campeachy. Jean Lafitte

Figure 3.13. Alleged slave token/identification tag.

allegedly built a house that came to be known as the Maison Rouge. There they operated under the flag of Venezuela. Once again, the Lafittes ran a very success-ful slave-dealing operation. As they had done at Grand Terre, the privateering brothers continued to capture Spanish slave ships off the coast of Cuba and bring the slaves to the barracoons or slave pens on Galveston Island (figure 3.13). The pens held a thousand or more slaves, who were then sold to people like the legendary Bowie brothers (John, Resin, and James) and sold directly to cotton and sugar planters in Louisiana.

American authorities caught up with the Lafittes in 1820 and forced them to leave the Texas coast. Their lawless activities were not to be tolerated by the Americans who had migrated westward. Lafitte and his buccaneers left the Bay of Galveston for the coast of Yucatán. He established a base at Campeche and continued attacks on Spanish ships. There are conflicting stories of what ulti-mately became of Jean Lafitte. Some believe that he died in Campeche on the Yucatán around 1826, while others say that he returned to Louisiana (Saxon 1930). That is how mysteries are born. Suffice it to say that with Jean Lafitte's departure from Louisiana, Grand Terre Island ceased to be the home of pirates and instead became home to the Lafitte legend.

Discovering the "Establishment"

In 1977, more than 160 years after Commodore Patterson's capture of Grand Terre and destruction of the "establishment," the New Orleans District of the U.S. Army Corps of Engineers began contracting for a cultural resource survey of the threatened barrier island. As a result of this work, the Lafitte Settlement site

(16JE128) was identified by Richard Weinstein on the north side of Grand Terre along the shore and in the shallows of Barataria Bay. He describes the site as a wave-washed shell midden 330 feet long (Gagliano et al. 1979). The site, revisited by Allen Saltus in 1989, produced an abundant scatter of early nineteenth century ceramics, including olive-green bottle glass, a fragment of tin-glazed earthenware, fragments from thirty-five different shell-edged pearlware rim patterns, and the butchered bones of domesticated animals. Importantly, a datum was installed and a base map was made, indicating a site 330 by 290 feet in area (Saltus and Pearson 1990).

More recent visits to the site in 1995 and 2001 by Earth Search, Inc., revealed that in less than a decade fourteen meters of the site had eroded into the bay. Observed in the shallows and redeposited along the surf line were ceramic fragments of creamware, hand-painted, transfer-printed, shell-edged, and annular pearlware, olive-green bottle glass, clay pipe stems, gunflints, wrought nails, and butchered animal bones. When taken as a whole, the artifact assemblage collected from the site appears to date between 1800 and 1820.

As part of the Earth Search, Inc., work, G & N Services, Inc., performed a submerged cultural resources survey using magnetometer, side scan sonar, and fathometer equipment. A Global Positioning System (GPS) was used to delineate the submerged portion of the site and to identify abandoned vessels. Conducted in December 2000, the survey identified the historic shoreline, a canal, and numerous wooden boards of various sizes protruding from the bottom of Barataria Bay. These boards may represent the tangible remains of the docks, warehouses, and habitations of the inhabitants of the establishment.

The information from 16JE128 supports the interpretation that this is the site of Lafitte's establishment. Earth Search, Inc., has found that in situ deposits remain and that the now submerged 800-yard-long Lafitte settlement site is eligible for inclusion in the National Register of Historic Places (Godzinski et al. 2001: 5-1–5-2, 7-1).

Lafitte's second lair in Texas was still extant some two decades after he had been driven from the region. His Maison Rouge was marked on the earliest plat of the City of Galveston in 1838. Over the past twenty years this site located on Water Street/Harborside Drive has been explored by the Lafitte Society of Galveston. Two projects directed by Sheldon Kindall in conjunction with the Houston and Fort Bend County Archaeological Societies have yet to yield conclusive evidence of Lafitte's activities.

Conclusions

Because of ongoing sea-level change, the future of the site of Lafitte's establishment on Barataria Bay is bleak. Erosion will lead to the inundation of the remaining terrestrial portion of the site within the next two decades. The treasure of Jean Lafitte is neither silver nor gold; it is the opportunity to find direct evidence of the nexus for his illicit activities. Certainly, many of the items discovered represent refuse associated with the hundreds of people who lived in the community. Perhaps there are items lost during the transfer to lighters or broken and deposited during the 1814 reduction of the lair. The site can serve as a counterpoint to the romance of pirates and smugglers. The reality is that they dealt in goods desired by the "law-abiding" citizens of New Orleans. There were no golden treasure chests. Instead, the wealth of these pirates was in human "cargoes" of slaves or such mundane items as cloth, salt, cocoa, bar iron, window glass, table glass, and ceramics.

We need only consider what is preserved in the archaeological record to recognize what we are missing from the systemic world. If the documentary record had been mute on the activities that took place on Grand Terre Island at the beginning of the nineteenth century, would we be able to recognize this as anything more than an early nineteenth century settlement? We do have historical documents, however, so an investigation of the site's terrestrial and submerged features and deposits could provide information on the organization and layout of a pirate settlement. Perhaps there is a pattern in the types or distribution of the artifacts that might be unique to this kind of site. Should a pattern be discerned, it could be tested in Galveston at Maison Rouge. Further investigations just may help move us a step closer to the factual world of the mysterious Jean Lafitte.

Acknowledgments

I am indebted to J. Barto Arnold of Texas A&M University and Tom Oertling of Galveston, Texas, for their help in tracking down Lafitte's "Campechy." I especially wish to thank Jeff Modzelewski, president of the Lafitte Society of Galveston, Texas, and Sheldon Kindall for providing background on the archaeological investigations conducted at Maison Rouge. Many thanks are also due to Russell K. Skowronek of Santa Clara University for his extraordinary support during the completion of this project. Figures 3.5–3.11 are courtesy of Godzinski et al. 2001. All other figures are by Joan M. Exnicios unless otherwise noted.

4

Contraband Traders, Lawless Vagabonds, and the British Settlement and Occupation of Roatan, Bay Islands, Honduras

J. David McBride

> The English took Possession of the Island of Rattan in the year 1742 during the War with Spain. On the Peace in 1748, Gov. Trelawney was ordered by Letter from The Duke of Bedford, Nov. 25, to withdraw from there the Companies of his Regiment & disband the Officers of that Garrison. Mr. Trelawney, in his letter of April 8, 1749, informs The Duke of Bedford of the receipt of that order, & his compliance therewith, but proposes to leave the Detachment on the Mosquito Shore, to protect the Trade there, & defend it from any Attack from the Spains Governors on Pretence that it belongs to Indians, or Contraband Traders, & Lawless Vagabonds.
>
> **Public Records Office, National Archives, 1749**

This quotation gives a tantalizingly brief summary of the 1740s occupation of the island of Roatan in the Bay of Honduras and the need to extend this occupation to "protect the trade there." But what was this trade, and what was this war with Spain (known as the War of Jenkins' Ear) about? In this chapter I investigate these questions and more particularly examine historically and archaeologically the British attempts to protect this trade, especially the important resource of logwood. The Spanish referred to British trade as piracy, since they claimed all of Central America (including the Mosquito Coast, the present Belize, and Roatan) as their territory.

In the 1720s British attempts to deal with piracy against their shipping in the Caribbean and the Atlantic became more successful. The most effective methods for eliminating piracy were passing more effective legislation, issuing pardons, and increasing naval patrols in the high piracy areas (Cordingly 1995:203). In 1720 there were more than two thousand pirates, but by 1726 the numbers had shrunk to only about two hundred (Cordingly 1995:203). Many pirates became logwood cutters in present-day Belize and were described, even by the British, as "contraband traders and lawless vagabonds" (Craig 1969; Joseph 1980).

The contraband trade in the Caribbean was a very serious threat to the British economy in Jamaica and was strongly fought by the Spanish. The contraband trade was a factor in the decline of Spain's empire in America (Brown 1928:189). Spain's response to the trade was to send privateers, known as Guarda-Costa, to seize British ships carrying "illegal" cargoes (Pares 1936:46–48; Temperley 1909:206). The British issued "Letters of Reprisal" to their privateers to recover the lost ships and cargoes. The privateer activities and contraband trading continued and eventually led to the War of Jenkins' Ear in 1739, which resulted in the British settlement of Roatan in 1742 (Davidson 1974:53; Pares 1936:46–48; Temperley 1909:206).

Early Settlement of Roatan

The location and physical conditions of Roatan and the other Bay Islands have allowed for settlement since prehistoric times (figure 4.1). Roatan is about thirty miles long and thirteen miles wide, located in the Bay of Honduras about thirty miles from the coast of Honduras. The Bay Islands lie in the tradewind belt, with constant winds between nineteen and twenty-six miles per hour (Davidson 1974:12). The settlement of Port Royal is on the southeastern side of Roatan. The harbor there provided protection to ships and settlements and was described by Thomas Jefferys, geographer to the king of England, as naturally fortified with rocks and shoals, with an entrance so narrow that only one ship could pass at a time (Davidson 1974:59). The island also provided fresh water and food, including wild hogs, deer, wild fowl, turtle, and fish.

Roatan was inhabited prior to the arrival of Europeans. Archaeological investigations thus far have not conclusively determined the cultural affiliation of the prehistoric inhabitants (Davidson 1974; Epstein 1959; Strong 1933). W. D. Strong (1933) believes these early inhabitants are Paya, while others have concluded they are Maya or Lenca or Jicaque (Davidson 1974:19). Based on ceramics, the occupation of Roatan began during the Late Maya Classic period and continued until the Historic period (Davidson 1974:24; Epstein 1959). Archaeological sites on Roatan include residential, burial, and offertory sites, and ceremonial sites have been located on both the Bay Islands of Utila and Guanaja (Davidson 1974:22).

The Spanish visited the Bay Islands during the sixteenth century. Christopher Columbus passed through the area during his fourth voyage (1502 to 1504) and provided the first written accounts of the area (Davidson 1974:25). The Spanish did not settle the Bay Islands, but the islands were subjected to Spanish slaving raids. In 1503 the queen of Spain authorized the capture of "Caribs" (Indians believed to be cannibals) as slave labor in the mines of Española (Davidson 1974:31; Sauer 1966:193–94). In 1516 Spanish slavers collected 400 Indians from Utila and another island for use in the mines of Santiago, Cuba. Other raids

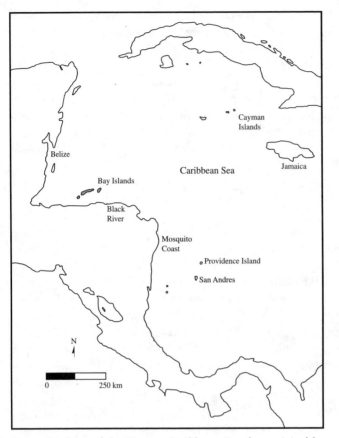

Figure 4.1. Map of the Western Caribbean. Based on original by William V. Davidson, 1974. Used by permission of William V. Davidson.

occurred in the 1520s, but precise numbers are not known. By this time slaves were also being imported from Africa for use in mines and in agricultural activities (Davidson 1974:33). Although Spanish slaving raids depopulated many islands in the Caribbean, native peoples were still living on Roatan and other Bay Islands when they were visited by English pirates in the late sixteenth century (Sauer 1966:194; Wright 1932).

Spain claimed all of the West Indies and Central America and the riches that they found there. English, French, and Dutch privateers and pirates were not far behind the Spanish and were not concerned with Spanish claims. Columbus took refuge at the Madeira Islands during his third voyage when he heard French corsairs were in the area. In 1522 the Viscount of Dieppe sent Captain Jean Fleury to capture the ships on which Hernán Cortés sent the treasure of

Moctezuma to Spain. Fleury was later captured by the Spanish and executed (Sauer 1966:51–52).

Pirates used islands without Spanish settlements like Roatan to obtain supplies and to careen and repair their ships. In August of 1577 an English captain with two ships, sixty men, and many cannon arrived at the island of Guanaja. The English took the native village and occupied it, while the inhabitants fled into the bush. The English pirates supplied themselves with food and overhauled their ships. A Spanish contingent including Captain Diego López and twenty men arrived from Trujillo after receiving word of the English occupation from the Indians. The ensuing fight left the English captain and ten of his crew dead, according to the Spanish. Captain López also reported that the remaining Englishmen may subsequently have sailed their frigate to Roatan and looted the Indian villages on the island (Wright 1932:198, 208).

In 1630 the Providence Company was incorporated in England to settle the West Indies (Newton 1914:86–87). The company consisted of English politicians and businessmen, including Puritan notables John Pym and the Earl of Warwick. Its main settlement was on Providence Island (now Santa Catalina) off the coast of Nicaragua. The island was settled primarily by Puritans, but the purpose of the Providence Company was always profit. Roatan, which was renamed Rich Island for Lord Henry Rich, the Earl of Holland, was also part of the Providence Company's holdings and was granted to William Claiborne of Maryland and Virginia in 1638 (Newton 1914:267). Puritan colonists arrived in late 1638 or early 1639 and remained there until they were expelled by the Spanish in 1642 (Davidson 1974:50–15; Newton 1914:315). Little is known of the settlement, although it may have been located at Old Port Royal, east of the island's eighteenth-century fort (Davidson 1974:49). If the Rich Island settlement was similar to the settlement at Providence Island, it would have focused on farming and trade with the Indians. Farming was not very profitable on Providence, and the settlers eventually turned to piracy. This may also have occurred at Roatan (Newton 1914:269).

As previously mentioned, the Spanish evicted the Roatan settlers in 1642, a year after their fellow colonizers at Providence Island were removed. The English Civil War began in 1642, essentially ending connections between England and the West Indies. In 1650 the Spanish removed the remaining Indians from the Bay Islands, hoping to discourage settlement or use of the island by pirates. For the next ninety years, the only visitors to Roatan were pirates, who used the island for supplies, careening, and the safety of the harbor (Davidson 1974:50–51).

In 1722 the pirate Edward Low kidnapped Philip Ashton, a twenty-year-old Massachusetts fisherman. After refusing to become a pirate by signing the pirate articles (their code of behavior), Ashton was kept as a prisoner aboard a ship. He escaped onto Roatan when the pirates stopped there to fill their water casks and clean their ships (Barnard 1976:18). Ashton describes the pirates' activities:

Roatan Harbour, as all about the Gulf of *Honduras*, is full of small Islands, which go by the General Name of the Keys. When we had got in
here, *Low* and some of his Chief Men had got a shoar upon one of these
small islands, which they called *Port Royal Key*, where they made them
Booths, and they were Carousing, Drinking, and Firing, while the two
Sloops, the *Rhode-Island*, and that which *Low* brought with him from the
Bay were cleaning. (Barnard 1976:19)

Ashton spent sixteen months on Roatan, living on coconuts and turtle eggs.
Although there was plenty of wildlife, such as fish and wild hogs, Ashton lacked
weapons to hunt them. He constructed a hut but did not give details. He also
complained about the "muskettos" (Barnard 1976:26). Ashton described the
pirates as "a vile Crew of Miscreants, to whom it is sport to do Mischief." Besides
being an unsavory lot, Captain Low and his men were also involved in the logwood trade, which became important to the next settlement on Roatan.

Based on the account of Philip Ashton, pirate captain Edward Low and his
men probably left little evidence of their visit to Roatan (Barnard 1976:19). The
pirates stopped long enough to get supplies and repair their ships. Ashton does
not say that the pirates camped or lived on the islands. It appears that Low and
his men stayed at Roatan for only a day or two (Barnard 1976:18–20).

Logwood and the War of Jenkins' Ear

The pirates continued to be held in favor by the English government in Jamaica
until after the treaty of Madrid in 1670. Under the treaty the Spanish accepted
English claims on settlements, including Jamaica, and the English promised to
cease commissioning privateer raids on Spanish ships and settlements. Unfortunately, word of the treaty did not reach Jamaica before Governor Thomas
Modyford authorized Henry Morgan and his fleet of thirty-six ships and 1800
pirates to sack Panama in late 1670. The rule of Morgan's clique in Jamaica
ended with the arrival of Sir Thomas Lynch as governor in June of 1671 and the
return of Governor Modyford to London under arrest (Newton 1933:270–77).
In 1682 Governor Lynch charged Captain Morgan with chasing many of his
former associates off the seas (Joseph 1980:69). As piracy and privateering went
out of favor, the English government turned to trade as a means to achieve foreign
policy goals and to enrich the state treasury (Newton 1933:276–77). At this very
time, a new "drug" or dye ingredient, known as logwood, was being heralded for
its commercial uses and profitability by English colonial officials and merchants
(Joseph 1980:69–70).

Logwood (*Haematoxylon campechianum*) is a small tree with a compressed
and fluted trunk, grayish bark, and irregular branches with stout spines. It is
found in coastal swamp areas of Campeche around Laguna de Términos and in
Belize along the Río Hondo, New River, and Belize River (Craig 1969:54; Offen

2000:135). The reddish brown heartwood of the tree was used for dyes for the woolen industries in Europe and America.

The earliest evidence for English interest in logwood was during the 1630s. Members of the Providence Company were interested in the islands of Tortuga and Hispañola because of the presence of dyewoods (Craig 1969:55; Parsons 1956:6). The first settlement in the Bay of Honduras was by a Captain Peter Wallis, who may have been a Puritan from Providence Island. Wallis and a sizable contingent of refugees from Providence may have settled in Belize as a result of the Spanish attack in 1642 (Craig 1969:55; Parson 1956:6). During the 1670s Spain was at the nadir of its power and in the worst financial depression of its history. The Spanish were unable or uninterested in colonizing the Yucatán marshes where the logwood grew and were unable to dislodge the English logwood cutters (Joseph 1980:72). Logwood cutting became an alternative occupation for pirates forced from the sea. Between 1670 and 1690 piracy and logwood cutting began to merge. In the early 1670s two-thirds of the English pirates would enter the profitable logwood trade, at either Campeche or the Bay of Honduras, according to the governor of Jamaica (Joseph 1980:74).

Life in a logwood camp in the 1670s was described by William Dampier (1906a, 2:18–19), a pirate, naturalist, and logwood cutter. The logwood-cutting settlements in the Bay of Honduras and the Bay of Campeche were initially very primitive. The cutters made palmetto-thatched huts that were "slightly" built, although the thatching prevented the sometimes violent rains from soaking in (Dampier 1906a:79). The huts were built near a creek and the logwood groves. The logwood was cut down to the heartwood, which was then taken to the edge of the creek to be transported to ships. On Dampier's trip to the bay his group hired the logwood cutters' boat (a periago) to transport the logwood to the ship. They paid the cutters in money, rum, and sugar. The logwood cutters numbered about 250 and grew "frolicksom" after drinking the rum punch made by Dampier and the crew. When the commercial transactions were completed, the logwood cutters entertained the pirate crew with a beef and pork barbecue with meat that they had hunted in the savannas (Dampier 1906a, 2:18).

The heyday of the logwood trade was between 1650 and 1750, when demand outran supply and prices reached 100 pounds sterling per ton (Joseph 1980:70–71). More than two hundred vessels entered the settlements in Campeche and Belize between 1671 and 1684 and brought over six hundred tons per year to Jamaica. From Jamaica, Yankee and Dutch traders would take the logwood to New England and the European continent, and English traders to England (Joseph 1980:70).

The War of Jenkins' Ear was over trade in the Caribbean, especially the logwood trade (Pares 1936; Temperley 1909). The Spanish government wanted this trade to stop; British merchantmen began to complain about Spanish depredations as early as 1714, as Spanish privateers, or the Guarda-Costas, seized their ships for carrying contraband. The Spanish continued to seize ships that they

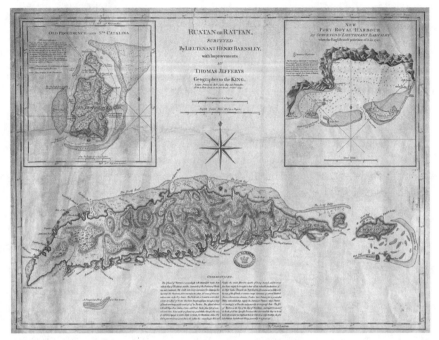

Figure 4.2. Map of Ruatan or Rattan. Surveyed by Lt. Henry Barnsley with improvements by Thomas Jefferys, 1775. The National Archives, Public Records Office. Used by permission of the National Archives, Kew, U.K.

believed to carry contraband, and the British continued to complain about the seizures and to trade in contraband until war was declared in 1739. Many British merchants and politicians argued for war. The final depredation came when the Spanish Guarda-Costa boarded a British merchant ship under the command of Captain Robert Jenkins and allegedly severed his ear with a cutlass in 1739 (Pares 1936:60–61; Temperley 1909).

The Roatan harbor that attracted the pirates in the seventeenth century also attracted the British military in the 1740s (figure 4.2). Roatan was described to Governor William Trelawney of Jamaica by Lieutenant Hodgson as one of the best harbors in the Bay of Honduras and a suitable refuge for the baymen and for agriculture (Davidson 1974:53; Pares 1936:103). In 1742 the island was occupied by 250 of Trelawney's Jamaica regiment of British regulars along with African slaves to erect the fortifications and protect the logwood trade (Davidson 1974:54). Roatan was to be a headquarters for all of the British and British shipping for the Bay of Honduras and the Mosquito Coast. It was also to be a starting point for contraband trade with the Spanish colonies in Central America and the Caribbean and a base for men-of-war to enforce the laws of navigation and drive the Dutch out of the logwood trade (Pares 1936:103).

The settlement at Port Royal, Roatan, consisted of the town of Augusta, the hamlet of Litchfield, Fort Frederick on the harbor mainland, and Fort George on the cay in the harbor. Fort George had twenty cannon and a large structure, perhaps a barracks or magazine. Fort Frederick, on the west side, had six cannon and outbuildings. Eighteenth-century maps suggest that Augusta had approximately thirty structures spread over thirty acres (Davidson 1974:56). William Davidson (1974:56) mentions some stone building foundations visible in the 1970s, suggesting substantial construction. Most buildings were probably made of thatch. Litchfield was a smaller cluster of houses on the next ridge west of Augusta; and the Henry Barnsley map (Public Records Office, National Archives [PRO, NA] 1742a) and the Thomas Jefferys map (PRO, NA 1775) show another cluster of structures on the east side of Port Royal. Davidson (1974:54) estimates a population of 800 to 1,000 in 1743.

Life at a military base in the Caribbean was not necessarily pleasant (Buckley 1998). The most serious problem was illness. One of the principal reasons for having slave labor in the Caribbean outposts was to limit the soldiers' exposure to the sun, which was thought to be a cause of the illness (Buckley 1998:131). The soldiers' diet was limited to salted pork, salted beef, bread, peas, and rice. They rarely, if ever, ate the local seafood. Craftsmen and camp followers may have accompanied the soldiers. Often women (either employed workers or slaves) did various jobs for the soldiers, including laundry and cooking. These women may have been slaves or the wives or consorts of the soldiers (Buckley 1998:153).

The settlement of Roatan did not progress as Governor Trelawney had envisioned. The island did not produce enough food for the settlers and soldiers, so they had to be supplied from Jamaica and William Pitt's cattle ranch at Black River (Davidson 1974:57). Major Caulfield, the commander of the companies at Roatan, wrote to the governor of Jamaica, informing him that only 50 of the 250 troops were fit for duty (PRO, NA 1745). Most of the farmers complained that the soil was poor (PRO, NA 1743). Critics of the settlement said that Roatan was out of the way for the logwood ships and that the Black River/Belize settlements were better suited as bases for contraband trade with the Spanish colonies. Trelawney lost interest in Roatan and began to neglect it when the safety of Jamaica was threatened (Pares 1936:104).

The Spanish never attacked Roatan during this occupation, but the English withdrew under conditions of the 1748 Treaty of Aix-la-Chapelle, in which Spain and England returned conquered territory (Pares 1936:540). Caulfield and his soldiers left in November 1749 (Davidson 1974:58; PRO, NA 1749). There was no mention of the condition of the abandoned settlement or fortifications.

Postwar Settlement of Roatan

Following the 1748 treaty, the English returned briefly to Roatan to graze mules from Trujillo on the Honduran mainland, under Spanish licenses, but did not establish a settlement (Davidson 1974:60). Occasionally the British Navy would visit the island. Admiral Burnaby made two large-scale maps of the island in 1765 (Davidson 1974:60). In the 1770s England and Spain began to make grand plans for the Caribbean and Central America. Spain hoped to remove the English from its settlements in Belize/Black River, in Honduras, and the Mosquito Coast of Nicaragua; and the English hoped to capture Nicaragua and build a canal between the Atlantic and the Pacific (Floyd 1967). Once again Roatan was to become a small part in these schemes. On October 5, 1779, the English ordered Colonel Dalrymple to occupy the island to provide protection for the logwood cutters on the mainland (Davidson 1974:61). Three weeks later the Spanish attacked the settlement at George's Cay, Belize, and 250 logwood cutters and slaves escaped to Roatan. When the Spanish attacked the Black River settlement five months later, 300 more refugees fled to Roatan (Davidson 1974; Floyd 1967; Kemble 1884).

Things were not going well for the English. They were pushed out of Belize and Honduras and were soon pushed out of the thirteen colonies in North America. The major English offensive in Nicaragua failed because they had to wait for additional troops and supplies; and many became sick or died of diseases (Floyd 1967).

The Spanish reoccupied Trujillo, a coastal city adjacent to the Bay Islands, uninhabited since it was sacked by the English in the seventeenth century. There they began to assemble troops and ships for an attack on Roatan. Over 600 regulars and militiamen were drawn from settlements all over Spanish America, along with two ships-of-the-line and ten other frigates, with forty cannon. These were placed under the command of Matías de Gálvez, president of Guatemala (Davidson 1974:61–62; Floyd 1967:156).

Gálvez left Trujillo on March 14, 1782, and sailed to Roatan. Fort George was defended by twenty cannon and men with small arms. The majority of Roatan's inhabitants were slaves and could not be armed. The Spanish arrived on March 15, and the men-of-war and frigates opened fire the next morning. Fort George returned fire; a fusillade lasted the whole day. The next day the English surrendered, suffering two casualties, both slaves. The English prisoners were sent to Havana to be exchanged, and the slaves were sent to be sold. The Spanish burned the town, dismantled the fort, and took the cannon aboard their ships. On March 20 Gálvez wrote to his brother that "The English establishment at Roatan has been destroyed" (Floyd 1967:156).

This second British settlement of Roatan was different from the 1740s occupation. The majority of the inhabitants were slaves, who were refugees from the Belize logwood camps. According to a map drawn by Davidson (1974:63) (figure 4.3) there were more structures in the 1780s at Fort George and Fort Frederick, indicating that military personnel may have been living there. The other structures were spread out along Port Royal, as opposed to the 1740s concentration at Augusta.

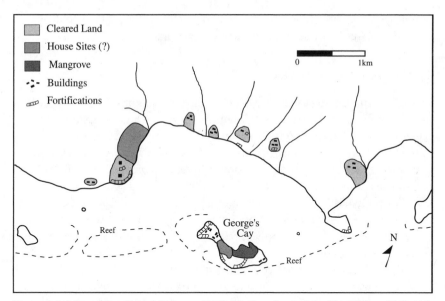

Figure 4.3. Map of Port Royal, Roatan, 1779–82. Based on original by William V. Davidson, 1974. Used by permission of William V. Davidson.

Roatan was uninhabited from 1782 until March 1797, when 5,000 Black Carib prisoners were transported by the English from St. Vincent and marooned on Roatan (Davidson 1974:65). The Spanish resettled most of the Black Caribs to areas around Trujillo; but some remained and settled at Punta Gorda on the northeast shore of the island (Davidson 1974:65).

In 1834 slavery was abolished in all British colonies, including the Cayman Islands. The Euroamerican Cayman Islanders feared a loss of power and property, and many immigrated to other parts of the Caribbean. They first arrived in Roatan in 1830; over the next twenty-five years more than 700 settlers relocated there (Davidson 1974:75–78). Most of the modern towns were founded during this period.

In 1852 the British claimed the Bay Islands again and set up a colony that lasted for seven years. This time it was not the Spanish but the Americans who were upset. After 1823 American foreign policy was based on the Monroe doctrine, which basically stated that the New World was no longer open to European colonization. After the British left in 1857, Roatan became part of Honduras. Commercial fruit companies built plantations in the 1860s, but they were wiped out in a hurricane in 1877 (Davidson 1974:93).

Agriculture and boat building were the major economic activities during the early twentieth century. In the 1960s tourism became an important part of the economy. One resort (Roatan Lodge) was located in Port Royal, and a marina was planned for the eastern part of the harbor. Several houses were built around

Port Royal, one directly on the site of Fort Frederick. In 1980 the old English town site of Augusta was under cassava cultivation.

The Archaeological Investigations

In 1980 an archaeological survey of the eighteenth-century British sites at Port Royal was conducted (figure 4.4). The primary research goal was to determine what remained of the settlements and if the 1740s occupation could be differentiated from the later 1780s occupation. A secondary goal was to find evidence of earlier seventeenth-century occupations. The survey consisted of surface collection and excavation of shovel test pits. It was focused on Augusta, the habitation site shown on 1740s historic maps, and Fort George, on George's Cay. We selected these areas because of their potential to answer our research questions and due to limitations in access and vegetation cover at other areas. We also hoped that individual house sites could be identified at Augusta and that soldier, slave, or British farmer occupations could be distinguished.

The Augusta site is situated on a ridge approximately 400 by 150 feet. A grid was established, and the area was surface collected. The portion of the area under yucca cultivation had visibility of 75 percent. Another portion of the area had recently been burned; here visibility was reduced to between 40 percent and 75

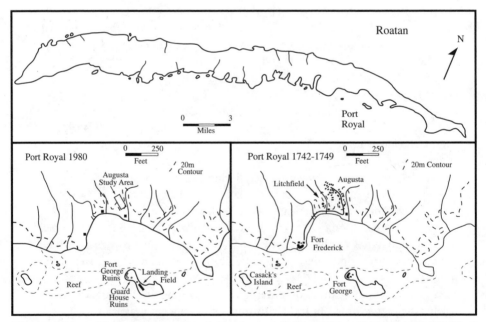

Figure 4.4. Map of Roatan and Port Royal. Based on original by William V. Davidson, 1974. Used by permission of William V. Davidson.

percent. The slopes and areas outside the grid had natural vegetation cover, limiting visibility to 10–50 percent.

Shovel tests were dug at 50-foot intervals, beginning at the datum point (W0N0) and running westward to W350 N0 (figure 4.5). The S50 east–west line was also tested. The slope of the ridge prohibited testing at the N50 line, but pits were dug at the N25 line. The shovel tests produced very few artifacts but did provide an understanding of the stratigraphy of the ridge.

A surface collection of the gully to the southwest of the ridge also resulted in the recovery of artifacts. The area had recently been burned off, and vegetation had not yet regrown. The gullies behind the western gully also contained some artifacts. Other gully slopes and ridges around the Augusta site were too overgrown to survey.

Three 5×5-foot test units and two 2×2-foot test units were excavated in the Augusta site. The 5×5-foot units (W310 S30, W280 S30, and W125 S0) were excavated in areas with surface indications of cultural activity. The test units provided some additional information, but not in the quantity hoped for. They all reflected similar stratigraphy with no visible features. The two 2×2-foot test units were also excavated as a result of surface conditions. One 2×2 unit, at W15 S5, was excavated inside the remains of a structure. The other, at W39 N0, was located at the bottom of a slope. The material recovered from the survey and testing includes delftware, bottle glass, and cannonballs and dates to the 1742 occupation by the British military.

Although the location of the seventeenth-century occupations by the Puritans or any pirate occupations is not well documented, Davidson (1974:49) thought that the 1642 Puritan settlement could be at Old Port Royal, east of present-day Port Royal. Part of this area was surface collected, but no seventeenth- or eighteenth-century material was recovered. Additional surveys, involving surface collection, were undertaken along the Port Royal beaches and in ravines, or bights, to locate any indications of pirate activity or the 1780 occupations by the logwood cutter refugees. These surveys were also limited by surface visibility. No artifacts that could be dated to seventeenth or early eighteenth century pirate occupations or from the late eighteenth century logwood refugees were recovered.

Augusta Survey Results

The artifacts recovered from the Augusta excavations and surface collections are presented in table 4.1. The most numerous artifact type was bottle glass, which composed almost 80 percent of the assemblage (figure 4.6). Ceramics included English delftware, Chinese porcelain, redware, and coarse earthenware (figure 4.7). Cannonballs, clay pipe fragments, a glass bead, window glass, bricks, and nails were also found.

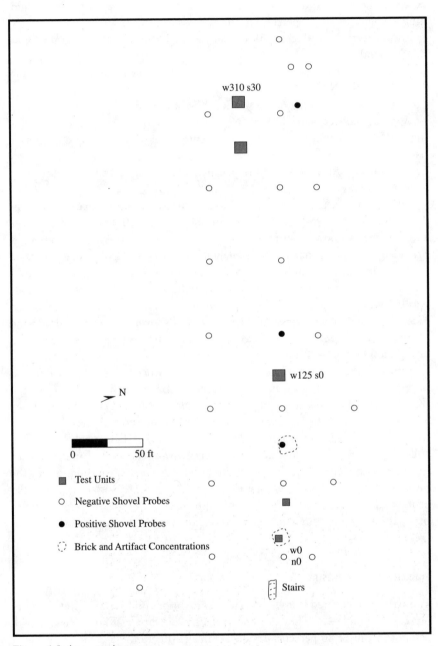

Figure 4.5. Augusta site map.

Table 4.1. Artifact Frequencies

Artifact	Number	Percentage
Bottle glass	272	80.9
Ceramics	28	8.3
Pipe fragments	9	2.7
Nails	5	1.5
Window glass	7	2.1
Cannonballs	6	1.8
Beads	1	0.3
Miscellaneous	8	2.4
Totals	336	100

Chronologically diagnostic materials from Augusta date from the first half of the eighteenth century and are likely associated with the 1740s British military occupation rather than the 1780s occupation. The blue hand-painted delftware designs with a tulip motif were chronologically widespread but most common on English sites before 1765 (Miller and Stone 1970:30; Noël Hume 1978:108). The bottle glass recovered was thick, dark-green glass indicative of eighteenth-century wine or liquor bottles; and the neck fragments and bases indicate that the bottles dated from the period 1736 to 1755 (Noël Hume 1978:98). The absence of creamware and pearlware, the most common ceramics on British sites of the late eighteenth century, suggests that the Augusta townsite area was not occupied in the 1779–82 period.

Figure 4.6. Bottle fragments.

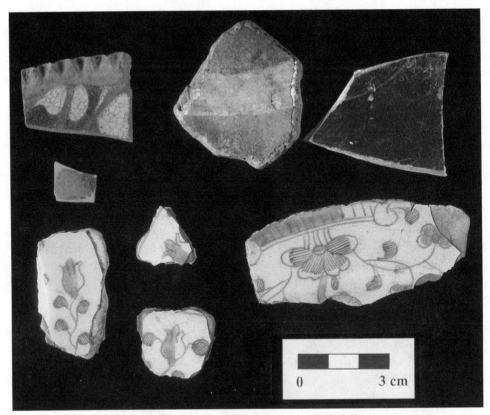

Figure 4.7. Ceramics. *Top row*: glazed redware; *bottom row*: British delftware.

Although the Chinese porcelain sherds are not a good temporal indicator, they are good indicators of high economic status and cultural refinement. Their presence at Augusta, particularly in the forms of plates and serving dishes, suggests upper-class tastes and behavior and the likely presence of officers or successful merchants or farmers. The bottle glass recovered is also indicative of the behavior of the eighteenth-century residents. The large assemblage of wine or rum bottles shows that drinking was an important activity for these early soldiers and trader/pirates.

While Davidson (1974:56) suggests that most structures at Augusta were thatched huts, architecture artifacts recovered from Augusta suggest more substantial buildings. These artifacts include bricks and brick rubble, five wrought nails, and seven window-glass fragments. The bricks found in shovel probe W85 S5 and unit W15 S5 are possibly the remains of foundations or chimneys. Brick rubble was also found in unit W125 S0. The bricks discovered in these units indicate substantial residences or government buildings at these locations. Also, the location of the buildings near the east end of the ridge nearest the harbor suggests that they were the regimental headquarters or officers' quarters.

Interestingly, the six cannonballs were found in the test unit at W125 S0, with the brick rubble. This may suggest the use of this building as a military storage facility and provide an explanation for its more substantial construction. It is also possible that this was the location of a gun emplacement. The cannonballs were all one-pounders, suggesting a gun that was used by infantry and could be moved by a horse or several men.

Fort George Investigations

Fort George was also explored, but excavations were limited because there was little soil development on the key. Architectural remains of the fort were the most significant finds. The walls of the fort, the remains of the guardhouse, and a well were recorded. Fort George is a Redan or a field fortification, with two parapets forming a salient angle (Hinds and Fitzgerald 1998:73). Seventeen cannon were located at the fort (Davidson 1974:54). The remains were not in a condition to allow determination of the number of gun emplacements (figure 4.8). A guardhouse is the only building shown at the fort on the Barnsley map (PRO, NA 1742a) and the Jefferies map (PRO, NA 1775). The Spanish destroyed many of the fortifications after the fort's capture in 1782 (Davidson 1974:62). Hurricanes and looting have also impacted the site.

Near the fort ruins are the remains of a stone structure that may be the guardhouse mentioned on the historic maps (PRO, NA 1742a, 1775) (figures 4.9 and

Figure 4.8. Fort George, looking southwest.

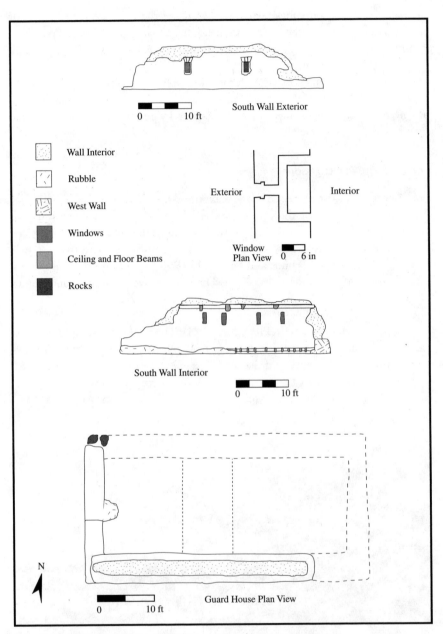

South Wall Exterior

0   10 ft

Wall Interior

Rubble

West Wall

Windows

Ceiling and Floor Beams

Rocks

Exterior   Interior

Window
Plan View   0   6 in

South Wall Interior

0   10 ft

N

Guard House Plan View

0   10 ft

Figure 4.9. Plan views and profiles of guard house at Fort George.

Figure 4.10. Guard house at Fort George: south wall, exterior.

4.10). Davidson (1974:57) suggests that this structure may have been the barracks, although the locals refer to it as the powder magazine. The structure is twenty-four feet wide and about fifty feet long, although only part of the building remains. The most interesting features are the windows: two on the exterior of the south wall and four on the interior. This configuration is commonly seen in illustrations of powder magazines but not in pictures of British barracks in the West Indies (Buckley 1998:152, 328). The size and configuration of the Fort George building ruin suggests that it was more likely the guardhouse.

Summary and Conclusions

The English occupied Roatan during three periods between 1638 and 1782, and pirates visited the island several times between the sixteenth and eighteenth centuries. The first settlement was by a group of English Puritans, with a grant from the Providence Company. There is very little documentation on the settlement, its size, or even its location. The later settlements were better documented, with maps showing structures in the 1740s and later. Historical documents also give population numbers, supply lists, and plans for future developments. A drawing of the 1782 battle between the Spanish and the English at Roatan shows the fort and houses.

The 1742 map by Lieutenant Henry Barnsley shows Augusta, Fort George, Fort Fredrick, a cooperage, and an area planned for a town. Fort George, on the key, includes the redan and a large structure described as a guardhouse. Fort Frederick was destroyed in the construction of a house in the 1960s (William Davidson, personal communication, 1980). No remains of the cooperage or of a town on the east end of Port Royal were located during the survey.

The survey focused on the Augusta site and on Fort George. The Barnsley map shows many houses at the location of Augusta, on a ridge overlooking the harbor. The layout of the town was not the typical military organization. Instead of rows of buildings, Augusta follows the topography of the ridge. During the survey we found foundations for two structures and numerous kitchen, architecture, and arms artifacts. Bricks discovered in an excavation unit, window glass, and nails were the only evidence of structures. The Augusta area was under cultivation, and the farmer could have removed bricks and building stones.

The Augusta site appears to be primarily a military habitation area occupied during the 1740s. Most of the ceramics recovered from the site were British Delft. After the 1760s the ceramics at British sites are typically dominated by creamware and pearlware. The lack of creamware and pearlware at Augusta places the occupation in the 1740s rather than the 1780s. The most numerous artifacts found were bottle glass. All of the bottle glass is typically described as from wine bottles, although the locals refer to them as "Pirate Rum Bottles." The forms recovered from Roatan are similar to those described by Ivor Noël Hume (1978:65–66) as dating between the 1730s and the 1750s. Two of the favorite leisure activities of the British soldiers were drinking and smoking (Buckley 1998:335). The relatively large number of bottle glass fragments could also represent the presence of soldiers. The structures correspond to the 1742 map of the island and indicate little modification during the 1780 occupation.

At Fort George Cay the ruins of fort, a powder magazine, and a well were observed to be in fairly good condition. No other remains of houses or other structures were found on the key. The only structures shown on the 1742 Barnsley map are the fort and a building called a barracks. Based on the substantial nature of the construction and its windows, it was probably a powder magazine rather than a barracks. There was no evidence of occupation by earlier pirates or the later logwood cutter refugees on the key. Habitation was probably limited to the vicinity around the fort, because of rocky conditions to the east and mangrove swamps to the west.

In 1779 refugees from the logwood camps in Belize came to Roatan. The structure of their settlements was much more dispersed compared to the earlier military settlement or town sites like Augusta. The majority of the logwood camps' population consisted of slaves, and the actual number of British solders is unclear (Davidson 1974:62). The Spanish attacked the island in 1782 with two ships-of-the-line and ten smaller ships. After exchanging cannon fire with the Spanish for more than a day, the British surrendered (Davidson 1974:62).

None of the British attempts to settle Roatan were successful. The first Puritan colonists, in the 1630s, were removed by the Spanish. Limited information is available on this settlement, but it was part of the Providence Company's plan to settle the region and expand English trade and the empire (Newton 1914). On Providence Island and perhaps Roatan farming was a failure, and the settlers turned to contraband trading and piracy.

The British left Roatan in 1749 after treaty negotiations ended the War of Jenkins' Ear. The British settlements at Belize and Black River remained, with many contraband traders and lawless vagabonds. When the Spanish gave up claim to Belize In 1763, the logwood trade became legitimate. Toward the end of the century logwood became less important for the dye-making industry, and mahogany became a more important product.

All figures are by J. David McBride unless noted otherwise.

5

A Mariner's Utopia

Pirates and Logwood in the Bay of Honduras

Daniel Finamore

Modern notions of pirate life are at once both alluring and horrifying; indulgence in hedonistic pleasures and freedom from economic and social oppression are immediately countered by immoral acts, everyday violence, and the promise of an early death. Any archaeological study of pirate life must contend with the romanticized and often unfounded notions of piracy that pervade the modern imagination in order to frame interpretations within the context of not only true pirate acts but also true motivations. Although ships were the theaters of pirate expression, communities also existed on the coastal margins of the European sphere of hegemony. At these terrestrial locales pirates acted out their distinctive cultural roles, recreating and reinforcing an unusual set of social relations that distinguished them from mainstream European society.

Archaeological investigations of pirate life that contextualize assemblages by taking into account the unconventional circumstances of site formation are most likely to yield robust interpretations. During the 1990s, excavations of a pirate encampment near the mouth of the Belize River were undertaken, which were greatly informed by firsthand accounts of life at the site but even more significantly by a broader understanding of social forces that fostered a community with a unified set of mores and an alternative way of life "beyond the line."

Piracy and Logwood

In the turbulent times following the 1667 Treaty of Madrid, in which the English Crown agreed to participate with Spain in the suppression of privateering and piracy, the choice for English mariners who had been engaged in that trade or who desired a life different from that of a "Jack tar" or common seaman suddenly narrowed. As summarized by the pirate/explorer William Dampier (1906b, 1:156), they could "either go to Petit Guavas, where the Privateer-Trade still continued, or into the Bay for Logwood." Many went to the coast of Belize, a remote part of Spain's New World empire, where there was no significant Spanish occupation and where logwood (a type of wood utilized to dye textiles and other products) grew in abundance.

Logwood is a small tree with a growth range restricted to the low-lying rivers and swamps around the peripheries of the Yucatán peninsula, most notably the Laguna de Términos in the Bay of Campeche, Cape Catoche in northern Yucatán, and the Belize coast along the western Bay of Honduras. During the sixteenth century, logwood (mostly under its appellations "campechewood" or "blackwood" and the Spanish *palo de tinta* and *palo de Campeche*) was shipped across the Atlantic by Spaniards and distributed to European merchants. It was sold at highly profitable rates, at one point for over £100 per ton (Gibbs 1883:24). The Spanish learned of the properties of logwood from the Maya, who called it *ek*.

Logwood was recognized by English mariners to be a commodity of value by the 1570s, when the buccaneer John Chilton commented on the lading of "a certeine wood called campeche (wherewith they use to die)" (Hakluyt 1927, 6:276). By the 1590s English pirates such as William Parker (Hakluyt 1927, 7:224) and George Clifford, third Earl of Cumberland (Purchas 1905–7, 16:22), staged raids on logwood-laden ship sailing out of Campeche.

Over the next hundred years, English pirates moved from attacking logwood-laden ships of Spain to settling on shore around the Yucatán peninsula to cut the wood themselves. They would eventually deplete those forests, with the exception of those at the western end of the Bay of Honduras, in what is today Belize. In 1677 the Dominican Friar Joseph Delgado was captured on this coast by English pirates under the command of Bartholomew Sharpe and was taken to their encampment on an island several miles from the Belize River mouth, most likely on St. George's Cay (Thompson 1988:28). Sharpe was not on the Belize coast for long, though; three years later he crossed the Isthmus of Panama and attacked Spanish Pacific coast settlements, whereupon he returned to England.

The British Crown attempted to do without logwood, and for most of the seventeenth century its use was actually illegal (Bancroft 1813, 1:340). Although the rationale for the prohibition was based on the ephemeral character of the dye, it seems likely that it had more to do with English-Spanish rivalry in the logwood-producing regions of the Caribbean than with government concern for English consumers. In the informal logwood economy that emerged, therefore, acquisition, transport, and use were beyond government control, effectively relegating the producers to the status of smugglers and thieves.

The life of a wood-cutter at this time is well documented as being a transient one. But by the 1680s some of the mariners began to remain as long-term settlers, with regular introductions of new populations, such as the mutinous crew of Captain John Coxon. They were sent to the Belize River to evacuate the logwood cutters but decided to join them instead (Joseph 1989:14; Burdon 1931–35,

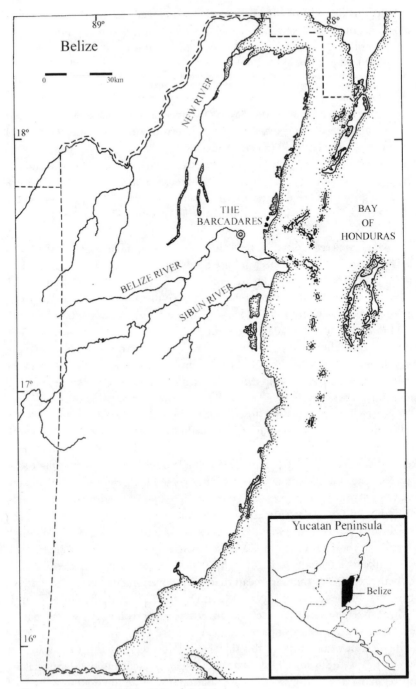

Figure 5.1. Map of Belize, Central America.

1:57). In 1705 "the River of Bullys" was described as the primary point of lading for English logwood ships (Burdon, 1931–35, 1:60).

Practical Geography

The geographical focus of this study has been referred to by a variety of names over the past three hundred years. The early eighteenth century community based around the Belize River (also spelled Balize, Balise, Valis, Wallis, and other ways) was most commonly called the "Bay Settlement"; because the Belize River flows into the Bay of Honduras, its occupants were called baymen.[1] The British settlement along the north coast of the present-day nation of Honduras was called the Mosquito Shore. In the late 1780s the British Mosquito Shore settlement was evacuated, and the independent nation of Honduras was established in 1838. Nevertheless, most nineteenth-century English-language references to "Honduras" actually pertain to the settlement that was the colony of British Honduras from 1862 to 1980, which today is the nation of Belize (figure 5.1).

Pirate Legends

The folklore regarding logwood cutters and pirates has had a powerful influence upon modern perceptions and myths of eighteenth-century Belize. The romantic but commonly held view of Belize history begins with a haven of free-spirited and adventuresome pirates who occasionally sneak out of hiding amid the cays and reef system to perform piratical acts of independence against Britain's economic oppression and Spain's cultural conceit. They eventually become attached to the place, so they find legitimate livelihoods, prosper, form a government, and are finally rewarded with the status of a colony of the British Empire.

It is much more likely, however, that logwood-cutting was considered to be a viable alternative to working either as a sailor or as a pirate—the latter being an extremely dangerous and increasingly untenable form of resistance to life as a laborer in the maritime industries. Popular and scholarly histories of Belize have perpetuated the legacy of pirate origins since the first treatment was attempted. In 1809 Captain George Henderson of the 44th Regiment wrote:

> The keys, it is also well known, were long the chosen haunts of the Buccaneers who infested this part of America; and from which at most seasons they could issue forth, equipped and supplied to carry on their depredations in the neighboring seas, or on the contiguous shores, and to which when pursued they might retreat, protected by the intricacy of a navigation where none dare follow, and, indeed, of which few at the time knew any thing but themselves. Of these hardy spirits and of their modes of life some traces yet remain. (Henderson 1811:25–26)

Henderson did not specify whether the "traces" he referred to were cultural remnants in the existing community or material ones on the ground. Even so, his reminiscences on pirate heritage offered inspiration at the outset of the project.

A Ship Master among Pirates

A key document in the historical record of the early Bay Settlement is the account of Nathaniel Uring, a merchant sea captain who was born in Norfolk, England, and went to sea at the age of fourteen. In 1720 on a voyage to the Bay of Honduras to load logwood, he wrecked his vessel, the *Bangor Galley*, on "Four Kee Reef," part of the extensive network of cays and coral that extends along the Belize coast. During his five-month stay, Uring chronicled the hard labor and tedium that characterized the everyday life of the baymen.

> In the dry Time of the Year the Logwood-Cutters search for a Work; that is, where there are a good Number of Logwood Trees; and then build a Hut near 'em, where they live during the Time they are cutting. When they have cut down the Tree, they Log it, and Chip it, which is cutting off the Bark and Sap, and then lay it in Heaps, cutting away the under-wood, and making Paths to each Heap, that when the Rains come in which overflows the Ground, it serves as so many Creeks or Channels, where they go with small Canows or Dories and load 'em, . . . and carry it to the Barcadares, . . . from whence the People who buy it fetch it. (Uring 1726:354–55)

The strong seasonality of flooding in the river valley meant that the job of cutting wood could be undertaken when the ground was relatively dry, and the cutters could pass the season of highest water on the high banks near the river mouth. Cutting the wood in up-river locations was generally conducted in small groups or even alone. Life near the coast, however, where the settlers brought the wood after the wet season began, was much more communal.

Aspects of Maritime Culture

Predominant anthropological approaches to frontier settlement in new lands most commonly explain existing social and political structures in terms of a "donor culture" adapting to new environmental influences. In the earliest times of the Belize settlement, the overarching commonality that unified the donor population was not ethnicity or geographic region of birth. Rather, the population was most strongly associated with a distinctive economic subculture of itinerant maritime laborers whose professional activities separated them both physically and socially from the majority of land-based society. Although the first settlers of Belize were undoubtedly members of the western European cultural tradition, and many were citizens of the British Empire, they cannot be characterized as merely an extension of a unified British cultural system implanted into an alien environment. They identified themselves as merchant seamen above any ethnic or land-based national affiliation; thus they had a distinctly different cultural identity from that of other migrants from seventeenth-century England (Weibust 1969). The first European settlers of Belize were opportunistic seafaring adventurers who came out of a long tradition of maritime mercantilism, in which social relations and economic organization were guided by maritime institutions far removed from those of the contemporary agriculturalist.

As Marcus Rediker (1987) has argued convincingly, these mariners came from a tradition of laborers who were unified by the strategies for survival that had developed over generations in a highly isolated and dangerous environment on the margins of mainstream European culture. Elements of this maritime social organization included a strong sense of *collectivism* among the lower ranks on board, based on the cooperative labor necessary for most activities; *egalitarianism* harking back to medieval principles of equal shares of rewards for equal risk in an enterprise; and an *antiauthoritarianism* linked to the collectivism of maritime existence (Rediker 1987:146).

What we can perceive of the original political organization in the European settlement of Belize conformed to these maritime ideals. Around the middle of the 1700s, a visiting British naval officer codified a set of laws that had long been used among the settlers to resolve disputes, recognize mutual rights, and punish violators. Called "Burnaby's Code," it operated without empowering individuals with titles such as judge or magistrate (Burdon 1931–35, 1:100–106). Within maritime communities, there is a well-known tradition of adopting general articles as a means of governance by common consent. A similar but more famous set of articles was printed in the August 8, 1723, issue of the *Boston News-Letter*. Those articles of agreement were purportedly signed by every participant on pirate vessels of the day. Like Burnaby's Code, they were also intended to recognize the collective goals of groups working without civil government on the margins of Western society. These pirate articles include one stating that if any gold or jewels are found aboard a prize they must be delivered up for equal division within twenty-four hours or else the finder will suffer whatever punishment the majority of the company thinks fit. Another allocates payment for various injuries suffered during battle, losses incurred for the common good. One article prohibits acts that are a threat to the common good, such as "snaping [sic] of guns in the hold."

Many settlers of Belize were familiar with the pirates' practice of signing articles. During his visit of 1720, Captain Uring noted that "the Wood-Cutters are generally a rude drunken Crew, some of which have been Pirates, and most of them Sailors" (Uring 1726:355). Two years later, Philip Ashton was captured by pirates while fishing off Marblehead, Massachusetts. He was taken to the Caribbean, where he encountered the pirate Ned Low, who "had been to Honduras, and had taken a sloop, and brought off several Baymen." According to Ashton these men had accepted Low's offer to "sign their Articles, and go along with them" (Knight 1976: 2n6). On another occasion, Ashton actually observed the bayman Thomas Grande join a group of pirates (Knight 1976:42).

Second only to the cutting of wood, the activity that dominates early descriptions of the settlement is the consumption of alcohol. Prodigious drinking bouts have certainly never been the exclusive domain of pirates or even of mariners. Nonetheless, shipboard life has long been inextricably associated with the consumption of alcoholic beverages (Pope 1989). Observing the drinking sessions of logwood cutters in Campeche, William Dampier noted the expectation that outsiders would treat the cutters with respect and acceptance of their undisciplined ways:

> If the commanders of [recently arrived] Ships . . . treat all . . . the first day with Punch they will be much respected; . . . but if he be niggardly, they will pay him with their worst wood . . . nay, they will cheat them with hollow Wood filled with dirt in the middle and both ends plugg'd with a piece . . . drove in hard, and then sawed off so neatly, that it's hard to find out the Deceit. (Dampier 1906b, 2:179)

In fact, Aaron Lopez of Newport found out that he had fallen victim to this ploy when he attempted to sell a cargo of logwood in Bristol, only to be informed by the merchants there that one ton of logs was filled with tar (Massachusetts Historical Society 1914–15. 1:116).

Captain Uring also took note of the drinking sessions he witnessed in Belize:

> Their chief Delight is in drinking; and when they broach a Quarter Cask or a Hogshead of Wine, they seldom stir from it while there is a Drop left: . . . keeping at it sometimes a Week together, drinking till they fall asleep; and as soon as they awake, at it again, . . . They paid me a considerable Deference; . . . but I should have been much more agreeable to 'em, if I would have kept 'em Company at their drinking Bouts. (Uring 1726:355–56)

Group practices of alcohol consumption are often explained by anthropologists and sociologists in terms of the socially integrative functions they perform and the sense of *communitas* they provide (Heath 1987:31–32). As emphasized by Mary Douglas (1991:4), "drinking is essentially a social act, performed in a recognized social context," following mutually accepted rules that create a feeling of fraternity among the drinkers. The baymen engaged in heavy drinking as an expression of group cohesion and also a means of symbolic communication with outsiders. By expecting a "gift" of liquor before any business was conducted, with the unstated assumption that they would reciprocate with an honest exchange of logwood, the baymen extended their social world to include the merchant captains who purchased their product, essentially requiring them to accept the baymen's lifestyle.

Excavations at the Barcadares

After suffering shipwreck due to what he viewed as inaccuracies in existing charts of the bay, Uring (1726:358) endured a forced association with the "crew of ungovernable wretches" who resided at the Barcadares, "where was little else to be heard but blasphemy, cursing, and swearing." He wrested control over his socially and environmentally menacing surroundings by drawing his own chart of the Bay of Honduras, with an inset map of the lower Belize River and the settlement of "the Barcadares" (figure 5.2).

Uring's description of the dwellings at the Barcadares indicates rudimentary structures that likely had no foundations and would leave little architectural evidence:

> The Manner of their Lodging is thus: They fix several Crutches in the ground about Four Foot high, and lay Sticks across, and upon those Sticks they lay a good Quantity of Leaves; and this is their Bed. There is also at each Corner of the Bed-Place, a tall Pole fixed, to which they fasten their Covering, which is generally made of Ozenbrigs; so contriv'd that it falls down on every Side, and serves not only for Curtains, but also keeps the Flies from disturbing them. (Uring 1726:182)

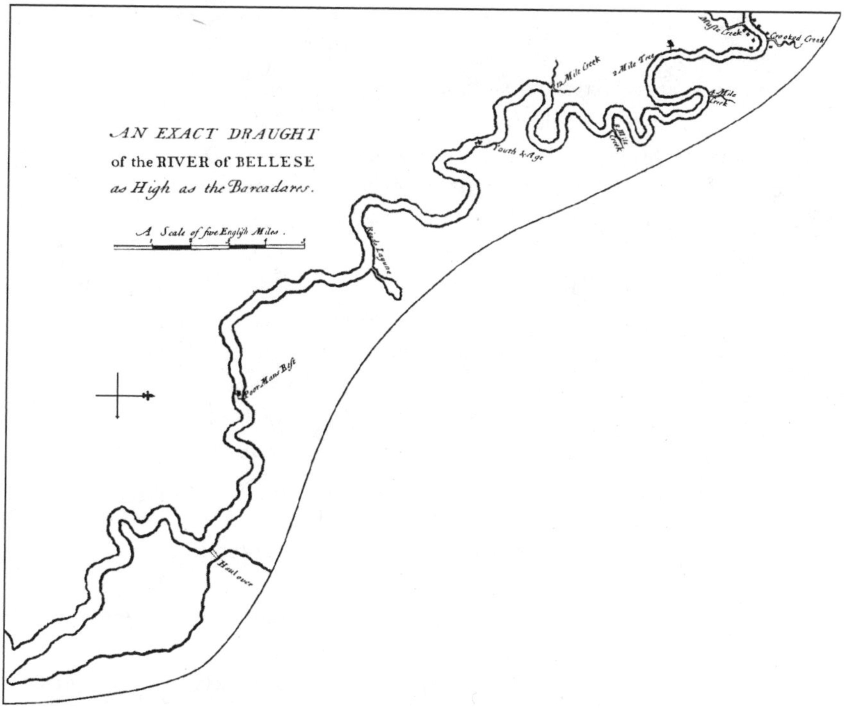

Figure 5.2. Uring's (1726) map of the lower Belize River.

Figure 5.3. A similar bush camp from Stedman's (1796) account of travel in Suriname.

This kind of dwelling without foundation or constructed floor of any kind has strong implications for artifact deposition and site formation at this locale. The lack of any significant architectural component in the archaeological record would greatly reduce the likelihood of encountering features or heavy artifact deposition within localized areas that would be expected with the long-term occupation characterized by a significant dwelling structure. Nonetheless, archaeological investigations were focused on identifying the location and extent of early settlement at the Barcadares (figure 5.3).

Uring's map depicts a locale that proved to be easily identifiable by correlating the meanders in the Belize River that he drew with those on a modern topographic map. The locale was far closer to the river mouth than the forty-two miles stated by Uring (twenty-two miles or thirty-five and a half kilometers as the river flows), at the modern village of Grace Bank. The site is also located just downstream from Little Falls, which was the first significant obstruction to navigation encountered when traveling up-river from the coast.

Following initial testing, archaeological investigations at the site of the Barcadares consisted of ten 1-m² excavation units. Excavations yielded artifacts distributed diffusely though the uppermost thirty to sixty centimeters of soil. The paucity of features or stratigraphically concentrated accumulations of artifacts indicates the influence of the architectural type on site formation processes as well as periodic episodes of flooding on site preservation. Additionally, many low-fired clay concretions ranging in size from one to five centimeters in diameter were recovered from the uppermost three strata. These concretions were determined to be naturally baked earth fragments from the hearths of open fires, created when the silty-clay soil of the Belize River valley was exposed to the heat of an open flame. No undisturbed hearths were uncovered at the Barcadares, only crumbled fragments—further evidence that the site had been subjected to some degree of disturbance.

Analysis

The preponderance of datable artifacts indicates that occupation at the Barcadares may have begun as early as the 1670s and that it had declined or ceased by the mid-eighteenth century, shortly after Uring's visit. This diachronically discrete deposit constitutes the earliest known site of the British Bay Settlement.

As anticipated, artifact densities at the Barcadares site were low, most likely because it was "home" for a relatively mobile population of small and fluctuating size, occupying semipermanent dwellings for only a portion of each year. Nonetheless, artifact concentrations in the ten excavation units were high enough to obtain an interesting window into life at the Barcadares settlement.

Artifacts recovered include many iron fragments, such as wrought nails (which were probably used in constructing the settlers' sleeping pavilions) as well as trunk or box hinges (possibly from sea chests), large spikes, wrought staples, and other unidentified hardware, some of which may relate to the activities of cutting and transporting logwood. Three sizes of lead gun shot were also recovered. Although a single large-musket ball may have played a roll in defense, the majority was small bird shot, which was undoubtedly employed for food collecting.

Fragments of smoking pipes of both Dutch and British origin were recovered. Stylistically, the bowls fit within the date range of 1680 to 1730 (Walker 1977), and one marked example is datable to manufacture between 1668 and 1688. The 339 fragments recovered constituted 27.8 percent of the site assemblage. Application of Lewis Binford's (1978) stem bore analysis to the 199 measurable fragments yielded a date of 1733.

These artifacts reflect the daily life and physical conditions under which these people lived, but it was the ceramics that most clearly illuminated the distinctive behavior of this society of mariners.

A total of 252 historical period ceramic vessel fragments were recovered at the Barcadares, representing 23.0 percent of the entire site assemblage. Only 39 (15.5 percent) of these fragments were identifiable to original vessel form. The gray salt-glazed stoneware fragments recovered included several that are probably from a single Westerwald-style stoneware porringer with twisted handles that was only partially reconstructible. This vessel form was not commonly exported to Britain or the British colonies during the late seventeenth and eighteenth centuries (Noël Hume 1967:353). The overwhelmingly dominant vessel forms from this site are large bowls and the related handled porringer. A small number of gray stoneware jug fragments, possibly Rhenish as well, are the next most dominant form. Bowls and jugs were commonly used during this period in the cooperatively organized activities of food preparation and consumption of the sort described by Uring (1726:356) (figure 5.4; table 5.1).

The vast majority of ceramic vessel fragments from the Barcadares were delftware, over one-third of which were hand-painted blue; 5.5 percent of those were also hand-painted red. Gray salt-glazed stonewares represent a much smaller

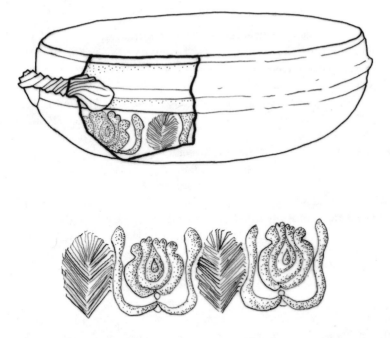

Figure 5.4. Partially reconstructed Westerwald-style stoneware porringer from the Barcadares (approximately 7 inches in diameter).

percentage within the distribution of wares, with the others only marginally represented. The nearly complete absence of other more functional earthenwares suggests that these high-style bowls were used on an everyday basis, instead of being reserved for display or use only on special occasions. The small quantities of creamwares and pearlwares are presumed to represent a later, ephemeral phase of occupation than indicated by the majority of the assemblage. These wares also account for the outlying vessel forms in the table below (table 5.2).

Five blue hand-painted Chinese porcelain fragments were recovered from the Barcadares, constituting 2.1 percent of the entire ceramic assemblage. One fragment of particular interest is a thin body sherd with blue underglaze decoration similar to that seen on Kangxi period (1662–1722) ceramics. It also possesses a preserved overglaze enamel trail in the form of a square mark. Similar maker's marks appear frequently within the basal rings of Chinese vessels. Though fragmentary and unidentified, this mark is unusual, because it appears on the decorated surface of the object and would have been considered part of the decoration. Such visible placement of the maker's mark is considered a characteristic of more high-style and expensive wares.

The mere presence of such exotic wares in the Bay Settlement and their particularly large representation at the Barcadares are notable. The prevailing view

Table 5.1. Identifiable Vessel Types from the Barcadares

Form	Number	Percentage of total
Bowl	19	67.8
Jug	5	17.8
Porringer	1	3.6
Plate	1	3.6
Saucer	1	3.6
Tea/coffeepot	1	3.6
Total	28	100.0

Table 5.2. Ware Types by Sherd Counts from the Barcadares

Ware	Number	Percentage of total
Tin-oxide glazed ware	221	91.7
Gray salt-glazed stoneware	6	2.5
Porcelain	5	2.1
Redware	3	1.2
White salt-glazed stoneware	2	0.8
Other gray stonewares	2	0.8
Creamware	1	0.4
Pearlware	1	0.4
Total	241	100.0

of this artifact class as functioning primarily as a socio-technic symbol of the social stature of its possessor was put forth by James Deetz (1977:60). The pattern of use of porcelain vessels in colonial sites is assumed to have differed significantly from that of the more common ceramic wares, but Julia Curtis (1988) has outlined the difficulties in explaining the economics of how porcelain made its way into English New World artifact assemblages. On preliminary examination, the high representation of porcelain wares in the early Bay Settlement might lead one to argue that this artifact class possessed little symbolic value as a means of class association. This contrasts with its role in elite homes in such well-studied contexts as the British colonies of Virginia and New England and the Dutch colony at the Cape of Good Hope. The Caribbean is notorious for having been the land of smuggled goods stolen from Spanish vessels that were transshipping exotic commodities from Asia via Philippine ports. Surely porcelain must have been common enough in the early-eighteenth-century Caribbean to be valued for its technomic function as a durable household item. Otherwise, why would the gristled working-class inhabitants of the Barcadares have paid more than necessary to obtain a piece of tableware solely to impress their peers? They of all people no doubt rejected the ceremonies of bourgeois competition and status negotiation involving tea drinking, formal dinners, and display that formed the central function of Chinese porcelain elsewhere (Hall 1992:387). If so, then what function did this exotic and expensive commodity serve?

There is one explanation that requires neither an alternative interpretation of the symbolic functioning of porcelain among the baymen nor an economic re-evaluation of the market supply of this artifact in the eighteenth-century Caribbean. This marginalized social class of maritime laborers had ample experience with the economic and psychological domination of the ship captains and owners for whom they had worked. Their calculated response, witnessed by their presence in Belize, was to resist that domination by escaping to the cultural and physical peripheries of the civilized world. Resistance to that economic domination involved not only physical distance but also materially manifested symbolic expressions of their independence from and rejection of the society that they had escaped. The uncouth baymen of Uring's narrative who slept on wooden platforms with mattresses of leaves also possessed Chinese porcelain of high quality. Martin Hall (1992:390) has described how the slaves who lived in the Castle at Cape Town possessed porcelain stolen from their repressors as an expression of symbolic resistance. The baymen did not need to hide their possessions and so carried their resistance to a greater extreme, exhibiting them for one another and for the merchant captains who visited them to buy their wood. Like the pirate who wore the fancy brocades and velvets that were forbidden him by European sumptuary laws (Ritchie 1986b:12), the bayman flaunted his independence from the oppressive social hierarchy of the maritime labor system by incorporating the symbolic trappings of upper-class British society into his isolated but autonomous world.

Counter to expectations prior to initiating excavations, the activity of copious drinking, which documentary sources indicate played a vital role in social interaction and group cohesion at the Barcadares, is not identifiable archaeologically through glass liquor bottles, the artifact category most directly associated with alcohol consumption. At the Barcadares, eighty-nine dark green bottle glass fragments were recovered, forming a scant 7.3 percent of the total artifact assemblage there. This could be due to the remote nature of this site, where other containers such as wooden hogsheads would have been the most efficient means for transporting alcohol, which could then have been transferred to any number of different types of vessels for ultimate consumption. In his satirical book *Adventures of Johnny Newcome in the Navy*, Royal Navy officer John Mitford (1819) noted that on long voyages at sea it was common for all of the glass tumblers to break, whereupon teacups would be substituted as the primary vessels used for alcohol consumption. This unconventional adaptation was considered to be a humorous idiosyncrasy of life at sea. The practice is also confirmed in a nineteenth-century caricature called "The Interior of a Midshipman's Birth [*sic*]" (figure 5.5). Mitford even penned a poem about it.

And none, When tumblers all had failed,
As *Neptune* the beaufet assail'd

Figure 5.5. "The Interior of a Midshipman's Birth [*sic*]. Drawn by a naval officer. Published by G. Humphrey, 27, St. James's Street, London, Aug^r 12, 1821." The caricature depicts sailors drinking alcohol from teacups (private collection).

> With grog, his tea-cup should renew
> Higher than to the stripe of blue,
> Which Wedgwood, in his niggard whim
> Oft brings an inch below the rim;
> For which in cockpits he gets curs'd,
> By Middys, gaping dry with thirst. (Mitford 1819:11)

The usual naval rum measure was replaced by the interior blue line on the teacup, which varied from cup to cup. In backwoods Belize, the lifespan of glass must have been as short as at sea, with similar accomodations made.

Although the range of artifacts recovered at the Barcadares was very limited, the large quantities of delftware, decorated stoneware, and high-quality porcelain and the near absence of undecorated utilitarian earthenwares indicate that a significant degree of wealth was invested in the baymen's personal possessions.

Conclusions

In his series of sketches called *The Encantadas, or Enchanted Islands*, Herman Melville speculated on what type of material culture would be left behind by a community of pirates. He wrote about remote islets beyond civilization that were "a secure retreat, an undiscoverable hiding place, where Buccaneers found that tranquility which they fiercely denied to every civilized harbor in that part of the world." Strewn across the beaches of these islands were "tokens of things quite in accordance with those wild traits, popularly, and no doubt truly enough, imputed to the freebooters at large," including "old cutlasses and daggers reduced to mere threads of rust, which, doubtless, had stuck between Spanish ribs ere now" (Melville 1984:232–34).

So was the early Bay Settlement really a mariner's utopia or merely a last-stop for debauched sailors? On first reflection, the material culture of the logwood-cutting mariners at the Barcadares appears to exhibit no attributes associated with the defining activities of pirate life, such as treasure or the cutlasses that Melville ruminated on. But interpreted within the context of Atlantic maritime culture, the assemblage reveals evidence of choice on the part of the residents and an active rejection of an authoritarian system of economic oppression. Withdrawing to the margins of civilization, they lived according to a system of values that deliberately repudiated the social rules and roles that they had escaped. Although the logwood cutters may have rejected the hierarchical values of British society by living and working cooperatively, they did not reject the accumulation and exhibition of wealth obtained through a combination of hard work and illegal pursuits.

So it seems there is a reality behind the prevailing myths of early Belize as a haven for pirates, although it is only fleeting. That romantic egalitarian community was rapidly superseded by a more conventional colonial system with a stratified social and political hierarchy. This accompanied a growth in the demand for mahogany, a forest product that (unlike the smaller logwood trees) required capitalization in the form of imported slaves for labor (Finamore 1994, 2004). The earliest known site of the British Bay Settlement survives as a curious archaeological anomaly of European colonial settlement in Belize and elsewhere around the world.

Acknowledgments

The research discussed in this chapter is based upon work supported by the National Science Foundation under Grant No. BNS-9013097. The author would like to thank Patricia A. McAnany and Mary C. Beaudry, both of Boston University, for their intellectual contributions to this project; John Morris, associate director of the National Institute of Culture and History, Belize, for logistical support; Elizabeth Schultz, professor emeritus at the University of Kansas, for her ruminations on Melville; George Schwartz for assistance with illustrations; and Matthew McDermott, Jeremy Bailey, and Eric Finamore for their "sweat equity." All figures are by Daniel Finamore unless noted otherwise.

Note

1. "The Bay" was commonly used as a term to refer to the informal British logwood settlement in the Bay of Campeche (at Laguna de Términos) as well. After it was largely evacuated in 1717, references to this locale were few; and the appellation was transferred to the settlement around the lower reaches of the Belize River.

Part 2

Pirate Ships and Their Prey

6

Piracy in the Indian Ocean

Mauritius and the Pirate Ship *Speaker*

Patrick Lizé

The so-called Golden Age of Euro-American Piracy lasted less than fifty years, from the closing decades of the seventeenth century through the 1720s. During this era the Caribbean Sea, Atlantic coast of North America, West African coast, and Indian Ocean were the main cruising grounds for pirates. This period of lawlessness came about just as the nation-states of Europe began to take on their modern borders and the trappings of centralized power—standing armies and fleets. The War of the Grand Alliance (King William's War, 1689–97) and the War of the Spanish Succession (Queen Anne's War, 1701–14) drew thousands of men into naval and privateering ships. While the central focus of these conflicts was preventing any one country from dominating the continent of Europe and upsetting the balance of power, these were truly worldwide wars. By the late seventeenth century the nascent European-focused world economy was beginning to take form. In the Americas, Africa, and Asia were the colonies and trading posts of England, France, the Netherlands, Portugal, and Spain. Along these long sea lanes flowed specie, spices, and slaves in the bottoms of European and local vessels. The capture of these valuable cargoes would not only enrich the lives of the victorious crew and their sponsors at home and in the government but would aid in crippling their enemy's economy and ability to wage war. These wars of empire often devolved into guerrilla warfare and piracy (Karraker 1953:29), where the adversaries would prey on enemy and neutral ships.

Part of this devolution came about because honesty cut into profits. As much as 60 percent of the value of a prize went to pay the royal share, custom duties, and court charges. One New York privateer returned to the colony in 1695 with £160,000 in stolen goods. He paid bribes of some £4,000 and so avoided the £32,000 royal share and other court costs. There was indeed a fine line between privateers and pirates (Lydon 1970:48, 56–57). Nonetheless, these were the "shock troops" of imperial expansion, who would act as patriotic colonizers and

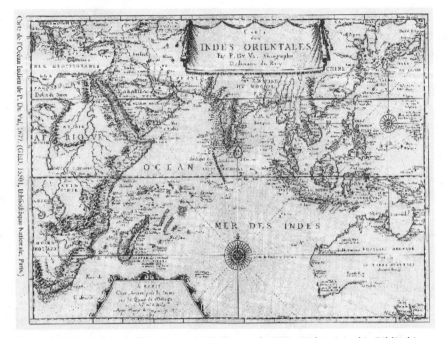

Figure 6.1. Map of the Indian Ocean, 1677. Drawn by P. Du Val (original in Bibliothèque National, Paris, GED.15501).

empire builders (Karraker 1953:55, 65; Lydon 1970:58). Nowhere was this more true than in the Indian Ocean and the Red Sea, a remote enough locale to ensure profits while keeping Atlantic insurance rates low (Karraker 1953:66).

From its epicenter on the island of St. Mary's off the coast of Madagascar east to the Straits of Malacca and south to the Cape of Good Hope, the Indian Ocean and its adjacent seas have been termed the "Piratechnic Institute," where the majors were "Commerce and Finance" (Karraker 1953:131) (figure 6.1). These pirate colonizers were known as "The Red Sea Men" because their main cruising area was the Red Sea. This was the haunt of the likes of Thomas Tew of Rhode Island, William Kidd of New York, and John Bowen of Bermuda.

John Bowen and the *Speaker*

In 1702 John Bowen was in his early forties. He was described by Daniel Defoe:

> We have learned from one who knew and frequently conversed with Bowen that he was born of creditable parents in the island of Bermuda who gave him a good education befitting him for the sea. The first voyage he made was to Carolina where some merchants finding him capable, sober and intelligent gave him command of a ship trading to the West Indies. He

continued in this employ for several years, until he had the misfortune to be taken by a French pirate, who having no artist (sailing master) detained captain Bowen for that purpose. After cruising some time in the West Indies, the French pirates shaped a course for the Guinea coast, where he took several good artists, they would not let captain Bowen go, and notwithstanding his great services to them, treated him as roughly as they did their other English prisoners . . .

After some time cruising along the coast, the pirates doubled the Cape of Good Hope, and shaped their course for Madagascar where, being drunk and mad, they knock'd their ship on the natives Elexa; the country thereabouts was governed by a king, named Mafaly [editor's note—Mafaly is actually the name of a region in southern Madagascar. The king's name was Babaw].

When the ship struck, captain White, captain Boreman, captain Bowen and some other prisoners got to the long-boat, and with broken oars and barrel staves which they found in the bottom of the boat, paddled to Augustin Bay, that is about 14 or 15 leagues from the wreck where they landed, and were kindly received by the king of Babaw who spoke good English.

They staid here a year and a half at the king's expense, who gave them a plentiful allowance of provision, as was his custom with all White men, who met with any misfortune on his coast; his humanity not only provided for all such, but the first European vessel that came in, he always obliged them to take in the unfortunate people, let be the vessel what he would; for he had no notion of any difference between pyrates and merchants.

At the expiration of the above term, a pyrate brigantine came in, aboard which the King obliged them to enter, or travel by land to some other place, which they durst not do; and of two Evils chose the least, that of going on board the pyrate vessel, which was commanded by on William Read, who receive them very civilly . . .

Defoe continues:

I find him cruising on the Malabar coast in the year 1700, commanding a ship called the *Speaker* whose crew consisted of men of all nations, and their pyracies were committed upon ships of all nations likewise. The pyrates here met with no Manner of inconveniences in carrying on their designs, for it was made so much a trade, that the merchants of one town never scrupled the buying commodities taken from another, tho' but ten miles distant, in a publick sale, furnishing the robbers at the same time with all necessaries, even of vessels, when they had occasion to go on any expedition, which they themselves would often advise them of.

Among the rest an English East Indian, captain Conaway from Benegal, fell into the hands of his crew, which they made prize of, near Callequilon

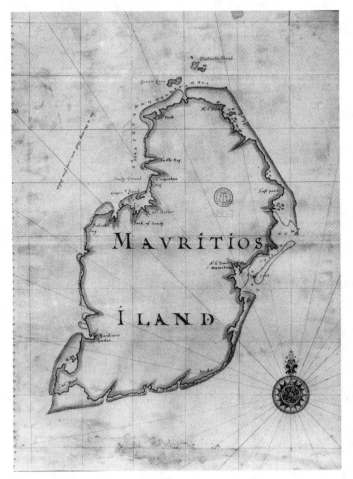

Figure 6.2. Historic map of Mauritius (original in Bibliothèque National, Paris).

[Quilon]; they carry'd her in, and put her up to sale dividing the ship and cargo into three shares; one third was sold to a merchant, native of Callequilon aforesaid, another third to a merchant of Porca, and the other to one Malpa, a Dutch Factor.

Loaded with the spoil of this and several country ships, they left the coast and steer'd for Madagascar: but in their voyage thither, meeting with adverse winds, and, being negligent in their steerage, they ran upon St. Thomas's reef, at the Island of Mauritius, where the ship was lost; but Bowen and the greatest part of the crew got safe ashore. (figure 6.2)

On January 7, 1702, after a violent squall, the pirate ship *Speaker* under the command of John Bowen sank near the "Swarte klip," now called "Ilot des Roches," off the eastern coast of Mauritius. The pirates put their boats to sea and hastily fashioned rafts, using the *Speaker*'s masts and yards. Each was heavily armed. They all safely reached the shore (Algemeen Rijksarchief 1702a, fol. 352v; Pitot 1905:298).

On January 9 two hunters discovered them and quickly alerted the governor of the island.

> They number some 170; 20 or 40 of them are Moors whose task it is to dry the weapons salvaged from the wreck. They have slaughtered three head of Company cattle, but otherwise have displayed no hostile intentions. (Algemeen Rijksarchief 1702b, fol. 366; Pitot, 1905:299)

Mauritius had belonged to the United Provinces since 1638. Then Governor Roelof Diodati, a "clever, crafty man, of dubious integrity" (Pitot 1905: 312), sent his lieutenant, Abraham Van de Velde, to determine how many pirates were actually on the island and to enter into negotiations with them.

"Should they attack us," said Diodati, while exhorting the colonists to assemble at his residence and to do their duty as honest citizens, "we shall defend the island and the fort for so long as breath of life remains in us. For we should prefer an honorable death to the shame of begging mercy of such miscreants, from whom we may expect only the worst" (Algemeen Rijksarchief 1702a, fol. 358; Pitot 1905: 301).

Diodati had his residence fortified against eventual attack. Muskets were cleaned and loaded, pikes were sharpened, and empty bottles were transformed into hand grenades (Algemeen Rijksarchief 1702a, fol. 353v). His men were set to work repairing, reinforcing, and elevating the dilapidated defensive wall that surrounded the fort. Diodati kept a watchful eye on all this activity, inspecting the workers' progress, urging them on, bucking up the flagging morale of his troops. The tiny army of fifty colonists, two slaves, and two convicts ("some of whom knew not even how to charge a gun, loading the ball before the powder") drilled on the beach (Algemeen Rijksarchief 1702a, fol. 353v).

Upon Van de Velde's return, Diodati called a meeting of his council:

> Whereas we now are certain that the pirates number 170 men (so reads the Resolution dated January 9, 1702) that they are heavily armed and could easily overrun and destroy the island; that 120 are White men; that they possess two small craft which take them back and forth from the wreck to shore; that among them are also 30 to 40 Lascares to Moors, who unload and polish the weapons, now spread out on the beach in great quantity; and whereas, for out part we possess only 46 muskets (most all but useless), 49 cutlasses, 4 guns and 12 cavalry pistols; our entire force consists of 52 men, including free colonists, 2 Blacks and 2 convicts, we cannot, therefore, attack the pirates and hope to overcome them. Be it then resolved, in order to prevent the pirates from ravaging the settlement and from going into the woods to forage for their food, to allow them instead to buy sweet potatoes

and meat from the colonists as indeed they have requested to do; and as they cannot otherwise leave the island, it has been further resolved to sell them a small sloop, the *Vliegendehart*, and to permit them to bring their sick to the Residence, where our surgeon can care for them. Should we succeed in convincing a goodly number of them to enter the Residence, we have determined to fall upon them and to murder them, so that we may later lay hands on the rest and put them to death as well. (Algemeen Rijksarchief 1702b, fol. 366v et seq.; Algemeen Rijksarchief 1702a, vol. 333; Pitot 1905:299)

Bowen preferred his own barber-surgeon to the company's and was given the material he needed to enlarge the *Vliegendehart*, so that he and his crew could depart as quickly as possible.

On March 4, with all in readiness, the pirates took official leave of the governor, presenting him with 2,000 piastres as a token of their gratitude. They then set sail for their hideout on Madagascar.

In 1704 we find Bowen again at the helm of another captured ship, the *Defiance*. Bowen pirated off the Malabar coast before retiring to Bourbon Island (Reunion Island) to live an honest life. Like many a pirate before him, he obtained—for a price—the favor of Governor De Villers. And so, duly pardoned, he settled down and became a colonist. Bowen did not long enjoy his newfound peace. On March 13, 1705, a sudden attack of colic carried him off, before he had the time to utter a single word.

No pomp marked his funeral. A simple grave dug in the underbrush was Bowen's final resting place. The colony's priest, Father Marquer, refused to bury Bowen, a heretic, in consecrated ground. Bowen left no heirs; he bequeathed to the company a 14-year-old slave. Nonetheless, he was one pirate who died wealthy; and that wealth did not go unnoticed, as the court clerk wrote down:

After having sealed his sea-chest at 10 o'clock in the morning, in the presence of several colonists, said box was later opened, and an inventory made of its contents:
—In gold, 750 Moorish and Arabian sequins, worth 1,500 ecus, or 2 ecus each.
—Old and used clothing, such as jerkins, shirts, caps, which was divided among those who had aided him in his illness, and those who had helped to bury him. (C2 Col, Item 11, Archives Nationales, Paris)

The *Speaker*

Contemporary sources described the *Speaker* as a former French warship captured by the English during the War of the League of Augsburg (King William's War). Unfortunately, its former name is unknown. Pirates are not renowned for keeping written records, and Bowen was no exception. Nonetheless, their victims left behind documents, which have allowed us to trace the *Speaker*'s itinerary and to know its size and the prizes it took.

In his deposition dated November 2, 1702, Thomas Towsey, who was held for six months and obliged to serve as a carpenter on the *Speaker*, says that the pirates robbed two Moorish ships belonging to Surat and one Dutch ship, the *Borneo*, a 300-ton vessel bound from Bengal to Surat.

We learn from Ashin Das Gupta (1979:101):

> On the 23 Sept. 1701, news reached Surat that Abdul Gafur's ship the "Hussaini" had been plundered by pirates off Daman and the Dutch cruisers escorting the Red Sea fleet, of which the "Hussaini" was one, had done nothing . . . Besides the "Hussaini," two other ships were missing. One of them, a vessel of Gafur's friend Mia Muhammad, turned up shortly after, thoroughly plundered, while the third, another of Gafur's remained missing.

Other documents give us information about the *Speaker*'s size. The Resolution of the Island Council of Mauritius, dated September 1, 1702 (Algemeen Rijksarchief 1702a, fol. 353v), tells us that the ship measured around 145 feet and carried 40 cannon. According to Conaway, the *Speaker* was a ship of 500 tons, mounting 40 guns and two patereroes (E-3-70 No. 8592; Hill 1919:32).

Finally, the documents left by the Island Council indicate that the *Speaker* sank near the Swarte Klip.

Discovering the *Speaker*

The island of Mauritius (61 km long and 47 km wide) is situated in the Indian Ocean about 1,083 km east of Madagascar (figure 6.3). Discovered by the Portuguese in 1511, the island remained uninhabited until 1638, when the Dutch colonized it as a base to refresh their ships traveling to or from the East Indies.

In July 1980 a French research team, in coordination with the National Commission of the United Nations Educational, Scientific and Cultural Organization (UNESCO), signed a draft treaty with the Mauritian government to investigate the wreck site. The site was investigated from September to December of the same year. Prior to the field aspect of the project, archival research relating to the loss of the *Speaker* was undertaken by M. J. Dumas and myself.

The wreck of the *Speaker* is located 1 km south of a small Rocky Island (Ilot des Roches), and some 2 km offshore from Grand-Rivière southeast (figure 6.3). The reef where the *Speaker* lies is covered with less than 5 meters of water and is exposed to heavy southeasterly swells. Periods when diving is possible occur from October to December and in March, unless, of course, unforeseen cyclones occur. As a result of these conditions the wreck is dispersed, poorly preserved, and especially hard to work. None of its timber structure survives. Instead, all that remains is a large debris-field covering some 5,000 square meters of reef,

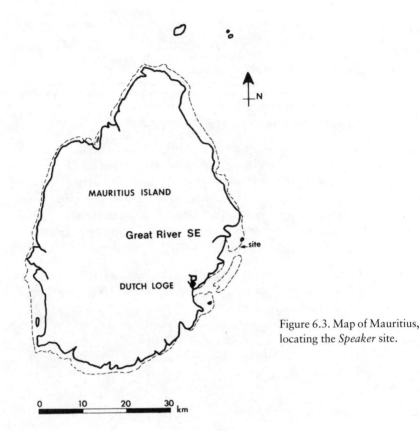

Figure 6.3. Map of Mauritius, locating the *Speaker* site.

consisting of durable artifacts encased in coral. The debris occurs in two main areas: around cannon number 30, where we found silver coins, a padlock, beads, lead ingots, a grindstone, rings, dividers, and a sundial; and around cannon number 7, where we found gold coins and gold bars.

The site (figure 6.4) occupies an area about 100 by 50 meters and is practically perpendicular to the reef. It is covered by a growth of coral that is fairly stunted, due to perpetual battering by the sea. A sandbank, edged on its northeast side by a bed of sea-plants, divides the site into two unequal areas.

The Artifact Assemblage

During the project the following artifacts were collected or noted.

Artillery

Thirty-one cannon measuring from 1.2 m to 2.5 m lay on the seabed (figure 6.5). One of them is unfinished (34 on figure 6.4) and was probably used for ballast.

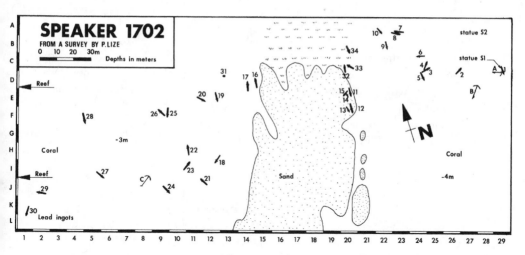

Figure 6.4. Site plan for the *Speaker*.

Figure 6.5. Detail of a bronze gun recovered in 1984.

Anchors

The three anchors indicated by A, B, and C in figure 6.4 measure 4 m, 4 m, and 3 m, respectively. One of the flukes of anchor A was broken by cannon 1 at the time of the wreck.

Ammunition

Ordinary lead musket balls were recovered in large quantities all over the site, as were many cannonballs of different sizes and hand grenades. The hand grenades found on the wreck (figure 6.6) are hollow cannonballs filled with black powder and pierced with a circular hold in which a bamboo tube was inserted to serve as a conduit for the fuse (description in Saint-Rémy 1702:1:305–13; 2:373). Similar grenades have been found in the *Evstafii* (Stenuit 1974:221–43) and the *Whydah* (Kinkor 1991; Clifford and Perry 1999b:223).

Navigational Instruments

Five pairs of brass navigation dividers in extremely fine condition were found (figure 6.7) They are of a classical type that can be opened and closed with one hand. Similar examples have been recovered from the *Lastdrager* (Stenuit 1974) and *Kennemerland* (Price and Muckelroy 1974).

Part of a compass dial (figures 6.8 and 6.9) was found. It consists of a graded brass disc with a folding gnomon. The complete instrument would be a canister or cylindrical bowl fitted at the upper part with this disc and at the bottom with a compass rose and magnetic needle protected by glass. The instrument found in the *Speaker* is a typical sundial from Nuremberg (Guye and Fribourg, 1970:figure 249). The container was usually made of wood, ivory, or gilded brass. The initials "PB" are probably those of the maker. Some very similar examples were found on the *Lastdrager* and *Kennemerland* (Price and Muckelroy 1974; Stenuit 1974).

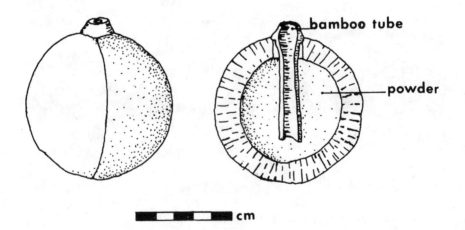

Figure 6.6. Hand grenade.

Figure 6.7. Brass navigation dividers.

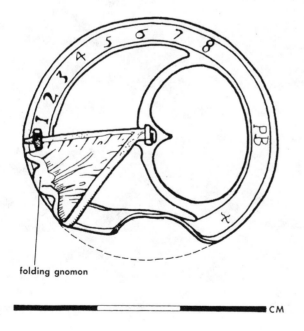

folding gnomon

CM

Figure 6.8. Illustration of a compass dial.

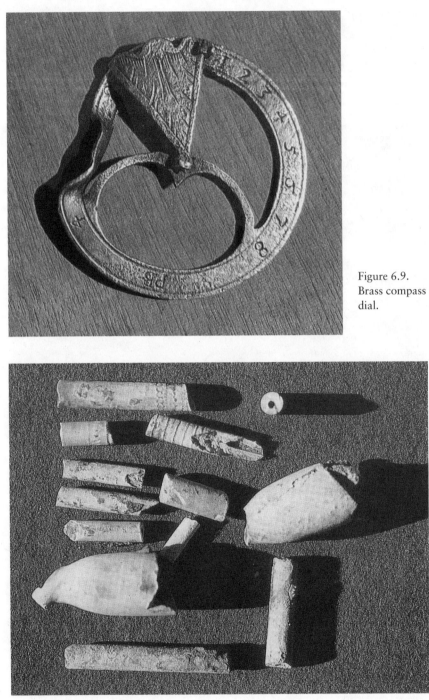

Figure 6.9.
Brass compass
dial.

Figure 6.10. Tobacco pipe fragments.

Clay Tobacco Pipes

The wreck held a large number of clay tobacco pipes bearing no mark (figure 6.10).

Padlock

A brass padlock 10 cm long was found on the wreck (figure 6.11). It is the Chinese type of lock (Eras 1974:43–45). The pin that goes through the two ears of the padlock is of a single piece, with the shackle and a bolt that bears the plate springs (figure 6.12). By simply pushing the shackle into the lock box, the springs are expanded, the spring-terminals are caught by two flanges, and the lock is thus secured. To open it the key must be slid into the box until it presses the springs down and frees the shackle.

Figure 6.11. Brass Chinese padlock.

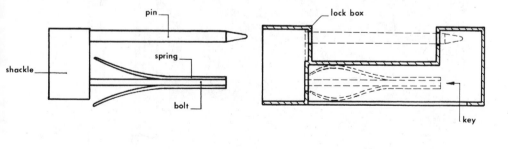

Figure 6.12. Illustration of the inner mechanism of a Chinese padlock.

Beads

A cache of trading beads was discovered on board the *Speaker* (figures 6.13 and 6.14). They are garnets, agates, and glass beads, which even today are referred to as *rassade* (because of their brilliance) or *contrebrode* (because of their resemblance to a black and white embroidered fabric).

Figure 6.13. Beads from the *Speaker*.

Figure 6.14. Garnet (*1*), agate (*2*), and glass (*3*) beads from the *Speaker*.

Rassade beads are large glass rosary beads of different colors and sizes. "They are of coarse glass. They are manufactured in large quantities in Venice. A white or black background is decorated with lines of different colors; a design that made the beads look as if they had been embroidered. Negroes use them to make belts composed of several strings of the beads, which young men wear around their hips, in lieu of clothing until they reach a certain age" (Labat 1730:28). Trade in these beads was considerable in the eighteenth century. In 1725 the Chevalier Des Marais brought no less than two thousand pounds of them into Guinea (ibid.).

The "samsam" variety is a large dark red agate striated with white, with a hole bored through, so it can be worn as a pendant (Lougnon 1956:111). The examples found on the *Speaker* are of two types. The first sort are spherical, 10 mm in diameter; the others are elongated, faceted beads from 20 to 30 mm long.

Statues

Two bronze statues were discovered close to anchors A and B but were too eroded to be identified with precision (figure 6.15). Still, one can say with certainty that they come from the south of India. One of them is distinguished by an undulating pose that brings to mind a dancer. The other, perfectly erect, seems to represent a divinity.

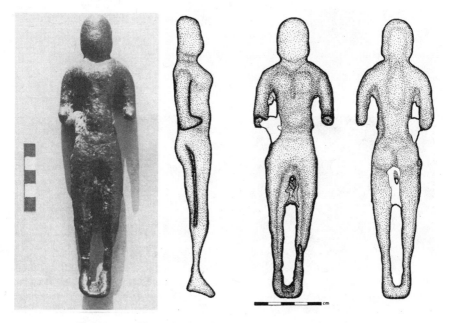

Figure 6.15. Bronze statue from south India and three-directional rendering.

Gold Ingots

Two small gold ingots, bearing no marks, were found at the site (150 g and 100 g). On both of them it is possible to make out the traces of the sand from the mold in which it was cast as well as the mark of a chisel blow, which indicates that they were split. Below is a list of coins found at the site:

1. A gold coin or dinar of the Ottoman Empire, minted in Cairo in the year 1053 of the Hegira (A.D. 1643–44) during the reign of Ibrahim (A.D. 1640–48) (figure 6.16) (British Museum Catalogue III:131, no. 358; Pere 1968:no. 429).

2. A gold coin or dinar of the Ottoman Empire, probably minted in Egypt during the reign of Mustapha I [also spelled Mustafa]. The coin is incomplete and double struck on both sides, the flan having turned over between the dies during the minting process. Neither the mint nor the date can be read.

3. A gold coin or dinar of the Ottoman Empire, minted in Cairo under the first reign of Mustapha I (1617–18) (figure 6.17) (British Museum Catalogue VIII:115; Pere 1968:no. 378).

4. A gold coin or dinar of the Ottoman Empire, probably minted in the year 1065 of the Hegira (A.D. 1654–55) under Mohammed IV, son of Ibrahim, who ruled 1648–87 (Figure 6.18).

5. Two Venetian ducats of gold, minted under Francisco Morosini, 108th doge of Venice, whose reign lasted from 1688 to 1694 (figure 6.19) (*Corpus Nummorum Italicorum*, VIII, pl. 19, no. 5, 94–99).

6. A silver taler, struck in Kremnitz in 1695 during the reign of Leopold of Austria (*Corpus Nummorum Austriacorum*, 1975, no. 86, a-7).

7. A silver coin from the Netherlands struck in the Dordrecht mint in 1602. (Delmonte 1967:no. 831)

Figure 6.16. Gold coin of the Ottoman Empire, minted in Cairo during the reign of Ibrahim (1640–48).

Figure 6.17. Gold coin of the Ottoman Empire, minted in Cairo during the reign of Mustapha I (1617–18).

Figure 6.18. Gold coin of the Ottoman Empire, minted during the reign of Mohammed IV (1648–87).

Figure 6.19. Obverse and reverse of a gold Venetian ducat minted under Francisco Morosini, 108th doge of Venice (1688–94).

Figure 6.20. Seventeenth-century silver eight-*real* "cob" from the Mexico City mint.

8. Four-*real* pieces, minted in Mexico, badly worn.
9. Two Spanish eight-*real* coins, minted in Mexico, badly damaged (figure 6.20).
10. A silver rupee from India (mounted as a pendant) minted in the workshop of Itawa (or Etawa) in the year 1102 of the Hegira (1658–1707).

11. Silver coin of Zaydi Imams of Yemen, of the reign of al-Mahdi Muhammad b. Ahmad, "Sahib al-Mawahib" (1687–1718), with the title "al Nasir li-Din Allah," minted at al-Khadra, date missing (Lowick 1983:307n31).

12. Silver coin of the same Imam, but with the title "al-Hadi li-Din Allah," minted in 1697.

13. Two silver coins of the Ottoman Empire, minted at Cairo under Sulayman II (1687–91), date missing.

14. Silver coin of Nayaks of Tinnevelly, sixteenth century or later (obverse: divinity standing under an arch; reverse: Tamil inscription).

Identifying the Wreck

The positive identification of the ship whose scattered remains have been found was made possible through the study of official records. As discussed above, the documentary evidence comes from the legal depositions of some of the *Speaker*'s victims. For example, the carpenter Thomas Towsey said that several ships of different cultural origin had been plundered by pirates. These numerous seizures, which seem to be the work of Bowen and his crew, might explain the diversity of the coins found at the site.

Other documents give us information about the *Speaker*'s size, an important element in identifying a ship. Those accounts say that the *Speaker* was a 500-ton ship armed with forty guns. During the project, thirty-three guns and three anchors of a size appropriate for use on a 500-ton ship were located. Finally, the Island Council indicates that the *Speaker* sank near the Swarte Klip, in the very area where the wreck was found.

All these factors, the lack of any other recorded shipwreck in this region, and especially the coins (which are all pre-1702) permit us to assume that the ship we found is indeed the *Speaker*.

Conclusion

The *Speaker* is of great historical and archaeological value as the first pirate ship to be investigated archaeologically. Had it not been for the documentary evidence relating to Bowen and the *Speaker*, nothing discovered on this wreck site would have told researchers that it was the remains of a pirate ship. Nonetheless, this salvage operation has allowed us to write a new page in the history of Mauritius.

Acknowledgments

At this end of this project, I have the honor and the pleasure of thanking those who participated in it—Jacques Dumas, Pascal Kainic, J. F. Leitner, and Yves Halbwacks—and all those who gave us their material help or moral support. Let me mention first of all Gérard Delaplace; Mrs. and Mr. De Fleuriot; Sir Raymond Hein; Mike Seeyave; Michel Camus; the Mauritian government, of course, especially the Ministry of National Education and Cultural Affairs; S. E. Kher Jagatsingh; David Ardill; the UNESCO Commission, particularly B. R. Goordyal, A. Murday, and G. Sooknah; and Mr. Tirvengadum, director of the Mauritius Institute. My thanks go as well to the experts and specialists who assisted us with the identifications: Mr. Curiel; Mr. Dhenin of the Cabinet of Medals of the Bibliothèque Nationale of Paris; Mr. Lowich of the Cabinet of Coins and Medals of the British Museum, London; Mr. Haudrere of the Centre National de la Recherche Scientifique (CNRS); B. Hutchinson, curator of the Department of Navigation and Astronomy, National Maritime Museum, Greenwich; Mr. Poirot from the Laboratory of the Diamond Exchange in Paris; Mrs. Prade, of the Museum Bricard in Paris; and Mr. Henrat, curator at the Archives Nationales in Paris. Many thanks to my colleagues in Portugal at the Centro Nacional de Arqueologia Náutica e Subaquática for their ongoing support. Finally, I wish to thank Nelly Mesclef for her help and also Charles Ewen of East Carolina University as well as Russell Skowronek, Demetra Kalogrides, Jessica Crewse, and Elwood Mills of Santa Clara University for their editorial review of this chapter. The translation is by Sheila Mooney-Mall, and the figures are by Patrick Lizé unless otherwise noted.

7

Christopher Condent's *Fiery Dragon*

Investigating an Early Eighteenth-Century Pirate Shipwreck off the Coast of Madagascar

John de Bry

Captain Kidd and the Pirates of Saint Mary's Island

In January 2000 an expedition was launched to search for the wreck of the *Adventure Galley*, a ship that belonged to the infamous Captain William Kidd of pirate fame. He was forced to abandon the ship in the natural harbor of the small island of Saint Mary's (referred to as Sainte-Marie Island in French texts and archival documents) off the northeast coast of Madagascar in 1698 (figure 7.1).

Saint Mary's was discovered by Arab seafarers in the twelfth century and subsequently by Europeans in the sixteenth century (by Diego Díaz in 1506). It lies 26 to 30 kilometers east of the Great Red Island (Madagascar) and is some 70 kilometers long; the width varies from 1 to 6 kilometers. It is a tropical paradise, sparsely populated. Pirates made their home on this island between 1650 and 1725. They used Saint Mary's as a base from which to launch raids on the Portuguese vessels and ships of the East India companies of England, France, and Holland and the richly laden Indian Moghul ships that sailed to India, Mocha, and Jeddah. Twice a year a fleet would take Muslim pilgrims to the port cities of Jeddah and Yanbu-al-Bahr for the pilgrimage to the Holy Cities of Jeddah and Mecca. The fleets entered the Red Sea through the narrow Bab al-Mandab Strait, between what is now Djibouti in east Africa and Yemen on the Arabian Peninsula. Pirate ships would wait in ambush to intercept the richly laden ships as they navigated through the dangerous bottleneck.

Madagascar had become a choice destination for English and other European merchants because slaves were cheaper than on the African continent and there was a great demand for firearms and all sorts of Western merchandise. Saint Mary's became a base for pirates for a variety of reasons. It was the place of

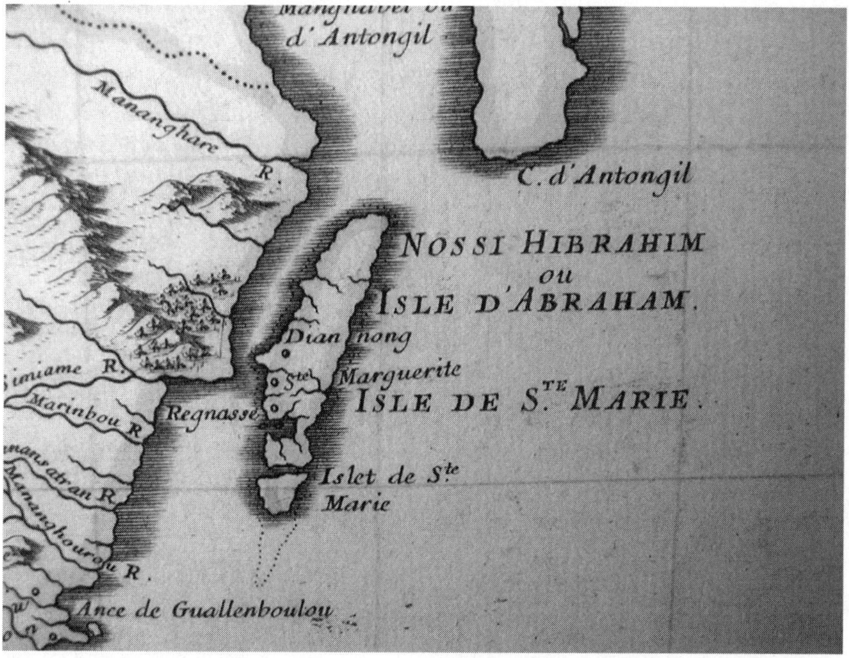

Figure 7.1. Map of Madagascar and St. Mary's Island, 1667 (detail). Courtesy of Service Historique de la Marine, Vincennes.

choice to water ships and take on supplies after having rounded the Cape of Good Hope and the perfect spot to wait out the monsoon winds (Rogozinski 2000:55). Saint Mary's also offered an excellent anchorage, with a naturally protected bay; a small island at the entrance of this bay created a perfect natural harbor and careening spot. Careening was the process of leaning a ship on its sides alternately, on a gently sloping beach, in order to clean, repair, and caulk the hull. This was especially necessary in warm subtropical and tropical waters, where wood from the hull was often attacked and eaten by teredo worms. These worm-like creatures, actually bivalve mollusks, use their greatly reduced shell to bore tunnels into wood. In the age of wooden sailing ships, this was a tremendous problem that often led to sinking.

The strategic location of St. Mary's made it an ideal location from which to launch raids on ships sailing back to Europe, loaded with rich cargoes of gold, precious stones, Chinese blue-and-white export porcelain, silk, spices, and drugs from India and the Far East. As early as the 1660s merchants from England were making the long and perilous journey to Madagascar, and in 1675 a ship from Boston came to trade with the Malagasy natives. Pirates were not far behind, arriving in the region about 1684 (Ritchie 1986a:83).

Piracy had become a major problem in the Caribbean. Tired of being attacked and robbed by these lawless seafarers, the European colonial powers decided not only to protect themselves better but to hunt down pirates aggressively and mercilessly. The Spanish treasure fleets became increasingly larger, better armed, and better protected and as a result suffered fewer losses (for the Spanish treasure fleet system and defense methodologies, see Phillips 1992). No such organized fleets sailed the Indian Ocean, leaving poorly protected ships at the mercy of roving marauders. Piracy surely had been practiced in this part of the world for centuries, but the uncertainties of tropical weather patterns, the fury of typhoons, and the treacherous passage around the Cape of Good Hope were of much graver concern to seafarers than isolated acts of piracy. The arrival and implantation of pirate companies in the 1680s introduced a new element of danger that would have a devastating economic impact on the region.

Because the vast majority of pirates were English, Indian and Chinese authorities felt that *all* pirates were English. Whenever a ship was attacked and taken, those authorities retaliated by closing down the trading posts of the English East India Company, putting the personnel under house arrest, and sometimes even imprisoning them. Until they were given monetary reparation for their losses by the English Crown, those operations would remain closed, resulting in heavy financial losses. The problem became so great that England decided to act: in 1696 a Scot by the name of William Kidd was granted a commission to hunt pirates in the Indian Ocean. He was born in Greenock, Scotland, around 1645, the son of a Presbyterian minister. Little is known about his early years, but by 1689 he was in the Caribbean. Kidd was a crew member on several ships, until he was made captain of the *Blessed William*, a 20-gun ship with a crew of eighty or ninety men (Ritchie 1986a:30). Kidd eventually became "respectable," married a well-to-do widow, and settled in New York City; they moved into a house on Pearl Street and even purchased their own pew in the Anglican Trinity Church. Perhaps influenced by his wife, William Kidd cultivated contacts in high places and became rather close friends with Scottish entrepreneur and politician Robert Livingston and provincial attorney general James Graham, also a Scot. Kidd and Livingston went into business together. As his circle of powerful friends grew, Kidd was eventually introduced to Richard Coote, the Earl of Bellomont, a member of Parliament.

It appears that Kidd and Livingston came up with the idea of a business venture that would involve hunting pirates. A group of partners would be formed, money would be invested and advanced, and an adequate ship would be purchased. Bellomont would use his high-placed connections to secure a privateering commission for Kidd from the king or the lords of the Admiralty, and Kidd would in turn share with his partners and investors the goods confiscated from pirates in the Indian Ocean. To make the size of the initial investment manageable and minimize expenditure, a crew of about a hundred seamen would be hired on a "no purchase, no pay" agreement, meaning that they would be paid only based on the value of the goods and vessels captured (Ritchie 1986a:52). The scheme seemed simple enough at the time to convince Kidd to go along with it, although his original goal was to secure a commission in the Royal Navy. Kidd in fact received two commissions: one to intercept and capture enemy merchant ships, the other to hunt pirates.

By February 1696 the deal was sealed. William Kidd took delivery of his new ship, the *Adventure Galley*, a 34-gun, 287-ton ship built at Castle Yard, Deptford. Once he reached the Indian Ocean, Kidd and his crew fell on hard luck, failing to find pirates or legal French prizes. (It appears that Kidd might have been reluctant to challenge and arrest pirates who were former shipmates or friends.) Desperate and under pressure from a rebellious crew of ex-pirates and ex-buccaneers, Kidd allegedly crossed the line and committed an act of piracy. On January 30, 1698, Kidd and his men captured the *Quedah Merchant*, a 400-ton ship from Surat (a city on the banks of the River Tapi, in northwestern India) bound for the Spice Islands (the Moluccas or Maluku Province in Indonesia) with a cargo of cloth, opium, sugar, and saltpeter worth an estimated £7,000 to £12,000.

Most of the *Quedah Merchant*'s cargo was the property of a high official at the Moghul's court. The ship was flying a French flag; so in order to intercept it Kidd ordered a French flag hoisted and, assisted by another vessel, the *November*, caught up with the *Quedah Merchant*. The English captain, uncertain about what was going on, came aboard the *Adventure Galley* and showed a French pass to Kidd. Once the cargo of the captured ship had been sold at Quilon (on the southwestern tip of India), the *Adventure Galley* sailed south, capturing and looting a Portuguese vessel and unsuccessfully chasing two English East Indiamen (commercial European ships trading with India and the Far East). Word of Kidd's piratical acts spread like wildfire, and soon the former pirate hunter was being branded a pirate himself and hunted.

Ironically, Commodore Thomas Warren first started spreading the rumor that Kidd was a pirate after an encounter in the south Atlantic with the *Adventure Galley* in December 1696, long before Kidd was involved in any action that could be perceived as piratical. With no safe place to seek refuge, the *Adventure Galley* limped into the natural harbor of Saint Mary's, where Kidd was forced to abandon his sinking ship. The vast majority of his disgruntled crew defected to other ships, joining pirate crews.

Kidd was reunited with some old crewmates turned pirates, such as Robert Culliford (one of Kidd's shipmates aboard the *Blessed William*, who had abandoned Kidd on the island of Antigua in January 1690). Culliford was a flamboyant homosexual who managed to escape hanging by taking advantage of a general pardon and had no difficulties in adjusting to the lifestyle of the pirate hideout.

In November 1698, six months after arriving at Saint Mary's, Kidd sailed for North America aboard the *Quedah Merchant*, now renamed the *Adventure Prize*. Upon reaching the Caribbean in April 1699, Kidd learned that an all-man hunt had been launched to capture him. After being refused protection from the Danish governor of Saint Thomas, Kidd sailed from island to island, stopping at

Mona Island and Hispaniola, in what is now the Dominican Republic. In an effort to cover his tracks, Kidd bought a sloop and left the *Adventure Prize* behind to be looted and burned. Making port in New Jersey and Long Island, Kidd finally reached Boston, where Bellomont, now governor, had him arrested in July 1699.

Sent back to England to stand trial, Kidd was convicted of murdering his gunner, William Moore, and robbing the *Quedah Merchant*. On October 30, 1697, Kidd had gotten into an argument with the gunner and struck him on the head with a wooden bucket. Moore died the next day from a fractured skull. Kidd argued that the *Quedah Merchant* was a legal prize and that his claim could be supported by the French pass, but the pass and other key papers entrusted to Lord Bellomont could not be found anywhere in time for the trial. William Kidd was hanged on Sunday, May 18, 1701, unrepentant and still proclaiming his innocence. Ironically, the missing pass and other important papers were discovered in London in 1911.

After Kidd

Kidd's departure and his ultimate demise did not spell the end of piratical activities on Saint Mary's. Rogues bent on making their fortune through depredation continued to flock to the Indian Ocean. Saint Mary's offered not only protection but also a seemingly endless supply of women. The island became a pirate hideout par excellence and the center of debauchery for many. Unscrupulous merchants sailing from New York, Boston, and Providence brought other supplies and necessities regularly. A surrealistic ambiance prevailed on the island. Pirates strolled about, dressed in outrageous clothing made of the finest silks, adorned with gold coins and precious stones. Their beautiful Malagasy women companions walked by their sides, wearing long silk saris embroidered with silver and gold and ostentatious jewelry made of gold, diamonds, sapphires, and rubies.

Several months at a time might be spent on land between raids, especially during the monsoon season, when sailing was either impossible or simply too dangerous. During those long periods, when not busy careening their ships on the islet at the entrance of the natural harbor, the pirates had plenty of opportunities to indulge in gambling, drinking, and, of course, sex. Games of chance and rum do not mix well; many fights, some with deadly outcomes, broke out. Women were also the cause of jealousy and quarrels. They frequently fought to gain the favors of the men they desired; but they often turned their anger toward scoundrels who abandoned them for another woman, either younger or prettier. This rather common practice was not taken kindly by the Malagasy women. They sometimes resorted to poisoning to take revenge, then fled Saint Mary's for the Big Island aboard dugouts, taking with them the riches that had been bestowed upon them by their male companions.

The pirates had settled on the north bank of Saint Mary's natural harbor and

Figure 7.2. Aerial view of the Bay of St. Mary's Island with the Ile des Forbans islet. Photo courtesy of the Discovery Channel.

along the shoreline to the north where the village of Ambodifotatra stands today. The hill that overlooks the small bay provided a vantage point from which to look out for enemy ships. The pirates lived in small wood and bamboo dwellings propped up on stilts, with roofs made of palm leaves, not so different from some of the huts that can be seen on the island today. Each pirate captain flew a flag that identified him. The pirate Adam Baldridge, who made his fortune as a merchant and trader on Saint Mary's, settled on the small island in the middle of the lagoon, still called Pirate's Island (Ile des Forbans) to this day (figure 7.2). He built a home and a fortified storehouse and trading post.

Baldridge might have built the system of mysterious tunnels (yet to be penetrated and explored). Before Kidd, a number of rogues based at Saint Mary's had made their fortune and left their marks in the annals of piracy. George Raynor had made off with some $40 million in 1690 and 1691 after taking two richly laden Portuguese galleons and an English East Indiaman. William Mason and his partner Edward Coats had plundered four Muslim pilgrim ships in the Red Sea in 1692 for nearly $20 million. Thomas Tew, an English pirate from Rhode Island, was even luckier, using his trusted and fast ship the *Amity* to attack and loot numerous vessels for an estimated $50 million worth of plunder. Dirk Chivers aboard the *Soldado* and Robert Culliford sailing in consort aboard the *Mocha Frigate* hit pay dirt when they captured the Indian ship *Great Mohammed* in the Red Sea on its way to Jeddah, finding the equivalent of $50 million in gold coins. Then there was William May, who had sailed aboard the *Blessed William* with William Kidd during the Nine Years War (1688–97). May returned to New York in 1697 aboard his ship the *Charming Mary* with an estimated $150 million. Of all the pirates operating out of Saint Mary's toward the end of the seventeenth century, none was as successful as the legendary Henry Every, who took two Muslim ships in the Red Sea, the *Fateh Mohammed* and the *Gang-I-Saway*, making off with at least $200 million in gold coins, jewels, silk, and fine Chinese porcelain. But the biggest robberies were to come in the first quarter of the eighteenth century.

The Robberies of Christopher Condent and John Taylor

Details of the early career of Christopher Condent (also known as John Condon, Congdon, Connor, and Condell; Ken Kinkor, personal communication, June 23, 2000) are sketchy. He is said to have been a native of Plymouth, England. We know that he was a quartermaster aboard a sloop belonging to a certain Mr. Simpson, a Jewish merchant from New York, and became engaged in illicit commerce and piracy in the Upper Antilles. Loosely based in New Providence in the Bahamas, Condent fled the island when Woodes Rogers, a former privateer, assumed the position of governor in 1718, with the mission of eradicating piracy in the region. Soon after leaving Nassau, Condent became involved in an incident that would change the course of his life forever. An Indian who had been beaten up by some of his fellow crewmen following a dispute decided to take revenge. After gathering arms and gunpowder in the forward section of the ship, he barricaded himself in the hold and threatened to blow it up. The crew suggested throwing grenades through the hatch to kill the Indian or force him to abandon his position, but Condent felt that was much too risky a proposition and decided to take matters in his own hands. Armed with a cutlass in one hand and a pistol in the other, he leaped into the hold. The Indian fired first and hit Condent, shattering his arm. Undaunted, Condent returned fire and killed the man, thus putting an end to a potentially catastrophic situation. Charles Johnson [Daniel Defoe] in his *General History of the Pyrates* wrote that when the Indian was dead "the Crew hack'd him to Pieces, and the Gunner ripping up his Belly, tore out his Heart, broiled and eat it" (1724:581).

Shortly after this affair Condent was elected captain. He crossed the Atlantic and reached the Cape Verde Islands, attacking and plundering several ships, including a Dutch ship off the island of Santiago, which he renamed the *Flying Dragon*. Crossing back to South America, he took several prizes. To mark his successes, Condent designed his own flag: a black flame with three skulls and cross bones (figure 7.3). Like other rogues before him, Christopher Condent eventually ended up in the Indian Ocean.

In late 1719, at Luengo Bay on the southwest coast of Africa, Condent spied a Dutch East Indiaman and English ship at anchor. As Condent maneuvered the

Figure 7.3. Christopher Condent's flag.

Flying Dragon closer for the kill, the alarm was sounded; the two ships cut their cables and attempted to evade the attacker. The English vessel *Fame* was wrecked on the rocky shore, while the Dutch ship ran aground on a shallow sandbar. Condent and his men were able to refloat the Indiaman and renamed it the *Fiery Dragon*. It was a magnificent ship armed to the teeth with forty guns in battery and twenty brass swivel guns as well as three cohorn mortars. The pirates, now 320 men strong, were ready to take on any ship that might have the misfortune of crossing their path.

In February 1720, while sailing off the treacherous Cape of Good Hope, the *Fiery Dragon* came upon the *Prince Eugene*, a richly laden ship from the Hapsburg Empire sailing from Canton, China, to Ostend, in present-day Belgium. After stripping the ship and its passengers of all valuables, Condent resumed sailing toward Saint Mary's, taking yet another Dutch East Indiaman in the process. At Saint Mary's Condent took on water and much-needed victuals and supplies and recruited additional men. Career criminals were not in short supply on this tropical paradise; many of the new recruits were seasoned veterans of the Indian Ocean, which made their addition even more valuable. When it left the harbor of Saint Mary's the *Fiery Dragon* had a complement of some five hundred men, including many black islanders.

On August 18, 1720, near Bombay, Condent and his company of pirates found their big prize, a pilgrim ship from Surat sailing to Jeddah on the Red Sea. The ship carried an astonishing treasure of gold coins, precious stones, fine porcelain and glass, spices, drugs, and silks worth £150,000, equivalent to $375 million today! Wisely, Condent gave the order not to abuse the prisoners, who had offered no resistance. They were put ashore at Malabar Hill near Surat, unharmed. The *Fiery Dragon* and its Indian prize returned triumphant to Saint Mary's, where wild celebrations were held.

John Taylor was an English pirate who had captured a number of prizes off the coasts of Africa and India. In 1720 he took his ship, the *Cassandra*, to Mauritius and Saint Mary's Island for repair. There Taylor struck a deal with Olivier La Buse, a French pirate from Calais who had made a name for himself in the Caribbean by successfully sailing in consort with other pirates (including Samuel Bellamy, who later captured the slave ship *Whydah*). La Buse's *Victory* and the

Cassandra, sailing in consort, eventually called port at Bourbon Island (Reunion) in April 1721, where they came across a large Portuguese vessel that was being repaired after weathering a storm. Aboard the carrack, named the *Nostra Senhora de Cabo*, were some 130 crewmembers and a large number of passengers, including wealthy merchants, the archbishop of Goa, and the Count of Ericeira, who was returning to Lisbon after serving as viceroy of Portuguese India. Seeing that the large ship was not only crippled but also poorly guarded, Taylor and La Buse hoisted English flags and sailed directly toward the carrack. As they were nearly upon the ship, they struck the English flags and replaced them with black flags, simultaneously opening fire. After a second volley the Portuguese surrendered. Boarding their prize, the pirates made an incredible discovery; the Count of Ericeira was carrying a hoard of diamonds valued at £500,000 and some £375,000 more in rare Asian products, the total equivalent to a staggering $400 million!

While La Buse was eventually caught and hanged for piracy in 1730, John Taylor returned to the Caribbean, where he negotiated a pardon from the governor of Portobelo, in Panama. He lived there for several years until retiring to Jamaica, where he married and fathered four children, having kept his share of the *Cabo* intact.

The Quest for the *Adventure Galley*

In late January 2000 an expedition to locate the wreck of the *Adventure Galley* was launched at the instigation of adventurer Barry Clifford and was funded by the Discovery Channel. I was invited to join the team as project archaeologist. Arriving on Saint Mary's Island on January 29, the team immediately began surveying the natural harbor adjacent to a small island named Ilot Madame (figures 7.4 and 7.5).

Two small islands were strategically occupied by pirates: Ilot Madame, at the entrance of the Baie des Forbans, or Pirates' Bay, and Ile des Forbans, or Pirates' Island, situated in the middle of the shallow bay. Pirates' Island was used as a storage depot and a place where pirates held their councils and divided their loot. Ilot Madame contained the port, various warehouses, and the careening area and was heavily defended with cannon. In 1643 the French East India Company (Compagnie des Indes Orientales) established a trading post on the small island and built warehouses. Forced by pirates to close operation in 1672, the company resumed its commercial activities in 1750, when France took possession of Saint Mary's.

The remote sensing survey was conducted with a Geometric 881 Cesium Vapor magnetometer and a Trimble GPS receiver. A differential GPS shore beacon was set up within a few meters of the harbor, and a single point-positioning algorithm to fix the coordinates of this reference station to within a few centimeters of true was used. A UHF radio link updated the mobile receiver with error

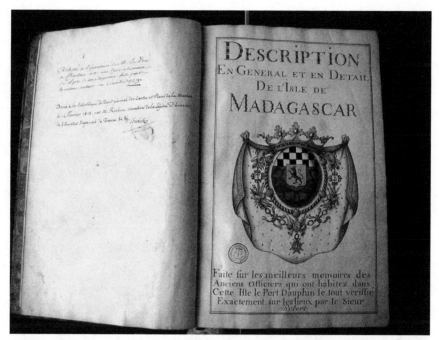

Figure 7.4. Manuscript on Madagascar, 1730, that yielded important historical data on pirates of Sainte-Marie Island. Courtesy of Service Historique de la Marine, Vincennes.

Figure 7.5. Undated manuscript chart of Ilot Madame and entrance to St. Mary's natural harbor. Courtesy of Centre des Archives d'Outre-Mer.

Figure 7.6. Blue-and-white Chinese export porcelain fragments scattered on top of the ballast stones of the *Fiery Dragon*.

corrections, providing absolute positioning in the harbor to about 50 cm accuracy. (The need for shore reference stations has decreased since this expedition due to the deactivation of Selective Availability by the U.S. government and improvements in receiver design.) Within a few days two ballast stone mounds were located just off the main dock at depths varying from 6 m to 7.6 m. The following day I inspected the sites. Upon closer examination it was noted that the smaller deposit was void of any visible cultural material; on the larger tumulus numerous blue-and-white Chinese export porcelain fragments and glass shards were observed, scattered over the entire mound (figure 7.6). They had been kept exposed by the prop wash of commercial vessels ferrying back and forth between Saint Mary's and the main island of Madagascar. During this initial survey four ceramic cup fragments were collected for the purpose of surface analysis and recording. The precise location of each fragment was carefully plotted and recorded, and the fragments were redeposited following the analysis and recording process.

The quality of the Chinese blue-and-white export porcelain, the stylistic floral designs, and the characteristics of the cup's feet suggested porcelain from the Kangxi period (1662–1722). The sinking of the *Adventure Galley* (1698) fitted nicely within the date range of the porcelain, and the resting place of the wreck closely matched the location of sunken pirate ships indicated in a 1733 manu-

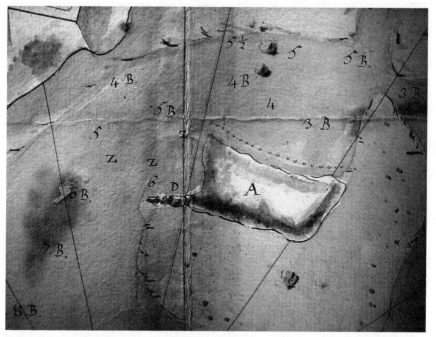

Figure 7.7. Detail of 1733 manuscript chart by Reynaud showing Ilot Madame Island and location of sunken pirate ships. Courtesy of Centre des Archives d'Outre-Mer.

script map (figure 7.7) that I located in a French archival repository (FM DFC XVII/28PFA/2, "Plan du Port de l'île de Saint Mary's de Madagascar, par Reynaud, 1733," Centre des Archives d'Outre-Mer, Aix-en-Provence, France).

Furthermore, contemporaneous documents mentioned that the *Adventure Galley* had sunk near the "careening spot." The same manuscript map showed that the careening area was indeed in close proximity to the ballast mound (figure 7.8).

The absence of ordnance seemed to strengthen the hypothesis that Captain Kidd's ship had been located. Eyewitnesses to the events surrounding the sinking testified that, as the ship was slowly filling up with water, it had been looted and stripped of almost everything that could be carried off, including the cannon (Public Records Office 1699). While all the pieces of the puzzle seemed to fit, it was nonetheless surprising to see that so much porcelain had been left behind.

One of the principal goals of this first mission was to produce a photo mosaic of the site—a true challenge, given the fluctuating and unpredictable visibility conditions in the bay. The mosaic would be tied to the Universal Transverse Mercator (UTM) grid. This is a worldwide rectilinear coordinate system based on the metric system. UTM coordinates are easily converted to geodetic coordinates (latitude/longitude) if required, and they are obviously very useful when trying to measure objects on the seabed. Charles Burnham of Advance Visuals,

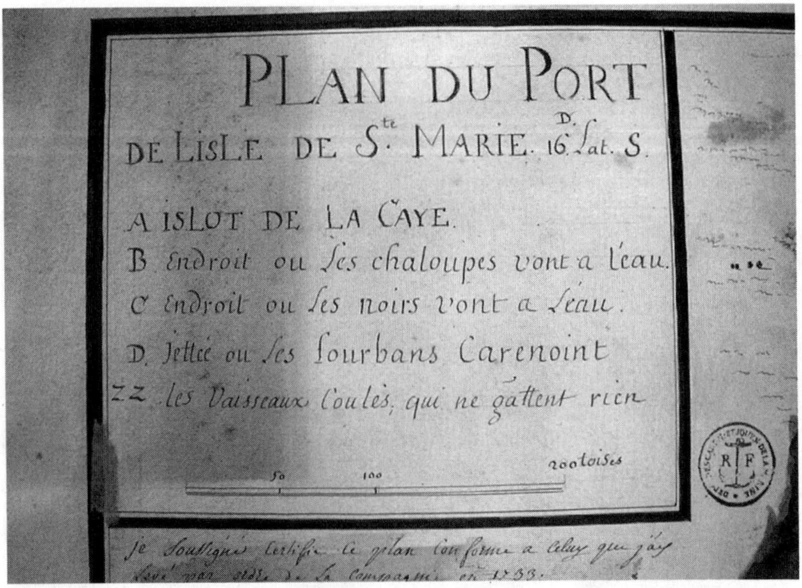

Figure 7.8. Cartouche of 1733 map. The two "Z"s indicate sunken pirate ships; "D" indicates the careening spot. Photo by J. de Bry; courtesy of Centre des Archives d'Outre-Mer.

Inc., of New York City performed that task. Using a Trimble GPS receiver, cinder blocks were carefully placed along three parallel lines on the wreck site. Block "A" was designated as the primary datum point and used to calibrate the other cinder blocks by tape measurements. Three lines of blocks rather than two were used because two distinct ballast stone deposits were present. The middle line, running true north south on the UTM grid, actually went between the two stone mounds. The southern boundary of the site was represented by a small cannon that lay several meters away from the visible extent of the wreck and did not seem associated with the primary wreck site. Three white polypropylene lines were set up between the blocks on the seabed and tagged every meter with a number, starting with 1 and ending with 20. Twenty blue strings (each about 25 m in length) were then positioned over the wreck to provide guidance for the camera operator and were virtually invisible underwater. Each guide string had a white square of tape attached every meter along its length. The end of each string was attached to a metal stake 25 cm tall.

The large ballast mound was in fact a three-dimensional site of 1 to 2 m vertical extent, which meant that the guide points (the little pieces of tape) were visually distorted by the shape of the mound. This distortion was taken into consideration in the final process of the mosaic data. The camera operator and two assistants, Wes Spiegel and Bob Paine, swam up and down the blue guide strings, ultimately recording slightly over two hours of video footage. When framing the guide marks, two marks were kept in frame at all times. Horizontal coverage was about 1.5 m. On especially good runs when visibility was at its optimum, all four marks were included in the frame. This would provide a rough meter scale when construction of the mosaic began. By not using a rigid photographic grid, the camera operator and his assistants were able to work quickly and with minimal interference with the archeological work that was being conducted simultaneously. Charles Burnham, who had used similar basic techniques when he mapped the site of the HMS *Titanic*, first produced a small mosaic of some of the timbers protruding from below the ballast stones using Adobe Photoshop and animated the results to give a fly-over effect.

The full mosaic would be more complicated. Photoshop artist Jane Finnerty and Burnham were faced with a technical challenge. Whereas the HMS *Titanic* had many straight lines and well-defined shapes, the Madagascar wreck site displayed mostly stone and silt. Other than the guide marks there was little else to go by. First, the 15 fps footage was downloaded to Adobe Premiere. This program allowed for the examination of every frame and exportation of the selected stills. Several criteria (visibility, lighting, guide marks, scale, and camera attitude) were used to select the best images for each square of the grid. All the selected frames were imported into Adobe Photoshop, and assembly of separate sections of the mosaic began. While the final product did not represent a calibrated scientific document and was not meant to supplant normal underwater archeological recording procedures, it provided a useful visual approximation of the overall wreck site (Charles Burnham, personal communication, July 2003). By February 10 the team had completed the initial survey and returned to the United States to prepare for a second expedition and an in-depth investigation of the wreck site.

Second Expedition and High-Technology Survey

We returned to Madagascar on May 24 and arrived on Saint Mary's Island the following day. New to the team were several scientists from Witten Technologies, Inc., of Boston, a high-tech firm that specializes in ground-penetrating radar imaging and Computer Assisted Radar Tomography (CART). Because an excavation permit had not yet been obtained, a noninvasive investigation technique was sought, and Witten Technologies, Inc. was chosen to develop it. The acoustic surveys were designed and carried out under the supervision of Douglas Miller and Jakob Haldorsen, who opted to perform a high-resolution seismic imaging of the wreck site. The Witten team was faced with a number of technical challenges: this type of acoustic survey had never been performed underwater on a shipwreck, there was no commercially available equipment to perform this task, and the survey would have to be conducted in a remote region of the world where no spare parts would be available—hence the need for a very robust and reliable system.

For high-resolution imaging through sediments saturated with saltwater, there are no practical alternatives to acoustic waves for the illumination of the object;

so the Witten scientists opted for a three-dimensional imaging system consisting of a commercially available sub-bottom profiler and a purpose-built lightweight conveyance system. They also brought a pair of hydrophones connected to a digital audio tape (DAT) recorder to be used for testing out concepts for a different acquisition system. In addition to the hardware a computer program to transform the acoustic reflection measurements into three-dimensional images also had to be designed. Taking into consideration the size of the area to be investigated and the degree of detail desired, the scientists decided to use a resolution of about 2 inches in the design of the system. This meant using a source capable of transmitting significant energy at 20 kHz. A small, light commercial source using a fixed 10–20 kHz chirp was chosen. The source was equipped with a fixed directional hydrophone that would record the reflected acoustic field.

With this high-frequency source it was felt that a reflection tomogram of the sub-bottom structure could be produced. The most critical section of the shipwreck could be covered with an acquisition grid of about 2 by 4 inches. This would allow the application of what is known in seismic exploration as "migration" processing to the data. Migration essentially transforms the data from a function of reflection times to a function of depth. For this technique to work, however, one has to know with some degree of accuracy the location of the source and receivers at the precise time of each record. In addition to positional accuracy, the image quality is also affected by the distribution of acquisition points on a spatially continuous acquisition surface. An even distribution gives the best results.

To meet these requirements for spatial accuracy, Cliff Evans of Schlumberger-Doll Research, from Ridgefield, Connecticut, designed a device—essentially a "frame" like an xy-plotter—that would allow divers to pull the source with the attached receiver (called a "fish") over the acquisition grid. To reduce the physical effort of the divers, the fish was equipped with an electric motor. In the interest of having a device that was small and light enough to fit into a single-engine airplane, the frame was made out of flexible lines that would be kept rigid using two additional lines stretched from each of the four corners. A large tent was set up on Ilot Madame Island, opposite the wreck site and packed with computer equipment. The processing units were connected to the in-water equipment by a thick cable. Originally the Witten scientists had planned to process the data and produce a three-dimensional picture of the buried vessel while still at the site.

As the sonar source was cranked back and forth, it became clear that the acquisition system needed to be modified. As it turned out, it was virtually impossible to keep the frame of the xy-plotter tight and rigid. The loose frame made it difficult to control or predict the motion of the fish. In addition to this, the gearbox transmitting power from the electric motor failed, forcing the divers to use a hand-crank for pulling the fish through the water. In doing so, it was difficult to keep it at a fixed speed, resulting in a variable and essentially unknown shot-point interval.

Figure 7.9. John de Bry (*right*) looks on as the fish containing the imaging sonar is lowered into the water. Photo by Chad Henning; courtesy of the Discovery Channel.

After experiencing problems with the link between the commercial acquisition system and the underwater conveyance system, the team finally settled for the simplest system that was available: the addition of the two extra hydrophones that were intended for experiments with alternative ways of positioning the sonar fish and as a backup to the acquisition components of the primary system (figure 7.9). Responses of the hydrophones were continuously digitized using a portable DAT recorder connected to a laptop computer. One of the hydrophones was attached to the source, and the other one was kept fixed at the end of the conveyance line. With the new configuration, sufficient measurements could be obtained to determine the geometry while using the signal recorded by receiver 1 for imaging purposes. Using travel times measured for ray paths connecting the source and receiver both directly and indirectly, and the known speed of sound in water, all the relevant positions could be calculated (position along a given pass, the depth of the source in the water for each recording position, the water depth at a given location, and so forth). The positional information allowed for migration processing of the data migrating one pass or line of data at a time. All migrated passes were collated into a three-dimensional cube. The outcome of this high-tech survey was spectacular. The resulting three-dimensional images clearly showed geometric shapes consistent with structural features of a large sailing vessel buried beneath the sediments. These images helped in visualizing the extent of the wreck site and will be most useful when a full excavation of the wreck is undertaken (Jakob Haldorsen, personal communication, July 2003).

While conducting the predisturbance survey, including the high-resolution seismic imaging of the site, and setting up the baseline, some architectural elements of the hull were observed protruding from beneath the ballast stones on the east side of the deposit. Hand fanning the silt away from what turned out to be floor timbers and fragmentary first futtocks, I recorded the framing arrangement (the way the first futtocks were fastened to the floor timbers). The framing pattern reflected a Dutch shipwright tradition instead of the expected English method.

In the English framing pattern the frame sets are made up of a floor, two first futtocks, two second futtocks, two third futtocks, and so forth, fastened together at each scarf using three treenails. The frames are set up so that they are touching each other; there is no space between them. This filling is extended to the level of the first futtock heads. From the head of the first futtock to the water line the frame timbers touch in some places, while in others there may be a space of 2.7 cm to 8.1 cm. From the water line up to the sills of the gundeck ports all the frames touch each other. Frames in the bow and stern extremities are canted (that is, they are not placed at a right angle to the keel).

Dutch frame sets are made up of a floor, a single first futtock, a single second futtock, a single third futtock, and so forth, fastened together using treenails. The treenails were made of fir rather than of oak as in France and England. The frames are arranged so that the first futtock fills the space between the floors and the second futtock fills the space between the first futtocks. The second futtocks do not meet the rung heads of the floors, however; nor do the third futtocks meet the rung head of the first futtocks. This leaves a space above and below each timber. While there is no space between frame sets, there is space within each frame set between the end of one timber and the beginning of another. Neither the Dutch nor the English used crotch frames; the lower futtocks are fastened directly to the rising (dead) wood in the bow and stern (Toni Carrell, personal communication, 2003).

Furthermore, as more and more blue-and-white Chinese export porcelain fragments were located, the decorative patterns suggested a period beyond the 1698 date for the sinking of the *Adventure Galley* sinking, closer to the end period of the Kangxi Dynasty, perhaps between 1720 and 1722. All this was puzzling to and did not fit Captain Kidd's flagship sinking scenario. Following the end of the second expedition on June 19, Ken Kinkor, a Cape Cod–based historian specializing in the history of pirates, was contacted and asked if he knew of other ships of European construction besides Kidd's *Adventure Galley* known to have sunk in the natural harbor of Saint Mary's Island between 1695 and 1725. His response was that the only other European built ship recorded as having sunk there during that period was the *Fiery Dragon*, which had belonged to the second most successful pirate in the Indian Ocean, Captain Condent (Ken Kinkor, personal communication, June 2000). (This ship has also been referred to as the *Flying Dragon*, but there is some confusion on the part of several chroniclers and historians. The *Flying Dragon* was the name of a previous ship owned by Condent; but, according to Ken Kinkor, in early 1720 Condent captured a Dutch ship named *Fame* at Luengo Bay in southwest Africa and renamed it the *Fiery Dragon*.) When asked if he knew where that particular ship had been built, Kinkor replied "Holland."

From this point on, I became convinced that the wreck found by Barry Clifford was the *Fiery Dragon*, not the *Adventure Galley*, and shared this opinion with Clifford and other team members. Understandably, there was some reluctance on everyone's part in accepting such a theory. After all, the shipwreck was simply too perfect to be anything but Kidd's ship, having been found in the right place with cultural material from the right period. What else could it be? There was only one way to provide a viable answer: to perform a test excavation of the site. The Malagasy government was once again contacted, and the Ministry of Culture was petitioned for an excavation permit. The former administration of now exiled president Didier Ratsiraka was plagued with corruption; and nothing moved very quickly, even with the gracious help of his daughter, Annick Ratsiraka. The biggest stumbling block to Barry Clifford's efforts to obtain the proper permission seems to have come from the Malagasy ambassador to the United States.

Finally, on October 8, 2000, special visas were granted to Clifford and his team. Ms. Ratsiraka affirmed that the excavation permit would be granted when we arrived in Antananarivo, the capital of Madagascar. The team arrived there on October 13; but the next day, at a meeting with the president's daughter, she announced that things had been delayed due to the absence of the minister of culture. She suggested that the group proceed to Saint Mary's Island and indicated that the permit would be granted in an official ceremony as soon as the minister returned, in just "a few days." Days turned into weeks; it was not until November 9, after countless telephone calls and meetings with Ministry of Culture officials, that the minister issued a permit for the test excavation of the shipwreck, limited to just ten days.

Test Excavation and Clues

The test excavation, begun on November 10, was performed on the southeast edge of the ballast mound where vestige of the ship's hull had been previously located. The purpose of the test excavation was to expose a larger section of the wooden structural elements of the ship and to record and analyze cultural material in an effort to confirm the suspected identity of the vessel. On the second day of excavation two small gold coins were located on top of a large floor timber (figure 7.10).

Both coins displayed Arabic writing (Ottoman reign of Mustafa II, A.H. 1106–

Figure 7.10. The first two gold coins in situ, resting atop a large timber. Note the hole on the coin to the left.

15/A.D. 1695–1703). One had been holed with what appears to have been a small square nail or tack. A Dutch gold coin minted in 1718 in Utrecht, the Nether-lands, was uncovered later that day among other artifacts (figure 7.11).

It was clear that the coins were not intrusive, just as it was clear that the wreck could not represent the *Adventure Galley*. Within the test excavation unit (2 m by 2 m), garboard, floor timbers, and fragmentary first futtocks were exposed. Upon close examination I confirmed that the oak timber layout and the way the first futtocks were arranged and fastened to the floor timbers reflected a Dutch construction tradition. During the course of the excavation project, ten more gold coins were uncovered, ranging in date from 1649 through 1718, minted in the Low Countries, Germany, Austria, Italy, and the Ottoman Empire (figure 7.12).

The variety of mints and nationalities represented in the numismatic assem-blage and the five coins with holes were holed, as well as the diversity of Chinese blue-and-white export porcelain ware types and styles, supported the tentative identification of a pirate ship rather than a commercial vessel. We have no reports of any significant amount of Chinese porcelain having been on board Kidd's ship; but the archival record shows that the *Fiery Dragon*, under the command of Captain Condent, captured two prizes in 1720. The *Prince Eugene* was taken off the coast of present-day South Africa in February or March 1720, and a richly

Figure 7.11. Gold ducat from the Low Countries dated 1718, minted in the city of Utrecht, Netherlands.

Figure 7.12. The eleven gold coins found on the *Fiery Dragon*.

Figure 7.13. Assortment of blue-and-white Chinese export porcelain found on the *Fiery Dragon*.

laden Mogul ship sailing from Surat to Jeddah was captured near Bombay in August of the same year. As noted earlier, the latter ship was reported to have carried a cargo estimated at the equivalent of $375 million in today's currencies (Rogozinski 2000:208). The porcelain and some of the gold coins provide us with a tantalizing link to the taking and subsequent looting of the *Prince Eugene*. Coming from Guangzhou (Canton), China, the ship was bound for Ostende in present-day Belgium, carrying an important cargo of silk, spices, exotic drugs, and Chinese porcelain. In addition to the coin minted in Utrecht in 1718, other coins were minted in West Friesland as well as in the Netherlands, in Frankfurt, Germany, and in Austria, all within the Hapsburg Empire. Two coins were struck in Venice, Italy, and three more within the Ottoman Empire.

Porcelain from the *Fiery Dragon*

The porcelain ware fragments found in situ on the wreck of the *Fiery Dragon* are extremely varied in styles as well as vessel types, which could suggest provenience from more than one ship taken as a prize and haphazardly loaded crates (figure 7.13).

Fragments from platters, plates, bowls, cups, and lids are scattered across the site and seem to be more numerous in the east portion of the wreck, identified as the starboard side. Some vessels have lobed rims; others scalloped ones. The most common decorations are flower and vegetal motifs, while a few display landscape scenes with pagodas (houses) and bodies of water. Fewer have animals (usually birds, such as the phoenix), and none depict human figures. Some geometric designs were also incorporated on some ware fragments, mixed with floral and vegetal motifs. Careful examination of some of the fragments revealed traces of patterns left by polychrome paint that had been applied over the glaze following the firing process. The over-glaze enamel paint did not resist long-term immersion in seawater; but the ghost image it left makes it possible to sketch the patterns and visualize what the vessels originally looked like.

All the fragments and an intact cup appear to have been fired in the kilns of Jingdezhen, in the province of Jiangxi in southern China, during the Kangxi period (1662–1722), based on the shape of the foot and the high quality of the porcelain (figure 7.14).

Stoneware had been produced in Jingdezhen since the tenth century, but the city made its reputation thanks to the introduction of *qingbai*, a white porcelain

Figure 7.14. Blue-and-white Chinese export porcelain cup with floral motif.

Figure 7.15. John de Bry recording a pewter tankard.

with a blue glaze that adheres to it perfectly and requires only a single firing. During the Song Dynasty (960–1279), potters from Jingdezhen began to exploit a new deposit called Gaoling (30 km northeast of the city) that provided an exceptionally fine clay, thus making the city's fortune. This refractory clay is feldspar formed of silica and alumina originating from the decomposition of an eruptive crystalline rock (aluminum oxide, Al_2O_3, occurring natively as corundum and in hydrated forms such as bauxite). In order to use this material in the manufacture of porcelain, it must be mixed with a substance known as *baidunzi* (meaning "little white bricks" in Chinese, the name derives from the form in which pulverized China stone was delivered to the kilns at Jingdezhen), which has the same structure as Gaoling but is less decomposed. Once pulverized, the resulting mixture is made into small blocks and placed in pits to decompose for several years. At the end of the decomposition period, the material has become flexible and malleable. During firing, the *baidunzi* melts to form a sort of cement that coats the kaolin particles. Mixed in equal proportions, the two components produced a beautifully pure white medium. The new genre, called blue-and-white, was created when an iridescent decoration made of cobalt oxide was added directly to the unfired surface using a brush. The entire piece was then coated with a special glaze and fired. The grayish cobalt oxide pigment would turn blue during the firing process. Thanks to this very dense glaze, the blue-and-white decoration was unalterable (Jean-Paul Desroches, personal communication, 1994).

The great Chinese export porcelain trade emerged during the reign of the Emperor Wanli (1573–1619), during the Ming Dynasty era. Blue-and-white porcelain is also designated as "kraak," from the Dutch term *Kraakpoorselein*, used to designate the first Chinese export porcelain first transported by carracks (a Portuguese type of ship). The quality and style of blue-and-white export porcelain from Jingdezhen is reflected in the porcelain material found on the wreck of the *Fiery Dragon*. The port city of Guangzhou (Canton) is located south-southwest of Jingdezhen. Guangzhou, strategically situated on the Xi Jiang River, became an active and important port that traded with India and the Muslim world as early as the seventh century and started trading with Europe in 1514. The first East India Company trading office was established there in 1684. It was the main port from which Chinese export porcelain was being shipped to Europe.

There is another tantalizing if not exceptional clue as to the identity of this particular wreck (figure 7.15). During the first predisturbance survey conducted in January and February 2000, a broken porcelain lid was recorded in situ. With an original diameter of 9 cm, the lid had a double-headed eagle or phoenix motif repeated three times, separated by foliage. Originally this motif was thought to be associated with the Augustinian Order (Jean-Paul Desroches, personal communication, February 2000). Thirty years after the first Jesuits arrived in Macao, three Spanish Augustinians arrived there on November 1, 1586, to establish a convent. Three years later, on August 22, the Portuguese Augustinians took over the Convent of Our Lady of Grace by order of Philip II of Spain, who then also reigned over Portugal. The heraldic device of the Saint Augustinian Order is a phoenix surmounted by a vegetal crown, standing on a heart pierced by two arrows (*Du Tage à la Mer de Chine,* exhibition catalogue, p. 158; Musée Nationale des Arts Asiatiques-Guimet, Paris, 1992). Only three Chinese porcelain objects adorned with the double-headed eagle are known to be extant, all three from the Wanli period (1573–1619).

The presence of this porcelain lid on Saint Mary's Island was surprising, because such items were thought to have been manufactured exclusively for the Macao market. We were dealing with a pirate ship, however, which could explain why the ship's cargo would not be typical of the cargo of East Indiamen. During the test excavation seven more porcelain cup fragments with the phoenix motif were found (figure 7.16).

Figure 7.16. Blue-and-white Chinese export porcelain cup fragments displaying the phoenix symbol.

There may be another explanation for this decoration. The coat of arms of the Hapsburgs was a crowned phoenix with a coat of arms on its chest. It is quite conceivable that those porcelain fragments represent a special order for the Hapsburg market (rather the Macao one) that was originally aboard the *Prince Eugene* when the *Fiery Dragon* seized it.

Miscellaneous Artifacts

Other artifacts uncovered during the course of the test excavation included an exquisite terra-cotta lion from Yixing, China, identified by its signature purple clay (figure 7.17). This distinctive clay was first mined around Lake Taihu in China during the Sung Dynasty (960–1279). Yixing acquired an international reputation for its production of purple clay wares, especially teapots. Yixing and the surrounding clay deposits are situated 193 km northwest of Shanghai in Jiangsu province.

A broken doughnut-shaped brown terra-cotta flask with several pieces missing was also found. It had two small handles, one broken and missing. This flask,

Figure 7.17. Terra-cotta Chinese dragon from Yixing.

called a pilgrim flask, is probably of Islamic origin, but no parallel has been found (figure 7.18).

We also discovered gargoulette (also known as kullal) fragments, from a type of lightly fired and porous small earthenware vessel for storing liquids (Avner Raban, personal communication, October 28, 1984); a small Chinese white porcelain figurine of a standing mandarin with his hands joined in a greeting gesture, possibly a game piece; numerous utilitarian ceramic ware fragments; and a beautiful ivory figurine of Jesus Christ, from a crucifix, missing its arms and feet (figure 7.19). The style suggests a late seventeenth century or early eighteenth century Spanish or Portuguese origin.

Organic Material

Collected wood samples used in the construction of the *Fiery Dragon* have been identified as European white oak, most probably *Quercus robur* or *Quercus petraea*. This wood, found on numerous wrecks, played a major role in European commerce and warfare and was the most commonly used wood throughout the history of seafaring (Steffy 1994). It is slightly lighter than *Quercus alba* (American white oak).

Two types of seeds found on the lowest level of the *Fiery Dragon* test unit have been tentatively identified as cf. *Prunus* sp. and *Myristica fragrans* (nutmeg; a tropical, dioecious evergreen tree native to the Moluccas or Spice Islands of Indonesia). The nutmeg may have come from the large Moghul ship taken near

Figure 7.18. Islamic "pilgrim" ceramic flask. No parallel for this doughnut-shape vessel has been found.

Figure 7.19. Ivory Christ in situ among ballast and cowry shells.

Bombay on August 18, 1720. This spice was much appreciated and in demand in Europe. A French Royal Ordinance dated September 9, 1726, directed French ship captains to bring back a variety of exotic plants, fruits, and spices whenever possible. Nutmeg was part of the extensive list given to sea captains sailing to the Americas, Africa, and the Orient. The other seeds belong to the genus *Prunus* of the Rosaceae family and closely resemble *Prunus dulcis*, the almond. The seeds examined do not appear to have the exterior pericarp shell present (which would greatly aid in identification because it contains the diagnostic pitting around the shell surface); they seem to represent the middle mesocarp shell that encircles the kernel or the almond. This also looks much like that of the apricot *Prunus armeniac*, also called the Chinese almond (Donna Rhule, personal communication, January 5, 2001).

Cowrie Shells

Large quantities of cowrie shells were found on the wreck of the *Fiery Dragon*, many cemented to the ribs of the ship. A number of the cowries have been identified as *Cypraea chinensis* (Indo-Pacific), *Cypraea walkeri* (Seychelles Island and the Maldives Islands), *Cypraea helvola* (Indo-Pacific), *Cypraea gracilis* (Indian Ocean), *Cypraea erosa* (Indo-Pacific), *Cypraea arabica* (Indo-Pacific), *Cypraea lynx* (Indian Ocean and west and central Pacific Ocean), and *Cypraea talpa* (Indian Ocean and central Pacific Ocean). Other species have yet to be identified, but the above-mentioned cowries were found to be the most numerous. The *Fiery Dragon* is known to have had a large quantity of cowries on board, as did other pirate ships in Saint Mary's (Public Record Office, CO 77/16; Deposition, fol. 292 recto and fol. 293 recto). Cowries were widely used in the region to trade as well as to purchase slaves. When placed within its historical and archaeological context, the cultural assemblage from this particular wreck provides all the necessary evidence needed to identify it as Captain Condent's *Fiery Dragon*.

Captain Condent and the *Fiery Dragon*

Christopher Condent often sailed alone with his pirate company without consorts. As the Caribbean became too dangerous, he migrated to the safer and often more lucrative Indian Ocean like other pirates, eventually sailing into the port of Saint Mary's Island in 1720 aboard his ship the *Fiery Dragon* (formerly the *Fame*, which he had captured in 1719). In August, after resupplying and signing on more men, Condent sailed for the coast of India, where he struck it rich by capturing a large ship laden with cargo reportedly worth £150,000 (as detailed in an earlier section).

Once the Indian ship had been fully looted, Condent and his crew returned to the safety and idyllic life of Saint Mary's Island. While they divided the rich booty and celebrated their good luck, the *Crooker* (a two-masted English merchant vessel called a snow) sailed into the small harbor to take on water. Perhaps inebriated and with a bit too much celebrating under their belts, Condent's crew boarded the *Crooker* and seized its supply of alcoholic beverages. Condent ended up compensating the ship's master, Captain Baker, for the spirits taken by his exuberant crew. The two men engaged in a civilized, if not friendly, conversation. Baker revealed that the French governor of Bourbon (present-day Reunion Island, named Mascarenha by Portuguese explorers and mariners about 1520) was offering a pardon to any pirate giving up his trade. A royal decree had given the island a legitimate right to pardon pirates and even encourage them to settle on the island. The only requirement was that they turn over or destroy their ships and turn over their weapons and ammunition. In return for a small fee each man would be allowed to bring in one black slave and settle on the island to lead a righteous and honest life.

Condent was very interested in this offer, especially after having taken such a rich prize and knowing that he would be allowed to keep his ill-gotten fortune. He asked Captain Baker to return to Bourbon and inquire as to the validity of this pardon offer. Condent was not unknown to Governor Joseph Beauvollier de Courchant, who was more than happy to see this menace off the water and under control. He quickly agreed to a general pardon for Condent and his men. In February 1721 Condent and thirty-two of his crew left Saint Mary's for Bourbon Island, burning the *Fiery Dragon* as it lay at anchor just before they departed. It is not clear what truly transpired, however. It is quite possible that there was disagreement among the 135 crew members about whether to accept the pardon and retire to Bourbon and that a scuffle broke out, resulting in the premature burning of the *Fiery Dragon*. That scenario would explain why so much cultural material remained on the ship. When an English squadron called port at Saint Mary's the following year, Captain Clement Downing reported finding "the Ruins of several Ships and their Cargoes piled up in great Heaps, consisting of the richest Spices and Drugs."

Christopher Condent distinguished himself while on Bourbon Island, acting as a negotiator for the governor when pirates took over a disabled Portuguese ship, the *Nostra Senhora de Cabo*, that had sought refuge on the island after weathering a devastating storm taking the viceroy of Portuguese India hostage (see the earlier discussion of John Taylor and Olivier La Buse). Condent managed to persuade the pirates to release the viceroy for a £400 ransom, although they kept the *Cabo* and took it to Saint Mary's Island. His handling of this delicate situation gained him the respect and friendship of the governor. In 1722, after marrying the governor's sister-in-law, Condent sailed for France and settled down in Saint-Malo, on the Normandy coast, where he became a successful and respectable businessman and ship owner.

Figure 7.20. John de Bry on the wreck of the *Fiery Dragon*. Photo by Nick Caloyianis; courtesy of the Discovery Channel.

While the name of William Kidd became synonymous with the word "pirate," his career was short; he was one of the less successful rogues who roamed the Indian Ocean. Christopher Condent, whose name is unknown to most, was the second most successful scoundrel who ever lived: he committed one of the largest robberies in history and got away with murder (figure 7.20).

All figures are by John de Bry unless noted otherwise.

8

The Pirate Ship *Whydah*

Christopher E. Hamilton

"There is no X to mark the spot, only Southack's crabbed writing over an area of the map that covers about ten miles of ocean" (Clifford and Perry 1999a:44). Finding that "X," the site of the wreck of the pirate ship *Whydah*, and proving that it was this vessel required historical research and oral histories from beach-combers, combined with remote sensing using a magnetometer and sub-bottom profiler and ultimately the excavation of test units using a dredge and a prop-wash diverter. The site, WLF-HA-1, was found in 1983. It lies some 1,500 ft (455 m) off Marconi Beach on Cape Cod in 20–30 ft (6–9 m) of water, under as much as 20 ft (6 m) of loose shifting sand on a cobble-strewn clay stratum. Once thought to cover 24,000 ft² (2,230 m²), it is now estimated to be scattered over twice that area (Kenneth Kinkor personal communication, January 17, 2003).

Historical Background

Whydah was a 300-ton, London built, ship-rigged galley designed for the slave trade. By the eighteenth century the term "galley" no longer referred to vessels that were rowed. Instead, it denoted a hull shaped for speed rather than cargo capacity, with no relation to the means of propulsion. Speed was all-important, because this ship was constructed to transport a highly perishable living "cargo."

Acting as a slave transport under the command of Captain Lawrence Prince, *Whydah* sailed from England to the Gold Coast of Ghana and the slave market town of Whydah, now in Benin, on the west coast of Africa. After loading its unfortunate human cargo, *Whydah* subsequently sailed to Jamaica in the Carib-bean Sea, where it sold these forced immigrants. At the end of February 1717, *Whydah* was homeward bound with a cargo of sugar, indigo, quinine, and the silver and gold specie earned from the sale of the enslaved Africans. *Whydah* was making its way north through the Bahamas when sighted by the pirate Samuel Bellamy. After a three-day chase, Bellamy and his crew took *Whydah* as a prize. *Whydah*'s captain and crew were set free in Bellamy's old ship, and Bellamy sailed the now pirate ship *Whydah* up the coast of North America, robbing other mer-

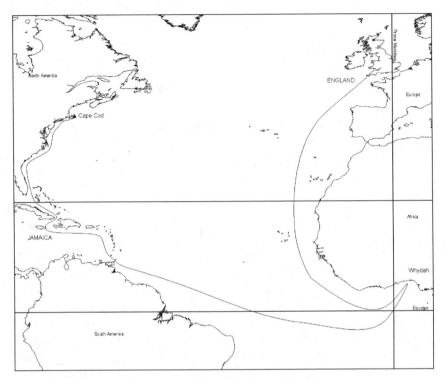

Figure 8.1. Journey of *Whydah*. Courtesy of Expedition Whydah.

chant vessels. It was bound for Richmond Island in what is today Maine. There they planned to careen the ship and clean it of the marine growth that had formed in warm tropical waters (figure 8.1).

Contemporary accounts suggest that *Whydah* mounted some 30 guns and carried between 130 and 200 men. It was reported that it also carried between £20,000 and £30,000 in silver and gold. On the morning of April 26, 1717, *Whydah* was east of Cape Cod and fell in with a merchant pink that was subsequently captured. Late that evening a roaring northeaster with heavy rain, thunder, and lightning blew in and drove the vessel into the shallows off Cape Cod. There the vessel caught on a shoal and was capsized and crushed (figure 8.2). Only two of the crew made it to shore. The body of their captain, Samuel Bellamy, was never found (Clifford and Perry 1999b:32).

A few days later, on May 1, 1717, Cyprian Southack was sent by the governor of Massachusetts to investigate the wreck. He found the remains of *Whydah*, "all in pieces North & South Distance from each other 4 miles" (Southack 1717). By May 8 seventy-two bodies had washed ashore, along with sixty pipes of wine and sections of *Whydah*'s hull that were subsequently burnt in order to retrieve the iron fittings for recycling. In the three centuries since its loss there have been

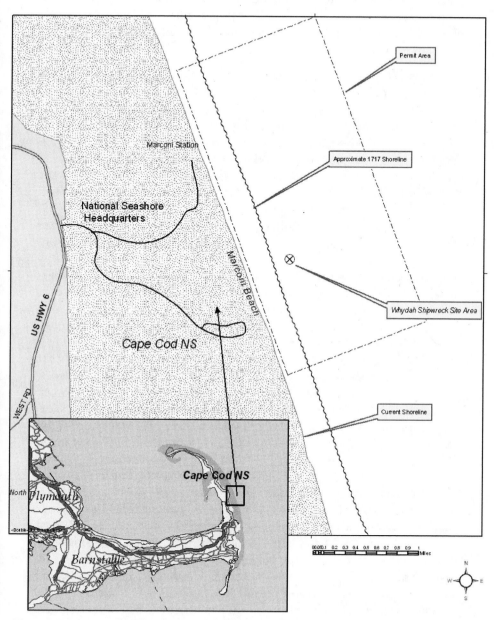

Figure 8.2. Location of WLF-HA-1, the *Whydah* wreck site. Courtesy of Expedition Whydah.

numerous reports of the discovery of various objects attributed to *Whydah* by the finders. Suffice it to say that because *Whydah* occupies a special place in Cape Cod folklore, such purported discoveries are by no means scanty.

Finding *Whydah*—Project Background

In 1978 Barry Clifford began historical background research on the sinking of the pirate ship *Whydah*. As the president of Maritime Explorations, Inc. (MEI), he led a group of private investors in the effort to locate the site of *Whydah*. In 1984 and 1985 the project was working with the archeological guidance of Edwin Dethlefson, followed by Warren Reiss, then Rob Reedy and myself, under permits from the Massachusetts Board of Underwater Archaeological Resources (MBUAR) and the U.S. Army Corps of Engineers (ACE), permit WLF-MA-85-176. This permit brought the project under the guidelines for implementation of section 106 of the National Historic Preservation Act of 1966 as amended, conditioned by the Memorandum of Agreement (MOA) by ACE, the Massachusetts Historical Commission (MHC), and the Advisory Council for Historic Preservation (ACHP). The courts voided the permit from the MBUAR in 1987; however, the ACE permit and the MOA remained in effect.

MEI conducted archaeological testing on the wreck site from 1983 through 1987. Over this period, twenty-two 8×16-foot test units and one 8×8-foot unit were wholly or partially excavated. Two of these units were opened but not significantly disturbed. The test units were excavated to assess site boundaries, integrity, and significance. Confirmation that the site was the remains of *Whydah* came during the 1985 field season with the dramatic find of the ship's bell, bearing the legend "THE † WHYDAH † GALLY † 1716." The results of the test excavations indicated that the site is under 20 ft (6 m) to 30 ft (9 m) of water, some 1,500 ft (455 m) off Marconi Beach in Wellfleet, Massachusetts.

In early 1987 the Whydah Joint Venture was formed by Rolland Betts and Tom Bernstein with MEI to conduct data recovery at the site. In 1988 MEI received approval of its Data Recovery Plan from the state and federal government for the conduct of full excavations at the *Whydah* shipwreck site. The 1988 field season began on May 24 and ended October 25, 1988. Within that period 113 days were spent in the field, with 86 days of excavation. During the 1988 field season a total site area of 4,192 ft^2 was excavated, yielding 20,851 artifacts and concretions. The excavated area consisted of approximately 17 percent of the 24,000 ft^2 of main site area as then estimated and reported in the Data Recovery Plan (Hamilton et al. 1988). The total area of the site excavated from 1984 (the initial discovery of the site) through 1988 was approximately 6,976 ft^2 or 29 percent of the main body of the site. The area excavated in 1988 was in excess of 300 ft^2 more than anticipated to be excavated for the 1988 and 1989 field seasons combined.

Field Methods

The boundaries for the site were identified with an intensive remote sensing survey over the area. Survey methods included sub-bottom SONAR and magnetometry. The purpose of the sub-bottom SONAR survey was to map the underlying topography of the clay and cobble strata beneath the sand overburden, while the magnetometer was used to identify magnetic anomalies.

Test pits varying in size from 8×8 feet to 8×16 feet were excavated across the site. The majority of the sand overburden covering the artifact-bearing clay and cobble stratum was removed using a propeller wash deflector device. A four-inch water induction dredge and later a two-inch airlift were used to remove the remaining sand. Excavation methods resulted in proveniences to within a foot for small items (Hamilton et al. 1992:119, 120). In 1988 a Data Recovery Plan was approved that allowed freedom to work in contiguous areas. Excavation of nearly 21,000 artifacts, including guns, the bow anchor, coins, lead shot, and many other artifact types, was completed in this season alone (Hamilton et al. 1992:124).

Site Formation

More than twenty-five years ago the late Keith Muckelroy (1978) penned a seminal volume in maritime archaeology. In it he identified the natural and cultural transformations that affect a ship and its contents as it passes from systemic (functional) to archaeological contexts. What survives the process is the result of the application of a number of "extracting filters," including the mechanical aspects of material loss to salvage, disintegration, seabed movements, and related forces. All of these variables dictate what survives and what does not in the evolution of a shipwreck. Muckelroy noted two extremes. The first occurs when the vessel sinks intact, dragged down by a combination of ballast, cargo, and inflowing water. The best example of this is *Vasa*, sunk in Stockholm harbor in 1628 (Franzen 1974). Things between decks were trapped, became waterlogged, and were eventually buried in the seabed. Wrecks of this kind are known as "continuous sites."

The other extreme that Muckelroy described was exemplified by the *Dartmouth*. This late seventeenth century ship disintegrated totally on the surface, spilling its heavy items onto the sea floor, while less dense objects floated away (Muckelroy 1978:166, 196). Debris can be scattered over a huge area. Wrecks of this kind are termed "discontinuous sites," because there is an absence of any defining architectural framework. Historic accounts and archaeological research indicate that this definition best fits the *Whydah*.

The storm that capsized and destroyed *Whydah* served as the first scrambling and extracting device of the ship as it washed ashore with practically all of its hull and other ship architecture, bodies, and even alcohol in the form of "sixty pipes

Figure 8.3. Silver *real* and .50-cal. round concreted together. Courtesy of Expedition Why-dah.

of wine" (Southack 1717). Seabed movement is the second scrambling and ex-tracting device in the formation of this discontinuous site. Muckelroy (1978: 176–77) notes:

> Within most marine sediments, there is usually an upper layer of deposit, anything between a few centimeters and several meters thick, which is in a state of semi-suspension, being lubricated by the surrounding water. Heavy objects will obviously drop through this, while less dense items caught in it are likely to be thoroughly jumbled and heavily abraded . . . This is the case with the Trinidad Valencera site . . . [where] a modern ring-pull beer can [was found] alongside a sixteenth-century timber at a depth of about 30 centimeters.

Yet (employing our understanding of the scrambling extraction filters in the high-energy coastal environment of Cape Cod), with the exception of the ship's architecture, integrity was found to be sufficient for reasonable interpretation of the site. Just as described above, there was a mixing and settling of heavy, high-density artifacts (for example, cannon) onto the clay and cobble strata of Pleis-tocene origin. Early eighteenth century artifacts associated with *Whydah* were found on the clay substrate immediately adjacent to and sometimes concreted to World War II–era ordinance (figure 8.3), thus demonstrating how dense objects sink while artifacts with lesser density (such as ceramics) are carried away and dispersed by these forces (Hamilton et al. 1992:465). Nonetheless, even a discon-tinuous site can yield important information on the ship and its contents.

To obtain information about how the ship and its contents were mixed as a result of the wrecking process, a principal component analysis was undertaken. The analysis was performed on the artifacts as grouped into twenty-six functional categories found within 8×8-foot units across the site (see table 8.1). Six principal components were derived and plotted with isopleths, using a distance weighted least squares regression formula on each component. The plots indicated potential artifact dispersion from the center of the site toward the south and particularly to the west. This analysis conformed to the understanding of the conditions of the wreck of *Whydah*, occurring in a northeast gale and subsequently augmented by later tide and long shore current movement, pushing items both west and south.

Along with the expected lateral movement of artifacts to the west and south, downward movement of the artifacts has occurred, caused by the deflation of the site area through storm-surge mixing of bottom sediments combined with coastal recession associated with the rise in sea level. The artifacts have been observed to be located beneath 1.5 m (5 ft) to perhaps 6 m (20 ft) of sand overburden. The precise rate at which artifacts have moved down through the sand overburden is not known. However, excavations have revealed .50-cal. rounds of World War II and slightly later vintage, concreted to silver *reales* from *Whydah* on the sub-bottom clay and cobble stratum (Hamilton et al. 1992:465).

While site formation may have left the majority of artifacts of dense material (such as lead, silver, and iron) from *Whydah* in the main body of the site, the natural forces of tide, current, and erosion have transformed the site by removing most of the light-density material (such as glass and ceramics) from the area. Final resting places for the artifacts would thus be expected to be the result of movement caused by tides and currents, with collecting places for artifacts found in depressions in the sub-bottom.

The influence of the shape and weight of artifacts was studied to determine whether the horizontal and vertical forces that transformed the site also sorted the artifacts. To test this hypothesis, three types of artifacts (iron round shot, lead small-arms shot, and silver *real* coins) were studied, because they were sufficiently numerous and of differing but regular shape and material densities.

These three types of artifacts with known provenience were counted and measured. The cannon shot types are iron round shot weighing one, two, three, and four pounds (PD1–PD4); the coin types are silver "cob" coins in denominations of half, one, two, four, and eight *reales* (REAL1H–REAL8); the lead small-arms shot is classified in twenty diameters (SHOT0–SHOT19). The small arms shot ranged from less than 1 mm (.04 in) to 19 mm (.75 in), measured with USA Standard Testing Sieves. The data for the analysis are presented in table 8.2. For reference it should be noted that the densities of iron, silver, and lead at 20° C are approximately 7.87 gm/cm^3, 10.49 gm/cm^3, and 11.35 gm/cm^3, respectively.

The Spearman Rank Correlation of the data indicates that *real* coins, iron round shot, and lead small shot are sorted according to their weight, though the

Table 8.1. Artifact Groups from *Whydah*

X	Y	1	2	3	4	5	6	7	8	9	10	11	12	13
-104	0	—	—	—	—	—	—	—	4	—	—	—	—	—
-96	48	—	—	—	—	—	—	—	1	—	—	—	—	—
-88	48	—	—	—	—	—	—	—	9	—	—	—	—	3
-88	56	—	—	—	—	—	—	—	4	1	—	—	—	4
-80	16	—	—	2	2	—	—	—	15	6	1	—	—	141
-80	48	—	—	—	—	—	—	—	—	2	—	—	—	9
-80	56	—	—	—	—	—	—	—	—	—	—	1	—	—
-72	-8	—	—	—	—	—	—	—	—	—	—	—	—	1
-72	0	—	—	—	—	—	—	—	—	—	—	—	—	1
-72	16	1	1	4	1	1	12	—	34	7	2	57	1	1,157
-72	48	—	—	—	—	—	—	—	—	—	—	—	—	—
-72	56	—	—	—	—	—	—	—	—	—	—	1	—	—
-72	80	—	—	—	—	—	—	—	—	—	—	—	—	1
-64	0	—	—	—	—	—	—	—	—	—	—	—	—	2
-64	8	—	—	—	—	—	—	—	3	3	—	—	—	31
-64	16	—	—	—	1	—	—	—	4	2	—	1	—	26
-64	24	—	—	—	—	—	—	—	7	—	—	—	—	80
-64	32	—	—	—	—	—	—	—	1	—	—	—	1	20
-64	48	—	—	—	—	—	—	—	3	—	—	—	—	11
-64	56	—	—	2	—	—	—	—	5	1	—	—	—	48
-64	64	—	—	1	—	—	—	—	18	—	—	2	—	26
-64	72	—	—	—	—	—	—	—	4	—	—	—	—	—
-64	80	—	—	—	—	—	—	—	1	—	—	—	—	—
-64	88	—	—	—	—	—	—	—	1	—	—	—	—	2
-64	96	—	—	—	—	—	—	—	—	—	—	—	—	1
-56	-8	—	—	—	—	—	—	—	6	1	—	—	—	1
-56	0	—	—	—	—	—	—	—	1	2	—	2	—	11
-56	8	—	—	—	—	—	—	—	4	—	—	—	—	26

14	15	16	17	18	19	20	21	22	23	24	25	26	Total
—	—	—	—	1	—	—	—	—	—	—	—	–	5
—	—	—	—	—	—	—	—	—	—	—	—	—	1
—	1	—	—	—	—	—	—	—	—	—	—	—	13
—	1	—	—	3	—	—	—	—	—	—	—	—	13
—	3	—	—	—	—	—	—	1	—	—	—	2	173
—	3	—	—	—	—	—	—	—	—	—	—	—	14
—	—	—	—	—	—	—	—	—	—	—	—	—	1
—	—	—	—	—	—	—	—	—	—	—	—	1	2
—	—	—	—	—	—	—	—	—	—	—	—	—	1
1	42	1	—	—	2	8	10	2	11	—	2	1	1,358
—	—	—	—	—	—	2	—	—	—	—	—	—	2
—	—	—	—	—	—	—	—	—	—	—	—	—	1
—	—	—	—	—	—	—	—	—	—	—	—	—	1
—	—	—	—	—	—	—	—	—	—	—	—	1	3
—	2	—	—	—	—	1	—	—	—	—	—	—	40
—	1	—	—	—	—	—	—	—	—	—	—	—	35
—	10	—	—	1	—	—	—	—	—	—	—	—	98
—	5	—	—	—	—	—	—	—	—	—	—	—	27
—	12	—	—	—	—	—	—	—	—	—	—	—	26
1	15	—	—	1	—	1	—	1	—	—	—	—	75
2	31	—	—	—	—	2	—	—	—	—	—	—	82
—	—	—	—	—	—	—	—	—	—	—	—	—	4
—	—	—	—	—	—	—	—	—	—	1	—	—	2
—	—	—	—	1	—	—	—	—	—	—	—	—	4
—	—	—	—	—	—	—	—	—	—	—	—	—	1
—	—	—	—	—	—	—	—	—	—	—	—	—	8
—	1	1	—	—	—	—	—	—	—	—	—	—	18
—	10	—	—	—	—	—	—	—	—	—	—	—	40

(continued)

Table 8.1—*Continued*

X	Y	1	2	3	4	5	6	7	8	9	10	11	12	13
-56	16	—	—	—	—	—	—	—	—	—	—	—	—	9
-56	24	—	—	—	—	—	—	—	6	—	—	—	—	39
-56	32	—	—	1	—	—	1	—	12	3	—	1	—	28
-56	40	—	—	—	—	—	—	—	8	1	—	—	—	14
-56	48	—	—	—	—	—	—	—	—	—	—	—	—	1
-56	56	—	—	1	1	—	—	—	35	2	—	—	—	77
-56	64	—	—	—	—	—	—	—	1	3	—	1	—	17
-56	72	—	—	—	2	—	—	—	9	—	—	—	—	1
-56	96	—	—	—	—	—	—	—	—	—	—	—	—	3
-48	0	—	—	—	—	—	—	—	15	—	—	3	5	2
-48	8	—	—	—	—	—	—	—	1	1	—	1	1	7
-48	24	—	—	—	—	—	—	—	173	—	—	—	—	95
-48	32	2	—	1	—	—	—	—	354	—	—	—	—	244
-48	48	—	—	—	—	—	—	—	—	—	—	—	—	1
-48	56	—	—	—	—	—	2	—	109	—	—	1	—	80
-48	64	—	—	—	—	—	—	—	66	1	—	—	—	13
-48	72	—	—	—	2	—	—	—	117	—	—	—	—	5
-48	96	—	—	—	—	—	—	—	21	—	—	—	—	2
-40	-32	—	—	—	—	—	—	—	—	—	—	—	—	2
-40	-24	—	—	—	—	—	—	—	—	—	—	—	—	1
-40	-16	—	—	—	—	—	—	—	—	—	—	—	—	—
-40	8	—	—	1	—	—	—	—	—	1	—	—	—	1
-40	16	—	—	—	—	—	—	—	—	—	—	—	—	7
-40	24	—	—	—	—	—	—	—	2	—	—	—	—	8
-40	32	—	—	—	10	—	—	—	323	4	—	—	—	231
-40	40	—	—	—	—	—	—	—	2	—	—	—	—	2
-40	56	—	—	—	1	—	—	—	12	3	1	3	—	19
-40	64	—	—	1	—	—	1	—	442	—	1	2	—	11
-40	72	—	2	—	2	—	—	—	204	—	—	—	—	6

14	15	16	17	18	19	20	21	22	23	24	25	26	Total
—	—	—	—	—	—	—	—	—	—	—	—	—	9
—	8	—	—	—	—	—	—	—	—	—	—	—	53
—	9	—	—	—	—	—	—	—	—	—	—	—	55
—	25	—	1	—	—	—	—	—	—	—	—	—	49
—	—	—	—	—	—	—	—	—	—	—	—	—	1
—	43	—	—	—	—	2	—	1	—	—	—	—	162
—	2	—	—	—	—	—	—	—	—	—	—	1	25
—	1	—	—	1	—	—	—	—	—	—	—	—	14
—	—	—	—	—	—	—	—	—	—	—	—	—	3
—	—	—	—	—	—	—	—	—	—	—	—	1	26
—	2	—	—	—	—	—	—	—	—	—	—	3	16
—	79	—	—	3	—	3	—	—	—	—	—	—	353
—	422	—	1	—	—	—	—	—	—	—	—	1	1,025
—	—	—	—	—	—	—	—	—	—	—	—	—	1
—	38	—	—	—	—	—	—	—	—	—	—	1	231
—	46	—	2	—	—	2	—	—	—	—	—	—	130
—	16	—	—	—	—	—	—	—	—	—	—	—	140
—	24	—	—	1	—	—	—	—	—	—	—	—	48
—	—	—	—	—	—	—	—	—	—	—	—	—	2
—	—	—	—	—	—	—	—	—	—	—	—	—	1
—	1	—	—	—	—	—	—	—	—	—	—	—	1
—	—	—	—	—	—	—	—	—	—	—	—	2	5
—	—	—	—	—	—	—	—	—	—	—	—	1	8
—	15	—	—	—	—	—	—	—	—	—	—	—	25
—	459	—	1	—	—	1	—	—	—	—	—	1	1,030
—	—	—	—	—	—	—	—	—	—	—	—	—	4
—	—	—	1	—	1	1	—	—	—	—	—	1	43
—	—	—	1	—	—	—	—	—	—	—	—	—	459
—	53	—	—	—	—	—	—	—	—	—	—	—	267

(continued)

Table 8.1—*Continued*

X	Y	1	2	3	4	5	6	7	8	9	10	11	12	13
-40	96	—	—	—	—	—	—	—	—	—	—	—	—	5
-40	104	—	—	—	—	—	—	—	—	—	—	—	—	3
-32	-8	—	—	2	—	—	—	—	49	2	—	—	—	69
-32	8	—	—	—	—	—	—	—	—	2	—	—	—	—
-32	16	—	—	—	1	—	—	—	3	1	—	—	—	24
-32	24	—	1	—	—	—	—	—	418	3	1	—	—	6
-32	32	—	—	1	—	—	—	—	543	4	1	1	—	53
-32	40	—	6	15	13	2	1	—	10,333	9	7	15	6	610
-32	48	2	4	3	30	—	—	—	16,318	9	6	87	2	282
-32	56	1	—	2	1	—	—	—	189	8	3	1	—	12
-32	64	—	1	1	—	—	1	—	11	2	1	20	—	1
-32	88	—	—	—	—	—	—	—	—	—	—	—	—	—
-32	96	—	—	—	—	—	—	—	1	—	—	—	—	16
-32	104	—	—	—	—	—	—	—	—	—	—	—	—	6
-24	-8	6	—	5	—	—	2	2	86	16	—	1	—	81
-24	32	1	1	10	56	2	1	—	3,050	18	3	56	1	603
-24	40	1	1	2	50	—	—	—	13,096	1	—	—	1	83
-24	48	—	1	—	27	—	—	—	8,821	—	—	2	—	24
-24	56	—	1	—	—	—	—	—	1,874	1	—	—	—	1
-24	96	—	—	—	—	—	—	—	5	6	—	—	—	13
-24	104	—	—	—	—	—	—	—	—	—	—	—	—	4
-16	-16	—	—	—	—	—	—	—	—	—	—	—	—	1
-16	-8	—	—	3	—	—	—	—	4	6	8	1	—	5
-16	0	4	—	6	19	—	—	19	1,247	5	9	46	—	580
-16	8	2	—	—	—	—	—	—	11	—	47	7	4	6
-16	48	—	14	—	4	—	—	—	9,945	—	—	1	—	1
-8	-16	—	—	—	—	—	—	—	—	—	—	—	—	—
-8	-8	—	—	—	—	—	—	—	22	—	—	—	—	—
-8	0	2	2	15	14	—	—	1	501	6	4	20	1	422

14	15	16	17	18	19	20	21	22	23	24	25	26	Total
—	—	—	—	—	—	—	—	—	—	—	—	—	5
—	4	—	—	—	—	—	—	—	—	—	—	—	7
2	194	—	—	1	—	6	—	—	—	—	—	2	327
—	—	—	—	—	—	—	—	—	—	—	—	—	2
—	7	—	—	1	—	—	—	—	—	1	—	—	38
—	56	—	—	1	—	—	—	—	—	—	—	1	487
—	294	—	—	1	—	1	—	—	—	—	—	—	899
—	1,082	—	3	1	6	7	—	2	6	—	8	2	12,134
—	133	—	3	7	1	3	—	—	5	—	2	11	16,908
—	1	2	—	3	1	—	—	—	—	—	—	—	224
—	—	—	—	1	—	1	—	—	—	1	—	3	44
—	—	—	—	—	—	—	—	—	—	—	—	—	0
—	7	—	7	2	—	—	—	—	—	—	—	—	33
—	—	—	—	—	—	—	—	—	—	—	—	—	6
—	2	—	2	62	1	2	—	8	—	4	7	10	297
3	398	1	3	2	2	10	—	2	4	5	18	—	4,250
—	437	—	1	—	—	1	—	—	1	—	—	6	13,681
—	169	—	1	—	1	—	—	—	—	—	—	—	9,046
—	7	—	—	—	—	—	—	—	—	—	—	—	1,884
—	18	—	1	—	—	—	—	—	—	—	—	—	43
—	—	—	—	1	—	—	—	—	—	—	—	—	5
—	—	—	—	—	—	—	—	—	—	—	—	—	1
—	3	2	1	1	—	—	—	—	—	—	4	24	62
1	1,112	—	4	28	4	129	—	1	9	—	8	15	3,246
—	1	—	1	3	—	12	—	1	—	—	16	3	114
—	191	—	—	—	—	—	—	—	—	—	—	—	10,156
—	—	—	—	—	—	—	—	—	—	—	—	1	1
—	—	—	1	—	—	—	—	—	—	—	1	—	24
1	579	—	4	24	2	39	12	6	1	5	14	—	1,675

(continued)

Table 8.1—*Continued*

X	Y	1	2	3	4	5	6	7	8	9	10	11	12	13
0	-104	—	—	1	—	—	—	—	—	—	—	—	—	—
0	-64	1	—	—	—	—	—	—	—	—	2	—	—	1
0	-56	—	—	—	—	—	—	—	—	—	—	—	—	2
0	-24	—	—	—	1	—	—	—	—	—	1	—	—	—
0	-16	—	—	3	—	—	—	—	971	3	2	—	1	16
0	-8	—	—	5	—	—	—	—	131	3	1	3	—	71
0	0	—	—	—	15	—	—	—	80	4	5	—	—	52
0	8	—	—	—	—	—	—	—	3	—	—	—	—	—
0	16	—	—	—	—	—	—	—	23	1	2	2	—	7
0	24	—	—	—	—	—	—	—	19	2	—	2	—	3
0	32	—	—	—	—	—	—	—	16	—	—	—	—	—
0	40	—	—	—	10	2	—	—	15,516	—	—	—	—	21
0	64	—	—	—	—	—	—	—	119	—	—	—	—	2
0	72	—	—	—	—	—	—	—	—	—	—	—	—	—
8	-16	—	—	—	—	—	—	—	2	—	—	—	—	2
8	-8	—	—	2	—	—	—	—	138	—	—	—	—	35
8	0	—	—	—	—	—	—	2	684	—	—	—	—	5
32	0	—	—	—	2	—	—	—	4	—	—	—	—	1
40	0	—	—	—	—	—	—	—	—	—	—	—	—	—
56	0	—	—	—	—	—	—	—	1	—	—	—	—	1
Total		23	35	90	265	7	21	24	86,271	156	108	341	24	5658

Note: Data from Hamilton 1992 with minor correction at SMAMM (-64, 56) from -5 to 5.
Artifact Group Examples:
1. CARP: Carpentry tools (e.g., hammers, adzes, awls).
2. FISH: Fishing devices (e.g., lead sinkers).
3. HTOOL: Hand tools (e.g., scissors, straight pins).
4. MANW: Manufacture waste (e.g., small lead fragments).
5. MEAS: Measuring devices (e.g., drawing compass, divider).
6. NAVI: Navigational aids (e.g., navigation rule, compass).
7. REST: Restraining devices (e.g., shackles).
8. SMAMM: Small arms ammunition (e.g., lead shot).
9. CANAMM: Cannon ammunition (e.g., roundshot).
10. CANN: Cannon (e.g., cannon and components).
11. FIRE: Firearms (e.g., musket, pistol, and components).
12. SWOR: Sword parts (e.g., rapier, cutlass).
13. COIN: Coins (e.g., *reales*, *livres*).
14. MERCH: Merchandise (e.g., bale seals).

14	15	16	17	18	19	20	21	22	23	24	25	26	Total
—	—	—	—	—	—	—	—	—	—	—	—	—	1
—	—	—	—	—	—	—	—	—	—	—	—	—	4
—	—	—	—	—	—	—	—	—	—	—	—	—	2
—	—	—	—	4	—	—	—	3	—	—	—	—	9
—	630	—	1	—	—	3	—	—	—	—	—	1	1,631
—	61	2	2	16	—	—	—	1	1	1	4	3	305
—	79	—	—	1	2	—	—	—	—	—	1	7	246
—	—	—	—	1	—	—	—	—	—	—	—	—	4
—	1	—	—	3	—	—	—	—	—	—	—	2	41
—	—	—	—	—	—	—	—	—	—	—	1	—	27
—	67	—	—	—	—	—	—	—	—	—	—	—	83
1	10	—	2	—	—	—	—	—	3	—	—	1	15,566
—	4	—	1	—	—	—	—	—	—	—	—	—	126
—	4	—	—	—	—	—	—	—	—	—	—	—	4
—	13	—	—	1	—	—	—	—	—	—	—	—	18
—	55	—	—	—	—	—	—	—	—	—	—	1	231
—	—	—	1	2	—	1	—	—	1	—	2	—	698
—	—	—	—	—	—	—	—	—	—	—	—	—	7
—	—	—	—	—	—	—	—	—	—	—	1	—	1
—	1	—	—	—	—	—	—	—	—	—	—	—	3
12	7,000	9	46	179	23	238	22	29	42	18	89	110	100,840

15. OCCUR: Other Currency (e.g., gold dust).
16. STOR: Storage Container (e.g., barrel and components).
17. FAUN: Faunal remains (e.g., animal bones).
18. GALL: Galley objects (e.g., bottle fragments, coal).
19. TABL: Tableware (e.g., plates, teapot).
20. APPA: Apparel (e.g., buttons, shoes).
21. PERS: Personal items (e.g., rings, seals).
22. RECR: Recreation (e.g., gaming pieces, tobacco pipes).
23. FURN: Furnishings (e.g., drawer knobs, candlestick).
24. OHARD: Other Hardware (e.g., hinge).
25. RIGG: Rigging elements (e.g., deadeyes, chain plate).
26. SHIP: Ship parts (e.g., anchors, bell).

Table 8.2. Standardized Location of Selected Artifacts for Distribution Analysis

Type	N	Count	Mean x	Mean y	Std x	Std y	Total std	Weight (grams)
Pd1	4	4	-38	42	13.7	10.1	23.8	453.6
Pd2	3	3	-56	8	24	13.9	37.9	907.2
Pd3	9	12	-50	34.7	22.4	28.2	50.6	1,360.8
Pd4	15	28	-39.4	10.3	30	17.3	47.3	1,814.4
Real1h	40	495	-40.1	26.5	20.3	17.7	38	1.6
Real1	55	944	-39.8	22.5	23.2	19.3	42.5	3.1
Real2	55	1,260	-45.2	23.4	23.6	17.9	41.5	5.9
Real4	41	501	-44.2	22.6	23.8	19.5	43.3	12.2
Real8	61	1,462	-43.3	20.2	26.1	23.5	49.6	24.5
Shot00	6	703	-25.8	39.5	3.4	3.8	7.2	0.004
Shot01	12	1,220	-24.8	40.5	4.2	4.9	9.1	0.008
Shot02	13	2,195	-24	41.5	5.2	5.6	10.8	0.013
Shot03	14	1,514	-23	42	6.9	8	14.9	0.021
Shot04	47	361	-23	42.2	9.8	12.4	22.2	0.056
Shot05	25	1,582	-16.2	32.6	15.1	23.9	39	0.089
Shot06	33	1,782	-25.9	40.1	12.9	18.4	31.3	0.097
Shot07	37	11,210	-14.7	42.3	14.2	9.8	24	0.15
Shot08	37	11,577	-17.1	42.7	14.6	12.5	27.1	0.3
Shot09	45	41,829	-22.2	42.3	11.6	10.7	22.3	0.596
Shot10	11	158	-26.9	37.8	11.7	12.8	24.5	1.521
Shot11	6	6	-28	32	28.1	19.6	47.7	2.5
Shot12	22	2,524	-27.4	42.3	9	8.3	17.3	2.9
Shot13	41	4,079	-21.7	42.4	12.1	10.5	22.6	4.5
Shot14	11	31	-22.5	28.6	17.5	20.8	38.3	7
Shot15	12	46	-26.3	30.3	14.9	21.2	36.1	12
Shot16	22	203	-28	37.8	11.2	18.8	30	16
Shot17	35	555	-27.7	33	15.6	19.7	35.3	19
Shot18	41	870	-24.7	30.7	14.9	21.3	36.2	28.59
Shot19	9	18	-17.3	19.1	19.1	23.6	42.7	40.918

Note: Lead shot, silver *reales*, and iron round shot with known locations.

lead shot is less well sorted than the coin or round shot. The combined results also suggest that shapes and/or material density influence the sorting of the artifacts as well. The weights of the three classes of artifacts do not appear to interact in the same manner with the tide and current forces that have dispersed them. Discoidal objects such as coins may be more sensitive to these environmental forces than spherical ones. The strength of the tide and current interaction with the artifacts on and within the sand column clearly must be considered. It is probable that the process of artifacts settling down through the sand overburden creates a different dispersal pattern and is more complicated than the process of artifacts sitting free and being dispersed across the bottom by wave and current action (table 8.3).

Table 8.3. Spearman Rank Correlation of Selected Artifacts

Material	Number	Correlation coefficient	Significance level
Lead shot	20	.687	< .01
Silver coins	5	.900	.05
Iron round shot	4	.800	> .05
Combined	29	.666	< .01

Note: Spearman Rank Correlation of total XY standard deviation and mean artifact weight by material type.

Insights into Pirate Social Systems

The relationship of the *Whydah* pirates was egalitarian—or perhaps "libertarian," if one emphasizes political orientation—relative to the class-oriented society of early eighteenth century Europe and its colonies. Status was achieved through demonstrated skill and specialized knowledge in navigation, gunnery, carpentry, medicine, capacity to lead and direct attacks on other vessels, and similar talents. Undoubtedly, force of will and fighting prowess also played a role in the achievement of rank or "Big Man" status for some individuals. In plotting the distribution of silver versus pewter and brass apparel remains (including buttons, cufflinks, and buckles), the mean point of dispersion for the silver items was closer to the stern of the vessel while that of pewter and brass was more centrally located on the wreck site. It is possible the silver apparel items were part of the "treasure" and were stored separately. More likely, the higher-status silver apparel items may be associated with storage in the stern, where the ship's captain, quartermaster, and other "officers" would have resided.

Some of the tools and technical implements used by individuals, often with special skills within the ship's company, have been found at the *Whydah* site. While they are sometimes prosaic in appearance, skill in the manipulation of these tools, as well as weapons, would be important in the achievement of status within the pirate ranks.

Mauls, caulking chisels, crows' feet pry bars, awls, hammers, and vises indicate the level of carpentry and blacksmithery attendant in the operation and maintenance of a vessel, particularly a relatively large pirate ship such as *Whydah*.

Numerous navigational devices (such as a ring dial, charting compasses, and stylus, among other items) are evidence of the importance of navigational instruments in ranging the seas close to dangerous shoals, reefs, and coasts while in search of likely victims or escaping from enemies.

A nested set of seven scale weights to measure gold or perhaps medicine would be used by the ship's quartermaster or doctor. Other individual lead and brass weights were also recovered, as well as a mortar used in grinding herbs and other

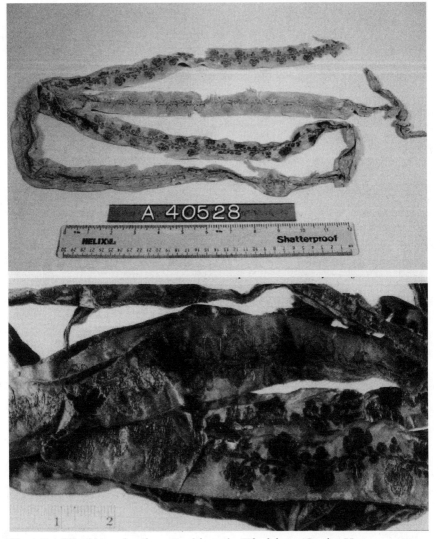

Figure 8.4. Silk ribbon taken from pistol from the *Whydah* site (Gordon Harvey, conservator). Courtesy of Expedition Whydah.

materials for medicine. The importance of producing fair shares of the loot, particularly with material like gold dust, is probably reflected by the presence of these items aboard *Whydah*.

Display of a particular dress or fashion also appears to have played a role in distinctly piratical behavior. Daniel Defoe reported:

> . . . in this, endeavoring to outdo one another, in the beauty and richness of their arms, giving sometimes at auction, 30 or 40 pounds a pair for pistols.

These were slung in time of service, with different colored ribbands [*sic*], over their shoulders, in a way peculier [*sic*] to these fellows in which they took great delight. (1972:211)

This account not only shows the concern with dress but also demonstrates the occasional wealth of pirate seamen. Marcus Rediker (1987) relates that the common "Tar" in 1717 could expect an average wage of £1.35 per month. At that rate, it would take over two years' wages for a common seaman to buy even one "fine" pistol.

The artifacts that best demonstrated the marriage between pistols and ribbons were found within a concretion. Inside was a French-made pistol, still in its hemp cloth holster, with a silk ribbon wrapped around its handle (figure 8.4).

Ship Architecture and Components

The architecture of *Whydah* and the various ship-related components could be understood through a comparison of the historical record with the archaeological record. As described to the royal governor of Massachusetts by Cyprian Southack and in trial testimony and similar sources, *Whydah* was a ship-rigged galley, approximately 300 tons, with an estimated length of 100 ft (30 m) to 110 ft (33.5 m) or more. The term "ship-rigged galley" indicates that there were three masts with square rigging (as opposed to fore and aft rigging, as on schooners or other rigging types). Also, a galley of the period would have two flush (continuous) decks (Botting et al. 1978).

The vessel may be divided into hull, rigging, and other components. The hull includes the outer shell, decks, fixed accessories (such as scupper liners for drainage), quarters, and internal supporting structures that divide the space and give buoyancy for movement over water. The rigging may be defined as the sails, masts, lines (ropes), deadeyes, blocks, and other tackle necessary for propulsion. Ship's components include the items added to a vessel that may or may not be permanently fixed, such as anchors, small boat(s), cannon, galley stove, and other materials or structures used by the crew during voyages.

As noted earlier, the hull of *Whydah* did not survive wrecking and salvage. Therefore, only a limited amount of information may be gleaned from the set of artifacts identified by the end of 1992. Important questions regarding the architecture of *Whydah* will remain unanswered until some undiscovered sections of hull are found (an extremely unlikely event) or until all artifacts have been removed from concretions and conserved and more closely scrutinized for evidence regarding the ship's structure.

Among the questions posed in the Data Recovery Plan (Hamilton et al. 1988) were whether *Whydah* possessed a ship's wheel (rather than a whipstaff for directional control) and whether a spritsail, indicating an archaic design, was used or whether use of the term "galley" meant that it could have been propelled by sweeps (long oars). These questions remain unresolved.

In confirmation of the historical record, it was found that the length of the distribution of the large concretions and artifacts was roughly 100 ft (30 m) along a northwest to southeast orientation, with the stern pointing to shore. The size of the main body of the wreck site follows Southack's description of the size of *Whydah*. The orientation of the wreck is explained by the direction of the wind and wave action as the ship was forced onto a near-shore sandbar by the gale.

Alterations to the architecture of captured vessels by pirates to improve their fighting qualities have been historically reported. The addition of cannon to *Whydah* is one aspect of pirate renovation. Eighteen cannon were on board *Whydah* when it served as a merchant vessel (Brown 1717). The depositions given by pirate captives aboard *Whydah* noted that between twenty-eight and thirty cannon were on board at the time of the wreck (Beer 1717; Merry and Roberts 1717).

Excavations recovered twenty-seven cannon as of 1992. Cyprian Southack recovered two cannon, among other wreckage later sold in Boston. At least one cannon remained on site, concreted to the base of the ships stove.

Bore diameter and trunion data from twelve of the cannon were reported in Hamilton et al. (1990). These cannon were reassessed with the remaining fifteen cannon sufficiently deconcreted to permit at least preliminary measurement of their bores.

The distribution of the cannon across the site fit a pattern that would match a vessel trimmed with the smaller three-pounder cannon situated in the far stern (3 cannon) and bow (2 cannon), the heavier six-pounder cannon tending to be placed closer amidship (4 cannon), and the more common four-pounder cannon placed throughout the length of the vessel (17 cannon). The locations of the cannon on the site are in agreement with historical documentation for arming ships.

The archaeological record has so far revealed some rigging elements, such as hawser line and other rope, deadeyes, chain plate, a urinal, scupper liners, lead patches, blocks, anchors, and other items. While some of the recovered ship components may be considered early and perhaps unique specimens, most have not been systematically examined with the goal of reconstructing *Whydah*.

Shipping System and Trading System

To place *Whydah* in its maritime context it is helpful to examine the shipping and trading system of the period. This direction of research is similar to that indicated by Immanuel Wallerstein (1974, 1980) in his development of a model of world economic systems and adopted by the Massachusetts Historical Commission as a method of organization and analysis of archaeological data. In his work on the systemic relatedness of the world economy, Wallerstein wrote that the Caribbean slipped from what he defined as a semiperipheral status relative to the European core of economic activity to a peripheral (or frontier) status. During this period, New England was promoted from peripheral to semiperipheral status.

In relation to the differing character of regions within the world economic system, Wallerstein (1974:350) noted:

> The division of a world-economy involves a hierarchy of occupational tasks, in which tasks requiring higher levels of skill and greater capitalization essentially rewards accumulated capital, including human capital, at a higher rate than "raw" labor power, the geographical maldistribution of these occupational skills involves a strong trend toward self-maintenance.

The most important link in the accumulation of capital (or resources) by areas within the European core and its semiperipheral and peripheral regions prior to the industrial revolution was through maritime trade. It was the exchange of raw products for manufactured products that basically motivated the shipping and trading systems. Even in the case of the projection of raw military power by Europeans with the goal of forced removal of intrinsically valuable materials (silver, gold, slaves, and so forth), the result was still the addition of material remains to the maritime archaeological record. The type of interaction may be discerned through the detailed examination of these archaeological materials.

In the particular case of *Whydah*, the presence of significant amounts of "treasure" associated with large amounts of *mixed* small arms and heavy ordnance, coupled with the scarcity of evidence of common trade items, leads to the conclusion of forced maritime exchange or piracy. This type of exchange is epiphenomenal to the necessary presence of long-range merchant trade through relatively uncontrolled waters, however, upon which maritime piracy relies for its existence.

Differences in the distribution of resources can be revealed by examining the material or historical remains of past shipping and trading activity. The Port Zone Model can help characterize the shipping and trading systems of the region and promote greater understanding of the setting of eighteenth-century European piracy.

The Shipping System

A Port Zone Model for shipping and trading was developed for the Port Zone of Boston, which includes Cape Cod. The model is most easily understood in graphic form. Figure 8.5, the Interzonal Model, illustrates the relationship of ship traffic in the shipping system between two contiguous Port Zones and the resulting shipwrecks. Note that the 50 percent proportion between Port Zones would only occur when external factors (such as weather, crew or ship fatigue) and similar forces are equal between the Zones. Current analysis indicates that ships entering a Port Zone may have a greater likelihood of wrecking due to these

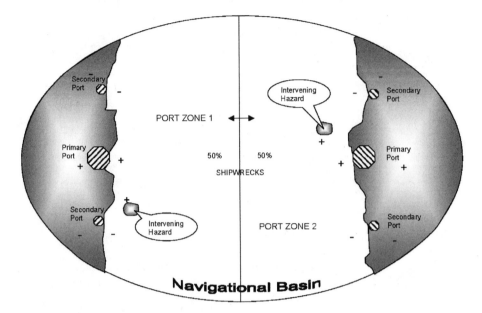

Figure 8.5. Port Zone Model: Interzonal Model showing theoretical distribution of population, shipping traffic, and shipwrecks. + = increase; – = decrease. Courtesy of Expedition Whydah.

factors. For instance, a ship's captain can decide not to leave port in foul weather that might endanger his ship; however, a vessel entering a Port Zone might arrive with no choice at that time and become wrecked. The preceding factors notwithstanding, a Port Zone Model should initially be applied with the expectation of equal proportions of shipwrecks between interacting Port Zones; subsequent alterations of the model may be based on historical and/or archaeological data accounting for intervening navigational hazards, distance, propensity of an area for foul weather, dangerous currents, warfare, pirates, and similar factors that would condition the presence or absence of shipwrecks.

Figure 8.6 shows the relationship of the types of cargos in the trading system with the theoretical relationship of the economic classes of occupations within the Port Zone. The economic classes include (1) primary—agriculture, mining, fishing, and other extractive industries, (2) secondary—manufacturing, trade, transportation, and service industries, and (3) tertiary—government, including military, and professional occupations. The preceding classifications may be altered, of course, to fit a particular analysis.

The elements of the model to be considered first are the variables of the shipping traffic of Boston, the population of Boston and outer Cape Cod, and the shipwrecks that occur in these two intrazonal areas. The purpose of the examina-

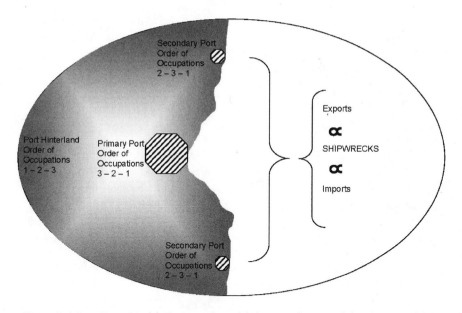

Figure 8.6. Port Zone Model: Intrazonal Model showing theoretical distribution of shipwrecks, shipping, trading, and occupations within a Port Zone ($\propto$ = proportional). 1 = primary sector occupations; 2 = secondary sector occupations; 3 = tertiary sector occupations. Courtesy of Expedition Whydah.

tion is to determine the place of Cape Cod as an area of intervening hazard within the Port Zone. Once it is established as an intervening hazard, the meaning of shipwrecks along the outer cape can be more securely tied to events and processes off-cape—in this case, Boston.

The results of the analysis indicate that outer Cape Cod is acting as an area of intervening hazard for the shipping traffic of Boston, the primary port of the zone. Therefore, shipwrecks occurring off Cape Cod should be examined and compared with an eye toward explaining events and processes not necessarily for Cape Cod but for the primary port.

The shipping system can be described as generally following population growth of the primary port. Boston's grew through the colonial period by exporting agricultural goods, fish, and other primary-sector material and importing manufactured and some agricultural materials, such as sugar. The early eighteenth century is marked by the addition of manufactured goods (for example, shoes) to the export trade and increasing immigrant traffic. Later trade is characterized by continued exports of manufactured goods and bulk products such as lumber, with imports of raw materials, oil, coal, and increased immigrant traffic. Finally, during more recent times, maritime trade dwindled to imports of oil matched by exports of scrap metal. For the current analysis we will assume that the occupations of the populace of the primary port and its hinterland are associated with the type of trade conducted as given in the Port Zone Model: Intrazonal.

A general review of some of the shipping and trading systems for the port of Boston was presented by Christopher Hamilton and Michel Cembrola (1991). Taking into account all historic periods, a review of their data indicates that the most likely type of vessel to be found off of Boston was a schooner-rigged vessel carrying either agricultural or mining cargos.

As the colonial period (1620–1775) is the era of interest with regard to the *Whydah* site, a similar examination of the data was conducted (Hamilton et al. 1992:499–500). Of those vessels with rigs recorded, the sloop (21) was the most common type of vessel wrecked, with schooners (17), ships (14), and brigs (11) followed by other types of rigs. The frequencies of the reported functional types of vessels wrecked off Massachusetts were merchant vessels (24), military (8), and whalers (4), followed by other types. The average size vessel for the early eighteenth century in the region was about fifty tons (Shepherd and Walton 1966).

From this study it would appear that *Whydah* was an unusual type for the shipping system as defined. *Whydah*'s size is revealed in history and in the distribution of the artifacts on the site to be 100 ft (30 m) long or more and about 300 tons. It was heavily armed with thirty cannon or perhaps more; even military vessels of similar size for the period carried only about twenty to twenty-two cannon (Lavery 1987). The cargo aboard *Whydah* appears to have been composed mostly of silver *real* coins, clipped African (Akan) gold jewelry (Ehrlich 1992), and relatively large numbers of unmatched navigational implements. This also helps to categorize the site as a statistical "outlier," given the more common cargos of manufactured imports and primary-sector exports noted for the region during the period. The possibility of the wreck site being identified as that of a privateer is also less likely because of its unusual cargo.

The numbers of merchant and military vessels for the period reveal the importance of the shipping system in moving goods between producers and consumers and the need to protect the vessels and their goods. The large number of merchant vessels wrecked off Massachusetts is assumed to reflect their approximate proportion within the shipping system. The need to protect the merchant vessels and other coastal installations is evidenced by the relatively high number of military vessels. The wreck site of *Whydah* provides us with a look at a predator of the many merchant vessels in the region and an antagonist of their military protectors.

The Trading System

Current understanding of the trading system indicates that reliance on trading primary-sector goods (such as agricultural, forest, and mining products) for secondary-sector manufactured products and luxury items may be considered one indicator of an early stage of economic development in a region. Even the trade in African gold jewelry can be viewed as the exchange of mining products for manufactured or luxury trade, in that the Europeans did not acquire this gold for its aesthetic value. Instead, the gold jewelry was clipped by the African traders and destined to be melted down by the Europeans for bullion. The manufactured goods or cowry shells that would have been traded in return fit the model. Cowry shells served as a luxury item among the African people who supplied the slaves represented by the shackles recovered at the site, who may be classified as a primary-sector "product," along with the clipped gold jewelry.

From a similar perspective, the silver *real* "cob" coins from *Whydah* represent a minimal effort on the part of colonial Spanish authorities to stamp out crude but usable coinage at a rapid rate. Cob coinage from the New World could then be considered primary-sector or perhaps secondary-sector items rather than representing the tertiary or government sector within the economic system.

As we have seen, *Whydah* was not a merchant vessel but a predator of merchant vessels. Thus an examination of the cargo and stores of *Whydah* revealed materials "sampled" from a number of merchant vessels working within the trading system. A large variety of sources for the cargo and stores might be indicative of a pirate vessel. Lack of comparative data makes this possibility difficult to prove, however.

The information inherent in large numbers of coins sampled during the early eighteenth century in the Caribbean and in nearby locations permits several comparisons. The individual weights of the *reales* and other coins by mint and denomination were determined. Examination of mean weights of the *real* "cob" coins showed they were less than expected for each denomination. The disparity in expected and observed weights for the silver coins has been attributed to corrosion of the silver while submerged on the site for over 270 years. The gold *escudos* from the site exhibited no such loss in weight, however, because gold does not corrode.

The mints for the *reales* were Potosí, Nuevo Rieno, Lima, and Mexico City. Other coins included *escudos* from Mexico City and Lima; shillings, crowns, and half-crowns from England; *centimes*, "silver Louis," *sous*, and one and half *écus* from France (Resmes, St. Menhold, Bordeaux, Paris, Limoges, and La Rochelle mints) and a Scottish bawbee.

Along with silver *real* cobs, gold *escudos*, and other coinage, more prosaic items of trade were also held in common by the pirates, the European homeland, and colonial settlements. These items include pewterware from Glasgow, Scotland and Penzance, England. Navigational instruments, some manufactured in Paris, France, were also among items recovered.

Accompanying these classes of artifacts are others with maker's marks or other features that make their origin identifiable, such as the clay smoking pipes from Bristol, England, and some of the small arms, including a carbine from London and muskets from Dieppe and Tulle, France. The handle of a French-

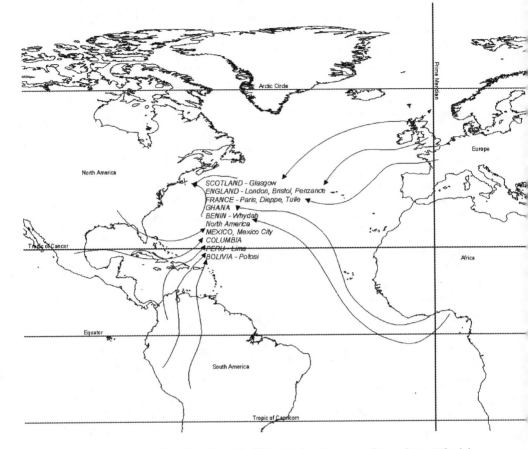

Figure 8.7. Sources of artifacts from the *Whydah* site. Courtesy of Expedition Whydah.

made pistol was carved from North American black walnut. The clipped gold jewelry from Africa was probably from the Gold Coast of Ghana, while the enslaved Africans were probably trans-shipped from the hinterlands of the slave market town of Whydah in modern Benin. The sources of these items illustrate some of the known complexity of the European trading system of the time (figure 8.7).

Reflections on Piracy and the Pirate Ship *Whydah*

The opportunities for advancement of knowledge in the fields of marine archaeology, history, and conservation are synthesized in the *Whydah* project. As the only securely verified and documented pirate ship ever discovered, *Whydah* provides a wealth of opportunity to explore the contrast between the myth and reality of this segment of the eighteenth-century population. Additionally, information about slave trading, weaponry, and shipbuilding has been obtained from the artifacts discovered. In short, the *Whydah* site is a window into a different time and poorly understood dimension of history and culture.

The interpretation of the archaeological data indicates that the site, even though located in a high-energy environment and suffering a very traumatic deposition process, contains sufficient information to model the general location of materials on the vessel as well as the stages of wrecking. The site has also yielded information that permits predictions about where other portions of the vessel or its contents might be.

The artifacts and historical data resulting from the excavation of *Whydah* reveal a picture of the life of pirates during the Golden Age of Piracy. Their life has been shown to be violent in the pursuit of a perceived need for personal freedom, fair treatment, and some degree of wealth beyond the general poverty of the common sailor.

The larger picture of piracy as represented by *Whydah* represents either anomaly or, more likely, an inevitable part of the developing shipping and trading system in the age of burgeoning European colonialism. The competition between nations in colonizing new lands vulnerable to European technology and advanced cultural integration at a national level is observable at least to some degree through the examination of the far-flung shipping and trading system of their colonies. *Whydah*'s pirate seamen were at first a part of and later predators of that system.

The development of capitalism and the political changes and realignments associated with that development in the Old and New Worlds can be seen in the changes in the shipping and trading system. These changes have been investigated by construction of a Port Zone Model for Massachusetts, using historical data. The results of the analysis indicate that the appearance of a pirate vessel in the shipwreck record of this developing shipping and trading system should not be considered unexpected and that such vessels generally should be recognizable by their material remains.

Added to the systemic association of *Whydah* is the potential of reinterpreting the particular historical setting in which it existed. The internal political struggle in the United Kingdom between mercantile and aristocratic interests as portrayed in conflict between Parliament and Stuart loyalists may well prove to be an important adjunct in understanding piracy during the Golden Age.

An examination of pewter plates from *Whydah* often yielded cut marks and graffiti of one sort or another (figure 8.8). One intriguing mark resembled a Romanesque "A": it may simply have been an initial, but it may be not a letter but rather a symbol. Making an admitted deductive leap, we could conjecture that the symbol may be the earliest depiction of the Freemason "Compass and Square." The schism between the Scottish Rite and English Grand Lodge versions

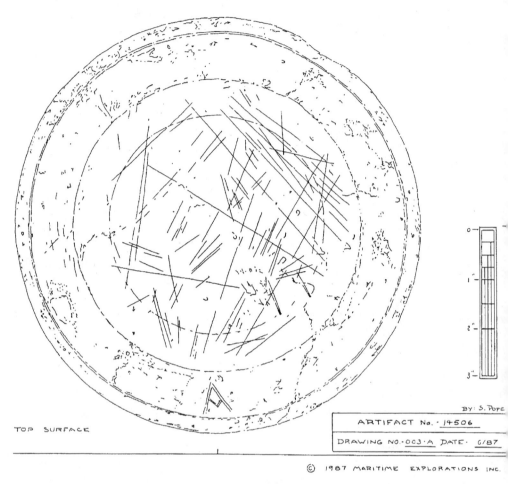

TOP SURFACE

BY: S. POPE

ARTIFACT No. · 14506

DRAWING NO.·003·A DATE· 6/87

© 1987 MARITIME EXPLORATIONS INC.

Figure 8.8. Pewter plate from the *Whydah* site. Drawing by Steven Pope. Courtesy of Expedition Whydah.

of Freemasonry occurred in this period, along with several Jacobite rebellions to restore the Stuart line to the British throne. Combined with the purported connection of the Stuarts to Freemasonry, the symbol might reflect a more serious connection between the Golden Age of Piracy and the struggle for the crown (Hamilton et al. 1992, Kinkor 1992b).

Despite substantial success in these broad-based investigations, further work is necessary. One problem for archaeology rests in the lack of complete or nearly complete excavations with associated detailed reporting, thus leaving wide gaps to be filled by few, often sparsely described shipwreck sites. These problems require a large degree of interpolation and extrapolation of the available data to achieve meaningful interpretations. These challenges are not uncommon in archaeology, however, and are unavoidable in our attempts to advance our understanding of human behavior. Continued research and analysis with cultural models is needed, using the archaeological sites and artifacts along with the information found in recorded history. The excavation, conservation, and interpretation of the *Whydah* site have been an effort to reconcile the two sources of information and make our understanding of the whole story of the ship and its crew greater than the sum of the material parts.

9

The Pirate Ship *Queen Anne's Revenge*

Mark U. Wilde-Ramsing

On a fateful day in November 1996 as researchers with Intersal, Inc., were winding down their search for shipwrecks in Beaufort Inlet, North Carolina, they discovered a room-sized mound of cannon, anchors, and ballast stones (figure 9.1). After a brief site visit and an inspection of the small collection of recovered artifacts, state underwater archaeologists agreed that the site was quite possibly the remains of *Queen Anne's Revenge*, (formally *La Concorde*), lost in 1718 by the infamous pirate Edward Teach (Thatch, Drummond, or other variation), popularly referred to as Blackbeard. The following months were filled with silence, during which an agreement was made between the private research company Intersal and the North Carolina Department of Cultural Resources. Well aware of the shipwreck's historical significance, Intersal agreed to relinquish rights to artifacts from the *Queen Anne's Revenge* site in order to keep this important collection intact for the people of North Carolina. Four months after the discovery, an official announcement came from Governor James B. Hunt Jr., evoking great fanfare and interest throughout the world. It was the biggest discovery in North Carolina's "Graveyard of the Atlantic" since the Civil War ironclad USS *Monitor* nearly three decades earlier.

Background

From the earliest colonial exploration, shipwrecks have been an important part of North Carolina's history; and in response the state has maintained one of the longest-standing underwater archaeology programs in the nation. Beginning in the early 1960s, state managers have been involved with a wide range of submerged cultural resources from prehistoric dugout canoes to sailing ships and steamers to twentieth-century motorboats. Throughout the years, state underwater archaeologists were often reminded that there was a possibility of finding physical evidence from the time when pirates frequented state waters. Local North Carolinians would inevitably claim that most any derelict lying in coastal waters contained cannon or forgotten treasure left behind by Blackbeard and his

Figure 9.1. Anchor A-1 is a prominent feature on the shipwreck site.

comrades. These sightings always turned out to be much more recent watercraft abandoned after being rendered useless.

Even the remotest chance of discovering pirate treasure stirs imagination and keeps local tradition alive. It is purported, for instance, that Blackbeard's sister lived in Grimesland, North Carolina (originally Boyd's Ferry), and hosted her infamous brother when he needed a break from seafaring (King 1911:23). Local residents are certain that Blackbeard buried treasure in his sister's backyard, as he reportedly did at every landfall he made in the state. Others claim that they are descended from Blackbeard because their family tree includes illegitimate children from the early eighteenth century. In one such case, the story has the pirate captain traveling well into the hinterland of southeastern North Carolina by way of the Trent River, where he had his way with the womenfolk—another recurring Blackbeard theme. Sometime later, the entire family migrated farther inland to a place they named Teachey in honor of the infamous pirate captain and progenitor (Smith 1997). Blackbeard's influence reached to the northern part of the state as well. In Rockyhock near the Chowan River, the Lynch homestead was reportedly "linked in tradition with 'Blackbeard' Teach, famed buccaneer" (*Wilmington News* 1929). Bath, an early-eighteenth-century capital of North Carolina, can rightfully claim an association with the pirate captain based on credible historical documentation; but it also has its share of suspect pirate lore (figure 9.2). A skeptical state historian could only shake his head when presented with genealogical evidence linking the pirate with the Beard family of Bath. The reasoning went that Captain James Beard, who resided in the colonial town, had a son who may have been "Black" Beard (Bailey et al. 2002).

A number of avowed landmarks connect North Carolina to the famed pirate and his exploits. Among them is his alleged property on Back Creek near the town of Bath, where countless holes have been dug throughout the years. There is also an old lookout on the lower Neuse River in Oriental named Teach's Oak, and Blackbeard was said to have killed a woman at Beaufort's Hammock House. Historical documentation to confirm these and other claims is scarce.

No evidence exists that the pirate captain visited the Carolina colony prior to June 1718, when he unceremoniously grounded his forty-gun ship *Queen Anne's Revenge* and the sloop *Adventure* on the shoals of Beaufort Inlet (formerly [Old] Topsail Inlet). According to testimony from several of his crew, Blackbeard was intent on ridding himself of the deep-draft vessel and significantly reducing the number of crewmembers, a move that today would be termed "corporate downsizing" (Herriot 1719). After wrecking, Blackbeard made his way to the colonial capital at Bath and engaged government officials in a convenient relationship based on bribery and tolerance. North Carolina's favorite pirate is known to have spent the days prior to his death moving about the rivers and sounds of the colony, using Ocracoke as his base of operation. This remote outer island provided a protected harbor and an advantageous location to monitor oceangoing commerce as it funneled through busy Ocracoke Inlet. Nor were the

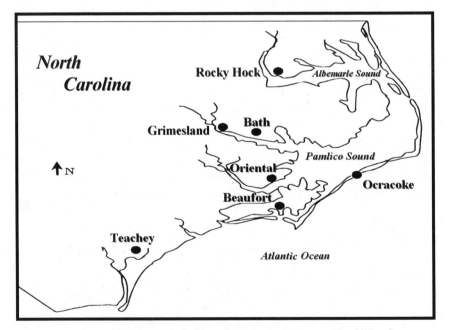

Figure 9.2. Reported locations of Blackbeard's activities in eastern North Carolina.

Figure 9.3. Springer's Point on Ocracoke Island may have been the site of Blackbeard's base of operation.

shipping lanes of the Atlantic seaboard far off. While some may have welcomed Blackbeard's presence, others apparently did not. William Bell, a planter living on the banks of the Pamlico River near Bath, accused Blackbeard of petty thievery and harassment (Cain 1984:85).

Historic documents, however, show that in late summer and fall of 1718 Blackbeard was not always in North Carolina. On August 11, 1718, Pennsylvania Governor William Keith issued a warrant for his arrest in Philadelphia (Pennsylvania 1840:45). Toward the end of August, the pirate captain was spotted cruising the waters of Bermuda (Lee 1977:79–80) A few months later, in October 1718, Governor Keith was so perturbed that he sent out an expedition to the Delaware capes to pursue him (Pennsylvania 1840:49).

Although Blackbeard received the king's pardon from North Carolina's Governor Charles Eden, some deemed his reformation nothing but a ploy. In response Virginia's Governor Alexander Spotswood sent a contingent of sailors under the command of Lt. Robert Maynard into North Carolina territorial waters to bring the pirate in dead or alive. In a bloody battle at Ocracoke Island (figure 9.3) on the morning of November 22, 1718,

> Blackbeard received a shot into his body from the pistol that Lieutenant Maynard discharged, yet he stood his ground and fought with great fury, 'till he received five-and-twenty wounds, five of them by shot. At length, as he was cocking another pistol, having fired several before, he fell down dead . . . Here was the end of the courageous brute who might have passed in the world for hero had he been employed in a good cause . . . (Johnson [Defoe] 1998:57)

Blackbeard's violent end fueled the embellishment of stories about him that today are an integral part of North Carolina lore. It is quite surprising, though, that the loss of *Queen Anne's Revenge* and *Adventure* off its shores is not a prominent part of this oral tradition, even though these shipwrecks are likely to represent the only physical remains of Blackbeard's activities that will ever be located and studied.

When *Queen Anne's Revenge* was lost, only a handful of families who depended heavily on the ocean for their livelihood inhabited Beaufort. In addition to fishing, as opportunities arose, they would have engaged in "wrecking"—salvaging cargo and equipment from vessels stranded along the coast. One can only wonder why the loss of Blackbeard's two ships was not imbedded in local lore and went virtually unnoticed until 1982, when researcher David D. Moore brought to light primary documents confirming their occurrence and location. In addition to Herriot's deposition given during the pirate trial in Charleston (Herriot 1719), Captain Ellis Brand of the HMS *Lyme* (in a letter to the Lords of Admiralty, dated 12 July, 1718) reported:

> On the 10th of June or thereabouts a large pyrate Ship of forty Guns with three sloops in her company came upon the coast of North Carolina ware they endeavour'd To goe to a harbour, called Topsail Inlett [Beaufort Inlet], the Ship Stuck upon the barr att the entrance of the harbour and is lost; as is one of the sloops. (Moore 1997b:36)

It was with this knowledge that Intersal, Inc., under the direction of president Philip Masters, made its discovery in the fall of 1996. Eight years before, the research firm had received a permit from the North Carolina Underwater Archaeology Branch (UAB) to search for the remains of *Queen Anne's Revenge* and *Adventure* in Beaufort Inlet. Intersal officials previously had been issued a permit to search the same area for the Spanish ship *El Salvador*, which was lost in 1750. For nearly ten years, the company conducted intermittent surveys in Beaufort Inlet with little result. In 1996 it hired Mike Daniel to direct field operations. Using historical accounts, Daniel selected a survey area that he felt encompassed the inlet's early eighteenth century entrance channel and outer bar (figure 9.4). Using a magnetometer and diver inspections, several sites were located, one of which represented a classic shipwreck, exhibiting a ballast pile with nine cannon and two large anchors. The Intersal team recovered several artifacts, including a brass blunderbuss barrel, cannonballs, and a bronze bell with the date 1705. While these items could not positively identify the shipwreck as one of Blackbeard's lost vessels, there was nothing in the extant historical records to dispute this claim.

At the time of discovery, the research files at UAB contained over 5,000 historically reported shipwrecks lost in North Carolina waters. In the Beaufort area there were nearly 200 shipwreck losses, 8 of which could be considered

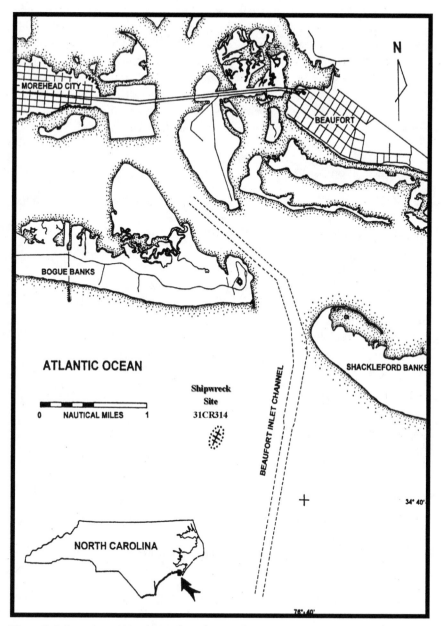

Figure 9.4. Location of North Carolina shipwreck 31CR314.

primary candidates for the Intersal discovery. All occurred during the eighteenth century in the immediate vicinity of present-day Beaufort Inlet (table 9.1). Among them was *Queen Anne's Revenge*, reported to be carrying as many as forty cannon when it ran aground and thus considerably larger and more heavily armed than other shipwreck losses in the area. The *Adventure*, an 80-ton sloop, and El *Salvador*, a 110-ton Spanish packet, each carried eight to ten cannon. Historical research indicates that the remaining shipwrecks from this period were unarmed coastal merchantmen (Masters 2001).

Initial Investigation

With this background, state underwater archaeologists began their investigations. In the early stages, the assessment process employed fundamental investigative techniques to retrieve the maximum amount of information with a minimal amount of disturbance to the site. Supported by temporary funding from the North Carolina General Assembly and a mixed crew of private, academic, and state personnel, a four-week expedition commenced in the fall of 1997 to analyze the shipwreck, designated North Carolina archaeological site 31CR314. The basic initial investigative objectives during the first field expedition were threefold: (1) to provide an opportunity for a wide variety of specialists to inspect the shipwreck, (2) to gain insight into the site's layout, makeup, and surrounding environmental conditions, and (3) to investigate key elements of the shipwreck to determine the likelihood that this was *Queen Anne's Revenge*. Site information was gathered from exposed portions of the wreckage using nonintrusive archaeological techniques, including photography, scale drawings, and artistic perspectives (figure 9.5). Manual probing and limited test excavations helped explore buried remains. Research divers collected wood and sediment samples as well as diagnostic artifacts.

The first objective of the 1997 expedition continued to be an underlying theme: to invite as many archaeologists, scientists, and individuals as feasible to examine the site to attain a full range of observations and opinions concerning the shipwreck. This multidisciplinary entourage included dozens of underwater and terrestrial archaeologists, coastal geologists, marine biologists, maritime historians, water-quality technicians, forensic specialists, and others (figure 9.6). Insight gained from opening the site, artifacts, and data to a wide inspection has enriched the archaeological findings at this intriguing shipwreck.

A second important objective of the initial fieldwork was to gain an understanding of the shipwreck and its surrounding environment. October turned out to be an excellent time of year to work at the site, because only one out of the twenty planned field days was lost to inclement weather. During this period winds were generally light and from the north; even as they increased to near gale force, the mainland offered a measure of protection.

Table 9.1. Eighteenth-Century Shipwrecks in Beaufort Inlet

Shipwreck	Guns	Tons	Type	Lost	Where
QAR	36–40	200–300	ship	06/—/1718	Topsail Inlet
Adventure	8–10	80	sloop	06/—/1718	Topsail Inlet
El Salvador	8	110	snow	08/30/1750	Topsail Inlet area
Susannah	0	30	schooner	04/02/1753	Old Topsail Inlet
Betsey	0	90	schooner	01/01/1771	Old Topsail Inlet
Unnamed	—	—	brig	05/—/1778	Old Topsail Inlet
Polly	0	< 64	sloop	07/16/1793	Ashore near Beaufort
Hero	0	94	schooner	02/09/1790	Beaufort Bar

The shipwreck lies at a depth of 23 feet below mean sea level, 1.3 miles off Fort Macon and 1,500 yards west of the present shipping channel of Beaufort Inlet. This barrier island tidal inlet provides access to historic Beaufort and the present-day shipping facility at Morehead City. The inlet is bordered by Bogue Banks to the west and Shackleford Banks on the east. The relatively stable inlet has remained open and navigable since 1672 and probably prior to 1585 (Fisher 1962:88).

Marine conditions during the fall 1997 expedition were conducive to underwater archaeological activities. Inlet currents were never strong enough to hamper investigators; and water clarity on the bottom was seldom less than two feet (only during short periods at tidal changes). Clarity was better a few hours before

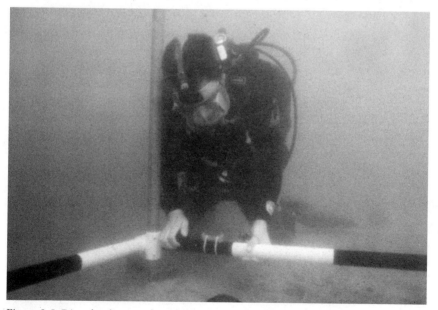

Figure 9.5. Diver leveling mapping frame.

Figure 9.6. Research vessels anchored at the site: R/V *Capricorn*, University of North Carolina–Chapel Hill (*foreground*); and (*left to right*) R/V *Pelican III*, Intersal; R/V *Snap Dragon*, North Carolina Underwater Archaeology Branch; and R/V *Seahawk*, University of North Carolina–Wilmington.

or after high tide, especially when easterly or southerly winds blew in the offshore waters. The downside of these winds, however, as opposed to winds out of the north, was an increased sea state due to fetch from the open ocean. This caused greater wave height and swell and deterioration in working conditions. At times during the expedition, divers were able to see in excess of twenty feet, a rare occurrence in North Carolina state waters. These clear conditions helped investigators quickly orient themselves and permitted detailed photographic documentation of the shipwreck (figure 9.7).

Wreckage exposed above the seabed measured 25 feet by 15 feet, and consisted of eleven cannon, two anchors, a grappling hook, numerous iron cask hoops, several rigging elements, a cluster of cannonballs, and a large amount of ballast stone and concretions. Elevations taken from a datum point tied to the site provided a series of profiles, showing the exposed portion rising on average 2 feet above the surrounding seabed. The highest point was one of the anchor flukes, which protruded 4.6 feet from the bottom.

A controlled excavation of a 6×3-foot unit prior to the recovery of cannon C-2 revealed the sedimentary nature of the sea bottom and the depth of buried remains (figure 9.8). Three detectable zones were identified. The upper horizon

Figure 9.7. Diver taking vertical measurements on the exposed remains.

consisted of 9 to 15 inches of poorly sorted, fine-medium sand. Below this zone was a 12-inch layer of very poorly sorted sand and coarse shell. This level contained the vast majority of small artifacts, most of which dated to the eighteenth century but which also included intrusions of nineteenth- and twentieth-century materials. The bottoms of the large objects as well as artifacts composed of heavy metal, such as lead shot and gold grains, were concentrated in the lower portions of the second strata and lay on top of a third zone, which consisted of well-sorted, stiff silty sand. This lowest zone was extremely hard packed and devoid of cultural materials.

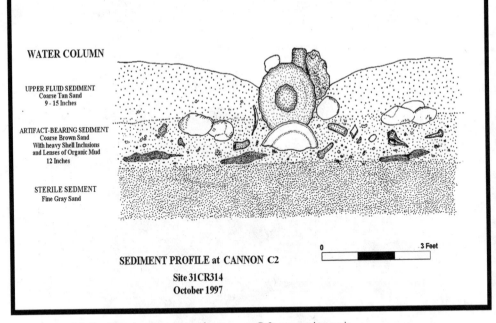

WATER COLUMN

UPPER FLUID SEDIMENT
Coarse Tan Sand
9 - 15 Inches

ARTIFACT-BEARING SEDIMENT
Coarse Brown Sand
With heavy Shell Inclusions
and Lenses of Organic Mud
12 Inches

STERILE SEDIMENT
Fine Gray Sand

0   3 Feet

SEDIMENT PROFILE at CANNON C2

Site 31CR314
October 1997

Figure 9.8. Profile of sediments at the cannon C-2 excavation unit.

In addition to cannon C-2, 284 individual objects were recovered from the test unit during excavation, including small amounts of ceramics, glass, wood and faunal remains, 2 pewter dishes (figure 9.9), numerous lead shot, 86 ballast stones, and 76 concretions. Concretions are a result of corrosion that forms around metals, particularly iron; in the process, sand, shells, and small artifacts become incorporated to create a hard, unrecognizable conglomerate. Based on the number of items recovered from this relatively small excavation, archaeologists began to realize that the shipwreck contained hundreds of thousands of individual artifacts. Furthermore, they expected many of these artifacts to be extremely delicate and to require a lengthy and costly conservation process.

Preliminary findings indicated that cultural materials covered an area approximately 150 feet by 90 feet. Limited test excavations identified additional cannon buried around the site, bringing the total after the first season to fifteen. While investigators failed to locate hull remains, the uncovering of the well-preserved wood stock on anchor A-3 (figure 9.10), located 50 feet north of the main mound, indicated that organic materials survived in the lower portions of the site.

The third objective of the October assessment and most pressing historical question was "Is this the *Queen Anne's Revenge*?" Preliminary findings from the first year provided some clues. Fifteen cannon clearly exceeded what was re-

Figure 9.9. State archaeologist John Clauser examines recovered pewter dish.

Figure 9.10. A large anchor (A-3) is located 50 feet north of the main site.

ported on any shipwreck candidate known to have been lost in Beaufort Inlet during the eighteenth century other than the pirate flagship. Most of the cannon at the shipwreck appeared to be six-pounders, with the exception of two that were slightly smaller. The numerous cannonballs recovered from the site were even more widely varied in size, apparently representing a vessel carrying an assortment of armament. One intriguing artifact was a concreted conglomerate of small lead shot, nails, and glass shards surrounded by fabric. This was suspected to be the remains of cannon bag shot, which would have been employed during close-range combat with the intent to kill and disarm enemy personnel.

The three large anchors located on the shipwreck were all of the size rated for a vessel of 250 to 350 tons and would have been too large for use on the much smaller *Adventure*, *El Salvador*, or other vessels reportedly sunk in the inlet (Curryer 1999:53). Diagnostic artifacts, including bottle fragments, ceramic shards, and pewter dishes, collectively dated to the late seventeenth and early eighteenth centuries. These and other remains also compared favorably with the assemblage recovered from the shipwreck *Whydah*, a pirate vessel remarkably similar to *Queen Anne's Revenge* lost off New England in 1717 (Hamilton et al. 1992). After the first season, archaeologists had found no "smoking blunderbuss" that would conclusively identify 31CR314 as the wreck of Blackbeard's flagship. Nor, however, had they found anything to suggest that it was not *Queen Anne's Revenge*, a well-armed, early eighteenth century merchant ship being operated by pirates at the time of its loss.

Extending Our Knowledge

The archaeological fieldwork conducted from September 14 to October 16, 1998, was a continuation of efforts begun in 1997 to assess the shipwreck lying in Beaufort Inlet. During the five-week project researchers were able to work nineteen days on site. In that time thirty-six divers conducted 501 dives for a total of 507 hours and 25 minutes on the bottom (numbers comparable to those registered the year before). Investigators again found that working conditions at the site during the fall were conducive to controlled archaeological research, except during periods of southerly winds. This was especially true during hurricanes—even those well out to sea.

Hurricane Bonnie passed over the site prior to the 1998 expedition and partially uncovered a section of intact hull structure lying on the north side of the exposed mound. During fieldwork archaeologists removed the remaining sand overburden from these wooden timbers, using an induction dredge to facilitate documentation. The 27×8-foot section consisted of frame timbers, exterior hull planking, and outer hull sheathing. The vessel's frame and planking were made of white oak (*Quercus* sp.), with some indications that they had Old World origins (Newsom 1999). A stronger connection to European shipbuilding comes from the sacrificial sheathing planks, positively identified as European red pine (*Pinus sylvestris*) (Miller 2003).

Exploration trenches transected the site to define the extent and nature of the artifact debris field (figure 9.11). In general, the farther away from the center of the site, the greater the depth of sand overlying artifacts, which reached nearly 4 feet in some places. These investigations indicated that the dispersion of buried artifacts was confined to an area 120 feet by 60 feet. If the site represented *Queen Anne's Revenge* (*La Concorde*), at an overall length of 90 to 100 feet, little horizontal movement of ship remains had occurred after the vessel was run aground. The shipwreck apparently deteriorated slowly and eventually became embedded in the seabed during a quiet period without the effect of a major hurricane event. If the wrecking event occurred in June 1718, historical records show that the shipwreck site was not affected by a hurricane for at least four years and that there were no major hits on the North Carolina coast for a decade after its loss (Ludlum 1963:192; Tannehill 1952:243). In this case, vulnerable portions of the hull would have been consumed by marine organisms and washed away by currents while the more resistant and heavier objects dropped to the seafloor, where they became encrusted and buried. That would lend credence to contemporary reports implying that *Queen Anne's Revenge* was run aground purposefully and to the timing of the event, which occurred in early summer, when prevailing southwest winds would have held the doomed vessel on the shoals (figure 9.12).

At the completion of the second season archaeologists confirmed that the shipwreck was oriented with its bow pointed toward shore. The large anchor A-3 found resting in the sand at the north end of the site would have served as a bower anchor. With its ring folded underneath, it had not been deployed or set. Recovered artifacts from the south end of the site included a large amount of lead shot, several ornamental upholstery tacks, parts of brass instruments, three pewter dishes, a medical syringe, and pieces of salt-glazed crockery and earthenware storage containers. A small amount of gold dust was also recovered during trench excavations (figure 9.13). Items of this sort traditionally would have came from the officer's quarters and/or magazine, both located in the stern of the vessel.

The wreckage appeared to lie in close proximity to where it grounded while navigating the shoals as it attempted to enter the inlet and reach a safe harbor. Evidence also suggested that after running aground and while relatively intact the vessel heeled to port and in the process spilled its deck load. This could be seen in the site layout, showing a scattering of cannon, in paired sets, along the west side of the main ballast mound. At the center of the site, ship's rigging (consisting of chain plate elements and deadeye rings) appeared to represent the main mast. The observed portion of hull structure was determined to be a forward section of the port side between the keelson and the turn of the bilge, or possibly a portion of the hull above the bilge. In either case the survival of structural elements was due to being pinned under the main ballast load. The discovery of a fourth anchor,

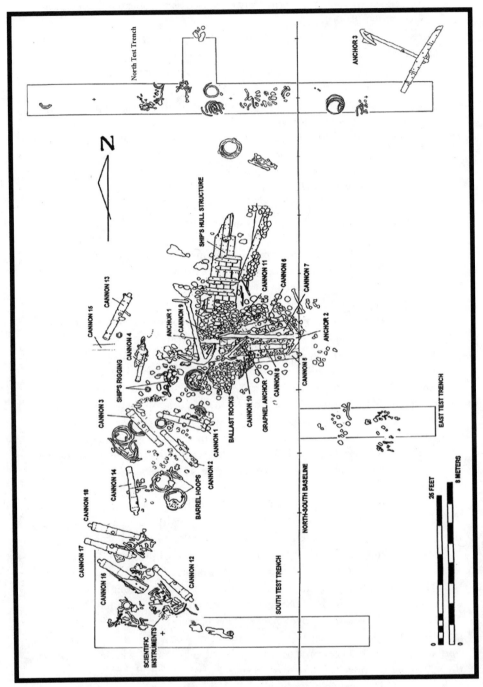

Figure 9.11. Archaeological site plan for 31CR314.

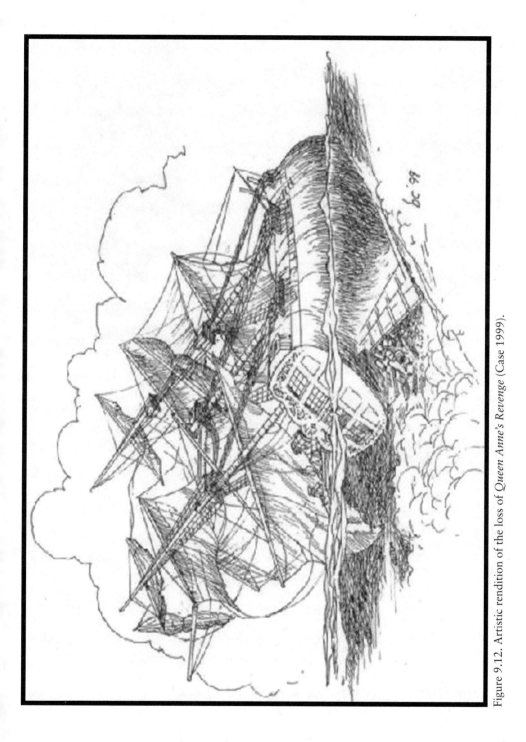

Figure 9.12. Artistic rendition of the loss of *Queen Anne's Revenge* (Case 1999).

Figure 9.13. Archaeologists Steve Claggett (*left*) and Wayne Lusardi examine gold dust.

located 420 feet south of the shipwreck site, led researchers to speculate that there may have been an attempt to free the vessel at the time of the loss. With a shaft length slightly less than 9 feet, the south anchor was approximately two-thirds the size of the three anchors at the main site. It also appeared to have been set in the sand with its shaft and ring pointing in the direction of the main wreckage. Assuming an association with the shipwreck, it may represent a kedge anchor used during an attempt to free the grounded vessel from the inlet shoal. This raised more questions than it answered in terms of why, when, and by whom this rescue attempt might have been made.

At the conclusion of the 1998 season, preliminary identification of the artifact assemblage (which included datable pewter, brass, ceramic and glass items) continued to fit neatly within the period of the late seventeenth and early eighteenth centuries. Several classes of artifacts—such as the lead upholstery tacks, an ornamental gun side plate, and cannon touchhole aprons—were nearly identical to those recovered from the pirate ship *Whydah* (Hamilton et al. 1992; Lusardi 2000). Preliminary analysis of the ballast rock samples indicated that they most likely originated from the Caribbean (Callahan et al. 2001:56), which suggested that the vessel operated in waters where both *La Concorde* and *Queen Anne's Revenge* traveled. An initial examination of gold samples showed that they were not found in the natural sediments at Beaufort Inlet (Pilkey and Bornhold

1970:C33; Craig et al. 2001:45–47) and thus represented a small amount of gold dust that was lost with the ship. The armament, which now stood at eighteen cannon, continued to provide strong evidence that this was Blackbeard's flagship; and two of the three recovered cannon were loaded, indicating that they represented armament not cargo or ballast.

Remote Sensing and Geophysical Interpretations

Early in the project archaeologists requested assistance from their colleagues in the field of marine geology to address some of the most pressing and interesting questions at the interface between archaeology and geology. For example, what was the environmental setting of the wreck site in the early 1700s (figure 9.14)? How had the site changed in the ensuing three centuries, and what were the natural forces that affected the archaeological record? Why were the artifacts now in 20 feet of water when the ship grounded in 10 to 12 feet of water, based on its estimated draft? Why was the shipwreck not discovered sooner in this shallow, heavily traveled location so close to shore?

Geologists began by digitizing twenty-five maps and charts to reconstruct the historic configuration of Beaufort Inlet and its relationship to the shipwreck over the last three centuries. The earliest charts showed that in the first half of the eighteenth century the entrance channel was on the western side. The projected location for shipwreck 31CR314 places it on the margin of the outer shoal just east of the historic inlet channel. The series of maps showed extensive offshore pivotal movement of the main navigation channel over three centuries (Wells and McNinch 2001:13–17). During this time, there were at least five distinct episodes when the inlet channel passed over the site, resulting in scouring and settling of the ship's remains to the depth where they are found today. As the channel moved away, shoaling resulted in total burial and kept artifacts covered until the inlet migrated back over the wreckage. Viewing the overall sequence of events, John Wells (Wells and McNinch 2001) estimated that the shipwreck was buried at least 80 percent of the time since its loss. During the early 1800s historic charts show that the sand overburden above the shipwreck was quite profound, because the water was only a few feet deep. A study of U.S. Army Corps of Engineers records shows that in 1927 the channel passed directly over the shipwreck and that inlet dredging took place that year to maintain its 20-foot depth. At that time wreckage most certainly was exposed; but sand quickly returned, and by 1930 the site was covered by only 6 feet of water. Since that time there has been a progressive loss of sand until it reached a depth of 23 feet and the partially exposed condition of the shipwreck observed at the time of its discovery (Suggs 2004). In another study, growth rates of mature coral collected from the site indicated an age of less than fifteen years and subsequently a relatively short period of exposure (Lindquist, personal communication, 1998).

Marine geologists collected data to study how periodic scour affected arti-

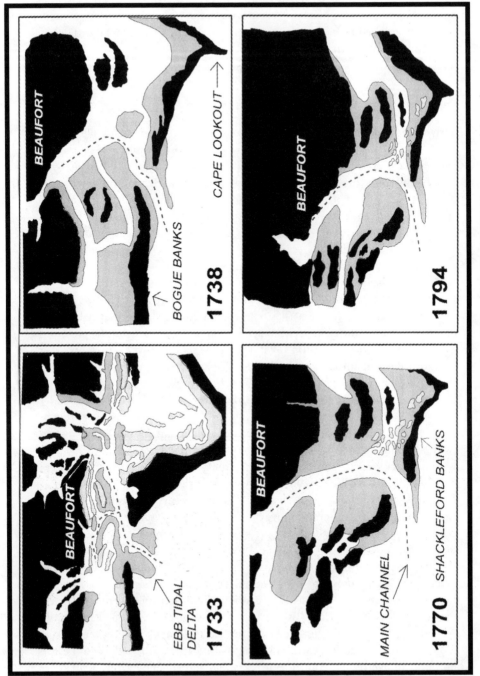

Figure 9.14. Eighteenth-century charts of Beaufort Inlet. Image from Wells and McNinch 2001:14; courtesy of the authors.

facts, predicated on three factors: near-bottom currents, sediment grain size at the seabed surface, and sedimentary characteristics of the underlying geology. This ultimately provided archaeologists with the tools to interpret the impact of environmental factors on the distribution of artifacts at the shipwreck site in the past as well as how these forces will continue to affect the site. An InterOcean S-4A electromagnetic current meter stationed near the site took continuous readings from May 1998 to April 1999. The instrument, anchored 1 meter above the seabed, recorded current velocity and direction and wave height and duration. During its deployment it captured a full range of data from calm periods to storm conditions, including northeasters, southwesters, and the direct impact from Hurricane Bonnie. Comparatively, only the hurricane-driven currents were strong enough to move significant amounts of bottom sediments, predominantly in a northeast direction. Geologists reported that during Bonnie "over the 50 hour storm period a volume equal to 2 dump-truck loads of sand was transported across a 1 square meter patch of seafloor in the immediate vicinity of the wreck" (McNinch et al. 2001:24) (figure 9.15).

Jesse McNinch further surmised that no appreciable change would be expected if sands moving into the area were equal to those moving out of the area. At the shipwreck, however, the exposed mound structure obstructed bottom flow and reduced the amount of sediment deposited on the side opposite the direction of current flow, which was in a northeasterly direction. Hydrodynamic effects further explained the scouring phenomena. As currents hit the raised mound of

Figure 9.15. Divers prepare to deploy the S-4A current meter (*foreground*).

Figure 9.16. One of two intact wine bottles discovered on the site.

artifacts, vortices and accelerated flows were created, similar to air stream flow behind large trucks on the highway. These currents and the shadow effect from the exposed mound resulted in a significant loss of the sediments on the north or lee side of the exposed wreckage.

Marine geologists also employed a series of high-resolution bathymetric and side-scan sonar surveys to detect and track changes at the shipwreck over the past several years. A highly accurate swath bathymetry system, one of only two such units available in the United States at the time, was used to map the bottom accurately to within 2 meters horizontally and 15 centimeters vertically. The results showed significant scouring after hurricane events and no subsequent reburial of the exposed mound (McNinch et al. 2001:21). In a scour-burial sequence, an object that rests on unconsolidated sands and is subjected to sufficient bottom flow will quickly settle into the hole created by current scouring and soon become level with the bottom. Once in that position, the object will no longer obstruct the current flow and will remain stable. During periods of calm, the scoured area around the object will eventually fill and complete the burial cycle (Trembanis and McNinch 2003:4–5). At shipwreck 31CR314, however, directly underlying the exposed wreckage was a hard-packed, scour-resistant sand layer that restricted burial. Sediment cores revealed that such an erosion-resistant layer increased the likelihood that artifacts were being disturbed during major storm events (Gibson 2004:11–15). Even with this disturbing news, delicate artifacts were found in a good state of preservation. A perfect example was the discovery of two intact hand-blown wine bottles nestled between two one-ton cannon (figure 9.16).

Archaeologists also employed remote sensing instruments. Magnetometers, which came into use during World War II, detect subtle changes in the earth's magnetic field caused by ferrous objects. These instruments have been particularly effective in locating shipwrecks, even wooden vessels, most of which contain substantial amounts of iron fasteners and hardware. A proton precession magnetometer used by the Intersal, Inc., survey team played a key role in the 1996 discovery of shipwreck 31CR314 by detecting a significant bipolar anomaly with peaks of +200 and −40 gammas over a distance of 200 feet as its sensor passed over the site. Divers confirmed the primary source was the numerous cannon and several anchors contained on the shipwreck.

A more recent innovation, the magnetic gradiometer, works the same way as the magnetometer but employs a sensor that contains two separate heads, approximately 2 feet apart. The instrument provides a digital readout of the difference or gradient between the two sensor heads. The readings therefore register only those ferrous objects that affect one sensor more than the other. Thus, large iron objects (which might normally distort site magnetics) can be effectively filtered out, because both sensors are influenced equally at a distance greater than a few feet.

Following a field test in June 1999, researchers returned to the shipwreck in the fall for eleven days to execute the gradiometer survey with an instrument provided by Surface Interval Dive Company, a North Carolina diver support group. During the survey, divers recorded 2,064 individual readings over the entire site (Lawrence and Wilde-Ramsing 2001:7). Using wireless communication gear to radio each position, divers moved the sensor-mounted sled down a graduated transect line (figure 9.17). At the time of the survey, sand accretion had buried most of the remains lying outside the main mound of artifacts. After recording and contouring the results of the gradiometer survey, archaeologists were able to overlay the site map and relate magnetic disturbances with previously recorded artifacts, such as cannon, anchors, and barrel hoops. Two anomalies in previously unexcavated areas were investigated, and the results confirmed the archaeologist's suspicion that each represented a cannon, bringing the total count to twenty (figure 9.18). Several more unidentified magnetic targets were likely to represent additional cannon. During the survey, the gradiometer also picked up ballast stones consisting of highly magnetic basalts as well as small iron objects. The maximum distribution of all artifacts was confined to a 110×55-foot area, based on the results of the gradiometer survey (Lawrence and Wilde-Ramsing 2001:7).

The examination of buried remains at the site using an array of remote-sensing instruments brought to bear technologically advanced methods. Analysis of these data helped researchers understand the nature and extent of the shipwreck's re-

Figure 9.17. Diver moves sensor-mounted sled down the transect line.

mains, the physical processes that affected its deterioration, and the potential impacts on artifact preservation in the future. Evidence continued to support identification of the shipwreck as that of *Queen Anne's Revenge* but also demonstrated how susceptible to disturbance artifacts have been and will continue to be during major storm events.

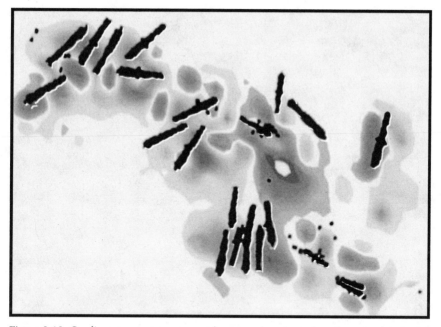

Figure 9.18. Gradiometer contour map with cannon locations plotted.

Mitigating Storm Impacts through Emergency Recovery

During the 1999 fall expedition, archaeologists were dismayed to find that considerable damage had been caused by a series of direct hits from hurricanes Dennis and Floyd. As marine geologists had predicted, wind-driven currents badly scoured the site on the north side of the main mound. Divers found a broad three-foot depression centering on the area of the previously documented hull structure. Intense currents had cast off sediment backfill and sandbags that had been placed on the articulated wooden components. Afterward, the hull itself sat on a pedestal of sand, with evidence of undercutting (figure 9.19).

In response, project managers began planning mitigative steps to record and recover artifacts from the affected area. This emergency recovery phase began in the last days of the fall 1999 expedition with the removal of an 8.5-foot-long hull plank and a ballast stone conglomerate, which became known as "Baby Ruth"—a giant version of the famous candy bar. As conservators cleaned this large concretion after its recovery, they were surprised to find that it contained not one but two small cannon, bringing the total count to twenty-one. This remarkable find added more evidence to the variable nature of the shipwreck's armament: cannon recovered from the site included two 6-pounders, one 4-pounder, one 1-pounder, and one ¾-pounder (figure 9.20). The smaller two cannon exhibited inscriptions,

Figure 9.19. Hull timbers exposed during hurricanes.

revealing that one was manufactured in England and the other in Sweden. Both cannon were loaded with powder charges and iron shot and packed with wads of fiber cordage.

The Swedish cannon also contained three worn iron bolts that had been placed in the barrel in front of the round shot. This artillery round was known as langrage. An eighteenth-century nautical dictionary provides the following definition:

> LANGREL, or LANGRAGE, (mitrailles, Fr.) a particular kind of shot, formed of bolts, nails, bars, or other pieces of iron tied together, and forming sort of a cylinder, which corresponds with the bore of the cannon, from which it was intended to be discharged. This contrivance is particularly designed to wound or carry away the masts, or tear the sails and rigging of the adversary, so as to disable him from flight or pursuit. It is never used in royal ships but very often by privateers and merchantmen. (Falconer 1870:121)

The last sentence is particularly significant with regard to distinguishing standard military practice from more adventuresome techniques, whereby gunners must have carried nearly as much risk as their targeted opponents (figure 9.21).

Investigators returned to the site the following spring to undertake emergency recovery of the threatened hull structure (figure 9.22). Unfortunately, prevailing

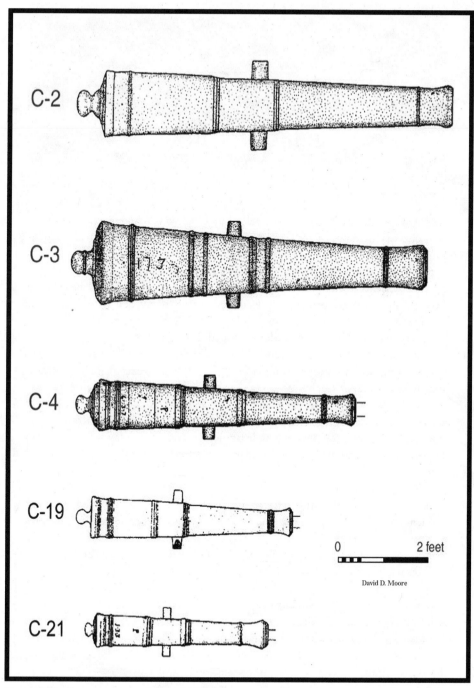

Figure 9.20. Cannon recovered from 31CR314.

Figure 9.21. Projectiles found in the Swedish cannon.

southwest winds during this two-week period limited actual site work to a total of four working days. In addition, researchers found that the hull structure was buried under 3 feet of newly deposited sand, making the task of uncovering it considerably more difficult. During the recovery, project divers disconnected ten frame fragments from the hull planks, wrapped them individually in plastic, and brought them to the surface. The four hull planks were each cut at the point where they disappeared under the main mound. The planks were placed one at a time on a padded aluminum ladder, strapped down, and lifted by several divers to the surface and then onto the recovery vessel. After the hull timbers were brought up, three additional thin planks, which served as sacrificial hull sheathing, were recovered in the same manner. While the frames showed extensive damage from exposure to the elements, the hull planks and sheathing that lay underneath were in an excellent state of preservation. The most important objective was completed: removal of fragile timbers out of harm's way should a future hurricane pass over the shipwreck. Time and conditions during the spring of 2000 fieldwork did not allow the documentation and retrieval of associated artifacts that lay beneath the hull structure. This work would wait until the fall.

From September 25 to October 13, 2000, a final major expedition was launched to complete the emergency recovery of artifacts affected by the catastrophic storms of the previous year. An area encompassing 125 square feet was completely excavated, with a total of 184 objects recovered and catalogued. A few disarticulated hull and sheathing planks (one nearly 18 feet long), a large amount of ballast stone, and a variety of concretions were among the finds. Individual artifacts were similar in some respects to those collected in the southern portions of the site, although not as numerous. Common artifacts included lead shot, a brass instrument (nested scale weight), and ceramics, which may imply that the ship was less compartmentalized than a traditional ship. It could be argued, however, that this was the result of exposure by strong currents, because artifacts were situated on a scour-resistant sediment layer. Artifacts recovered during the fall 2000 expedition would have been located under the previ-

Figure 9.22. Divers recovering a hull plank.

ously recovered hull planking and must have migrated to this position due to erosion and settling after the vessel wrecked. While a scour-burial model implies vertical movement of objects down through the surrounding sediments, localized conditions may also affect their relative horizontal position.

The emergency recovery effort was deemed a success in many ways. Obviously, the documentation and removal of artifacts in areas that are prone to suffer disturbance and damage from storms satisfied a site preservation concern. Hurricane forecasters continued to predict the likelihood of major storms for the foreseeable future. Archaeologists were also able to confirm the sediment profile that was seen on the south side of the exposed mound during cannon C-2 excavations. In general, site sediments consisted of three layers: a coarse sand overburden that became suspended and mobile during periods of strong current action; a partially disturbed zone made up of sand and shell where the shipwreck remains and associated artifacts were found; and an underlying fine, hardpacked sand, which kept artifacts from going any deeper. Also noted were the occasional lenses of fine black silt indicative of prior scour events.

Education Outreach

Public outreach and media coverage has been a major part of investigations at shipwreck 31CR314. It was with this in mind that the recovery of a second ballast-laden object, Baby Ruth II, lying in the excavated area was delayed until

Figure 9.23. Baby Ruth II recovery event, with a U.S. Army Reserve landing craft in the background.

the following spring. This object, containing the site's twenty-second cannon, was successfully recovered during a media event for nearly 150 people. These guests represented the tremendous and varied support that the project had received during research efforts. University chancellors and college presidents from participating institutions, state and local government officials, and foundation and local donors were all invited to ride to the shipwreck site in a U.S. Army Reserve landing craft and circle the recovery vessel as the concreted artifact broke the surface for the first time in nearly three centuries (figure 9.23).

From the time its discovery was announced, the shipwreck thought to be *Queen Anne's Revenge* has commanded extraordinary public attention, due to its potential association with Blackbeard and piracy. This interest enabled the project to obtain funding for some unique educational outreach initiatives. Most notable was an interactive Internet program called *QAR DiveLive*. First conducted in the fall of 2000, the weeklong event was primarily designed to reach North Carolina precollegiate classrooms. Videographers Bill Lovin and Rick Allen proposed a five-day broadcast from the shipwreck, modeled after a land-based program being offered by the North Carolina National Estuarine Research Reserve in Beaufort, North Carolina. The challenge was to relay a signal from 23 feet below the Atlantic Ocean up to a surface vessel, send it from there 2.75 miles to a shore station, and then digitize it for relay to the Internet, where school

Figure 9.24. An archaeologist conducts an underwater tour during *QAR* DiveLive.

groups and the general public could watch and participate. Lovin and Allen's mix of microwave and computer technology, video and audio expertise, and resourcefulness accomplished the task in a remarkably professional and cost-effective manner (Eslinger and Wilde-Ramsing 2001).

QAR DiveLive began with little publicity and fanfare in October 2000; but by the end of the week an estimated 1,600 schoolchildren from across North America had tuned in (figure 9.24). Students were able to log onto the *Queen Anne's Revenge* website to watch twice-daily live broadcasts and ask the archeologists questions as they worked on the ocean floor. The general public was invited to observe from home. Thousands of hits were received; the server crashed near the end of the week due to an overload of participants—a sign of its success.

In October 2001 the *Queen Anne's Revenge* project again went live from the shipwreck site. The response was more than double that of the year before, both in registered classrooms and from the general public. The first two and a half days focused on the archaeologists working offshore and underwater. Then the program took students into the project conservation laboratory to see firsthand how artifacts were cleaned and preserved for future study and exhibit. It was important to convey this point, because that was where a majority of the actual archeological investigation was taking place. Laboratory activities involved U.S.

Figure 9.25. U.S. Marine Corps technicians use X-ray technology to examine concretions.

Marine Corps technicians from the Explosive Ordinance Disposal Unit at Cherry Point, who X-rayed twenty-four concretions that had been previously recovered during excavations at the shipwreck (figure 9.25). Radiographs of these heavily encrusted objects allowed archaeologists and conservators to view the interior and increased the chances that fragile artifacts would not be damaged or destroyed during the cleaning process.

Students also visited with geologist Dr. James Craig, who was sifting through sediments collected during recent excavations at the shipwreck site. His careful work resulted in the discovery of numerous lead shot, emphasizing the need for this level of recovery. Researchers also took the students down into the muzzle of one of the recovered cannon using a video camera mounted on the end of a long flexible extension. This exercise confirmed that the cannon was loaded and provided details on the condition of the wad of cordage that held the cannonball in place.

QAR DiveLive events provided direct student access during a live question and answer period with scientists at the shipwreck site and in the conservation laboratory. It successfully provided an exciting blend of archaeological study, historical research, and shipwreck exploration.

Interpreting the Evidence

In addition to archaeological investigations and conservation activities, it should not be forgotten that historians were unearthing clues of their own in archives and libraries located on both sides of the Atlantic (Butler 2000; De Bry 1999; Ducoin 2001; Moore 1997a; Moore and Daniel 2001). Vital for interpreting archaeological findings, their research provided historical context within which to view artifacts from shipwreck 31CR314. Their findings on the origins and life of the vessel known as *Queen Anne's Revenge* can be summarized as follows.

While Blackbeard's early life and career are sketchy, the fact that he captured the French vessel *La Concorde* in late 1717 is well established. *La Concorde* first appears in 1710 during the War of Spanish Succession or Queen Anne's War (1701–13) as a privateer of 280 tons, equipped with 26 guns by owner René Montaudoin (Ducoin 2001). After the war the prominent merchant put *La Concorde* into service as a slave trader, which subsequently made three voyages in 1713, 1715, and 1717 (Mettas 1978:56). Each trip began from Nantes, France, in the spring, carrying trade goods for the west coast of Africa, where enslaved Africans were purchased. The ship then continued toward its New World destination, taking approximately two months to complete the transatlantic voyage. After unloading its human freight, *La Concorde* picked up a cargo from the West Indies, predominantly sugar, and returned to France. The third voyage, however, ended quite differently.

On March 24, 1717, *La Concorde* left Nantes with Captain Pierre Dosset in command, headed for the African port of Judah (Ouidah or Whydah). At that time it was listed as a 200-ton ship armed with sixteen cannon, carrying a crew of seventy-five. In Africa 516 human captives were taken on board, in addition to twenty pounds of gold dust. The transatlantic voyage, known as the Middle Passage, then began. In November 1717, as *La Concorde* approached its destination of Martinique in the West Indies, the ship was overtaken and boarded by Blackbeard and his company (figure 9.26). The pirate took the vessel, the gold dust, fourteen French crewmen (including three surgeons and two carpenters), and perhaps as many as a hundred enslaved Africans into his possession (Ernaut 1718).

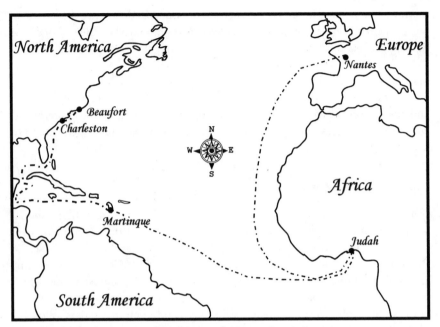

Figure 9.26. The final voyage of *La Concorde/Queen Anne's Revenge*.

With his new vessel, Blackbeard captured several other vessels over the next few weeks on his way to the Bay of Honduras. Several months passed before the pirate renewed his attacks on commercial shipping and began adding to his fleet, which eventually consisted of the flagship, three sloops, and several hundred men (Moore 1997a). During this period, Blackbeard may have switched his French flagship *La Concorde* for a forty-gun English ship, based on a deposition reporting a third-hand account (Morange 1718). While there is no further historical documentation to corroborate this vague mention, the possibility cannot be dismissed, thus adding to the uncertainty surrounding the origins of the vessel known as *Queen Anne's Revenge*.

As his flotilla made its way up the Atlantic seaboard in May 1718, the pirate captain sealed the port of Charleston, South Carolina, and prevented shipping traffic from entering or leaving. In an amazing display of contempt for New World authority, Blackbeard seized several vessels and detained a number of influential citizens, threatening them with death if they did not convince city officials to produce a chest of medicine (Lee 1997). Once ransom was paid, the pirate flotilla continued sailing up the coast. Within a few days the flagship and its consort *Adventure* were run aground and abandoned at Beaufort Inlet.

While no single definitive finding has yet surfaced to confirm Intersal's discovery, in many respects archaeological evidence from shipwreck 31CR314 accords with what might be expected of a well-armed ship lost in the early eighteenth century, as *Queen Anne's Revenge* reportedly was. More importantly, extensive research has not brought to light evidence to the contrary. Overall the site has yielded artifacts that date to the correct period, represent comparable armament and ship parts, and suggest the layout of a vessel that ran aground and deteriorated at that location. Based on thorough historical research, no other reported shipwreck in the general vicinity qualifies as a valid candidate. In addition to historical documentation, detailed remote sensing surveys and site explorations conducted in the vicinity of the Beaufort Inlet's historic bar over the past two decades have failed to locate an eighteenth-century shipwreck, other than shipwreck 31CR314, that approaches the size and armament of *Queen Anne's Revenge* (Masters and Levin 2004; Watts 1992, 1997).

An understanding of the maritime shipping activities of the period provides a historical prospective on the loss of *Queen Anne's Revenge*. The town of Beaufort served as a minor shipping port from its incorporation in 1723; nearby Cape Lookout served as a protected anchorage for ships even earlier. Maritime traffic in the area would have consisted almost exclusively of small coasting vessels (less than 100 tons) during the eighteenth century. While the early shipping records do not exist for Beaufort, the port was visited by only one vessel above 200 tons during the entire second half of the eighteenth century (Angley 1997). Larger ships employed in the transatlantic trade traveled well offshore from the treacherous North Carolina capes as they headed to Europe with their bulk cargoes of sugar and tobacco, the primary colonial exports during the early eighteenth century (Davis 1973:267–97). Normal colonial maritime patterns suggest that the presence and subsequent loss of ships greater than 200 tons during the early eighteenth century would be unlikely in the Beaufort area.

Yet without an artifact that relates directly to *La Concorde* or Blackbeard's exploits following its capture, project archaeologists must rely on carefully developed research and interpretation of circumstantial evidence regarding the nature, the period, and ultimately the identity of the shipwreck lying in Beaufort Inlet. With the uncertainties surrounding the origins of *Queen Anne's Revenge* and the undocumented activities of its renegade crew, an intriguing question arises that represents common threads throughout this book. Is there some clue, some reliable indication in the archaeological record, that can tell us when we have found a pirate ship? How does this evidence differ from what might be expected on a nonpirate vessel? Would a wide variety of cannon (both in size and in origin of manufacture) imply a pirate's stolen armament? Or was this standard practice for any captain or owner wanting to improve his ship's defensive capabilities when given the opportunity? The cannon were loaded, offering a glimpse of the crew's preparedness. Is this evidence of pirates or does it represent a general state of readiness that might be expected of any ship traveling during uncertain times, especially when sailing in pirate-infested waters? What can we say about the makeshift ingenuity and gunnery tactics seen in ordinance that includes a mixture of lead shot, nails, glass, and the occasional large iron bolt? Would only a pirate

Figure 9.27. The pirate captain Blackbeard. Printed in the 1725 edition of Charles Johnson's *A General History of the Pyrates* (London).

send such a nasty load swirling toward an unyielding victim? Or was it simply common practice applied by all in desperate situations? Would we expect to see less compartmentalization on a ship manned by pirates as a result of their relatively loose social stratification and would that show up in the archaeological record? What other artifacts and relationships might differentiate a pirate vessel? Some argue that archaeologists may never be able to detect unique "pirate" patterns, because ultimately pirates were trained seamen in a world where traditions were long-standing and order was essential to stay afloat (Babits 2001).

The basic question lingers: is this *Queen Anne's Revenge*, the ship that Blackbeard lost in Beaufort Inlet nearly 300 years ago? While by nature they take a skeptical approach, project archaeologists and associates working closely with the project find little reason to believe shipwreck 31CR314 is anything but the remains of the pirate captain's flagship. Through their detective work, researchers will continue to examine the whole range of mysteries surrounding the site. For while the pirate association is an added bonus, this rare eighteenth-century site provides a unique glimpse into maritime activities during this dynamic period of American history and seafaring. Its discovery in North Carolina waters and subsequent investigations have opened an exciting chapter in underwater archaeology. What state could be more deserving, after all the time its citizens have spent telling tales of pirates, digging for lost treasure, and erecting roadside attractions in honor of the infamous pirate Blackbeard (figure 9.27)?

Acknowledgments

Many people have helped in numerous ways with the preparation of this chapter from initial fieldwork to final editing. To all of them I am grateful. I specifically want to recognize Jeffrey Crow, Steve Claggett, Richard Lawrence, Nathan Henry, David Moore, Chris Southerly, Jim Craig, and Sim Wilde for their editorial comments and support. Julep Gillman-Bryan and Rick Allen took the underwater photographs, and Karen Browning provided graphic support. All other figures are by me unless otherwise noted. Thanks to Russell K. Skowronek and Charles R. Ewen for bringing this book together.

10

The Beaufort Inlet Shipwreck Artifact Assemblage

Wayne R. Lusardi

Since the discovery of Beaufort Inlet shipwreck 31CR314 off the North Carolina coast in 1996, state archaeologists have conducted approximately four months of combined field research on the site from 1997 to 2004. Preliminary analysis of the artifact assemblage and site location has led some researchers tentatively to identify the shipwreck as the pirate Blackbeard's flagship, *Queen Anne's Revenge*, known to have been lost near the inlet in 1718. Definitive evidence, however, is lacking; and a positive identification cannot be made based on scant circumstantial evidence alone. In fact, many artifacts and their relationship to the site are not consistent with known historical accounts of Blackbeard's flagship.

Background History

René Montaudoin, one of the most successful slave traders in Nantes, owned *La Concorde*, a 300-ton French Guineaman. Nothing is known of the vessel until its first recorded voyage, which began when it sailed from Nantes on April 13, 1713, under Captain Isaac Thomas, commanding a crew of 62 men. The vessel sailed to Judah on the coast of West Africa, transported 363 slaves to the Caribbean island of Martinique, and arrived back in France on July 31, 1714 (Thomas 1714; Mettas 1978:16–17). *Concorde*'s second slaving voyage began on February 27, 1715, under the command of Captain Mathieu Denis, with a crew of 60 men. Nearly 300 enslaved Africans from Gabingue were traded at St. Domingue in February 1716. After a brief stop at Bermuda, the vessel returned to Nantes on September 23, 1716 (Mettas 1978:37). The ship's final transatlantic voyage began on March 24, 1717, under the command of Pierre Dosset, with a crew of 75 men. On July 8, 1717, 516 Africans were loaded aboard at Judah (Dosset 1718; Ernaut 1718). Destined for Martinique, the ship was captured by pirates, presumably under the command of Edward Thatch or Teach (better known as Blackbeard), near the island of St. Vincent on November 28, 1717. The pirates released the French crew on the island of Bequia and gave them a smaller sloop called *Mauvaise Rencontre* (Mettas 1978:56). Blackbeard then continued to prey upon shipping in the eastern Caribbean, where he captured or plundered *Great*

Allen, Mountserrat, New Division, Margaret, Land of Promise, and an unidentified sloop. He then moved his operation west to present-day Belize and Honduras, where he captured among others *Protestant Caesar* and *Adventure* (Moore 1997a:appendix 1).

Blackbeard increased *Concorde*'s armament to as many as forty guns and renamed the slaver *Queen Anne's Revenge*. After taking a number of prizes, including a small turtle boat off the Caymans and an unidentified sloop off Cuba's northern coast, he sailed northward into the Bahamas and eventually toward mainland North America (Lawrence and Wilde-Ramsing 2001:3). With his flagship *Queen Anne's Revenge*, three smaller sloops, and 300–400 men under his command, Blackbeard blockaded the colonial port of Charleston, South Carolina, in May 1718. After plundering a dozen ships at the harbor's mouth and receiving a ransom of medical supplies, the pirates continued northward and arrived off the coast of Beaufort, North Carolina, in early June. The three smaller sloops safely entered Topsail Inlet (present-day Beaufort Inlet), but the pirate's flagship ran aground and foundered on the outer bar (Herriot 1719:45–46). When Blackbeard ordered one of the smaller sloops, *Adventure*, to assist *Queen Anne's Revenge*, it too was lost. Captured pirates later claimed that *Queen Anne's Revenge* and *Adventure* were grounded intentionally to break up the large company of pirates (Herriot 1719:46).

After losing his two ships and dismantling and marooning part of his crew, Blackbeard sailed a small sloop to the colonial capital of Bath, where he received a king's pardon. He then proceeded to Ocracoke, where he set up a base of pirating operations for the next few months, captured several prizes, and was eventually confronted and killed in November 1718 by an expedition led by Royal Navy lieutenant Robert Maynard (Lawrence and Wilde-Ramsing 2001:3).

1996 Discovery

The treasure hunting firm Intersal, Inc., operating under a state-issued search and recovery permit, located the remains of several historic shipwrecks near Beaufort Inlet, North Carolina, during a magnetometer survey in 1996. Treasure hunters removed thirty artifacts from site 31CR314 without recording provenience immediately following the discovery of the wreck. Unfortunately, many of these were the most diagnostic artifacts found to date, including a dated bronze bell, stamped musketoon barrel, and inscribed sounding lead.

1997 Field Season

The 1997 field season primarily consisted of postdisturbance survey and mapping of the exposed portions of the shipwreck. Archaeologists compiled a site-plan that included the main ballast pile, three anchors, fifteen cannon, and miscellaneous exposed concretions. Several test units were excavated around the periphery of the ballast pile to evaluate the extent of the site, as well as to determine what types of artifacts would be encountered beneath the surrounding sediments. Test units were also excavated over the north anchor stock to facilitate the collection of a wood sample and determine its condition and in the areas surrounding the two cannon that were later raised. Also recovered from the test units were 333 small artifacts including cannon shot, ballast stones, barrel hoop concretions, and intrusive materials, though their exact provenience was not recorded.

1998 Field Season

The 1998 field season was designed as a continual assessment of the site and a means to further determine the extent of the debris field (Lusardi 1999). A new baseline aligned north–south was placed to the east of the main ballast pile, and three transects were excavated by divers using airlifts and dredges. The northern transect contained ballast stones, barrel hoops, deadeyes, and a small quantity of lead shot. Although the eastern transect produced only a few large ballast stones and ceramic sherds, the southern trench revealed an abundance of cultural materials, including three additional cannon. In all 409 artifacts or groups of artifacts were recovered. Archaeologists also concentrated on an area of the site where a large section of wooden hull structure was partially exposed through disturbance erosion (figure 10.1).

1999 Field Season

In June and October 1999 archaeologists revisited the shipwreck and conducted a diver-positioned magnetometer survey of the site. Numerous ferrous objects were detected, including another cannon just to the north of the southern transect. A large ballast-covered concretion was recovered; when opened in the laboratory, it revealed two additional cannon and forty-eight associated artifacts. Fifty-one miscellaneous small artifacts recently disturbed by hurricanes were also recovered.

2000 Field Season

A large section of wooden hull structure was disassembled and recovered in May, and excavation of sediments located below the wooden elements was completed in October. Five 5×5-foot units were completely excavated to sterile strata, and 117 artifacts or groups of artifacts were recovered.

2001 Field Season

No archaeological work was conducted in 2001, though divers installed a permanent datum on the site and videographers relayed live Internet transmissions. No artifacts were recovered.

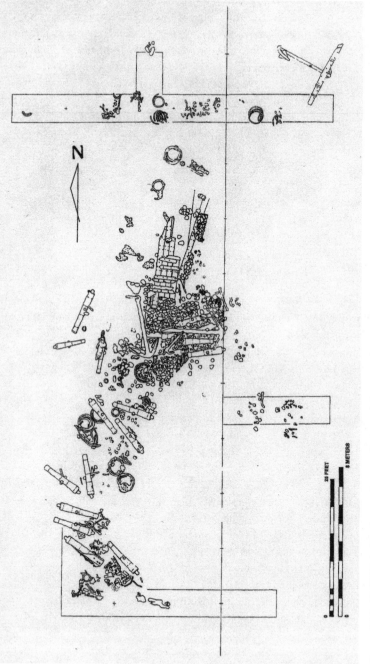

Figure 10.1. 31CR314 site plan at the completion of the 1998 field season. Many of the most diagnostic artifacts were removed prior to any field documentation. Drawing by W. R. Lusardi and D. Moore.

The Artifact Assemblage

Since the discovery of the Beaufort Inlet shipwreck in November 1996, over 2,000 artifacts have been recovered and conserved, while an estimated several thousand more await removal from concretion and treatment in the laboratory. Although the recovered artifacts represent less than 2 percent of the total known on the site, the assemblage already reflects many aspects of early eighteenth century maritime culture. Ship parts and equipment, arms, scientific, navigational and medical instruments, personal effects, and food preparation and storage items have been recovered from the shipwreck (Lusardi 2000:59–60).

Ship Parts and Equipment

The extant structure consists of ten or more composite frames held together by four white oak group (*Quercus* sp.) outer hull planks, some with red pine (*Pinus sylvestris*) sacrificial sheathing still in situ. Additional structure remains on site, buried under the main ballast pile. The components are fastened together laterally with iron drift pins, and each frame is attached to each underlying plank with two iron nails and two wooden treenails (figure 10.2). Wooden sheathing was attached to the hull's exterior over a layer of cattle hair with small square-sectional iron nails. A single red cedar (*Juniperus* sp.) frame may indicate a New World repair (Newsom 1999).

A cast bronze ship's bell dated 1709 was one of the first clues that an early eighteenth century shipwreck had been discovered. It features the Roman Catholic invocation "IHS [Iesus Hominum Salvator] MARIA" and the word "ANO" preceding the date, perhaps indicating a Spanish or Portuguese origin (figure 10.3). The artifact is considerably smaller than contemporary ship's bells and may have been used as a secondary watch bell.

Several wrought-iron hooks seized with rope were recovered from the site, though all were completely corroded, leaving only hollow molds in surrounding concretions. Conservators cast the empty molds with epoxy resin, revealing hooks that resemble those used extensively in ship's rigging and tackle as well as in the manipulation of cargo and heavy ordnance. Wooden deadeyes, iron strops, chain-plates, chain links, and cordage were also found scattered about the site. Distribution patterns of rigging elements suggest a two-masted vessel.

Hundreds of iron nails varying in length from 1.5 to 4 inches were removed from concretion attached to one of the cannon. The nails are square in section, flare or spoon slightly at the tip, and were probably contained in a box or bag that has since deteriorated. Fifteen decorative 1-inch lead tacks were recovered from the southern transect. The shanks are square in section and taper to a point, while the heads are decorated with a rosette or flower with a central boss. The tacks (too soft to be hammered) were probably used to decorate upholstery, furniture, leather-lined boxes, or chests (Hamilton et al. 1992:397). Identical

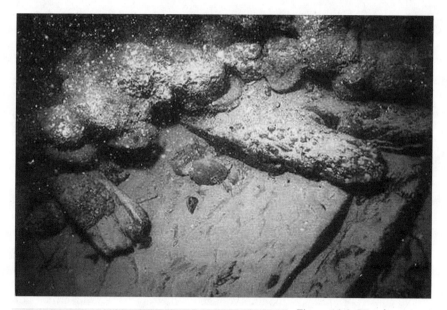

Figure 10.2. Wooden scantlings, futtocks, and sheathing protruding from under the ballast pile. The hull appears lightly built for a transatlantic vessel. Photo by North Carolina Division of Cultural Resources.

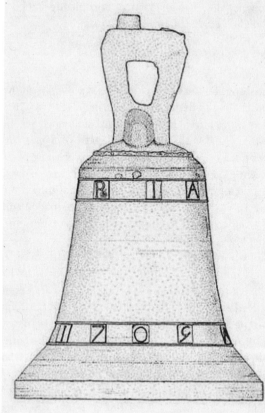

Figure 10.3. Bronze bell inscribed "IHS MARIA" and "ANO DE 1709." The presence of a Spanish bell on a supposed French slaver has not been explained. Drawing by North Carolina Division of Cultural Resources.

tacks are reported from the contemporary pirate vessel *Whydah*, lost off Cape Cod in 1717 (Hamilton 1992:397).

A perforated semicircular lead pump sieve with three flanges was found in 1996, and a second sieve fragment was recovered in 1999. Both fragments resemble sieves found on *El Nuevo Constante*, wrecked off Louisiana in 1766 (Oertling 1996:31–33). Two pierced lead strips, possibly remnants of draft markers (numerals I and X), were found near the structural remains in 1998. Several nondiagnostic lead strips and patches containing cattle hair and pitch were also recovered from the southern transect (Scott Cummings 1999). Ground tackle present on the site includes two stowed anchors and a five-fluke grapnel hook on the main ballast pile, a bow anchor with intact wooden stock near the northern transect, and a kedge anchor with intact stock and puddening located 420 feet south of the main site. The anchor stocks are of the white oak group (*Quercus* sp.) and tropical bloodwood (*Brosimum* sp.) (Newsom 1999).

Perhaps as many as fifty tons of variously shaped and sized river cobbles were stored in the ship's hull as ballast. Several hundred stones have been collected from different areas of the site to identify patterns in loading and deposition. The stones consist primarily of basalt, although geologists have also identified porphyritic to felsic-intermediate volcanics, volcaniclastics, hornblende gabbro, amphibolite, and limestone (Callahan et al. 2001:49).

Arms

Twenty-two cast-iron muzzle-loading cannon have so far been discovered on the Beaufort Inlet shipwreck site; according to data acquired during a 1999 magnetometer survey, additional guns may be buried in surrounding sediments. Seventeen cannon appear to be six-pounders, with an average length of 8 feet. All feature trunnions mounted low on the tube, suggesting a manufacture date prior to the middle of the eighteenth century. Five cannon have been recovered to date, all differing in length, weight, style, or caliber; this may indicate that they came from a variety of sources (figure 10.4). Four of the five cannon were loaded and ready for action, and all had wooden spiles in the vents to prevent rain and seawater from entering the touchholes (Lusardi 2002:34–35).

Cannon C-2, an unmarked six-pounder, is 8 feet 2 inches in length, weighs 1,840 pounds, and is the only cannon recovered to date that was not loaded. The gun's origin is unknown. Another six-pounder, cannon C-3, is 7 feet 8 inches in length and exhibits crudely chiseled numbers "17 3 0" running lengthwise along the first reinforce. According to Angus Konstam (2000), C-3 may have originated in France; if so, "1730" may represent the year of manufacture. Eighteenth-century French cannon were often chiseled with a date near the breech (Peterson 1969:74). Although peculiarly oriented and without hyphenations, the numbers may alternatively represent the weight of the cannon in old English hundredweights, quarters, and pounds (17[112] + 3[28] + 0 = 1,988 pounds). Knowing

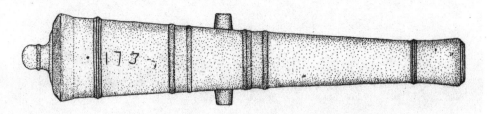

Figure 10.4. Cannon C-3, inscribed "17 3 0" on the first reinforce. The numbers may represent a weight mark or a date. Drawing by North Carolina Division of Cultural Resources.

the weight of each gun was crucial aboard ship because ordnance had to be distributed evenly to maintain the vessel's stability (Munday 1998:5). The actual weight of the cannon and the chiseled weight, however, differ by several hundred pounds. Cannon C-3 was in the process of being unloaded, and fragments of an exterior wad of cordage have been removed from the bore.

A smaller cast-iron British cannon (C-4) was covered with concretion, containing hundreds of artifacts including nails, ship's rigging, gun parts, pig bones, and ceramics. C-4 measures 6 feet ½ inch in length and features the numbers 6-3-7 stamped laterally on the breech (6[112] + 3[28] + 7 = 763 pounds). The letter "P" for "proof" (Gilkerson 1993:59, 63) also appears on the top of the first reinforce just behind the trunnions. Although the cannon's bore (3 ½-inch diameter) was heavily fouled, the contents were well preserved. A solid cast-iron ball (weighing 3¹⁄₆ pounds) was sandwiched between wads of cordage. The outer wad served to hold the shot in place while at sea (Gooding 1986:49; Munday 1998:8), and the inner wad created a better seal between the gunpowder charge and shot (Munday 1998:7). Fragments of a stitched paper cartridge and gunpowder residue were also removed from the bore. A similarly sized cannon (C-20) remains on the wreck site.

Divers raised a 1,000-pound concretion encased in dozens of ballast stones in 1999. When it was opened in the conservation laboratory, two cannon (a half-pounder and one-pounder) were discovered. Artifacts found in association with the guns include two kaolin tobacco pipes, cannon shot, a gunflint, wood, and rope fragments. The one-pounder (C-19) measures 4 feet 5¾ inches in length and, although comparatively small, is considerably too heavy (333 pounds) to be a rail-mounted gun. Its right trunnion was cast with the letters "IEC," representing the foundry of Jasper Ehrencreutz, whose family operated the Ehrendal Cannon Works in Sweden between 1689 and 1750 (Kennard 1986:70; Peterson 1973:156–57). The left trunnion is dated "[1]713." Following removal of the wooden tompion (*Pinus* sp. section *Taeda* American group), C-19 was found to contain a wad of cordage, three wrought-iron drift pin fragments (6⅜, 6⅞, and

Figure 10.5. Cast-iron grenades, one revealing interior powder chamber and wooden fuse.

8 inches in length), a second wad, a solid round shot (⅞ pound, 1⅞ inches in diameter), a third wad, and powder residue (Newsom 2001). No cartridge remains exist, so the gunpowder may have been poured with a copper ladle or contained in a paper wrapper that has since deteriorated. The combination of solid shot and drift pins was designed as an antipersonnel or antirigging load.

The half-pounder (C-21) is 3 feet 9 inches in length and features the numbers "1-3-3" stamped laterally on the breech (1[112] + 3[28] + 3 = 199 pounds), and a "P" for "proof" on the first reinforce. It also has an intact wooden tompion and was loaded with a single, solid round shot sandwiched between two wads of cordage. Fiber fragments from a cloth powder cartridge were also removed from the bore. The British gun is the smallest so far discovered on the site; if equipped with a wrought-iron yoke and tiller, it could have easily been rail mounted.

Munitions associated with the cannon include cast iron solid round shot (weighing ½, 1, 3, 4, 6, and 24 pounds), bar shot fragments, the drift pins removed from cannon C-19, and bag shot filled with lead balls, glass, and iron shrapnel. Several lead cannon vent aprons have also been recovered from the wreck. Designed to keep rain and seawater from entering the touchholes, all are flanged and contain square nail holes for attachment lines (Bingeman 1985:203; Blackmore 1976:218; Brown 1997:105; Clifford and Perry 1999b:201; Manucy 1949:73). Although no intact gun carriages have yet been discovered, possible carriage hardware consisting of breeching ringbolts and roves was found attached to cannon C-2 and C-4. A wooden wedge-shaped object, possibly a carriage quoin, was also found on the site.

Two baseball-sized hand grenades were found attached to a pewter dish nestled beneath cannon C-12's muzzle (figure 10.5). The grenades consist of imperfectly cast, iron spheres packed with gunpowder and pierced to accept a hollow wooden fuse. The fuse contained powder and a match and would have

Figure 10.6. Musketoon barrel breech with view, proof, and maker's marks arranged bottom to top.

been lit and thrown at the enemy, with devastating results (Darroch 1986:80–81; Marsden and Lyon 1977:16–19). Analysis of the residue removed from the interior of a broken grenade failed to detect any original powder constituents, such as saltpeter (potassium nitrate), carbon, or sulfur. The fuses were found to be either sycamore (*Platanus occidentalis*) or American beech (*Fagus grandiflora*) and may indicate a colonial American origin (Newsom 2001). Similar grenades were found on the pirate ship *Whydah* (Kinkor 1991) and on many other contemporary shipwrecks (Darroch 1986:76–86; Marsden and Lyon 1977:16–19).

Small arms from shipwrecks are far more rare, because most could be re-moved before sinking. A brass musketoon barrel, however, was one of the first artifacts recovered from the wreck in 1996 (figure 10.6). Blunderbusses and musketoons were commonly issued to boarding parties or used by mariners to defend a ship and quell mutinies (Gordon 1967:77; Moller 1993:276). The barrel (27⅛ inches long) is of cylindrical bore, flared just after a single baluster ring at the muzzle to 2½ inches, and was designed to shoot scatter loads. The breech is threaded, though missing the plug and tang ($^{13}/_{16}$ inch in diameter), and features a raised lip on the upper edge. London Gunmakers' Company view (V crowned) and proof (GP crowned) marks dating between 1672 and 1702 are stamped on the upper left quadrant of the breech (Blair 1962:116–17; Hawtrey Gyngell 1959:11), and a maker's mark consisting of the letters "TH" below a crown identifies an unknown London gunsmith (Blanch and Rywell 1956:151–52). The underside of the barrel that would have been concealed by the stock was left unfinished and exhibits coarse file scratches and two barrel lugs 5¾ and 18¾ inches from the muzzle. The Roman numeral "V" was crudely chiseled into the underside of the barrel at the breech, probably representing an assembly notation to be matched to components with similar marks (Bailey 1997:23; Patten 2000:23).

A brass side plate in the form of a sea serpent was found in concretion attached to cannon C-4 (figure 10.7). Although missing the forward fastener hole, the side plate (6⅛ inches long) is otherwise intact. The back is etched with an assembly numeral "II," and the center fastener hole is pentagonal in form. The artifact resembles Type G side plates found on English trade guns, used extensively in North America and French Canada (Brown 1980:283–84; Hamilton 1968:15–17, 1987:66–67, 71; Russell 1980:128), and several side plates recovered from the pirate ship *Whydah*, lost off Cape Cod in 1717 (Hamilton et al. 1992:251–64). Dragon or serpentine side plates with looping tails also occur on blunderbusses and musketoons (Gordon 1967:79). A flat brass butt plate found in close proximity to the side plate features three countersunk fastener holes and a simple, unnotched tang resembling the later sea service musket style (Bailey 1997:29, 46). Musket furniture is not uncommon on sea service blunderbusses of the same period (Gilkerson 1993:100; Moller 1993:281). A badly corroded iron lock plate was also recovered from the wreck.

A concretion found in the middle of the site may be the remains of a small wooden box or container consisting of a slat of wood, with a pile of small-caliber lead bird shot, three variously worked gunflints, three pieces of chert debitage, and a pewter spoon on top. The debitage suggests that gunflints were produced on board the ship. The pewter spoon may have aided in the preparation of cartridges or may have been intended for melting and recycling into shot. Another gunflint and several large chert cores, possibly used to produce additional gunspalls, were found scattered about the site.

Several thousand small-caliber lead round shot were also found on the ship-

Figure 10.7. Brass serpentine side plate typical of later eighteenth-century French trade guns.

wreck. The larger caliber musket (0.45–0.70 cal.) and pistol shot (0.20–0.40 cal.) were gang cast, and many still exhibit sprues and unfinished flashing. The smaller caliber shot (0.02–0.15 cal.) is of the Rupert style and features a characteristic dimple in one side, produced when molten lead was poured through a colander and allowed to drop 1–3 feet into a pool of water (Baird 1973:83–85; Hamilton 1976:35). Lead shot of various diameters was often mixed and used in scatter loads for cannon, blunderbusses, and musketoons.

Although no edged weapons have yet been found, a rectangular whetstone and quarter section of a grinding stone exhibit considerable usage patterns along the edges. These were used to sharpen cutlasses, knives, boarding axes, or other edged weapons and tools.

Scientific, Navigational, and Medical Instruments

Several surveying instruments were recovered in 1998, including a brass universal staff mount, probably used to affix a plane table, transit, or circumferentor to a tripod (Stone 1723:127–28). The staff mount consists of a rectangular pierced plate and socket connected by a universal ball joint. A worm screw rotates an internal gear, which in turn exerts pressure on a leather gasket, thus fixing the ball in place. Decorative setscrews also fix the mount in position. A brass sight for a surveying device was found 3 feet from the pivotal mount; the two pieces likely came from the same instrument. The sight is slotted twice for rough and pinpoint aiming, and the larger slot is bracketed by two holes that would have held a crosshair. A setscrew attaches the sight to an index that, when intact, would have held a second sight with opposing slots. According to Edmund Stone's English translation of M. Bion's eighteenth-century treatise (Stone 1723:128): "There are also two Sights to screw on, or slide up and down the Index, like those belonging to the Index of the Plain-Table; as likewise a Spangle and Socket screw'd on to the back-side of the Circle, for putting the Head of the Staff in."

A brass sector features two logarithmically scaled arms joined at a pivotal hinge (figure 10.8). Used with a pair of compasses, the sector made it possible to

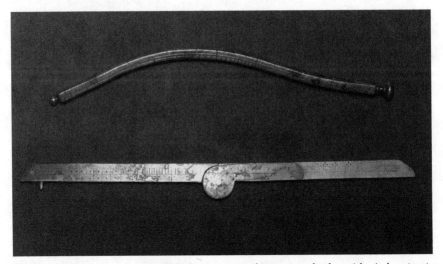

Figure 10.8. Brass instruments including a sector (bottom) and a logarithmic bar (*top*). These valuable instruments were left on the abandoned vessel.

solve problems involving proportions instrumentally (Waters 1958:417). Although no numbers are present, recessed dots or needle holes in sets of two, three, or four bracket some of the line spaces. A line of English inches (2.54 cm) occurs on the inside edge of one arm, while the back edge of both arms when opened is divided evenly into eight French inches (2.75 cm); the first block of both scales is further divided into twelve increments. A small set pin ensures that the arms line up when the instrument is closed.

Logarithmic scales also occur on three out of four faces of a brass bar surmounted by decorative finials on both ends. Each of the scales is numbered by fives; two from 0 to 24, and the third from 0 to 60. A six-pointed star is stamped near the end of the bar. Although outwardly resembling several known instruments—such as gunners' tally sticks and daggers, used to calculate shot and bore diameters, and Gunter's scale (De Maisonneuve 1992:21), which compares line of numbers (0–10), sine (0–90), and tangent (0–45)—this artifact is not an exact match to any and may represent an altogether different instrument.

A flat, brass key-like object pierced at one end resembles an identification tag for a survey chain. Survey chains typically consisted of steel links 12 inches in length; each fifth, sixth, or tenth link is marked with a tag held in place by a small metal ring. A rolled brass tube with a square brass rod soldered along the seam has so far avoided identification.

Navigational instruments from the Beaufort Inlet site include a set of brass dividers that still operate at the pivotal hinge. A sounding lead engraved "XXI" (21 pounds) and two smaller lead weights, both carved with a bladed tool, have been recovered. Though similar to fishing weights, both of the smaller weights

Figure 10.9. French-made pewter urethral syringe. This is the only positively French artifact from the shipwreck site.

feature hollowed bases typical of most sounding leads and may well have been
used to determine depth and bottom characteristics in shallow water. There is
also the possibility that these weights were used as counterbalances for scales or
plumb bobs for surveying instruments.

A urethral syringe with curved funnel tip was designed for the administration
of mercury to treat venereal diseases (figure 10.9; Rule 1982:192–93). Electron
microprobe analysis of residue recovered from the interior of the syringe revealed
a high concentration of mercury (10,000 parts per million) along with pewter
corrosion products (Craig et al. 2001:45). The plunger ring features two marks,
the first consisting of the letter "P" below back-to-back "C"s surmounted by a
crown. Historical sources reveal that French pewterers were required to stamp
their wares with a quality mark and place of origin, beginning in 1643. A
crowned "P" identifies pewter originating in Paris, while the two "C"s back-to-
back are indicative of "common quality" (*étain commun*) French pewter (Cotterell 1972:50; Riff 1972:76–77; Stará 1977:19). The second mark on the
plunger ring features the letter "P" (again for Paris) beneath unidentified maker's
initials, perhaps a date, and a crown.

A brass apothecary nesting weight and medicine bottleneck fragment with
cork still in situ were also found on the site.

Personal Effects

Personal effects recovered from the shipwreck include a kaolin clay pipe stem
fragment (bore diameter 2.8 mm), intact and partially intact pipe bowls that have
yet to be removed from concretion, a brass sail needle, a wooden bead, and a
gold-plated silver button back or spangle (figure 10.10). Three brass 1-inch
straight pins were found within a concretion that also contained a fragment of
stitched fabric, and four similar pins were removed from the cannon C-4 concretion. The pins feature straight shanks that taper to a point and a head fashioned
from a second piece of wire wrapped around the shank and flattened into a

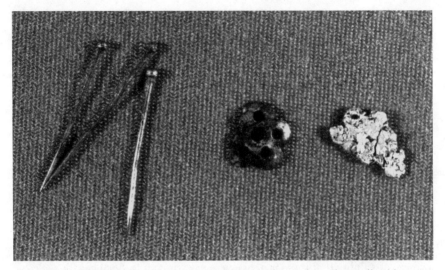

Figure 10.10. Personal effects: brass pins, a silver-plated spangle, and a small gold nugget.

button. Straight pins and other sewing instruments are often found on archaeological sites and do not necessarily represent gender distinctions (Hill 1995:90; Noël Hume 1982:254).

I found approximately 100 natural gold flakes, small nuggets, and crystals weighing 2 g in a concentrated area in the southern transect. Additional nuggets were found in sediments beneath the wooden hull structure. Analysis of eight flakes shows the interiors to be between 65 and 91 percent gold, with impurities consisting of silver and mercury. The surfaces are nearly 100 percent pure gold, and this differential layering is typical of grains found in stream placer deposits (Craig et al. 2001:45–47). Gold in this form does not occur naturally off the North Carolina coast, so its association with the shipwreck is undisputed.

Food Preparation and Storage

Two pewter plates have been recovered from the site, and two additional plates remain attached to cannon C-16 on the seafloor (figure 10.11). The first plate was found in test unit 1, level 2, and is 9½ inches in diameter. "LONDON" is stamped centrally on the base near a secondary mark featuring a crowned Tudor Rose within a London crest and a circular mark that exhibits the faded letters "GE." A set of four hallmarks stamped on the upper, single-reeded rim includes a rampant lion, a leopard's face, a unicorn head, and the initials "GH." Hallmarks were intended to identify the maker and give an official appearance to pewterware (Kerfoot 1924:188–89). This plate has been attributed to George Hammond, a craftsman known to have worked in London, beginning in 1693. Hammond was made steward of the Worshipful Company of Pewterers in 1709

Figure 10.11. Pewter charger and plate.

(Cotterell 1985:225), and his mark also occurs on several pewter basins recovered from the wrecked English slaver *Henrietta Marie*, lost off Key West, Florida, in 1700 (Mel Fisher Maritime Heritage Society 1995:56).

A second single-reeded pewter plate was found sitting within a fragmented pewter charger. The plate is 9⅜ inches in diameter and features basal marks with the word "LONDON," a London and Tudor Rose secondary mark, and the partial name of "[GEO]RGE HAMM[OND]." Beside his name is his symbol, a flexed arm wielding a short sword or dagger.

Two pewter dishes and three pewter chargers in various states of preservation have been recovered from the wreck, all differing in diameter and the nature of the markings. A single-reeded dish 17¼ inches in diameter was found beneath the muzzle of cannon C-12. It is the only piece of flatware recovered from the wreck that exhibits scratch marks indicative of use-wear. The base is stamped with the word "LONDON" within a sunken cartouche and illegible touch and secondary marks. An unusual line of square fastener holes penetrates the well of this dish from both directions. The function of these holes remains undetermined, though they clearly suggest a secondary function for this serving vessel. Analysis of the corrosion product revealed the presence of romarchite (SnO), a mineral not often reported in the archaeological record and perhaps only occurring on deteriorating pewter in submerged environments (Craig et al. 2001:44; Dunkle et al. 2001:A128).

The most degraded dish found on the site is 16⅜ inches in diameter. It was discovered beneath an accumulation of rigging elements (deadeye strops and chain-plates) in the middle of the site. Although no maker's marks are evident, the letters "IY" are stamped on the upper single-reeded rim. The letters probably represent the initials of the owner of the dish.

The first charger found on the wreck was situated beneath cannon C-2's cascable in test unit 1, level 2. The charger is 18½ inches in diameter and is stamped on the base with George Hammond's mark, the third of seven pieces of pewter flatware recovered from the wreck bearing his touch. The broad, single-reeded rim features four hallmarks: a rampant lion, a leopard's face, and two unidentified initials.

Another charger is 20¼ inches in diameter; despite a small puncture hole created by a sharp piece of green glass, it is the least damaged of the seven flat-ware objects recovered thus far. The underside of the broad triple-reeded rim exhibits the word "LONDON" bracketed by two circular marks, one identifying the maker (though it is not legible), and the other a London secondary mark. A rampant lion and two unidentified hallmarks are stamped on the marly, as is the owner's monogram "B^{S}A" arranged in a triad. This arrangement denotes a man with a given name beginning with "B," his spouse with a given name starting with "A," and the surname beginning with "S." A search of officers and crewmen of vessels captured by Blackbeard, as well as residents of Charleston, has not yet revealed a couple matching these initials (South Carolina 1983:225, 237).

A single-reeded charger 22 inches in diameter was found between cannon C-17's breech and cannon C-18's muzzle. Concretions attached to the charger's rim contained impressions of coarse fabric, possibly remains of packing material. The base is stamped with the name "IO. STILE" within a sunken cartouche. Stile's name appears again above a feathered crest bracketing an eagle clutching a snake. His hallmarks (a rampant lion, a leopard's face, and an eagle atop a snake) are also stamped on the base. Hallmarks were moved from the marly to the bases of flatware early in the eighteenth century as single-reeded forms gradually replaced triple-reeded styles (Cotterell 1985:51; Peal 1971:107–8). "LONDON" is also stamped on the charger's base near a crowned Tudor Rose dating from 1649–94 (Gwynn-Jones 2001). Stiles produced pewterware in London beginning in 1689 (Cotterell 1985:315), and the royal cipher was no longer used after Mary's death in 1694, thus establishing a five-year time frame (1689–94) for the charger's date of manufacture (figure 10.12).

Three isolated pewter fragments found on the site contain somewhat diagnostic features that allow vessel form determinations. A single-reeded charger rim section is 2⅛ by 1³/₁₆ inches, averaging ⁷/₁₆ inch in thickness, with a projected diameter of approximately 22 inches. Another pewter fragment (6⅜ by 2⁹/₁₆ inches) represents the bouge portion of the vessel that connects the rim to the well of a deep charger or shallow basin. A third fragment also represents the bouge between the rim and well of a shallow charger.

Figure 10.12. John Stiles and London marks on the back of a pewter charger.

The partial remains of a pewter spoon were found in a concretion that appeared to consist of a wooden box in which gunflints and lead shot were also kept. The spoon's handle is lozenge in cross-section and is bent (perhaps intentionally) near its slightly flaring end. A short rattail attaches the handle to the remnants of a circular bowl. Cast in two-piece molds, rattail pewter spoons were inexpensive and easy to mass-produce during the eighteenth century (Moore 1987:10–16; Noël Hume 1982:183). The back of the handle or interior of the bowl was often stamped with the maker's or guild mark. Unfortunately, this specimen is too fragmented to determine its origin or intended use.

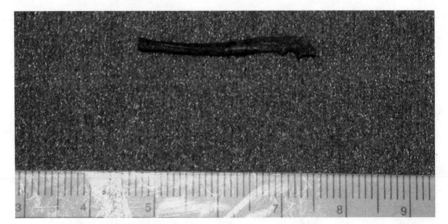

Figure 10.13. Rat ulna.

Two intact green glass onion bottles were found adjacent to one another between two cannon. Several additional necks and bases from similar wine bottles
have also been recovered, along with fragments of square, case gin bottles. When
compared with Noël Hume's (1982:64) colonial Virginia typology, the wine
bottles most nearly match those dated to 1710. Several intrusive nineteenth-
century bottle fragments were also found on the wreck.

To date, the ceramic assemblage from the Beaufort Inlet site includes two tin-
glazed, red-bodied faience rim sherds, a small piece of majolica, five pieces of
salt-glazed stoneware (including the base of a Rhenish jug), olive jar body sherds,
and several rim, base, and handle fragments from one or more large red-bodied
earthenware oil jars. When intact, the jars would have resembled several recovered from colonial Virginia that date to the early eighteenth century (Noël Hume
1982:143). A nineteenth-century ginger beer bottle was also recovered from the
site.

The majority of provisions appear to have been stored in wooden barrels or
casks. Hundreds of iron bands occur around the site, many in stacks of twenty or
more. The large quantities of associated hoops suggest that the barrels were
unassembled and the hoops bundled for easier storage. No wooden staves or
barrelheads have yet been identified.

Two-dozen well-preserved animal bones have so far been found on the shipwreck. Most are long bones, ribs, and skull fragments from immature pigs and
perhaps represent living animals kept on board the ship for food. Two cattle
bones featuring cut marks also derive from foodstuffs (White 1999). The right
ulna of a rat reflects an unwanted guest on the ship (figure 10.13), while several
bones from marine fish, reptiles, and mammals are likely intrusive to the site but
were collected for further identification.

Conclusion

Analysis of the archaeological and artifactual data has failed to provide definitive evidence for the identification of the Beaufort Inlet shipwreck site. Circumstantial evidence amounts to stating that the wreck is *Queen Anne's Revenge* because it meets the following criteria (Lawrence and Wilde-Ramsing 2001:9):

- the wreck dates to the appropriate period,
- the wreck is located where that vessel is known to have grounded,
- the wreck represents a heavily armed vessel, and
- there are no other candidates meeting the above criteria.

Unfortunately, circumstantial evidence alone does not warrant a positive identification.

Date

Many artifacts recovered from the Beaufort Inlet shipwreck date the site to the first half of the eighteenth century. A bronze bell dated 1709 and a cast-iron cannon dated 1713 establish a *terminus post quem* for the site. Ceramics and glassware fit within dated typologies, pewterware was produced by craftsmen known to have worked in London from the 1690s to 1720s, a musketoon barrel was proofed between 1672 and 1702, and surveying instruments compare exactly with a treatise published in 1723 (Lusardi 2000:66). If the markings on cannon C-3 represent a date, however, the *terminus post quem* is advanced to 1730, over a decade after the loss of *Queen Anne's Revenge*.

Location

By superimposing historical charts, researchers have determined that the Beaufort Inlet shipwreck is located on the edge of the offshore bar near the entrance to the early eighteenth century channel (Wells and McNinch 2001:17). The site location corresponds with historical accounts of the loss of *Queen Anne's Revenge*. According to Captain Ellis Brand of HMS *Lyme*, for example: "On 10 June or thereabouts a large pyrate Ship of forty Guns with three Sloops in her company came upon the coast of North Carolina ware they endeavour'd To goe in to a harbour, call'd Topsail Inlett, the Ship Stuck upon the bar at the entrance of the harbour and is lost; as is one of the sloops" (Brand 1718). David Herriot, who sailed with Blackbeard, also deposed that "the said Thatch's ship *Queen Anne's Revenge* run a-ground off of the Bar of Topsail Inlet" (1719:45).

   Ten other eighteenth-century vessels are known to have been lost in the area of Cape Lookout and Bogue Banks (Wilde-Ramsing 1998:57–58). The Beaufort Inlet shipwreck site is located along busy trade routes, adjacent to a navigable inlet and in an area with extensive maritime history. Several wrecks have been found in close proximity, and nine cannon, numerous anchors, and rigging elements from another unidentified early eighteenth century ship occur only a few miles west of the Beaufort Inlet site. I discovered an intact early eighteenth century olive jar on another ballast heap located inside Beaufort Inlet north of Bogue Banks (Tidewater Atlantic Research 1998:19–23). In addition to *Queen Anne's Revenge*, *Adventure*, *El Salvador*, *Susannah*, *Freedom*, an unknown brig, and the sloop *Betsy* all wrecked near Beaufort Inlet before 1772 and thus are all potential candidates. Wilde-Ramsing (1998:58) ruled these vessels out, stating all were smaller, lightly armed merchant ships, though historical research has failed to produce arms manifests or structural descriptions for any of these vessels with the exception of *El Salvador*.

Armament

The existing hull structure, rigging elements, quantity of ballast, and ground tackle represented in the archaeological remains suggest a ship of light construction with perhaps as few as two masts. The number and the diversity of the cannon indicate a heavily armed vessel, though the overall cannon count falls considerably short of the number reported to be on *Queen Anne's Revenge*. The French slaver *Concorde* was originally outfitted with fourteen to sixteen guns before Blackbeard increased the vessel's complement to as many as forty cannon. According to Henry Bostock (1717), master of the sloop *Margaret* captured by Blackbeard on December 5, 1717, *Queen Anne's Revenge* was mounted with thirty-six guns. Walter Hamilton's (n.d.) deposition claims that "the ship say some has twenty two others say she has twenty six guns mounted but all agree that she can carry forty." With only twenty-two confirmed cannon on the site, questions arise as to the location of the remaining eighteen guns.

Claims that *Queen Anne's Revenge* was the most heavily armed ship in the New World during the eighteenth century (Stewart 2000:11) are grossly under-researched. A sampling of Spanish vessels, for example, shows that many of the 1715 Spanish plate fleet ships were armed with substantial numbers of cannon. The *Nuestra Señora del Carmen* (72 guns), *Nuestra Señora de la Regla* (50 guns), French warship *Grifón* (40 guns), and the fleet's *Almiranta* (54 guns) all outnumbered *Queen Anne's Revenge* (Burgess and Clausen 1982:9). The quicksilver galleon *Nuestra Señora de Guadalupe* (1724) was armed with 74 cannon (Smith 1988:85–90). The three largest vessels of the 1733 New Spain fleet, *El Rubí*, *El Gallo Indiano*, and *El Infante*, each carried 60 guns, while 15 merchant vessels attached to the same fleet were each armed with 20–36 cannon (Johnson 1733; McIver 1733). *Nuevo Constante* (1766) boasted a complement of 22 guns, 18 of which were eight-pounders (Pearson and Hoffman 1995:21).

The fact that all five of the Beaufort Inlet site's recovered cannon are somewhat different from each other does not necessarily constitute a piracy material culture. Diverse assemblages of cannon are not uncommon on ships, especially during times of war, when captured ordnance was put to use (Munday 1998:12). Merchant vessels, in particular, were often armed with antiquated guns from a variety of sources. Because England and Sweden exported such large quantities of cast-iron cannon, the presence of guns from either country does not help to identify the nationality of the ship (Brown 1997:104; Peterson 1969:62). A variation in cannon size does not necessarily indicate different sources; shipboard guns could range considerably in size and type, each requiring its own shot and powder charge (Phillips 1986:144). Many eighteenth-century royal warships were equipped with dozens of guns of varying sizes (Howard 1979:207–14). British Gun Establishment records from 1716, for example, list six-pounders ranging from 6 feet in length up in increments of 6 inches to 9 feet in length (Howard 1979:212; Peterson 1969:42).

Contrary Evidence

No objects have been found that identify the Beaufort Inlet wreck by name or nationality. The majority of artifacts that can be attributed to particular countries are English. Two, possibly three, of the five recovered cannon are English; one is Swedish; and one is undetermined. All of the pewter chargers, dishes, and plates are English. The musketoon barrel is English. Only the syringe is French. It seems improbable that of the thousands of artifacts recovered from a French slaver, only one single item can be definitively identified as being French.

The presence of a Spanish bell on the site is also intriguing. It is not inscribed with the name *Concorde* or *Queen Anne's Revenge* or the name of any of the known prizes that Blackbeard captured prior to running aground in Beaufort Inlet. Seldom were bells used on more than one vessel, each being made for a particular ship (Wede 1972:6); so it is not likely that the bell belonged to Blackbeard's flagship. The date on the bell (1709) also does not correspond with the *Concorde*'s date of building.

Pewter flatware that was part of the ship's stores was occasionally stamped with the initials of the vessel to which it was assigned. A plate from the British slaver *Henrietta Marie* (1700), for example, has "HM" stamped on the base (Mel Fisher Maritime Heritage Society 1995:56; McNair-Lewis 1992:17; Sullivan 1994:67), and a plate from the pirate vessel *Whydah* (1717) features the initials "WG" (Hamilton et al. 1992:370; McNair-Lewis 1992:17). None of the Beaufort Inlet pewterware has the initials "LC" (for *La Concorde*) or "QAR" (for *Queen Anne's Revenge*).

The absence of slave trade goods should also be evaluated. Pewter jugs, basins, and tankards were often exported from Europe and exchanged for slaves, gold, and ivory in West Africa (Hatcher and Barker 1974:268–69; Sullivan 1994:60). Sources report that at times the market was inundated with pewterware, and leftover trade goods remained on board slavers for the eventual return to Europe (Barbot 1746:459–60). Dozens of pewter basins, tankards, bottles, and spoons (packed inside a pewter flagon), for example, were recovered from the slaver *Henrietta Marie*. This vessel was lost in the western Florida Keys after it had traded its cargo of slaves for New World products such as sugar, tobacco, cotton, and logwood in Jamaica (Shaughnessy 1995:49–50; Sullivan 1994:42, 60–67). Substantial quantities of leftover trade goods, including tens of thousands of glass beads, lead mirror frames, and iron bar stock, were also found on *Henrietta Marie*. *Whydah* was also a slaver before being captured by the pirate Sam Bellemy. It eventually sank in a storm off Cape Cod in November 1717. A large collection of leftover trade goods for the African market was found on this ship as well (Hamilton et al. 1992). *Queen Anne's Revenge* was originally a French slaver that operated along routes similar to those of *Henrietta Marie* and *Whydah*, though not a single trade item has yet been identified on the Beaufort Inlet wreck site.

Objects reported taken in depositions by Henry Bostock and others do not occur on the site. Where are the medical instruments from the French surgeon's kits or those received as ransom in Charleston? Where are the navigational instruments reportedly taken from various prizes? Where is the silver plate reported by Bostock (1717)? If these objects were removed from *Queen Anne's Revenge* prior to its abandonment, why were so many valuables left behind? Many of the cannon, particularly the smaller guns, could easily have been salvaged. The idea of a pirate leaving small arms and ammunition on a grounded vessel is perplexing, yet many abandoned items occur in the archaeological record. How does one explain the presence of a 24-pound cannonball, far larger than any of the ordnance on site? Why were gold nuggets and gold dust left on the ship? Why were valuable instruments and pewterware abandoned? If the ship was intentionally grounded, as many accounts in the *Tryals of Major Stede Bonnet* attest (Bonnet 1719), how does one explain the presence of a kedging anchor set in a position to assist the vessel off the sandbar? If Blackbeard sailed *Queen Anne's Revenge* for any length of time in semitropical waters without careening, why is the sheathing found on site without any teredo damage?

Although the identity of shipwreck 31CR314 cannot yet be positively established, there is considerable reasonable doubt for its identification as Blackbeard's flagship. If it is indeed *Queen Anne's Revenge*, the artifact assemblage does not reflect in any way a distinctly piratical material culture. The Beaufort Inlet shipwreck can be considered indistinguishable from any contemporary heavily armed merchant vessel trading in the Americas during the first half of the eighteenth century.

All figures are by Wayne R. Lusardi unless noted otherwise.

11

Going to See the Varmint

Piracy in Myth and Reality on the Ohio and Mississippi Rivers,
1785–1830

Mark J. Wagner and Mary R. McCorvie

Tales of pirate attacks on late eighteenth and early nineteenth century flatboats and keelboats have long formed part of Ohio and Mississippi River Valley folklore. Issuing forth from remote hideouts located along these two rivers, pirates such as Colonel Plug, Captain Samuel Mason, and the murderous Harpe brothers reportedly plundered an untold number of passing river craft (Ashe 1808; Flint 1830a, 1830b; Hall 1828). The folklore regarding river pirates continued to grow into the twentieth century (Botkin 1955:204–8; Coates 1930; Rothert 1924), with colorful but highly inaccurate depictions of Ohio River pirates in widely popular films such as *Davy Crockett and the River Pirates* (1956) and *How the West Was Won* (1962).

The river pirate legend reached its cinematic peak in the *How the West Was Won*, in which fictional pirate Colonel Jeb Hawkins robbed and murdered passing river travelers from his hideout at Cave-in-Rock, a large natural cave on the Ohio River. In the famous pirate scene from this film, Hawkins (played by Walter Brennan) lures mountain man and trapper Linus Rawlings (Jimmy Stewart) into the cave by pretending that he has a "varmint . . . [like] no man in these parts has ever seen before" imprisoned in a pit in the cave. When the hapless Rawlings goes into the cave "to see the varmint," he is stabbed in the back and thrown into the pit by the pirates; fortunately he escapes and vanquishes Hawkins and his gang in a violent fight on the riverbank in front of the cave.

The power of the river pirate legend has continued to the present day, as illustrated by a recent article in a folklore magazine regarding the discovery of an early nineteenth century flatboat found eroding out of the banks of the Ohio River in southern Illinois (figure 11.1).

This wreck, which to our knowledge represents the first remains of a flatboat yet discovered along the Ohio or Mississippi rivers, was interpreted by its discov-

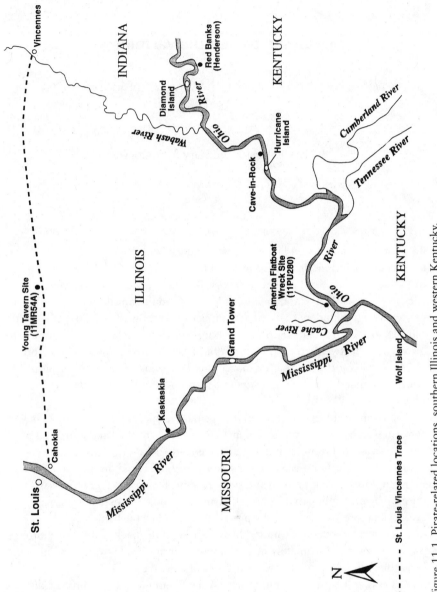

Figure 11.1. Pirate-related locations, southern Illinois and western Kentucky.

Figure 11.2. *America* flatboat wreck, summer 2002, following removal of fill.

erer within the context of Ohio River pirate folklore as representing the remains of a boat plundered by the legendary pirate Colonel Fluger or "Plug" (Schwegman 2000).

Subsequent investigation of this wreck by Southern Illinois University Carbondale (SIUC) archaeologists revealed that this flatboat (which we named the *America* after a nearby early nineteenth century town of the same name) most likely sank as the result of an accident (figure 11.2; Wagner 2003).

The suggestion that the *America* had been attacked by pirates, however, led us to investigate the extent to which piracy actually existed along the lower Ohio and Mississippi rivers ca. 1785–1830. Was it indeed possible that the remains of pirate-looted boats might be found along the shores of these two rivers? We present the results of our research in this chapter, starting with an examination of the types of people, vessels, and cargoes that traveled along the Ohio and Mississippi River during the late eighteenth and nineteenth centuries. This provides a historic context for the results of the archaeological documentation of the *America* shipwreck and the evidence for the existence of piracy along the Ohio and Mississippi rivers. We examine in detail the career of Captain Samuel Mason, a man long identified in folklore as a notorious river pirate. We use these historic and archaeological data to examine the archaeological implications of river piracy. Finally, we consider the problem of the recognition of the archaeological remains of pirate-looted vessels along the Ohio and Mississippi rivers.

Historic Context

The Ohio and Mississippi rivers represent the two largest rivers of eastern North America. From its headwaters in Minnesota, the Mississippi flows southward for over 2,300 miles before draining into the Gulf of Mexico. The Monongahela and Allegheny rivers combine at Pittsburgh, Pennsylvania, to form the Ohio, which flows southwest for almost a thousand miles before draining into the Mississippi at present-day Cairo, Illinois. These two rivers have represented major transportation routes for the movement of people, goods, and ideas throughout eastern North America for thousands of years (Muller 1986). The rivers retained their importance during the colonial period, as French, British, and Native Americans traveled the lengths of these two rivers in canoes, bateaux, galleys, barges, and other vessels. New Orleans, located near the mouth of the Mississippi River on the Gulf Coast, became the entrepôt for goods produced in the interior as early as 1702 (Wagner and McCorvie 2003).

The Louisiana country became a Spanish possession at the end of the Seven Years War in 1763. During this same period thousands of British colonists began establishing settlements in the upper Ohio River Valley near present-day Pittsburgh (Dunbar 1915:268–70). The Ohio River became a natural migration route for immigrants bound to the present-day states of Kentucky, Ohio, Indiana, and Illinois, who descended the river in large boxlike flat bottomed boats variously called "flatboats," "Kentucky boats," "arks," and "family boats" (figures 11.3 and 11.4).

Convoys of such one-way boats, sometimes containing several hundred people, descended the Ohio, carrying emigrant families, their goods, and animals to new homes in the west.

Flatboat cargoes consisted of every type of item produced in the Ohio and Mississippi Valleys, including flour, corn, wheat, potatoes, tobacco, fruit, whiskey, beans, and onions as well as live animals such as horses, cattle, pigs, sheep, and chickens. Flatboats carried manufactured goods such as brooms, buckets, glass, farm machinery, lumber, and coal (Scheiber 1969:277–79). Others carried human cargoes in the form of African-American slaves intended for sale in the lower Mississippi Valley (Anonymous 1806). Early nineteenth century flatboat operators who successfully reached New Orleans or other downriver ports sold their cargoes and boats for whatever the market would bear then traveled overland along the Natchez Trace back to their homes in the Ohio Valley. Extending from Louisiana on into Mississippi and Tennessee, the Natchez Trace was little more than a dirt path that stretched for hundreds of miles through the thinly populated interior lands of the Mississippi Valley.

Thousands of flatboats descended the Ohio and Mississippi River annually from the late eighteenth century to the start of the Civil War. Flatboat travel continued on a reduced scale on both rivers following the end of the Civil War, with the last recorded voyages to New Orleans taking place in the 1890s. Other

Figure 11.3. Late eighteenth century Ohio River flatboat. Image from Georges-Henri-Victor Collot, *Voyage dans l'Amérique Septentrionale*, 1826.

Figure 11.4. Nineteenth-century emigrant flatboat *Picturesque America*. Image from William Cullen Bryant, *Picturesque America* 1874.

vessel types on the Ohio and Mississippi ca. 1790–1830 included keelboats, bateaux, military barges and galleys, sailing brigs and ships, rafts, and steamboats (which made their first appearance on the Ohio in 1811). Flatboats, however, were by far the most prolific vessel type on the two rivers ca. 1790 to 1830 and probably outnumbered all other vessel types combined in any given year during that period.

Traveling down these two rivers in rudimentary shoebox-shaped boats was an extremely hazardous enterprise that resulted in hundreds, if not thousands, of wrecks over the ca. 130 years of the flatboat era. Natural hazards included submerged and floating trees, rocks, sandbars, collapsing riverbanks, storms, ice floes, earthquakes, whirlpools, treacherous currents, and tornadoes. Cultural factors that resulted in wrecks included inexperienced crews, poor workmanship, attacks by Native Americans, collisions with other vessels, and piracy. Timothy Flint, writing in 1826, gave the impression that innumerable boat wrecks littered the shores of the Mississippi. As he noted: "I do not remember having traversed this river in any considerable trip, without having heard of some fatal disaster to a boat, or having seen a dead body of some boatman . . . The multitude of carcasses of boats, lying at the points, or thrown up high and dry on the wreck-heaps, demonstrate palpably how many boats are lost on this wild . . . river" (Brooks 1968:69).

The *America* Wreck

This wreck represents the partial remains of the stern section of a shell-built edge-joined flat-bottomed vessel that is exposed only when this portion of the Ohio River drops 24 feet below flood stage (figure 11.2). During periods of high water, the wreck is covered by as much as 50 feet of water. The wreck is located approximately 1 mile below the abandoned early nineteenth century town of America, after which the boat is named. Local citizens who discovered the wreck in 2000 received permission from the landowner to excavate the boat (Schwegman 2000). This they did, recovering a suite of early nineteenth century artifacts, including pewter spoons, a redware milk pan, clothing buttons, kitchen utensils, and iron boat tools (figures 11.5 and 11.6).

The discoverers did not record the boat construction in detail, prompting us to undertake this work in 2002, when low water levels once again exposed the wreck (Wagner 2003).

Our work revealed that the *America* represented approximately two-fifths of the very bottom of a pre–Civil War flatboat (figure 11.7).

The now-missing bow section was oriented upstream, indicating that the boat had turned around before it came to rest on the shoreline. Surviving structural elements (all made from oak) included two log chine-girders (called gunwales by early nineteenth century flatboat builders) that formed the sides of the hull, the aft sections of two bow-to-stern stringers, parts of three cross-ties that extended

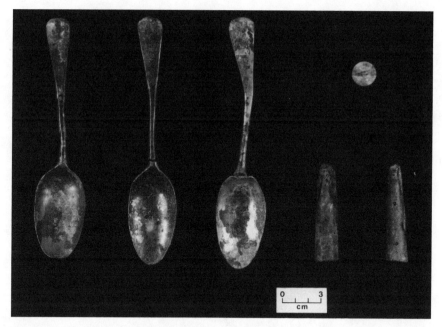

Figure 11.5. Pewter spoons, bone-plated utensil handles, and a pewter button from the *America*.

Figure 11.6. Iron felling ax, caulking iron, and possible iron candleholder from the *America*.

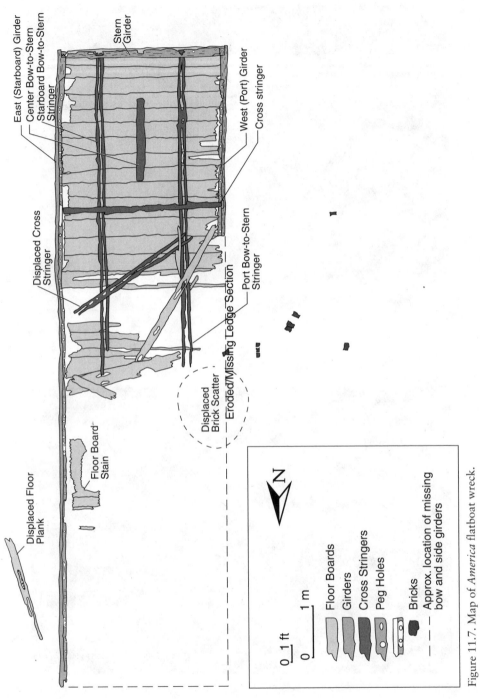

Displaced Floor Plank

Displaced Floor Plank

Floor Board Stain

East (Starboard) Girder
Center Bow-to-Stern Stringer
Starboard Bow-to-Stern Stringer

Stern Girder

West (Port) Girder
Cross stringer

Displaced Cross Stringer

Displaced Brick Scatter

Eroded/Missing Ledge Section

Port Bow-to-Stern Stringer

N

0 1 ft
0 1 m

Floor Boards
Girders
Cross Stringers
Peg Holes

Bricks
Approx. location of missing bow and side girders

Figure 11.7. Map of *America* flatboat wreck.

transversely across the wreck, a stern girder, a stern plank, floor planks, and displaced hand-made bricks that once formed part of a firebox or chimney. The floor planks, which were intact near the stern, became progressively fragmentary toward the forward section of the boat, eventually disappearing altogether. The wreck measured 12 feet (3.7 m) wide by 44.3 feet (13.5 m) long along the starboard gunwale. The starboard gunwale appeared to be virtually intact (possibly missing only a few inches off the forward end), indicating that the boat originally measured about 12 feet wide by 45 feet long.

The two rectangular gunwales consisted of chine-girders split out of a single oak tree. The smooth outboard sides of the gunwales lacked visible axe or saw scars, while the inboard sides contained a ledge (3 inches thick by 4 inches wide) to which the floor planks were attached by using wooden pegs or treenails. In addition, the ledges served as supports for the bases of a series of vertical wooden stanchions (none of which survived), to which the side planks of the hull would have been attached. These stanchions had been placed every 4 feet along the sides of the vessel and every 3 feet along the stern. The spacing of the stanchions was determined on the basis of a series of holes drilled through the sides of the upper parts of the two gunwales and the stern planks. These holes once held wooden treenails inserted through the thinned top portions of the gunwales in order to hold the stanchions in place.

Our research also revealed that the boat builders cut a series of rectangular mortises in the bottoms of the two gunwales and the stern girders at regular intervals. These mortises served to hold the tenon ends of a lattice-work arrangement of longitudinal stringers and cross-ties that held the boat framework together. The longitudinal stringers consisted of roughly trimmed oak saplings or branches 6 inches wide by 4 inches thick, spaced at 3-foot intervals. The aft sections of the port and starboard stringers survived intact, while only a small fragment of the center stringer still remained. The tenon ends of these stringers had been pegged into the bottom of the stern girder using wooden trenails. Pairs of eroded holes in the displaced floor planks in the forward section of the vessel revealed that the stringers also had been pegged to each of the floor planks for the entire length of the vessel. The cross-ties consisted of crudely trimmed oak saplings spaced approximately 11 feet apart. Like the longitudinal stringers, the thinned tenon ends of the cross-ties had been inserted into mortises cut into the bottoms of the gunwales and pegged in place. Unlike the stringers, however, the cross-ties were not pegged to the vessel floor planks, which would have severely weakened whichever floor planks the individual cross-ties extended along.

The wreck contained the remains of 25 floor planks and a single stern plank. Each plank measured approximately 11 feet 10 inches long, 12 inches wide, and 1 inch thick. The boat builders had laid the ends of the floor planks into rabbets (4 inches wide by 1 inch deep) cut into the inboard sides of the two gunwales. The depth of the rabbet cuts combined with the 1-inch thickness of the floor planks created a flush bottom across the entire width of the boat. Two holes spaced 4 to

6 inches apart then were drilled through the end of each plank into the gunwale ledge bottoms. Wooden pegs inserted within these holes completed the connection of the plank floor to the gunwales. The stern plank remained the only surviving example of the strakes or rows of oak planks that once formed the sides and ends of the boxlike hull. Similar in size to the floor planks, the stern plank was once pegged to three stanchions set within mortises cut into the rear sides of the stern girders. If the plank sides of the boat measured 6 feet high (a typical dimension for flatboats), six strakes of 1-foot-wide planks would have been required.

The *America* wreck lacked any oar, sweep, or other steering parts. It also contained no interior features identifiable as the remains of a cabin or shelter, with the exception of a brick scatter. When the wreck was first discovered, this brick scatter was located along the port gunwale to the north (forward) and south (aft) of the southern most cross-tie (Schwegman 2000:23). This jumbled scatter extended east from the inboard side of the port gunwale toward the middle of the boat. It is our belief that these bricks once formed part of a brick firebox located within a cabin similar to one sketched by the artist Charles Leseueur in 1828 (Wagner 2003:figure 3.6).

Artifacts included kitchen, clothing, and tool-related items that appear to have represented the personal possessions of the boat crew (figures 11.5 and 11.6). No trace of the boat cargo was recovered, suggesting that these items either floated away during the wreck or were salvaged and removed by the boat crew or passersby. One of the pewter spoons contained an 1801–11 hallmark, indicating that the *America* had to have been constructed no earlier than 1801. In addition, a tree-ring date obtained from one of the boat gunwales returned a date of 1857 (Wagner 2003:94–95). This date was based on a single match, however, and did not exhaust all possible matches within the Ohio River Valley. Based on the recovered artifacts, we feel that this date is too late and that a date range of ca. 1801–30 for the *America* is more likely.

Piracy on the Ohio and Mississippi Rivers, ca. 1785–1830

The initial discoverers of the *America* wreck suggested that it represented the remains of a pirate-looted vessel (Schwegman 2000:25). Historian Michael Allen (1990:83), however, has argued that the danger of piracy along the Ohio and Mississippi rivers in the early 1800s was greatly exaggerated by later popular writers. He notes that he did not find a single firsthand account of a pirate attack on a flatboat, although scattered secondhand historical accounts of bandit attacks on flatboats on the lower Mississippi River prior to 1820 exist (Allen 1991:112–13). Allen (1990:80–81) concluded that a "kernel of truth" must exist beneath the "tangle of folklore and fact" created by later writers regarding pirate attacks on such boats.

While we agree with Allen that the extent of piracy along these two rivers has been greatly exaggerated, it also is clear that pirates *did* operate at various locations along the Ohio and Mississippi rivers prior to 1830. Our research uncovered several firsthand accounts of piracy along these two rivers in court trial transcripts, government correspondence, travel accounts, diaries, and pioneer reminiscences (Anonymous 1817:20–22; Hamilton 1953:93; Mason Trial Transcript 1803). Piracy along these two rivers appears to have started in the late eighteenth century, as the dramatic increase in river traffic to New Orleans made this form of banditry economically profitable. Very little settlement existed along the lower Ohio and Mississippi during this period, with the cities of Louisville, Natchez, and New Orleans being notable exceptions. Instead the rivers flowed through a largely unpopulated countryside broken only occasionally by smaller pioneer settlements and towns. Piracy appears to have largely ended by 1830, as increased settlement in the lower Ohio and Mississippi River valleys led to the formation of state and county governments, courts, and law officers.

The first mention of piracy along the Mississippi River that we are aware of occurs in a 1785 letter from Francisco Cruzat, then Spanish governor of St. Louis, to the Virginia (American) authorities on the Illinois side of the river. Cruzat referred in his letter to "insults and unlucky attacks [on merchant boats] from the rebels and pirates who infect the Mississippi . . . because they did not go down or come up with a convoy" (Alvord 1909:373–74). Cruzat was silent as to the nationality of the "rebels and pirates" infesting the Mississippi, but they may have included American adventurers like Captain Samuel Mason, who began drifting down the Ohio into Kentucky and Illinois following the end of the Revolutionary War. One group of pirates reportedly operated near Grand Tower on the Mississippi River (figure 11.1) until captured by the Spanish in 1788 (Baldwin 1941:117).

In 1789 a pirate attempted to attack a small convoy of American vessels carrying a cargo of tobacco down the Ohio River to New Orleans. The convoy had wintered in Louisville, Kentucky, where a "renegade . . . or decoyer who lived among the Indians and whose job it was to lure boats ashore for the purposes of murder and robbery" had learned the name of the man (Major Samuel Forman) commanding the convoy as well as the type and value of its cargo. The man then preceded down river, where he and a group of Indians attempted to set up an ambush below the mouth of the Tennessee River. Calling to Major Forman by name, the man begged him to pull into shore and rescue him. As the boats began to pull in, the major spotted Indians hiding along the shore and steered back to the center of the river, escaping the ambush (Forman 1888:37). The use of white prisoners or renegades as decoys to lure boats to shore had long formed part of the pattern of warfare between Native Americans and European colonists in the Ohio Valley. What set this particular attack apart from those earlier ones, however, was the leading role played by the "renegade" in planning the attack and his apparent interest in seizing the cargo of the boats rather than just destroying them and their passengers.

Governor Cruzat's and Major Forman's accounts of piracy along the lower

Ohio and Mississippi rivers are given added significance by the fact that both fall within the period (1782 to 1803) when the notorious pirate Captain Samuel Mason operated along these same two rivers. Mason is the only inland river pirate whose career has been documented in detail, primarily due to his having been captured by the Spanish on the lower Mississippi River and tried as a pirate in 1803 (Mason Trial Transcript 1803).

Samuel Mason, more than any other inland river pirate, resembled the "formidable characters . . . [from] the great age of piracy" of the saltwater oceans of the world (Cordingly 1995:xix). Born in 1739 in Norfolk, Virginia, to a respected family, Mason had embarked by the late 1760s on what would be a 40-year criminal career of horse and slave stealing, robbery, counterfeiting, murder, and piracy (Mason Trial Transcript 1803; Rothert 1924:164). By the early 1770s he had moved over the mountains to western Virginia, where he took part in the violent frontier wars between the American Indians and colonial settlers of the upper Ohio River Valley (White 1991:355). A fellow soldier described him as an "ignorant man . . . utterly unfit for any command . . . except [for] being rashly brave, and a good rifleman" (Bancroft 1835:308). Mason proved this assessment correct in 1777, when he led fourteen soldiers into a Shawnee ambush, with Mason himself escaping death only by hiding beneath a fallen tree (Thwaites 1895: 223–24; Thwaites and Kellogg 1912:65).

Mounting debts led Mason to abandon his farm in the upper Ohio River valley in the mid-1780s for the Holston River settlements along the Virginia-Tennessee border. Accompanied by a gang of "several worthless louts . . . [none of whom] were known to work," Mason and his family angered the well-known frontier leader General John Sevier by stealing items from slaves (Draper n.d.a:313). Ordered out of east Tennessee by Sevier, Mason and his gang, including a notorious killer by the name of Bassett who was to remain with Mason until his death in 1803, drifted into southwestern Kentucky in the late 1780s. Mason later bragged that Bassett was the "greatest robber of horses and negroes" that he had ever known and that over the years he had furnished Bassett and another outlaw with all they needed to go on "campaign[s] . . . [to] steal horses, negroes, and everything else" in return for part of the profits (Mason Trial Transcript 1803:33–34).

By 1791 Mason and his followers had set up shop at Red Banks (now Henderson), Kentucky. Red Banks at this time was a pioneer settlement of a few houses, taverns, and stores located along the Ohio River on the southern edge of the American frontier (figure 11.1). The location of Red Banks directly on the Ohio River enabled Mason and his followers to broaden the scope of their criminal activities to include piracy. Witnesses at Mason's 1803 trial testified that while at Red Banks he had been involved in the disappearance of a flatboat and its captain in 1791. Another witness told the court that he had heard a slave woman belonging to Mason recount how in 1798 "on the river Cumberland [Mason had made her help] to drag to the river a man that Samuel Masson [*sic*] had killed to have [his] valise in which was plenty of money" (Mason Trial Transcript 1803:106). One of Mason's own gang members also testified that Mason had bragged that together with Basset and another man he had "killed [people] on the . . . Cumberland and that . . . [the three of them] robbed [people there] and divided together the prizes" (Mason Trial Transcript 1803:33).

Mason's activities made Red Banks notorious within a few short years following his arrival. A traveler who stopped at the town in 1794 commented on its bad reputation, calling it a "refuge for horse thieves, rogues, and outlaws [including Samuel Mason] . . . I was informed that many boats had been robbed by the Red Banks people and many persons swindled out of their cargoes" (Bond 1922:49). In response, the state of Kentucky appointed Revolutionary War veteran John Dunn as constable of Red Banks in 1792. Mason and his gang challenged Dunn's authority in 1795, beating him senseless and throwing his apparently lifeless body over a fence. Tensions between Mason's gang and the more law-abiding elements of the town steadily escalated until Mason's followers murdered Dunn in 1797 (Starling 1887:27, 95). In response, local settlers organized a vigilante-style posse that swept through southwestern Kentucky, killing some bandits and driving others away. Mason and his gang reportedly fled down the lower Ohio,

Figure 11.8. Photograph of Cave-in-Rock, Illinois, ca. 1950, by Southern Illinois historian John Allen. Used by permission of Special Collections, Morris Library, Southern Illinois University, Carbondale.

Figure 11.9. Pirate-related locations, lower Ohio and Mississippi river valleys.

where they apparently stopped for a short time in 1797 at Cave-in-Rock, a 200-ft-long one-room cave on the Illinois shore (figure 11.8; Audubon 1897:232–33; Corning 1929:22; Blowe 1820:577; Peck 1823:99).

The increased vigilance of law officials in both Illinois and Kentucky appears to have prompted Mason to leave the Ohio River and emigrate to the Spanish lands of the lower Mississippi River Valley in 1800 (figure 11.9).

After assuring Spanish officials that he was only a simple farmer with an undeserved bad reputation, Mason—now known as "Mason of the Woods" or "Father Mason"—and his gang occupied camps in Spanish Louisiana, from

Figure 11.10. Murder of a traveler along the Natchez Trace. Image from Robert M. Coates, *The Outlaw Years*, 1930.

which they launched attacks on American boats and land travelers along the Natchez Trace in Mississippi Territory for the next two years (figure 11.10).

Information regarding Mason's piratical activities during this time is contained in the testimony of one of his gang members, John Sutton, at Mason's 1803 piracy trial. Sutton testified that Mason proposed to him that they "stop [a] few flat boats and beat to death the master of the flat boat—and through [*sic*] them in the bottom of the water, and after to plunder the flat boat . . . [and] then burn the flat boat." They then would take the looted merchandise to dishonest storekeepers in various towns who would give them "half of their worth," while stolen horses could be sold for one-third their actual value. Sutton also testified that the Mason gang sometimes worked in two groups. One group of pirates would pose as legitimate buyers, paying a flatboat captain in cash for his cargo and carrying it away. The other gang members would then stop the boat at a point farther down the river and rob the captain of his cash, leaving him penniless and without a cargo. In another case of subterfuge the pirates pretended to be interested in buying rifles from a flatboat captain but then turned his own guns on him and "pillaged the flatboat" (Mason Trial Transcript 1803:22, 34, 42, 49).

Mason's undoing came as the result of a series of robberies in 1802 in which he attempted to rob the same traveler twice. The would-be victim identified Mason by name, prompting the American governor of Mississippi Territory to offer a reward for his capture (Mattern et al. 1986:224–25). Adding to the alarm, the Spanish governor in New Orleans indicated that he had information that the notorious frontier mass-murderer Wiley or "Little" Harpe was one of the gang (Claiborne 1880:225–27). Accompanied by gang member John Sutton, Mason and his immediate family occupied some empty cabins on the Spanish side of the river in present-day southeastern Arkansas, where they attempted to disguise themselves as farmers. Their alarmed neighbors instead informed the Spanish militia that they believed them to be "Masson [sic] and his band . . . who are always on the bank of the river, of whom every bodies [sic] are complaining to have been attacked by them . . . [including attacks on] several boats." The Spanish surrounded the cabins, capturing Mason and his family on January 13, 1803 (Mason Trial Transcript 1803:1–3).

At a preliminary hearing in New Madrid, Missouri, Mason attempted to clear himself by once again posing as an innocent settler. He could not explain, however, the presence of over $7,000 in bank notes and twenty bundles of "hairs . . . from human creatures . . . that were not cut voluntarily" (that is, scalps) among his possessions. Believing the human scalps to be evidence "of several murders," the court sent the Masons to New Orleans for further investigation (Mason Trial Transcript 1803:91). There the Spanish governor ordered them to be turned over to the American governor in Mississippi, as all of Mason's piratical activities appeared to have taken place on the American side of the river (Baum and Troncoso 1935:54). In March 1803, while being transported up river to Mississippi, Samuel Mason and Sutton overpowered their guards and disappeared into the woods. In response to a reward offered by the American governor for Mason's recapture, Sutton and another gang member killed him and brought his head in to claim the reward. There they were recognized by a flatboat owner as two of the pirates. As a result they received a different sort of reward than they had anticipated. Sutton and the other man were arrested, tried in federal court, found guilty of piracy, and hanged in Greeneville, Mississippi, in early 1804 (Bancroft 1835:309; Claiborne 1880:531; Draper n.d.a.:317–18; Hamilton 1953:93; Rothert 1924:247–51).

Mason's death appears to have largely ended organized piracy along the lower

Ohio and Mississippi rivers. Attacks on travelers continued after this date (Allen 1990:83–84; Baldwin 1941:132); but no one appears to have risen to take Mason's place as the leader of a wide-ranging gang of pirates. Botanist Thomas Nuttall (1819:295–96) reported that prior to 1811 "there existed on the banks of the Mississippi, a very formidable gang of swindling robbers . . . about 80 in number . . . under the direction of two captains . . . usually stationed at the mouth of the Arkansa [sic], and at Stack Island"; this may be a garbled account of Mason's activities a few years earlier. Other post-1803 banditry accounts include one recorded by John James Audubon in his diary during an 1820 flatboat trip down the Mississippi River. During this trip the flatboat captain pointed out a bend in the river where he had found the bodies of two "dead men shot through the head" on a previous voyage (Corning 1929:33). In 1817 a party of flatboat travelers found the body of a man floating in the Mississippi River that showed signs of a violent death. These same travelers were accosted near Walnut Hills on the Mississippi, one of Samuel Mason's old haunts, by three men in a canoe who demanded that they pull over so the men could search their flatboat for a "stolen" dog. Suspecting the men to be up to no good, one of the flatboat crew fired a bullet over their heads, causing the possible pirates to give up the chase (Anonymous 1817:20–22).

Another instance involved James Ford, a dishonest ferry operator and tavern keeper suspected of numerous robberies and murders along the lower Ohio River in the 1820s and 1830s (Rothert 1924:283–306). In 1832 Ford placed an advertisement in an Illinois newspaper, seeking the return of a runaway slave who had "both ears cut off close to his head, which he lost for robbing a boat on the Ohio River" (Anonymous 1943:423). The most famous account of a "late" pirate attack on a flatboat is the one involving future United States president Abraham Lincoln. In 1828, as a young man, Lincoln and a friend took a flatboat down the Mississippi River to New Orleans. Lincoln noted that below Baton Rouge "one night they were attacked by seven negroes with intent to kill and rob them . . . [we] were hurt some in the melee, but succeeded in driving the negroes from the boat, and then 'cut cable' and 'weighed anchor' and left" (Lincoln 1953:62).

Archaeological Implications of River Piracy

Site Types

Despite the historical evidence for piracy in the region, archaeologists have yet to identify a single definite pirate-related archaeological site in either the Ohio or Mississippi River valleys. A 1970s archaeological survey of Cave-in-Rock State Park in Illinois, an area known to have been frequented by Mason in the late 1700s, failed to identify any sites that potentially could be linked to this type of criminal activity (Jon Muller, personal communication, May 15, 2003). Archaeological investigations have yet to be conducted within the low-lying cave itself, which floods on an almost annual basis (figure 11.8). Any cultural deposits associated with Mason and other pirates, even if they could be distinguished from those of other river travelers of the time, may lie deeply buried beneath the layers of river-deposited sediment that cover the floor of the cave.

Documents associated with Samuel Mason indicate that pirate-related sites in the two valleys potentially should include the remains of camps, farms, rural houses, taverns, and stores as well as boat wrecks. In Kentucky the Masons are reported to have occupied camps "at the mouth of Highland Creek" and on Diamond and Hurricane Islands in the Ohio River (figure 11.1), while in the lower Mississippi River they lived at camps on Wolf and Stack Islands (figure 11.9) as well as camps located "along the banks of the river" (Audubon 1897:232; Draper n.d.a.:312; Mason Trial Transcript 1803:1). Mason's predilection for such remote camps was so well known that the Spanish nicknamed him "Mason of the Woods." Occupation of such secluded camps allowed the pirates to watch for passing flatboats, shielded their activities from law-abiding citizens, and made it difficult for law officers to find them. When the Spanish finally did apprehend Mason and his family in 1803, it was because they had left the security of the woods temporarily to occupy a vacant house in a frontier settlement, where their alarmed neighbors immediately reported them to the authorities.

Habitation and commercial sites linked to river piracy include rural houses, taverns, and stores. Both in Tennessee and present-day Arkansas the Masons lived in "abandoned" houses or cabins that they occupied without permission. Mason also may have been living on a farm during the time he lived in Red Banks, Kentucky, in the late 1780s and early 1790, although surviving records simply refer to him as living outside of town. Commercial sites linked to river piracy include frontier taverns and stores, with Samuel Mason himself reportedly operating a tavern while he lived near Pittsburgh in the early 1780s (Rothert 1924:163). The Masons made "the tavern of Nicholas Welsh, a man of bad reputation . . . [their] headquarters when in [the] town [of Red Banks]" in the 1790s (Draper n.d.b.:14). Mason also secretly sold his ill-gotten "plunder" and "prizes" to dishonest frontier merchants such as storekeeper Hugh Glass of Nogales, Mississippi, for one-half to one-third their actual value. The Spanish suspected that Mason had similar arrangements with dishonest merchants in at least five other lower Mississippi Valley settlements (Hatfield 1965:347; Mason Trial Transcript 1803:32, 42).

Caves and rock shelters or overhangs figure prominently in river pirate folklore, although the extent to which they actually were used by such outlaws is unclear. No firsthand accounts, for example, exist of any river travelers encountering Mason or other pirates at Cave-in-Rock (figures 11.1, 11.8). Nor did any of the pioneers interviewed by frontier historian Lyman Draper (n.d.a, n.d.b) in the early 1800s make any reference to Mason having been located at Cave-in-Rock. Numerous river travelers of the 1810–25 period, however, recorded stories prevalent in the lower Ohio at the time that the Masons had occupied Cave-in-

Rock in 1797 (Blowe 1820; Corning 1929:21–22; Peck 1823:99; Schultz 1810: s201). This is the same year that the regulators chased Mason out of Red Banks, Kentucky, and it is indeed likely that he and his gang fled to Cave-in-Rock for a short time. Cave-in-Rock, however, is a highly prominent landmark that was visited by virtually every late eighteenth to early nineteenth century Ohio River traveler. Rather than making such a public place their headquarters, it is more likely that Mason and his followers periodically occupied Cave-in-Rock as one of a series of shifting short-term river camps, similar to the pattern that they later followed in the Mississippi River valley.

Surviving documents consistently refer to the vessels attacked by Mason as "flatboats" or simply "boats" (Draper n.d.a.:313; Mason Trial Transcript 1803). Mason's apparent concentration on attacking flatboats may simply reflect the much greater frequency of this vessel type, as opposed to keelboats, the other most frequent early nineteenth century river boat. Mason also may have been deterred from attacking keelboats due to the difficulty of subduing their larger crews (Baldwin 1941:56–90). The fate of flatboats attacked by Mason varied from being robbed and allowed to proceed on their way to being plundered and burned (Mason Trial Transcript 1803). Diaries kept by early nineteenth century river travelers indicate that wrecked and abandoned flatboats were such common features along the Ohio and Mississippi rivers that passing boats seldom stopped to investigate the cause of their sinking (Anonymous 1806). The Masons may have burned some flatboats after robbing them because these boats may have exhibited clear evidence of pirate attack such as rifled cargo and dead bodies that they wished to disguise. Mason and his gang did murder some river and overland travelers, as clearly evidenced by the twenty human scalps that the Spanish found among their possessions in 1803 as well as by testimony offered at their trial (Mason Trial Transcript 1803).

Material Culture

How does one identify a site occupied by pirates as opposed to nonpirates? As noted above, Mason, his family, and other gang members are known to have used or frequented farms, rural houses, taverns, stores, camps, and caves. But how does one distinguish the archaeological remains of a house lived in by river pirates from one used by law-abiding citizens? Are there distinctive artifact patterns that are characteristic of this type of criminal behavior?

In this section we use two different types of data sets—archival and archaeological—to address these questions. The first consists of two inventories of the material possessions of Samuel Mason, his family, and John Sutton compiled by the Spanish authorities at the time of their capture on January 13, 1803. In combination, these inventories represent a unique source of information on the material possessions of the most notorious band of early nineteenth century river pirates in the lower Ohio and Mississippi River valleys. A party of Spanish militia

Table 11.1. Mason Family Possessions by Functional Category

Clothing	Arms	Personal	Sewing	Transportation
Coats	Lead	Handkerchiefs	Linen cloth	Horses
Shirts	Shot	Razors	Flannel cloth	Horse shoes
Pants	Powder	Leather strop	Calico cloth	Saddles
Shoes	Bullet mold	Comb	Cashmere cloth	Bridles
Socks	Carbine	Soap	Silk cloth	Halters
Waistcoats	Shotguns	Watch	Wool cloth	Girths
Vests	Pistols	Pocket knife	Velvet cloth	Leather ropes
Gloves	Butcher knives	Child's toy	Goat's hair (wool)	Blankets
Silver buckles		Beaded bags	Nankeen cotton cloth	
Leggings		Portmanteaus	Baizin felt cloth	
Child's cloak		Money	Unsewn clothing	
		Human scalps	Thread	
			Buttons	
			Scissors	

Kitchen	Hunting	Tools	Furnishings	Food
Campaign stove	Deer hide	Axes	Clock	Flour
China teapot	Bear skins	File	Blankets	Potatoes
Boiler (tin kettle)	"Cat" skins		Sheets	Corn
Tin cup	Other skins			Cow
Pewter item				Heifer
				Swine
				Salt
				Beans
				Spice

took the Masons by surprise at the "Little Prairie" settlement in present-day northeast Arkansas, capturing them as they attempted to flee on horseback. The Spanish meticulously inventoried the clothing, equipment, and personal belongings of the captured prisoners, even down to the color and pattern of their socks. One of these inventories was completed on January 13, 1803, at the Little Prairie settlement, and the other was made thirteen days later, following the transportation of the prisoners to New Madrid. In addition, the January 26 inventory also includes an estimate of the value of the various items. Slight variances exist between the two lists, because some items such as clothing and cooking equipment were given back to the prisoners for their use while in jail. Nonequine livestock such as cattle, pigs, and chickens also apparently were left behind at the Little Prairie settlement. Finally, the Spanish omitted from the January 26, 1803, inventory several stolen items, including a saddle and two saddle pistols that they intended to send to New Orleans as evidence of the Masons' guilt.

The archaeological data set consists of the artifacts recovered from the Young Tavern (11Mr54) site in southern Illinois (Wagner and McCorvie 1992). The Young Tavern (1813–19) was operated by Samuel Young, a Revolutionary War veteran whose name appears on a list of frontier outlaws masquerading as tavern keepers in southern Illinois in 1818 and 1819 (figure 11.1). The members of the "Goings Gang," headed by William Goings, operated a series of about a half-dozen taverns strung out along the St. Louis–Vincennes Trace or Road, which extended for 150 miles across southern Illinois (Mason 1915:40). Goings and his gang of "land pirates" engaged in criminal activities similar to those of Samuel Mason, including horse and slave stealing, robbery, and the murder of overland travelers. The violence of their crimes steadily escalated until 1819, when a group of regulators captured and whipped several of the gang, after which they were ordered to leave the area. Samuel Young, although reportedly a gang member, was permitted to stay in the county for some unknown reason. We completely excavated the former location of his 1813–19 tavern in 1988 prior to its destruction by a highway realignment project (Wagner and McCorvie 1992:37–43).

We separated the items found in the Mason's possession in 1803 into functional categories, following Stanley South (1977) with some modifications (table 11.1). We then ranked these functional categories by value following Dean Anderson (1994), using value estimates listed on the January 16, 1803, inventory (table 11.2). We would note that the rankings in table 11.2 are skewed somewhat by the fact that the Spanish did not provide value estimates for the kitchen items (stove, kettles, and cup) that they returned to the Masons for their use, farm animals and foodstuffs left behind at the Little Prairie, and items such as the horse pistols and saddle that the Spanish believed to be stolen. We also did not include as part of the personal category the $7,060 that the Masons had in their possession when captured or the twenty human scalps, which have no obvious monetary value.

The information contained on table 11.1 reveals that the Masons were traveling light, with a minimum of belongings at the time of their January 1803 capture. Particularly notable in this regard is the limited range of kitchen items. Notably absent are kitchen items typically found at early nineteenth century American frontier sites, such as ceramic plates, bowls, cups, and other containers; tableware, including forks and spoons; and glass bottles and other containers. Instead, the Masons had only a single portable "campaign" stove, one or two tin kettles or "boilers," one tin cup, a refined earthenware "china" teapot, and a pewter item of unknown type. The arms and personal categories tell a similar story. Although well-supplied with powder, shot, and lead, the Mason party carried a very limited range of weapons. The weapons found on them at the time of their capture consisted entirely of three carbines and shotguns, one of which had a broken stock; three butcher or scalping knives; and two stolen pistols. The three oldest Masons (Samuel and sons John and Thomas) each appear to have carried one scalping knife and a carbine or shotgun, while the two younger sons (18-year-old Samuel Jr., and 16-year-old Magnus) apparently went unarmed. John Sutton (whom the Masons distrusted and tried to shift the blame to for their various crimes at their trial) carried no weapons of any kind.

Table 11.2. Ranking of Mason Family Possessions by Functional Category and Value

Functional Category	Value ($)	Percent
Transportation	470.40	67.81
Clothing	84.50	12.18
Arms	45	6.49
Sewing	38	5.48
Food	25	3.60
Personal	15.80	2.28
Furnishings	12	1.73
Tools	2	0.29
Hunting	1	0.14
TOTAL	693.70	100.00

The men of the Mason party also may have shared various personal items rather than loading themselves down with excess baggage. At the time of their capture they had only one each of the following personal items: a comb, razor, leather razor strop, pocket knife, and watch. The January 26 inventory credits them with owning five razors, indicating either an error in the initial inventory or that their captors gave them additional razors in the intervening two weeks. The Masons carried few tools, having only two small camp axes and a file at the time of their arrest. Transportation items consisted entirely of six horses and their accoutrements: saddles, blankets, bridles, girths, and a set of horseshoes. As with their weapons, the quality of these items as listed in the trial transcript varied, with one horse being "rather old," the bridles listed as "good and bad," and one saddle consisting solely of the wooden frame of a "savage's" or Indian saddle. Their party consisted of seven adults and three children and only six horses, so at least some of the group must have traveled on foot part of the time.

The variety of domesticated animals and foodstuffs in table 11.1 presents a misleading picture of the numbers of these items typically associated with the Masons. Virtually all of the farm animals as well as the corn and flour had been purchased by the Masons following their arrival at Little Prairie on December 31, 1802, as part of an apparent plan to disguise themselves as farmers (Mason Trial Transcript 1803:2, 86, 88). The clothing and sewing categories provide a great deal of information about the appearance of the Mason gang as well as how they obtained their clothes. The presence of linen, nankeen, and woolen cloth; partially finished but unsewn coats, pants, shirts, and waistcoats; and scissors, thread, and numerous buttons among their possessions suggests that Margaret Mason, wife of John Mason, who was also one of the prisoners, made many of their clothes. The quality of some of the cloth—silk, velvet, and cashmere—is atypical of the plain linen, wool, and cotton clothing worn by many early nineteenth century frontier settlers, suggesting that some of it may represent loot from robberies. The Mason men dressed in blue, green, and gray woolen and cloth coats; linen shirts; gloves; leather, nankeen cotton, velvet, and cashmere pants; striped, checkered, and plain nankeen cotton and wool waistcoats and vests; silk and cotton socks; and shoes. Other clothing items included a "Prince Albert"–style coat (a long double-breasted frock coat) and a pair of "leggings" similar to those worn by Native Americans (Mason Trial Transcript 1803:8–11, 81–88).

Ranking of the various functional categories revealed that the transportation category (horses and their equipment) constituted 67.81 percent by value of all items owned by the Masons at the time of their capture (table 11.2).

This high ranking largely is the result of the combined value of their horses, which the Spanish estimated at $380. Even if the horses are omitted, however, the combined value of the horse equipage (blankets, saddles, bridles, girths, and so on) is still higher at $90.40 than the value of any other functional category. The combined value ($122.50) of the clothing and sewing categories indicates that clothing, cloth, and sewing equipment were the next most valuable items owned by the Masons, at 17.66 percent of the value of all functional categories. Arms-related items (a class of artifacts that one intuitively would have expected pirates to own a large number of) represented only 6.49 percent by value of all items owned by the Masons. Putting this in a comparative perspective, the value ($45) of all the weapons owned by the Masons was approximately half the value of their horse equipment ($90.40), a little more than half that of their clothing ($84.50), and only $7 more than the value of their sewing supplies ($38) (table 11.2). The remaining functional categories—furnishings, personal, food, and hunting—comprised a very low combined 7.75 percent of all artifacts owned by the Masons by value. The value of the kitchen-related items, which were given back to the Masons by the Spanish, is unknown; but we doubt that the combined value of these few items could have been more than $25.

The Masons had been at the Little Prairie settlement for less than two weeks prior to their capture by the Spanish on January 13, 1803. Thus we suspect that the items they possessed at that time (table 11.1) are probably more representative of those that they used when living in the woods, moving from camp to camp, rather than when they occupied a house in a rural settlement. Many of these items, particularly clothing, would leave little in the way of archaeological remains. The types of nonperishable remains that we believe potentially might occur at an early nineteenth century pirate-occupied camp are presented in table 11.3. This table assumes that examples of all the artifact types possessed by the Masons in January 1803 (with the exception of domesticated food animals) were used and discarded during the time when such a camp was occupied. Although precise numbers obviously are lacking, it is readily apparent that the transportation, clothing, and sewing categories appear to decrease in importance, while the arms-related category increases. Due to the probable nonpreservation of clothing items and fabric, the clothing and sewing categories would diminish to buttons and buckles as well as scissors and other metal sewing items used in their manufacture. Conversely, the discarding of broken weapons and the casting of lead

Table 11.3. Potential Archaeological Remains of Mason Family Camp by Functional Category

Clothing	Arms	Personal	Sewing	Transportation
Buttons	Melted lead	Razor blades	Buttons	Horse shoes
Buckles	Shot	Comb fragment	Scissors	Saddle parts
Bullet mold	Watch parts		Bridle parts	
	Carbine parts	Knife blade		
	Shotgun parts	Beads		
	Pistol parts	Portmanteau latch		
	Knife blades	Smoking pipes		
	Gun flints			

Kitchen	Tools	Furnishings	Food
Metal stove parts	Ax blade	Clock works	Deer bones
Ceramic teapot sherds	File		Bear bones
Tin scraps			"Cat" bones
Pewter scraps			

bullets cause the arms-related category to rise, due to the increased number of iron and brass gun parts, lead sprue from making bullets, and gun flints present at the site. The food category probably also would rise significantly due to the butchering of wild game and the discarding of their remains on the ground at the camp.

The archaeological remains projected to occur at pirate-occupied camps are strikingly similar to those found at certain Native American–occupied sites of the same period. Archaeological investigations at the Windrose site (11Ka326), an early nineteenth century Potawatomi settlement in northeastern Illinois, recovered many of the same types of artifacts as in table 11.3, including gun parts, lead sprue, gun flints, bullet molds, kaolin pipes, files, metal containers, axes, files, beads, scissors, knife blades, horseshoes, horse bridles and bits, and wild animal remains. Also similar was the very low representation at the Windrose site of Euro-American kitchen-related ceramics and cutlery, such as forks and spoons (Wagner 2001). These marked similarities raise the possibility that in the absence of archival or historical documents specifically identifying a particular location as a pirate camp, such a camp could be misidentified as the remains of a Native American settlement during the historic period. Native American–occupied sites, however, also should exhibit several distinctive characteristics that would serve to identify them as such, including a much lower frequency of clothing buttons and buckles due to use of traditional clothing; presence of handmade stone smoking pipe fragments; occurrence of silver trade ornaments; and the recycling of broken brass and iron kettles into ornaments, tools, and other artifact types (Wagner 2001).

The artifact assemblage projected to occur at camps occupied by river pirates such as the Mason family also is notable for the absence of any type of artifact

Table 11.4. Young Tavern (11Mr54) Site Artifacts by Functional Category

Clothing	Weapons/ Hunting	Personal	Sewing	Transportation
Bone buttons	Gun flints	Smoking pipes	Pins	Hame hook
Metal buttons	Lead shot	Coins	Antler awl	Harness ring
Shoe heel	Lead balls	Marbles		Halter strap bolt
Buckles		Watch part		Horse (bones)

Kitchen	Architecture	Tools	Furnishings	Food/Fauna
Brass kettle	Nails	Hammer	Lamp glass	Cattle
Iron ketttle	Iron lock bolt	Wedge	SW grease lamp	Swine
Cutlery	Iron thumb latch	Hoe	Sheep	
Pot hook	Window glass	Wrench	Chicken	
RFE Plates	Brick	File	Elk	
RFE saucer	Clay daub	Whetstone	Squirrel	
RFE bowls			Deer	
RFE sauce boat			Turkey	
RFE tea pot				
RW jar				
RW pot				
RW pitcher				
RW jug				
SW jug				
Glass bottles				

Source: Data from Wagner and McCorvie 1992.
Note: RFE = refined earthenware ceramics, RW = redware ceramics, SW = stoneware ceramics.

patterning indicative of this type of criminal activity (table 11.3). The two items found on the Masons that confirmed their identity as pirates in the mind of their Spanish captors—$7,060 in paper currency and twenty human scalps—would leave no archaeological remains except in extraordinary circumstances. The high-quality silk, cashmere, and velvet clothing worn by the Masons also would leave little or nothing in the way of remains. As in the case of correct identification of early nineteenth century frontier camps as being Native American or Euro-American in origin (discussed above), it may be impossible to identify a river pirate–occupied site as such in the absence of corroborating documents.

The artifact assemblage from the Young Tavern (11Mr54) also lacks any identifiable archaeological signature of criminal activity (tables 11.4 and 11.5).

Samuel Young and his family operated their 1813–19 pioneer homestead as a "latchstring" tavern, a private home that had no official tavern license, at which travelers might spend the night if the occupants agreed to take them in. Thus the artifact assemblage from the site is largely characteristic of an early nineteenth century southern Illinois pioneer farmstead. The assemblage deviates from that of a typical farmstead in containing a relatively high proportion of refined earth-

Table 11.5. Proportions of Functional Categories, Young Site (11Mr54)

Functional Category	Ceramics	Metal	Glass	Bone/Antler	Stone	Daub/Brick	Total	Percent
Kitchen	1,630	18	381				2,029	52.79
Food/Fauna				1,210			1,210	31.48
Architecture		57	27			231	315	8.20
Transportation		3		166			169	4.40
Furnishings	3		61				64	1.67
Clothing		29		2			31	0.81
Personal	7	2					9	0.23
Tools		8			2		10	0.26
Arms		3			2		5	0.13
Sewing				1			1	0.03
TOTAL	1,640	120	469	1,379	4	231	3,843	100.00

Source: Data from Wagner and McCorvie 1992, p. 364.
Note: Transportation-related faunal remains consist entirely of horse skeleton bones.

enware serving vessels such as pitchers that would have been needed at a tavern. Also unusual for a farmstead of this period was the presence of artificial lighting devices, including grease and other lamps that would have been needed in the evening to provide light for tavern patrons. In contrast to the Mason family possessions, kitchen and food remains were well represented at the Young Tavern, constituting 52.80 percent and 31.49 percent of all artifacts recovered from the site, respectively (table 11.5). If faunal remains are not considered, the proportion of kitchen-related items rises to 82.25 percent, followed by the architectural remains of the Young Tavern at 12.77 percent (table 11.6).

The sole possible indicator of criminal activity at the site, which is extremely tenuous and not conclusive by any means, is the high quality and cost of the refined earthenware ceramics recovered at the site. Comparison of the socioeconomic ranking of the Young site through the use of mean ceramic values derived from both sherd and whole vessel counts revealed that the site ranked higher than eleven nineteenth-century Illinois non–tavern related farmsteads (Wagner and McCorvie 1992:273). Simply put, all this means is that tavern operator Samuel Young had more disposable income to spend on the purchase of higher quality and more expensive consumer goods than did contemporary and slightly later Illinois farm families. It does not indicate whether he and his family acquired the money to purchase these items through the slightly illegal operation of an unlicensed tavern or through the more violent criminal operations of the outlaw gang of which they are reported to have been members (Mason Trial Transcript 1803).

Conclusions

Pirates clearly did attack and rob flatboats and possibly other vessels along the Ohio and Mississippi rivers during the late eighteenth and early nineteenth cen-

Table 11.6. Proportions of Functional Categories, Young Site (11Mr54), Excluding Fauna

Functional Category	Ceramics	Metal	Glass	Bone/Antler	Stone	Daub/Brick	Total	Percent
Kitchen	1,630	18	381				2,029	82.25
Architecture		57	27			231	315	12.77
Furnishings	3		61				64	2.59
Clothing		29		2			31	1.26
Personal	7	2					9	0.36
Tools		8			2		10	0.41
Arms		3			2		5	0.20
Transportation		3					3	0.12
Sewing				1			1	0.04
TOTAL	1,640	120	469	3	4	231	2,467	100.00

turies. Thus the remains of pirate-looted boats potentially still could exist as shipwrecks along the banks of these two rivers. It may be extremely difficult archaeologically to distinguish the wreck of a flatboat that sank due to pirate attack from one that sank due to natural causes. The only firsthand account of the methods used by river pirates to attack flatboats comes from John Sutton's testimony, where he stated that Samuel Mason asked him to help rob "[a] few flat boats and beat to death the master of the flat boat—and through [*sic*] them in the bottom of the water, and after to plunder the flat boat . . . [and] then burn the flat boat" (Mason Trial Transcript 1803:40). Based on this account, pirate-attacked flatboat wrecks should exhibit marks of extreme violence, such as the presence of lead musket and pistol balls embedded in the boat timbers, the skeletal remains of the murdered crew, or indications of an attempt to burn the boat in order to destroy all evidence of the crime. They also should date from the period (ca. 1785–1830) when pirates are known to have been most active along the Ohio and Mississippi rivers. The wreck also should not exhibit any evidence that it sank from some other cause than piracy.

Was the *America* indeed attacked and burned by pirates? In contrast to the conditions outlined above, we found no evidence that the *America* met a violent end. Rather than being burned, the bottom of the flatboat was in an excellent state of preservation (figures 11.2 and 11.11) except at the junction of the stern girder and starboard gunwale, where the boat timbers exhibited evidence of rotting. Inspection of this joint revealed that the peg hole intended to connect the gunwale and stern girder had been drilled badly off-center, barely connecting these two structural elements. Early nineteenth century boat yards located on the Ohio River near Pittsburgh were notorious for their use of rotten wood and poor construction, leading river guidebook author Zadok Cramer to urge repeatedly that federal inspectors be stationed in these yards to oversee their abysmally poor work (Cramer 1811:33, 34). If the *America* was built in one of these yards, it is

Figure 11.11. The *America* flatboat wreck following refitting of displaced stringers, summer 2002.

entirely possible that poorly drilled joints and rotten wood formed part of its construction.

We concluded that the *America* already may have been leaking badly at the stern due to this bad joint by the time it reached the lower Ohio (Wagner 2003). This stretch of the river contained numerous navigation hazards during the early nineteenth century, including shoals, sandbars, and rocks as well as floating and submerged tree trunks. The orientation of the wreck (bow facing upstream and stern pointed downstream) is the correct position for a docked flatboat, leading us to surmise that the crew attempted to swing the stern of the vessel around in an attempt to beach the boat after hitting an obstacle on the river. The boat appears to have sunk before this maneuver was completed, so that it was partially or fully submerged beneath the river. The cargo may then have been salvaged by the crew and placed on another boat or floated off as the boat sank. The types of artifacts that we did recover (clothing items, boat tools, and kitchen supplies) may not have been worth salvaging or may have been impossible to find on the bottom of the submerged wreck (Wagner 2003). The superstructure of the wreck may have been quickly dismantled by passing boat crews or local settlers for the lumber. It also could have broken off and washed away during one of the fall or spring rises of the Ohio River. The gunwales and floor planks, mired in the river bottom, eventually silted over and disappeared from sight for almost 200 years (figure 11.11).

The story of piracy in the Ohio and Mississippi River valleys has yet to be fully documented from either a historical or an archaeological perspective. Neglected by historians, this topic was taken over at an early date by folklorists, who selectively used historic documents to weave a romantic but inaccurate tale of piracy in the two river valleys. As we have tried to show in this chapter, however, primary archival documents such as the Mason Trial Transcript have the potential to provide a great deal of information on the locations and types of Ohio and Mississippi River pirate-related sites as well as the kinds of artifacts associated with this form of criminal behavior. We also suspect that many additional but as yet unexamined documents relating to Ohio and Mississippi River piracy exist in Spanish, French, and American archives. Future research into such documents, in combination with archaeological investigations at other shipwreck sites and land-based sites potentially associated with river piracy (such as Cave-in-Rock), may one day lead to a more accurate assessment of the history and archaeology of piracy within these two great river systems.

Acknowledgments

The documentation of the *America* could not have been completed without the assistance of a large number of volunteers, including landowner Charles "Chuck" Kiestler, county engineer Nick Niestrath, and John Schwegman, who discovered the wreck in 2000. SIUC administration and faculty members who volunteered their time include John Haller, vice-president of academic affairs, and assistant professor Robert Swenson of the Department of Architecture and Interior Design. Brian Butler, director of the SIUC Center for Archaeological Investigations, and Paul Welch of the SIU Anthropology Department provided much appreciated help and advice in the completion of this project. We wish to acknowledge Ann Haaker, Illinois deputy State Historic Preservation officer, and archaeologist Joe Phillipe of the Illinois Historic Preservation Agency (IHPA) for providing funding for the documentation of the *America*. We would also like to thank Don Ball and Jan Hemberger of the Louisville District Corps of Engineers (COE) office for their assistance in helping secure the necessary federal permits for the investigations. Finally, we wish to thank Terry Norris, St. Louis District COE archaeologist, who visited the wreck site early in the project and conclusively identified the *America* as the remains of an early 1800s flatboat. All figures are by Mark J. Wagner unless noted otherwise.

12

Identifying the Victims of Piracy
in the Spanish Caribbean

Russell K. Skowronek and Charles R. Ewen

"Yo Ho, Yo Ho, a pirate's life for me!" The song from the Disney theme parks' Pirates of the Caribbean attraction has echoed across the decades since it opened at the flagship site of Disneyland in 1968. After a cruise past the skeletal remains of pirates and a booming admonition that "Dead Men Tell No Tales!" visitors are transported back to what seems to be the Golden Age of Piracy at the turn of the eighteenth century (Botting et al. 1978:14–41; Konstam 1999:94). They pass between a stone Spanish fortification and a pirate ship, exchanging gunfire. Within moments the town is taken, and the Spanish inhabitants are being forced to surrender their "treasures" to the jolly rogues. The ride ends with a drunken debauch and an all-consuming fire. As discussed in this volume, there appears to be little basis for these images, so can evidence of piracy be found in the archaeological record?

From Disney's "imagineering" to some 140 swashbuckling theatrical and made-for-TV Hollywood films (Parish 1995), the popular picture of piracy has been decidedly skewed for more than a century toward swarthy cutthroats who were a potent force in the Caribbean during the early modern era (Hoffman 1980:1–3). The question remains, however: just when and how did the presence of these interlopers alter the way of life for the Spanish colonial residents, who were the victims of piracy, in the Caribbean basin? Were the reports of smuggling and pirate attacks hyperbole to gain the attention of the Spanish Crown or were they accurate accounts of the depredations of these seafaring "terrorists"? In the following pages we examine the material evidence both pro and con for the modern view of the Pirates of the Caribbean.

Background

The sixteenth century was a watershed in the development of the modern world economy, bringing monumental changes to Spain and Western Europe (Wallerstein 1974). At the time of the first voyage of Columbus, Spain consisted of little more than its present Iberian holdings and a few overseas possessions such as the Canary Islands. We must not forget, however, that at this time Spain was already linked by wide-ranging trade networks to the rest of Europe (Croft 1983; Curtin 1984:2; Davis 1973:64; Hurst 1977). In less than half a century, from 1510 to 1550, alliances, conquests, and dynastic ties via Charles I (or V) to the House of Habsburg would link Spain to the Antilles, New Spain (Mexico), and Tierra Firme (South America); the Low Countries; Burgundy; Austria; Franche-Comte (eastern France); parts of Germany; and half of Italy, including Naples, Sicily, Milan, Genoa, and Venice (Elliott 1963:165; Tannenbaum 1965:133).

In the latter half of the sixteenth century, the empire would feel some contraction in Europe due to the split of the House of Habsburg at the abdication of Charles I and the war with the Netherlands. Still, the additions of the Philippines and the Crown of Portugal with its far-flung holdings made sixteenth-century Spain the most powerful global European empire by the end of the sixteenth century (Haring 1947:313; Tannenbaum 1965:99, 133).

It is this burgeoning empire of Spain in the sixteenth century and its influence on shaping the modern world that many anthropologists and even some historians forget. Although commercial capitalism and mercantilism were in their infancy, raw materials, finished goods, and peoples were moving within the empire and between the nascent nation states (see table 12.1; Davis 1973:51, 64; Gerhard 1981:64–65, 89; Lister and Lister 1982:13, 69–71; Lynch 1984:148–55). Spain derived over two-fifths of its revenue from Antwerp, which was the economic capital of Western Europe from the beginning of the sixteenth century until 1585 (Lynch 1984:143), and the rest of the Low Countries, (Davis 1973:65; Tannenbaum 1965:134). To this and other Habsburg Old World ports of call, including Seville, sailed Hanseatic, English, Italian, and French ships (Haring 1947:295). This trade was to continue with Holland and England and other such "heretic" nations even during the religious and dynastic schisms of the last third of the century. War then was not total, and indirect trade could and did take place in ports such as Rouen and Nantes in France (Lynch 1984:145,154; Tanguy 1956).

Trade between Spain and its New World colonies is equally well chronicled. This "Columbian Exchange" (a term coined by Crosby 1972) brought Spain great wealth from the New World in the form of dyes, such as annetto, indigo, and cochineal; hides and other cattle by-products such as tallow; and fish from Labrador. There were tropical luxuries such as cotton, tobacco, medicines, and cacao. From the Philippines came silks and porcelains. From Nueva Cadiz came pearls (Willis 1976), and from Cuba there was copper for bronze guns. Exotic New World ceramics like Mexican Red Painted wares (Deagan 1987:43–44; Smith 1949) were imported and were popular in still-life paintings of the era by artists like Juan Bautista de Espinosa, Juan Van der Hamen, and Francisco de Palacios (Jordan 1985:93, 137, 205). Finally, there were the "cultigens," which

Table 12.1. Spanish Old World Political and Commercial Ties

Area	Dates
England	1558–1625
France	
Alsace/Lorraine	1504–circa 1680
Burgandy	1504–1678
Franche-Comte	1504–1678
Navarre, Béarn, Rousillon	1504–circa 1659
Holy Roman Empire	1519–56
Austria	1519–21
"Germany"	1519–31
Rhenish Provinces	1519–1614
Italy	
Florence	1529–76
Liguria (Genoa)	1528–1684
Lombardy (Milan)	1535–1713
Naples	1516–1707
Sicily	1516–1713
Low Countries	
Belgium	1504–1714
Netherlands	1504–1578
Philippines	1565–1898
Portugal	1580–1640

Sources: Croft 1983; Elliott 1963; Haring 1947; McAlister 1984; Tannenbaum 1965; Wallerstein 1974.

would cause the largest change in the lifeways of Europe. These were the most important harvests: silver from Mexico and Potosí and gold from the islands and mainland (Crosby 1972:170; Haring 1947:293; McAlister 1984:364–66; Tuck 1985:42; Wolf 1982:140).

The effect of these new products on the economy and lifeways of Spain and the Old World created great upheavals. This can be seen not only in soaring rates of inflation (e.g., Hamilton 1934; Lynch 1984:129–36) and population growth (Crosby 1972:165–202) but also in the outward signs of class distinction, such as sumptuous displays of clothing and tablewares and conspicuous consumption of exotic foods (Braudel 1973:125, 137–39). The opulence of this era for the elite is forever captured in portraiture and still-life art that preserves the material markers of this commerce (e.g., Jordan 1985).

Possibly the most important impact that the New World imports had was allowing Spain to pursue its imperial ambitions in the Old World. A large part of this New World income was squandered on wars to create a new Holy Roman Empire. Since the close of the Reconquista in 1492, Spain had been nearly continuously involved in wars with one or more adversaries who were not eager to be part of a Catholic state. Along with costly foreign campaigns came a concomitant rise in defensive expenditures. Spain's enemies were not content to wait to be attacked. As the sixteenth century progressed, the Crown was forced to extend this protection to its holdings overseas, which were its chief source of revenue.

Trade between Spain and the New World, which brought these exotica, during the opening and closing thirty years of the sixteenth century was a monopoly of the city of Seville and its port at San Lucar (Elliott 1963:179; Haring 1947:303). During the intervening forty years, Coruña, Bayona, Aviles, Laredo, Bilbao, San Sebastián, Barcelona, and Malaga traded directly with the Indies. These ports were already part of the extensive intracontinental European trade (e.g., Tanguy 1956). No doubt it was a combination of Spain's growing inability to meet the material demands of its colonies with Spanish produce (Haring 1947:294; Tannenbaum 1965:127) and the established commercial connections of these ports that led at least one historian to comment that by the 1540s trade ceased to be insular and became continental in scale (Lynch 1984:169).

The story of the rise of the Spanish hegemony begins in the islands of the Caribbean. During the first quarter of the sixteenth century, Spanish wealth, commerce, and settlement focused on the Greater Antilles—Cuba, Hispaniola, and Puerto Rico. The earliest settlements were founded on Hispaniola, the island where Columbus left the majority of the crew from the wrecked *Santa María* in 1492.

Hispaniola

Hispaniola is a land of rugged mountains, deep valleys, and broad plains. Although it lies in the tropics, all of the island was not equally lush. Uneven rainfall produced environments ranging from tropical rain forest to virtual desert. In the northeastern quarter and on the Guacayarima peninsula, where rainfall is greatest, were tropical rainforests and deciduous and semi-deciduous forests. These forests were heavily lumbered by the Spanish in the sixteenth century for dyewoods, including the prized *brasilium* or brazilwood, pines and pine resins and gums for naval stores, and medicinal plants such as *Cassia fistula* (used as a purgative) and wild cinnamon (Sauer 1966:92, 93, 98, 99; West and Augelli 1976:45–48).

In the modern era, the island of Hispaniola is known for the production of nickel, iron, bauxite, salt, and copper (Augelli 1965:252–53; West and Augelli 1976:97). In the fifteenth and sixteenth centuries the mineral that lured the Spanish to occupy Hispaniola was gold. On December 12, 1492, Columbus formally claimed Hispaniola for Spain. At that time he first saw, and captured, one of the natives, described as a "very young and beautiful woman" clad only in a *gold* nose-plug (Morison 1942:283). It is difficult to ascertain, half a millennium later, which aspect of the woman's déshabillé concerned the Spanish sailors' sensibilities more that day, but let it be noted that the following day was to witness the first European prospecting trip on the island (Morison 1942:284). From these humble beginnings began the first gold rush in the New World. Placer deposits of gold would be found along the Haina and Ozama Rivers in the eastern half of the island, and the source lodes were discovered later in the interior (Floyd 1973:32, 44, 66; Sauer 1966:61, 77–79, 153–55). When Columbus reported to the Crown in 1494: "There is more gold here than iron in the Biscay," the reverberations were felt throughout the Iberian Peninsula and Europe (Floyd 1973:24).

Copper was another mineral exploited by the Spanish, though it was most appreciated because its presence usually signaled the presence of gold in the deposits as well. Greg Smith (1995:337) notes that some of the first African slaves imported to the New World were intended for work in the copper mines near Puerto Real in the early sixteenth century. Copper not only had intrinsic value but also was an essential component for the bronze that was crucial in the casting of artillery for the defense of the empire (Hoffman 1980:59–62).

The third major mineral to be exploited by the Spanish was salt. Mined from the Enriquillo–Cul-de-Sac Depression and shipped through their port of Azua, salt served not only as a table seasoning but also as an important preservative for hides and meats (Floyd 1973:11). Indeed, it was the quest for a reliable source of salt for their fishing fleets that led the Dutch to trespass on the islands off the coast of Venezuela by the end of the sixteenth century. The Dutch did not sail empty vessels to gather salt but arrived with a "ballast" of illegal trade goods (Parry and Sherlock 1971:46).

The Spanish settlement of Hispaniola in the fifteenth and sixteenth centuries would best be defined as a colonial extractive cosmopolitan frontier where the exploitation of local resources was the primary function (Skowronek 1989). Its rapid evolution and transformation from initial exploration to cosmopolitan plantation colony is best seen against the larger expansion of the empire into the New World and the colony's response when faced with a huge investment in physical plant and falling returns from its initial trajectory of investment and growth. By 1520, less than thirty years after Columbus' landfall, the colony was maturing, with fifteen officially incorporated villas with coats of arms and city governments and growing demographic and economic stability (Lockhart and Schwartz 1983:16–180; McAlister 1984; Skowronek 1989:99–116).

By 1520 the Spanish New World empire had grown far beyond the confines of Hispaniola to include the islands of Puerto Rico, Cuba, and Jamaica and parts of modern Venezuela, Panama, and Mexico. By the end of the century Spain's presence would be felt from Labrador to Tierra del Fuego—but Hispaniola would remain an administrative hub in the New World (Lockhart and Schwartz 1983:84).

Territorial expansion encouraged emigration not only by Old World Spaniards but by many residents of Hispaniola as well. As the gold resources in Hispaniola began to dry up and new strikes were made in the new territories, many citizens of Hispaniola's *villas* joined in the rush (Floyd 1973:223–32; Moya Pons 1976:72, 75, 77). The end result of this population drop was the abandonment of many of the *villas* that had been established earlier. Hispaniola's success as a colony would now be based on the exploitation of tropical plants. This was the birth of the New World plantation system. By 1546 the 5,000 Spanish inhabitants of Hispaniola were outnumbered by 12,000 black slaves (Moya Pons 1976:80). Those *villas* that remained took on a greater degree of permanence with the construction of rectangular stone structures for public and private religious and secular use (Council 1975; Ewen 1991; Floyd 1973:221; Goggin 1968; Willis 1995). By the end of the century Spain had abandoned the western third of the island (today's Haiti) and maintained only a handful of agricultural settlements in what would become the Dominican Republic.

Colonies and Corsairs—Ending the Spanish New World Monopoly

The mid-sixteenth century change in the origin of materials exported from the Old to the New World coincides with the end of the initial wave of booty-driven Spanish conquests and with the entrance of other Europeans into the New World. At this time all Western European cultures were more similar than dissimilar (Gerhard 1981:56), sharing common economic, political, and religious philosophies over local ethnic variations. As Fernand Braudel (1973:123) succinctly put it: "Man is a creature of desire and not of need." While all of Europe was indirectly benefiting from Spain's colonial expansion through increased intracontinental trade, there were some who wanted more.

In 1494 Pope Alexander VI made the Spaniards the sole "proprietors" of the lands to the west of the line created by the Treaty of Tordesillas. This did not sit well with the rest of Europe. Francis I, king of France, declared that, as "the sun shines on me as well as on others, I should be very happy to see the clause in Adam's will which excluded me from my share when the world was being divided" (Galvin 1999:31; Williams 1963:207). To secure a larger share of the New World profits, France issued privateering letters of marque. Privateers sailed privately owned ships authorized by a commission from a recognized sovereign to attack designated enemies, in this case the Spanish. They became known as corsairs, from the Spanish word *corsario*, meaning "one who cruises." For the Spanish, it meant anyone who entered the Indies without a license from the Casa de Contratación or who attacked Spanish vessels. The vast majority of these attacks took place west of the Azores and north of the Tropic of Cancer. It has been said:

> There was indeed "no peace beyond the line," and it was taken for granted there would be hostilities in the Caribbean area no matter how friendly international relations might be in Europe. Acts of violence "beyond the line" were not regarded as acts of war, and atrocities which would have been condemned in the comparatively chivalrous warfare which still existed in Europe were scarcely noticed when they occurred in America. (Burns 1954:140–41)

The earliest French attacks in the Americas were aimed at both settlements on Hispaniola and the Greater Antilles and the ships that sailed between them and the Old World. The Antilles have been described as a "curving fence with five main gates: the Straits of Florida, the Windward Passage, the Mona Passage, the Anegada Passage, and the Galleon's Passage north of Trinidad" (Galvin 1999:26; West and Augelli 1976:26). In addition to these portals there are at least another dozen "choke" points that became the focus of attacks (Galvin 1999:24–26). Communities that were unfortified or weakly fortified were repeatedly pillaged. For example, Havana was taken three times before 1555, while the relatively well-fortified ports of Santo Domingo on Hispaniola and San Juan, Puerto Rico, remained unscathed. From 1535 through 1563 there were thirty-four corsair land attacks in the Antilles, twenty-one attacks on the Spanish Main, and five attacks in Central America (Hoffman 1980:47). By way of comparison, in the decade between 1536 and 1547 more than sixty ships were lost to corsairs in actions "across the line." During the next fifteen years more than eighty others would be lost (Hoffman 1980:26, 66).

To defend against these depredations a growing amount of money was spent on building and garrisoning defensive fortifications for coastal communities, building and manning a coast guard, and mandating an annual convoy system for commerce between the Old and New Worlds (Galvin 1999:34–37; Hoffman 1980:124–25, 176–77). Even so, the defense of the Indies was a real bargain for the Spanish Crown. At its most expensive, it was less than what was spent to maintain the royal household. In 1586, before Francis Drake raised the level of violence when he fielded 1,000 men in the capture of Santo Domingo, the defenses provided security for the major towns, for some coastal shipping, and for all transatlantic shipping, while providing a nominal policing of the region for illicit trade. Some twenty to forty corsairs are thought to have operated in the Caribbean each year, but they did not operate in large squadrons and rarely constituted a force of more than one hundred men (Hoffman 1980:235–36).

This leaves us with a question about the real significance of these attacks on Spanish colonial settlements. How many settlements were abandoned because they were destroyed by corsairs? How many settlements were abandoned because of a conscious decision to congregate the populace in a more defensible location? And how many settlements were abandoned because they were no longer profitable and new opportunities existed?

It appears that few settlements were permanently abandoned due to pirate attack. The Spanish response was to fortify the more important towns like Santo Domingo, Cartagena, and Havana. The response of the citizens of the less important, unfortified towns was to hide in the woods and pay a ransom for the pirates to go away. So the Spanish colonists developed a pattern to deal with this menace, and pirate attacks became part of the cost of doing business in the Caribbean. In fact, for the average colonist, the pirates might actually be the only trading partner available.

Puerto Real is an interesting example of the Spanish Crown's extreme measures to curb smuggling. In 1566 Philip II abolished the hide trade along Hispaniola's north coast. The north coast was not on the route of the Spanish treasure fleets, and thus the northern towns had little access to Spanish seaborne commerce. Hides were Puerto Real's chief export, so the decree was largely ignored, prompting the Crown to forbid ship registry of any kind to be carried out with Puerto Real in 1570. Still having no luck in controlling buccaneer activity, it ordered Puerto Real abandoned in 1579, followed by the entire western third of Hispaniola in 1605 (Hodges and Lyon 1995:105–8).

Material Evidence for Corsair Attacks and Illicit Trade in the Sixteenth Century

There is evidence in the archaeological record of corsair attacks or the fear of corsair attacks. For more than a quarter of a century Kathleen Deagan has found evidence of Francis Drake's 1586 attack in the form of charred posts, fired daub, and other burnt refuse layers identified in wells of St. Augustine (Deagan 1985). While Puerto Real is reported to have been sacked and burned in 1566 by the French pirate Jean Bontemps (Johnny Goodtimes would be the English translation), there has been little evidence of that incident detected in the archaeological record. Likewise, there is little evidence of the sacking of Panama Viejo by Henry Morgan in 1671 (Mendizábel 1999). Raymond Willis (1995:163–65), however, was able to detect evidence of a squatter occupation at the site postdating the Spanish occupation of Puerto Real. The Spaniards abandoned Puerto Real in 1579 due to the inability of town officials to curb the smuggling that was rampant along the northwestern coast of Hispaniola. It appears that the buccaneers made use of the abandoned site as one of their hideouts (Hodges and Lyon 1995:109).

Perhaps the most obvious legacy of the "fear factor" in both the archaeological and systemic contexts is found in fortifications. Beginning in the sixteenth century fortifications were strengthened at San Juan, Puerto Rico (figure 12.1); Santo Domingo (figure 12.2) and Puerto Plata on Hispaniola; Santiago and Havana, Cuba (figures 12.3 and 12.4); San Juan de Ulúa, Mexico; Trujillo and Puerto Caballos, Honduras; Nombre de Dios, Panama; Cartagena, Colombia; and sites in Florida (Hoffman 1980:152–69). For example, at St. Augustine, Florida, at the Fountain of Youth Park, archaeologists from the University of Florida have found evidence of the initial fortifications built by Pedro Menéndez de Avilés to defend the settlers from French attacks (Waters 1997). The seventeenth- and eighteenth-century Castillo de San Marcos (figure 12.5) and Fort Matanzas (figure 12.6) are the linear descendants of these earlier fortifications. Farther north, in what is today South Carolina, Stanley South has identified in Santa Elena, Florida's sixteenth-century capital, Forts San Marcos and San Felipe (South 1980, 1982, 1983, 1984, 1985).

Figure 12.1. Eighteenth-century plan of the fortifications of San Juan, Puerto Rico.

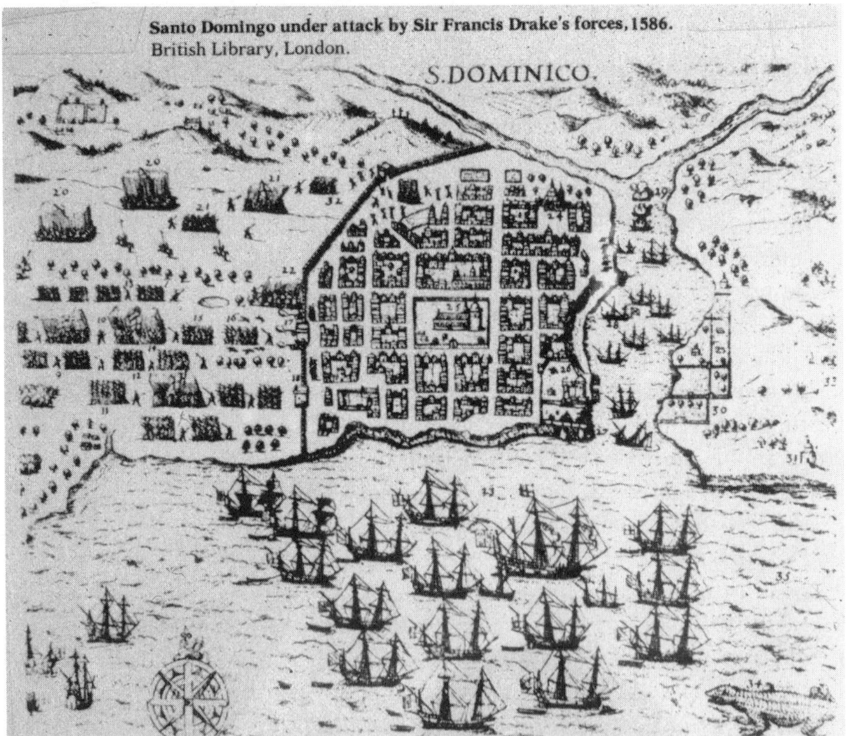

Santo Domingo under attack by Sir Francis Drake's forces, 1586.
British Library, London.

S. DOMINICO.

Figure 12.2. Sixteenth-century engraving of Santo Domingo on the island of Hispaniola being attacked by Sir Francis Drake. Courtesy of the British Library, London.

Figure 12.3. Sixteenth-century Castillo San Salvador de la Puerta in Havana, Cuba.

Figure 12.4. Castillo de los Tres Reyes del Morro in Havana, Cuba.

Figure 12.5. Castillo de San Marcos, St. Augustine, Florida. Courtesy of the National Park Service.

If the evidence of "fear" can be documented in the form of the public architecture associated with fortifications, is there compelling evidence for illicit trade? Although contraband trade was widespread in the seventeenth and eighteenth centuries (for example, Harman 1969:47–63) some researchers (such as Elliott 1963:190; Haring 1918:231–57, 1947:308) have projected the roots of this vast contraband trade and its negative effects on the empire back into the sixteenth century. Yet, given Spain's sixteenth-century strength, other researchers have pointed out that the effect of interlopers on legitimate trade represents less than one-twentieth of the total returns (for example, Lynch 1984:163, 172). Importantly, Spain's colonial monopoly remained largely intact until the 1630s, at the height of the Thirty Years War (Wolf 1982:152). Because of these different historical views, it is unclear whether foreign interlopers did or did not intrude upon Spain's New World mercantile monopoly in the sixteenth century. To determine the validity of either of these diametrically opposed views requires an objective examination of the material culture from the era.

Figure 12.6. Fort Matanzas, south of St. Augustine, Florida.

Illicit Trade—Fact or Fiction?

Accurately ascertaining and quantifying the impact of foreign interlopers in the commerce of colonial Spain requires linking it to archaeologically recoverable materials, such as ceramics, whose points of origin are identifiable. Thus, the frequency of tablewares produced outside of the Spanish Empire should correlate with the role of foreign interlopers in the trade of each colony. The historical record indicates that perishable items accounted for much of the contraband trade. "Contraband goods documented to have entered Puerto Real included slaves, fine cloth, linens, various dry goods, soap, wax, and mercury" (Hodges and Lyon 1995:105). It is difficult to account for these items in the archaeological record, however, so we will focus here on the ceramic assemblage.

To examine this problem the Spanish sixteenth-century colonial sites of Puerto Real (Deagan 1995; Ewen 1991) and Santo Domingo (Council 1975; Goggin 1968) in Hispaniola and St. Augustine (Deagan 1985) and Santa Elena (South 1980, 1982, 1983, 1984, 1985) in Florida are considered here, because of their contemporaneity, the presence of archaeological collections, and, in the case of the former colony Hispaniola, the documented occurrence of contraband trade by foreign interlopers. Additionally, information from the 1554 *flota* (Arnold and Weddle 1978; Skowronek 1987) and the Baños de la Reina site in Seville (Mc-Ewan 1986, 1988) is utilized. These sites represent contemporary examples of Old World Spanish mercantile trade and settlement and, as such, act as "contraband-free" controls for the study.

Table 12.2. Sixteenth-Century "Spanish" and "Non-Spanish" Tablewares

Location	Number	Percent
Hispaniola		
Santo Domingo (*Convento de San Francisco*)[a]		
Spanish	1,016	99.7
Non-Spanish	3	.3
Total	1,019	100.0
Puerto Real[b]		
Spanish	15,413	98.8
Non-Spanish	191	1.2
Total	15,604	100.0
Spanish Florida		
St. Augustine[c]		
Spanish	614	82.6
Non-Spanish	129	17.4
Total	743	100.0
Santa Elena[d]		
Spanish	9,845	97.85
Non-Spanish	216	2.15
Total	10,061	100.00
The *flota* and Spain		
1554 *flota*[e]		
Spanish	53	82.8
Non-Spanish	11	17.2
Total	64	100.0
Baños, Seville[f]		
Spanish	1,904	99.4
Non-Spanish	11	0.6
Total	1,915	100.0

Sources: a. Council 1975; Goggin 1968; Willis 1995; b. Ewen 1991; McEwan 1983; Willis 1995; c. Deagan 1985—excludes Mexican-produced Fig Springs Poly., San Luis B/W, Ichtucknee B/W, Mexico City White—post-1590 deposition; d. South 1979, 1980, 1982, 1983, 1984, 1985; e. Skowronek 1987; f. McEwan 1986, 1988.

The types of ceramic tablewares recovered from these sites include honey-colored lead-glazed wares and Columbia Plain majolica, Yayal Blue on White, Isabela Polychrome, Santo Domingo Blue on White, Santa Elena Mottled Blue on White, Santa Elena Green and White, Sevilla White, Sevilla Blue on White, and Caparra Blue, among other decorated majolicas. It is worth noting that Puebla-produced majolicas would not be exported from Mexico to the rest of the empire until the beginning of the seventeenth century (Goggin 1968:210; Skowronek 1987:106). Ceramics that are not Spanish in origin include tin-glazed earthenwares and brown "Cologne" stonewares from Germany and the Low Countries as well as Ligurian Blue on Blue, Montelupo Blue on White, and Montelupo Polychrome tin-glazed wares from northwestern Italy. Ming porcelain from China was available via the Philippines and the Manila galleon trade after 1573.

It should be noted, however, that this ware was only available through Portuguese smugglers from 1550 to 1573 (Deagan 1987). Stonewares and lead- and tin-glazed earthenwares were manufactured in Nantes and the hinterlands of Brittany and sent from the southern manufacturing centers of Uzes and Dieulefit to Spain and thence to the New World (Skowronek 1992).

In table 12.2 these tablewares are grouped into "Spanish" (including colonial-made exports such as Mexican Red Painted) and "non-Spanish" ceramics by count and frequency. Inspection of the frequencies shows that at four of the sites—Santo Domingo, Puerto Real, Santa Elena, and Baños—so called non-Spanish imports represented less than 3 percent of the total ceramic assemblage. These "non-Spanish" imports, however, include Cologne stoneware and Italian majolicas from Liguria, Montelupo, and Faenza, all of which originated in areas that the Spanish controlled or monopolized. Only at the site of Puerto Real are "French"-made and "Dutch"-made tin-glazed earthenwares and pre–Manila galleon trade porcelain reported (Ewen 1991). While these sherds make up less than 1 percent of the total assemblage of 15,604 fragments recovered from the site, they may possibly indicate illicit trade. It is also possible that they may represent aspects of normal commerce from the Spanish Netherlands or Spanish-controlled parts of France or Spanish-made imitations ("knock offs") of these wares.

At St. Augustine and the 1554 *flota*, "non-Spanish" imports make up 17 percent of their respective assemblages. "Non-Spanish" types represented at these sites include Oriental porcelain, Cologne stoneware, and Italian-made Ligurian Blue on Blue, Montelupo Blue on White, and Montelupo Polychrome. All these wares were either made in Spanish-controlled lands or carried by the Spanish *carrera* and thus are not directly attributable to illicit activities.

Piracy and Smuggling in the Seventeenth and Eighteenth Centuries

The Spanish New World hegemony began to unravel at the end of the sixteenth century with the attacks of the English "heroes" Francis Drake and John Hawkins. To the Spaniards, Drake and Hawkins were the terrorists of the worst sort (viewed very much as Americans currently regard Osama bin Laden and Saddam Hussein). The Spanish bulwark would be permanently breeched in the seventeenth century during, and as a result of, the Thirty Years War (1618–48). Early in the century the Lesser Antilles and parts of Hispaniola began to attract Protestant Dutch, English, and French squatters.

Originally these interlopers made their living hunting the feral cattle that abounded on Hispaniola and selling the meat to passing ships. These were "master-less men—marooned or shipwrecked sailors, deserters, escaped felons, runaway indentured servants, and all such that disliked organized society" (Parry and Sherlock 1971:82). They became known as *boucaniers* or "buccaneers" be-

Figure 12.7. Seventeenth-century engraving of a *boucanier* with his *boucan*, or grill.

cause the meat from the animals they hunted and killed was smoked and cured on a grill known as a *boucan* (figure 12.7). Not content with the meager profits to be made from the sale of beef jerky, these trespassers soon began to expand their bottom line by preying on the smaller merchantmen that plied those waters. These settlements were viewed not only as interlopers on Spanish territory but also as heretics against the Catholic faith by the Spanish, who frequently attacked them.

The buccaneers soon established a stronghold on the island of Tortuga off the northwest coast of Hispaniola in the late 1620s. From this base and a growing number of other settlements in the Antilles they attacked Spanish settlements and commerce. One of the islands that fell to the English under the command of William Penn's father was Jamaica in 1655. To give a sense of the magnitude of these attacks, it has been calculated that fifty-seven cities, towns, and villages were sacked on the Spanish Main in the sixteen years following the capture of Jamaica (Haring 1910:267). At the same time France, England, and the Netherlands were establishing colonies on the North and South American mainland and beginning to roll back the Spanish frontier. To every attack, whether by buccaneers, privateers, or regular naval and military forces, Spain reacted with ever increasing defenses. For example, the destruction of St. Augustine and the outlying missions to the Apalachee and Timucua Indians of Florida was met with the construction of the Castillo de San Marcos and Fort Matanzas. These coquina-block edifices were never overcome by attack and still guard the water approaches to St. Augustine. Similarly, many of the great "castles" that defend the harbors of Havana, Cartagena, and San Juan date from this era.

In the New World the first legitimate international contact between the Spanish colonies and England was formalized in 1670 (Harman 1969:5). This concession allowed British ships in distress to call at Spanish American ports, where illegal trade often took place under the pretext of reprovisioning and repairs (Harman 1969:5–6). In 1713, at the conclusion of the War of Spanish Succession, England was granted another concession. The Treaty of Utrecht allowed an *asiento* with England for trade at Portobello and other ports. This treaty, like those before it, did little to stem English smuggling activity. These violations included keeping the single ship at Portobello perpetually supplied with merchandise and trading with other "closed" Spanish ports. By this time it hardly mattered, however: the foreign powers all had footholds in the Caribbean, and trade, while not officially condoned, was common.

Florida was no different from the rest of the Spanish Empire in its desire for high-quality, lower-priced merchandise and was further impelled to develop trade relations in an attempt to acquire the necessities of life (Tepaske 1964:89). The uncertain supply forced St. Augustine to look for other non-Spanish sources to obtain goods. Until the 1750s, when a more open trade was legalized, all of St. Augustine's governors condoned this illicit trade (Tepaske 1964:72).

Much as the earlier sixteenth-century Spanish settlers of Hispaniola had traded their local produce (cow hides) to the European smugglers, the eighteenth-century Spaniards had a valuable commodity for trade: then, as today, Florida "gold" was oranges. Introduced in the colony in the sixteenth century with grapes, figs, and other fruits and crops, the orange thrived in the mild, temperate climate (Harman 1969:23). St. Augustine traded cargoes of up to 38,000 oranges to Charleston, Georgetown, Hampton, New York, Philadelphia, Providence, and Savannah (Harman 1969:15, 21, 23). With this "Florida gold" went other fruits, sweetmeats, fish, and deer skins. In exchange British colonial traders supplied pork, beef, flour, rum, cheese, butter, salt, wine, tallow, wood, slaves, nails, hoes, axes, grindstones, and diverse European goods (Harman 1969:83–91). At least one load of these "diverse European goods" from Charleston in 1756 included clothes, blankets, silverware, *china*, and mirrors (Tepaske 1964:74). By the mid-eighteenth century there were also private Spanish merchants selling goods from Cuba directly to St. Augustine.

While British traders openly walked the sandy streets of St. Augustine, the harbor serviced French ships and sent provisions to the French colonies of Louisiana and Canada (Harman 1969:63–64; Tepaske 1964:88). This trade in naval stores eventually reached as far as Vera Cruz and only ended with the Spanish evacuation of the colony in 1763.

Finally, Spanish St. Augustine went beyond the open entertainment of smugglers and entered the gray world of privateering during the second quarter of the eighteenth century. In both King George's War (aka the War of Jenkins' Ear) and the Great War for Empire (the Seven Years War) Spanish privateers based in St. Augustine obtained much needed goods from attacks on English vessels. Their forays took them as far north as New York and netted them cargoes of rice, sugar, coffee, fruits, fish, pork, wine, and flour. Even in times of war, however, the illicit trade between the colonies continued in spite of both British and Spanish restrictions (Harman 1969:37, 39, 41, 68, 72).

Identifying Illicit Trade in the Archaeological Record

Comparison of this sixteenth-century material with ceramic evidence from the first third of the eighteenth century provides a scale for interpretive reference. Remains from the 1733 *flota* and eighteenth-century St. Augustine, Florida, are considered as assemblages that respectively represent the Spanish mercantilist monopoly and a port with documented illicit trade (Deagan 1983; Harman 1969:47–63; Skowronek 1984:182–98). The St. Augustine assemblage represents an economic cross-section of the community. In addition to imports produced and traded in the Spanish Empire, such as majolica and porcelain, Rhenish and English white salt-glazed stonewares, French-produced faience, and English-made delft, Astbury, and slipwares are present (Skowronek 1984:176–78). While 32 percent of St. Augustine's ceramic tablewares are "non-Spanish" in origin, these imports represent less than 2 percent of the 1733 *flota*'s assemblage (table 12.3).

These frequencies of foreign ceramics at eighteenth-century St. Augustine reflect Spain's economic weakness at this time. The illusion of mercantile monopoly was borne in the highly visible sailings of the *carrera*; but supplying the hinterlands was more difficult for the declining empire to achieve and thus was left increasingly to foreign interlopers. A comparison of the sixteenth-century and eighteenth-century data reveals the marked impact of illicit trade in the eighteenth century in the empire's hinterlands. Even though there was a doubling of Spain's New World empire from the sixteenth to the mid-eighteenth century, the thirty-fold increase in the frequency of "non-Spanish" produced or traded wares over this 150-year period quantifiably illustrates changes in Spain's commercial

Table 12.3. Eighteenth-Century "Spanish" and "Non-Spanish" Tablewares

Location	Number	Percent
1733 *flota*[a]		
Spanish	2,910	98.5
Non-Spanish	45	1.5
Total	2,955	100.0
St. Augustine (SA 7–5, 7–4, 16–23)[b]		
Spanish	1,467	68.1
Non-Spanish	688	31.9
Total	2,155	100.0

Sources: a. Skowronek 1984:176–78; b. Deagan 1983.

strength and helps clarify the limited role of contraband trade in the sixteenth century.

Summary and Conclusions

The ideas presented here underscore the value of examining popular notions regarding the significance of illicit trade and interlopers in the Spanish colonial world. Our views of what represents "Spain" and "Spanishness" in the early modern era and what represents the role of foreign interlopers in the Spanish colonies require a historical knowledge of trade networks and patterns—illicit and legal—in both the Old and New Worlds in the sixteenth through eighteenth centuries.

It is clear that a "culture of fear," beyond a mere defensive response, did develop as a result of pirate attacks during the early modern era. The fortifications that were erected, enlarged, and modified are a material expression of the victims' fear of attack. Given the location of most of these edifices—guarding harbors and the communities that stood there—it is clear that they feared a seaborne threat. The Spaniards' goal was to construct a structure that could repel an attack or withstand a siege until a relief force could be mounted. The Castillo de San Marcos (figure 12.5) in the backwater of St. Augustine, Florida, served just that purpose in 1702 and 1740 when the city was put under siege by English colonists and Indian auxiliaries from Georgia and South Carolina.

The place of illicit trade is another issue. As noted in Braudel's (1973:123) dictum cited above, "Man is a creature of desire and not of need." Expatriates living in the hinterlands of a colonial system do not "go native" if they have other options. They attempt to the best of their abilities to transform their new home into a facsimile of the old. Their ability to effect this transformation is related to the amount of commercial contact the settlements enjoyed with the mother country (Skowronek 2002:297–300). The resulting compromise, as studied archaeologically at Spanish colonial sites, is known as the "Spanish Colonial Pattern" (Deagan 1983; Ewen 1991).

Communities whose heyday was past (such as Puerto Real in the second half of the sixteenth century) or whose sole *raison d'être* was defense (such as St. Augustine) were backwaters that had little contact with the Spanish *metropole*. To make up for the shortfalls in desired material goods, other sources were sought. This resulted in an illegal trade within the idealized structure of the Spanish colonial world but was tolerated due to the realities of the inadequate supply system. To find evidence of smuggling and piracy and to evaluate their significance in the lives of people requires being able to differentiate objects that were obtained legally from those that appeared through other channels. Few items other than historic ceramics are directly identifiable as to point of origin unless they bear a maker's mark.

Quantification of ceramic tablewares from terrestrial and shipwreck sites in the Old and New World whose national origin is highly identifiable has laid the foundation for an index capable of measuring changes in Spain's commercial strength. A measure for intra-empire commercial and military control is discernible through changes in the frequency of the presence and absence of "Spanish" and "non-Spanish" produced or traded wares. As more work is completed in other parts of the empire and other periods, a finer index of these changes will emerge.

Finally, these data also suggest that, given the extent of Spain's political control and trading relations, it is more reasonable for researchers to associate most sixteenth-century exotic, non-Spanish, Old World materials with legitimate and normal channels of trade rather than viewing them as the physical manifestations of foreign interlopers dealing in contraband. Of course, these exotica must always be considered in the context of the rest of the collections associated with the site and, more importantly, in the context of the milieu in Spain and its colonial expression in the early modern era to understand the ramifications of their presence on an archaeological site.

"Dead men," or more specifically their past actions, "do tell tales" through the objective interpretation of their material culture. The holistic approach that characterizes historical archaeology not only provides knowledge of the realities of the colonial world through an examination of direct and indirect observations of human behavior (for example, archaeological and documentary evidence) but also provides the framework for exploring the idealized goals, views, and beliefs that the colonists held about their own behavior in the colonial setting (for example, contemporary accounts). It is this conjunction that allows a balanced view of these processes (Schuyler 1977). The documentary record has several deficiencies: (1) the context of the actions is unknown; (2) there is a bias toward the world of commerce; (3) it only represents elite views of colonial life; and (4) sometimes people lie to cover up personal inadequacies or illegal behavior—such as smuggling. An examination of the daily lives of the colonists requires more direct evidence of human behavior—archaeological data.

Archaeologically derived information provides measurable units of comparison that are useful in determining the role of piracy and illicit trade in the Spanish colonial world. Every archaeological site contains numerous classes and functional groups of artifacts that can be categorized for pattern recognition within and between communities (for example, South 1977:95–96). A more nuanced picture of the past is coming into focus through historical archaeology. And it is every bit as fascinating as the highly fictionalized pirate stories that we all grew up with as children.

All figures are by Russell K. Skowronek unless noted otherwise.

Part 3

Pirates in Fact and Fiction

13

Pirate Imagery

Lawrence E. Babits, Joshua B. Howard, and Matthew Brenckle

As pirate shipwrecks continue to be sought, found, and investigated, a close look at what might constitute a distinctive pirate assemblage is necessary. The act of piracy, a legal construction, rather than any concrete artifact distinguished pirates from everyday sailors. Three lines of nondocumentary evidence exist: the personnel, the ship itself, and the artifacts. While sailors were distinguished from landsmen by their clothing and tools, there is little artifactual evidence to distinguish sailors from pirates. What survives in a shipwreck is not likely to demonstrate conclusively that the wreck was manned by pirates.

The Beaufort Inlet wreck site publicly identified as Blackbeard's *Queen Anne's Revenge* by the governor of North Carolina has the same problem. While Governor Hunt had obvious reasons for claiming that *Queen Anne's Revenge* had been found, he was responding to an older popular imagery that we are all familiar with, even if the objects did not survive nearly 300 years under water. A similar observation can be made for the *Whydah*, a known pirate vessel identified by its bell and its public imagery, including one book about its discovery, *The Pirate Prince* (Clifford 1993).

Today's children know what a pirate looks like long before they learn any names or details about piracy. In part, this is attributable to James Barrie's *Peter Pan* (1987; originally published in 1904) and Robert Louis Stevenson's *Treasure Island* (1965; originally published in 1883). Captain Hook is relevant here because he was Blackbeard's bosun (Barrie 1987:44). Aside from an "iron claw" replacing his right hand, Hook's distinguishing attribute was that "he somewhat aped the attire associated with the name of Charles II" (Barrie 1987:52), a flamboyant, late seventeenth century style that included much lace. Hook's pirates were a "villainous-looking lot," one in particular with "great arms bare, pieces of eight in his ears . . . [a] gigantic man" (Barrie 1987:50–51).

As they get older, children graduate to Robert Louis Stevenson's *Treasure Island* and Long John Silver. Captain Silver's distinguishing attributes (depending on the written version rather than films) produce a standardized pirate figure, but with one leg and a Devonshire accent, drawing out the *r*s until they are almost words in themselves. It is not simply Silver's appearance that is striking. The book begins with nautical references and Captain Billy Bones, "a tall strong, heavy, nut-brown man, his tarry pigtail falling over the shoulders of his soiled blue coat, his hands ragged and scarred, with black, broken nails, and the sabre cut across one cheek" (Stevenson 1965:11). The description continues: "[H]is great sinewy arm . . . was tattooed in several places. 'Here's luck,' 'A fair wind,' and 'Billy Bones his fancy,' were very neatly and clearly executed on the forearm; and up near the shoulder there was a sketch of a gallows and a man hanging from it" (Stevenson 1965:22).

Bones was being stalked by his former crew mates, led by Long John Silver, "the ship's cook, Barbecue, as the men called him" (Stevenson 1965:66). "His left leg was cut off close by the hip, and under the left shoulder he carried a crutch . . . He was very tall and strong" (Stevenson 1965:54). "Aboard ship he carried his crutch by a lanyard round his neck, to have both hands as free as possible" (Stevenson 1965:66). "He was tricked out in his best; an immense blue coat, thick with brass buttons, hung as long as to his knees, and a fine laced hat was set on the back of his head" (Stevenson 1965:122). The long coat fits within late seventeenth- and early eighteenth-century styles, and the wooden leg is typical of ships' cooks retained after injury in the Royal Navy (figure 13.1). Silver owned a parrot named Captain Flint that squawked "Pieces of eight! Pieces of eight" (Stevenson 1965:67). Silver, Captain Hook, and Blackbeard are linked via Israel Hands, a known Blackbeard crewman. In *Peter Pan*, Captain Hook was said to have been Blackbeard's bo'sun and "the only man of whom Barbecue [Silver] was afraid" (Barrie 1987:44, 51).

Stevenson's pirates included Black Dog, "a pale, tallowy creature, wanting two fingers of the left hand, and though he wore a cutlass, he did not look much like a fighter. I had always my eye open for seafaring men, with one leg or two, and I remember this one puzzled me. He was not sailorly, and yet he had a smack of the sea about him too" (Stevenson 1965:18). Blind Pew lost his eyesight in the same broadside that took away Long John Silver's leg. "He was hunched, as if with age or weakness, and wore a huge old tattered seacloak with a hood that made him appear positively deformed" (Stevenson 1965:27). Others are described as "mahogany faced," muscular and tattooed; but if they were not identified as pirates, the descriptions would fit law-abiding sailors.

The television film *Goonies* includes many pirate caricatures, including One Eyed Willie, clothed in Jacobean finery, sitting at a jewel-laden table on board his vessel. Popular imagery is fairly consistent in showing a pirate leader as a flawed gentleman and his crew as tarred, sunbronzed, tattooed, hook-armed, wooden-legged, eyepatch-wearing seadogs. This image translated to a terrestrial funeral in *Cold Mountain*, when a dead preacher has two pennies placed on his eyes when one eye started to open, because "to have covered the opening eye would have looked strange and piratical" (Frazier 1997:30).

Figure 13.1. "The Sea Cook" by Thomas Rowlandson, ca. 1780. National Maritime Museum, Greenwich, England.

Walking the plank is one part of the popular image of piracy. Although this action has been discounted as myth, at least one example from a later period involving mutinous privateers does exist:

> . . . two Days ago Capt. Davise in the employ of Mr. Stanly arrived from the french West Indies—he brings an acct of a matter similar to this exactly— a vessel of the United States put into St. Thomas's the Capt. went ashore & the majority of the seamen being English they mutinied lashed a plank on

the Bows and told the mate to take his choice either to walk over Board or navigate that vessel into Tarbola, the latter alternative of course was embraced . . . the young Gent son of our printer and of exceeding good character offers to make oath to and I believe has or is to do. (Nash 1777:719–20)

While twentieth-century images are well known, they follow the tradition of earlier pirate imagery. Charles Johnson's 1724 book *A General History of the Pyrates* (1972; Charles Johnson is assumed to be a pseudonym for Daniel Defoe) went through many editions; as styles changed, so did the book's illustrations. Johnson's illustrations showed popular sailor images and identified them as pirates. Without this identification, they would just be sailors.

A pirate's clothing and accoutrements were no different from those of law-abiding sailors on a merchantman or man-of-war. The sailor's short clothes distinguished him from the landsman, with his long clothes (Lavery 1989:204; Rodger 1986:64). As sailor styles changed, similar clothing was worn by pirates, who, after all, were sailors. In fact, pirates are often shown dressed in later clothing more typical of a book's publication date than of their own time.

Images of Blackbeard are a case in point. The 1724 image shows him wearing a thrumm (figure 13.2), the seventeenth-century sailor's hat (Johnson 1972:72). In 1740 (figure 13.3) he is wearing a low cocked hat (Botting et al. 1978:136); but by the 1780s he has a full cocked hat (Cordingly 1995). His coat length also varies according to current styles.

While sea officers' clothing tended to change more rapidly, in keeping with current styles, sailors were notoriously conservative in terms of their functional clothing, although they often wore garish items when going ashore. Traditional clothing elements like loose trousers, short jackets, and monmouth caps or thrumms readily identified sailors. A fan (ca. 1740) in the collections of Colonial Williamsburg shows both sailors and soldiers in typical attire. The sailors had short jackets, caps, and loose breeches or very short trousers, while the soldiers wore longer coats and tight-fitting breeches (Baumgarten 1986:45, 66). The weaponry is too vague to identify precisely, other than as flintlocks.

Pirates thus are impossible to tell from common sailors by their dress (figure 13.4). At Ocracoke Inlet, where Blackbeard was killed, one of Lieutenant Maynard's crew was shot by a fellow Royal Navy sailor, who took "him by mistake for one of the pirates" (Lee 1997:122). Sailor's clothing alone (buttons, hooks, eyes, buckles, and so forth) therefore cannot be linked with piracy either. A pirate's personal weaponry reflects that available to any sailor.

The generalized imagery is all well and good for the public but insufficient for scientific archaeological reporting. For an archaeologist, faced with differential preservation, the popular image is of little help. Cloth rarely survives in the archaeological record, wood floats away, and iron decays. That takes care of the flag, eye patch, wooden leg, and hook. Unless a fortuitous site formation process

Figure 13.2. "Black-beard the Pyrate," 1724. Printed in the original edition of Charles Johnson's *A General History of the Pyrates* (London, 1724).

Figure 13.3. Blackbeard, ca. 1740. Printed in the 1725 edition of Charles Johnson's *A General History of the Pyrates* (London).

Figure 13.4. Sailors boarding a pirate ship. Courtesy of Maritime Heritage Society.

occurred, as in the sinking of the English collier *General Carleton of Whitby* in 1785 (Babits and Ossowski 1999), little identifiable clothing will survive.

When the *General Carleton* sank on September 1785 in the Baltic Sea, a barrel of birch tar spilled over several clothing items, including hats, gloves, jackets, vests, breeches, stockings, shoes, and at least one shirt. As part of the wrecking process, the tar mixed with sand and metallic artifacts, resulting in a concretion from which the clothing was later extracted. Wool and leather clothing survived, along with a silk ribbon; cotton, hemp, and linen material did not survive, leaving some items disassembled because the thread was linen (Babits and Ossowski 1999). These clothing items exhibit damage, repair, or adjustment, indicating that they were being used by sailors rather than stowed for later issue or sale. As a collection of clothing items in everyday use, the *General Carleton* assemblage is as remarkable for the eighteenth century as the *Mary Rose* (McKee 1972; Rule 1982) and *San Juan* (Davis 1997) are for the sixteenth century, the *Vasa* (Franzen 1966; Kaijser et al. 1982; Skenback 1983) and *Kronan* (Einarsson 1997) for the seventeenth, and the *Bertrand* (Petsche 1974) for the nineteenth.

Piracy is robbery at sea without a letter of marque and reprisal or commission. As a physical activity, piracy does not survive in the archaeological record. So how does one tell a pirate from a sailor in terms of a wreck's artifacts? More importantly, how does one tell if a wreck is a former pirate ship? An examination of what survives, has been documented, and has been found on "pirate sites," such as Beaufort Inlet and the *Whydah*, might prove instructive.

Any vessel used by pirates may or may not have been modified. Modifications included cutting down the forecastle or the stern castle, adding gun and sweep ports, and shifting masts (Botting et al. 1978:133; Johnson 1972:64). Although many archaeologists will not admit it, most nautical archaeology has very little to do with a vessel above the bilge, except in those unusual instances where a vessel was quickly buried or lay in very cold water. Human activity was concentrated and distinctive embellishment was placed well above the waterline in most vessels. When ships burned, wrecked, or rotted away, only the lowest portions survived in the mud or sand. If a wreck was accessible, it was repeatedly scavenged for usable material.

With the exception of a ship that came to rest on its side or was rapidly buried, virtually the only evidence of typical pirate modifications would be mast steps, timbers attached to the keel or keelson (the spine of a vessel) to support the mast. Masts were also inserted into a mortise on the keel or keelson. How does one tell if mast steps were added or put out of use, much less that they were a modification to convert a merchant vessel to a pirate ship? An armed merchantman, especially a slaver or a privateer, has many similar attributes (speed, large human spaces, heavy armament), for precisely the same reasons.

Artifacts may provide clues. If a vessel's history is known, any recovered artifacts should reflect that history. For the *Queen Anne's Revenge* and the *Whydah*, artifacts should reflect a ship outfitted in Europe for the slave trade that made voyages to the Caribbean via West Africa and returned (Clifford 1993; Lee 1997:14; Mettas 1978:16, 37, 56; Moore 1989). Most basic ship accoutrements should be English or French. Other artifacts should relate to the slave trade. The *Henrietta Marie* might well serve as a starting point for comparative purposes, because it contained numerous items used in the slave trade (Moore 1989). The *Whydah*, a slaver before being converted into a pirate vessel, contains artifacts linking slavery with piracy (Clifford 1993). Again, the question can be raised, what if the captured slaver *La Concorde* was swapped out for another vessel, which then sailed north as the *Queen Anne's Revenge* to terrorize Charleston? There ought to be items taken from European and American vessels after a slaver turned pirate. A listing of captured vessels should reflect these origins.

The Beaufort Inlet Wreck and *Whydah* sites yielded ceramics, including salt-glazed stoneware and redware. These are typical ceramics from Western Europe for the early eighteenth century and appear on terrestrial sites from Rhode Island to Brazil. There were also pewter objects and lead sounding weights. The barrel hoops and anchors are not distinctive, at least as far as they have been examined. The artifacts represent a generic nautical assemblage, except for the bell and the pewter plates.

Weaponry may provide clues because it is large, resistant to decay, and diagnostic for time and place. Pirate weaponry might include weapons of several nationalities and sizes. In contrast, an armed merchantman, privateer, or man-of-war would have adequate shot for a set of standardized guns. Pirates might be presumed to have a variety of weapons, captured as they upgraded their vessel and personal weapons. They may have shifted weaponry from one vessel to another to create a more powerful armament. A mix of older pieces as well as up-to-date cannon might be found. This interpretation is partially based on a 1718 pirate vessel inventory (Pennsylvania 1718) and an Alabama pirate inventory (Sands 1818) (tables 13.1 and 13.2).

The Pennsylvania inventory shows ten cannon, two swivels, and three patereros. The patereros were obsolete by 1718, but they had particular value as rapid firing, lightly charged, antipersonnel breech loaders. The Pennsylvania inventory also suggests that the pirates planned on fighting on only one side of their ship because there were only four sponges and five pass boxes. The Pennsylvania inventory also shows thirty muskets, five blunderbusses, five pistols, and seven cutlasses, plus fifty-three hand grenades (Pennsylvania 1718). A hundred years later, an Alabama pirate vessel had a similar diverse weapons assemblage, described as "11 old guns, 10 pistols, 2 Sords [*sic*]" (Sands 1818).

A number of weaponry-related artifacts have been recovered from both the Beaufort Inlet wreck and *Whydah* sites. For Beaufort Inlet, these include seven cannon, touch-hole covers, smaller shot, and cannonballs ranging in size from two to twenty-four pounds. The touch-hole aprons on both sites are virtually identical (Hamilton et al. 1992:66–71), and their curvature fits recovered cannon vents. Two recovered *QAR* cannon are six-pounders. Preliminary measurements

Table 13.1. Pennsylvania Pirate Inventory, 1718

10 Great Guns & Carriages	4 Sponges
2 Swivel Guns	2 Crows
3 Pateraroes	0 Organ Barrels
4 Chambers	7 Cutlasses
30 Muskets	5 Great Gun Cartridge Boxes
5 Blunderbusses	8 Cartridge Boxes
5 Pistols	for small arms
53 hand Granadoes	4 Old Chambers
2 Barrl. Powder	20 Guns Tackles
4 Caggs of Catridge	10 Breechins
2 Powder Horns	2 Guns, Worm & Ladle
	Acct. of Sails, Rigging & Stores
1 Main Sail	2 Runners & Tackles
1 ffore sail	a Small Quantity of Tallow
1 Jib	& Tobacco
2 fflying Jibbs	3 Compasses
1 Top Sail	1 Doctor's Chest
1 Sprit Sail	1 Black fflagg
1 Square Sail	1 Red fflagg
1 boat Main Sail & ffore Sail	2 Ensignes
22 Spare Blocks	2 Pendants
1 Topmast Stay	8 Stoppers
1 ffore halliards	1 fflying Jibb halliards
1 Topping Lift	1 main Halliards
2 Grinding Stones	1 main Down Hall
24 Water Casks	1 Jib Sheet, the other for
1 barl. of Tar & a peice [sic]	Bow fast
30 barl. of Powder	1 Flying Tack
7 Dead Eyes	1 Fish Hook & Pendant
1 Kittle	2 Pump Spears
2 iron potts	1 Broad Ax
3 Anchors	1 Wood Ax
1 Cables [sic]	1 hand saw
1 old piece of junk	1 pair of Canhooks
13 planks	1 hammer
2 Top Sail Sheets	1 Auger
1 Boom Tackle	1 plain
13 bbr. of Beef & pork	Some Iron work & Lumber

Source: Pennsylvania 1718.

on the cannon, including at least seventeen still on site, suggest that, while there are several lengths, the bores all seem to be about four inches or two inches. These are consistent with six-pounder to nine-pounder cannon and lighter swivel guns. The range of cannon seems fairly uniform and may reflect the original armament that might have been carried aboard the slaver *La Concorde*. For Beaufort Inlet, upgraded weaponry might be questioned, because the *La Concorde* was well armed, and any newer, larger guns may have been saved prior to abandoning the

Table 13.2. Alabama Pirate Inventory, 1818

4 Mosquito Bar	2 pr Pantaloons
1 Piece Gingaws	2 Vest & one Coat
1 Bed Sack	9 Bags
11 Old Guns	10 Pistols
1 Spade and Hatech [sic]	2 Sords [sic]
1 Quadrant	2 Compasses
2 Charts	8 Kegs
1 Sail Bag	1 Boat with 3 sails & 9 oars
2 Hatchets	1 Hammer
1 Hand Lead	1 Small box containing Sundry Articles

Source: Sands 1818.

Queen Anne's Revenge. But what if the *La Concorde* was exchanged for a better, cleaner vessel, uncontaminated with the human waste left on a slaver, before Blackbeard ran his flagship aground off Beaufort?

Cannonballs certainly reflect the diversity expected aboard a large vessel with upgraded armament, but this is misleading. The 24-pound shot on the Beaufort Inlet wreck may be intrusive, since nearby Fort Macon had eighteen 24-pounders. In 1862 Union forces attacked Beaufort Inlet and exchanged artillery fire with Fort Macon for almost two days. During the bombardment, Fort Macon's gunners fired 24-pound shot at the Union fleet standing 1.25 miles offshore, the location of the Beaufort Inlet site. Unless a 24-pounder cannon is found on site, it is more likely that this cannonball is an 1862 Confederate projectile.

The 6-pound balls match some recovered cannon. The smaller shot could have been grape shot or have been used in the lighter swivel guns common to eighteenth-century vessels. Two possible QAR hand grenades might be misinterpretations. They were not solid balls; cloth impressions were on both clusters' outer matrix; and X-rays showed a variety of shot present. The *Whydah* did have hand grenades, hollow iron balls with wooden fuse plugs. Pirates also used bags of shot more than men-of-war did because they were made up easily. They wanted to capture vessels, not sink them; a premium was thus placed on disabled rigging or maimed crewmen. Bag shot was certainly used on the 1718 *Whydah*, a vessel positively identified as a pirate. Bag shot was used on privateers as late as 1814, however: "a twenty-four pounder . . . was loaded with an immense quantity of grape and buck shot, balls and bullets of every description" (Savannah 1814:3).

Further examination of lead shot in concreted clusters shows several size groups, including swan shot, buck shot, and two larger ball types in the .54–.60 and the .69–.88 caliber ranges. The shot diameters provide keys about other weaponry on board, including shoulder arms. Gun experts can identify at least three musket sizes and two pistol sizes in these ranges. Far more interesting is that all the shot above a half-inch diameter is very poorly mold cast, often misshapen, and many still have sprues. These shot were probably wasters; but instead of being recast, they were bagged for antipersonnel use.

The only *QAR* firearm recovered is a blunderbuss that could take many different shot sizes, including all those found. Other small arms have been identified by parts found in concretions, including at least one musket. Statements about the identity of the Beaufort Inlet site are confirmed by examining the *Whydah*, where guns, pistols, weapons parts, a cartridge box, and shot were found.

Knives and cutlasses should be found as well, but it is hardly valid to suggest that these were present only on pirate ships. An unknown 1779 North Carolina armed merchantman that ran aground yielded a pair of swivels, several small arms, pistols, blunderbusses, and cutlasses (Virginia Gazette 1779). This salvaged goods list reads much like a pirate inventory, confirming the similarity between the two groups of seafarers:

> Sundry dry goods, consisting of a variety of articles, a parcel of nails, several small arms, pistols, blunderbusses, cutlasses, and a quantity of powder, and many other articles saved from the brigantine Dispatch, William Sarjeant master, lately chased on shore, and stranded on the coast of North Carolina. And on Thursday the 14th of October, will also be sold at the South Quay, a quantity of rum, molasses, nails, canvas, osnabrugs, etc. also the rigging and sails, part of which are quite new, with a ten inch cable also new, an anchor of 800 wt. and a pair of swivels, also saved from the said brigantine. It is hoped that the skippers on the said vessels will be so obliging as to attend at Petersburg on the above day that some measures may be adopted for adjusting their respective proportions in the value of goods saved. (Virginia Gazette, 2 October 1779)

Information recovered to date is insufficient to support any specific identification of pirates from an artifact assemblage. Thus far, the mix of artifacts on the Beaufort Inlet site is not diagnostic for Blackbeard, except for the date. On the *Whydah*, the ship's bell was recovered, thus identifying the wreck as a ship used by pirates. Although the Beaufort Inlet artifacts may have been used by pirates, so far nothing has been identified that is specifically diagnostic for pirates as opposed to seamen in general.

Any suggested pirate ship or pirate artifact model includes precisely those items that an armed merchantman would have: a mix of cannon of different sizes, often from different nations, loaded with shot designed to damage a vessel's rigging and personnel. Personal weaponry such as pistols, cutlasses, and knives would be found on any vessel. Sailors' clothing is different from landsmen's but is neither uniform nor identifiable specifically as a pirate's. Without supporting documentation and artifacts clearly linked to a specific vessel identified as a pirate vessel, attributing any artifacts to a pirate crew is very subjective.

To return to the public imagery of pirates, what we need to find is subject to differential preservation—but it could be found. We might find a purser's cabin preserved because a barrel of tar soaked its contents. Here we might find arm hooks, wooden legs, and eye patches. If so, we might also expect the skeleton of a wooden-legged seafarer draped over the wheel, with a parrot skeleton on his shoulder. In many ways, the imagery is summarized by Clive Cussler in *Trojan Odyssey*:

> She was a square-rigged barque with three masts and a shallow draft, a favorite vessel of pirates before the seventeen hundreds. The foresails and topsails were billowing in a nonexistent breeze. She mounted ten guns, five run out on the main deck on both sides. Men with bandannas around their head were standing on the quarterdeck, waving swords. High on her mainmast, a huge black flag with a fiendishly grinning skull dripping blood stood straight out as if the ship was sailing against a headwind . . . "Look at the man in the scarlet suit and tell me what you see" . . . "A man with a feathered hat" . . . "He has a peg leg and a hook on his right hand." "Don't forget the eye patch" . . . "all that's missing is a parrot on one shoulder" . . . "A bit stereotyped, don't you think?" . . . captain with his Treasure Island Long John Silver peg leg, Peter Pan hook and Horatio Nelson eye patch. And then there was the flag. (Cussler 2003:210–12)

Digression into fiction is not flippant. Pirate imagery was largely generated by fictional and semifictional accounts. Pirates were sailors first, and their vessels were in contemporary use. Even if it is not a pirate ship, the Beaufort Inlet site is important because it is the oldest wreck yet found in North Carolina. Pirates are just extra titillation to generate public interest and funding. Only after asking very specific questions about just what specifically distinguishes a pirate's belongings from a legal sailor's material culture will we know what is diagnostic for pirate vessels.

14

X Marks the Spot—Or Does It?

Anthropological Insights into the Origins and Continuity of Fiction and Fact in the Study of Piracy

Russell K. Skowronek

The complex societies of early modern Western Europe were set apart from their predecessors by their growing economic linkages beyond the political and cultural boundaries of the region. This nascent "European-centered world economy" was established first through the importation of luxury items and later through bulk produce (Wallerstein 1974:15–63). The basis of this "world economy" was the European "core" states' economic capture and/or political control of "peripheral" areas that produced these desired commodities.

A transformation began to take place in the late eighteenth and early nineteenth centuries that is visible from the Caribbean to the Pacific. Steam technology as part of the nascent Industrial Revolution shrank the globe through the construction of canals, railroads, and steam-powered vessels. The ability to create and rapidly move European produce led to global "democratization" such that more people had economic access to European material goods and Europeans had access to goods once considered luxuries for the elite. Instead of costing silver, plantation-produced comestibles (such as tea, coffee, chocolate, and sugar) and other materials (like hides, tallow, tobacco, and cotton) could be had for the produce of Staffordshire. As time passed, the cultures that produced the exotica of Africa and Asia would come to be seen as a lower form of society within the unilinear evolutionary scheme of the early social Darwinists. In its former place of prominence was the capitalism of Europe and the United States. The material products of Europe replaced "luxury" items from Asia and even locally produced utilitarian items. As a result, the goal was no longer to imitate Asia but to capture it for its market potential. The shock troops of this new invasion made it perfectly clear that they were Europeans first and foremost in language, diet, and material culture, and they expected to enjoy commerce free of the danger of pirates (Skowronek 2002).

Beginning with the reduction of the North African Barbary States at the turn of the nineteenth century and continuing through the proclamation of the Monroe Doctrine and into the 1830s, the United States Navy worked assiduously to clear the Atlantic Ocean and Caribbean Sea of smugglers and pirates. In Asia the Royal Navy did the same, following the British defeat of China in the Opium Wars and the establishment of their naval base in Hong Kong. As a result the late nineteenth century world had radically changed. The rule of law as dictated by remote governments would regulate trade and thus regulate the people's lives, which were already becoming increasingly regulated in the shift to wage labor in factories.

Pirates that were so much a part of the accounts of the early eighteenth century (e.g., Executive Journals, Council of Colonial Virginia, May 5, 1720) had largely disappeared by the mid-nineteenth century. In the West the growing strength of the state and industrialists, which left the proletariat fearful of reprisals by their employers or the state should they not "toe the line," may have made many long for an earlier, freer, time. Escape to that time would come through one of the pluses of life in the controlled world of the West: literacy.

Transformation

Studies of bandits in Sardinia and the Mafia in Sicily have shown that the mid–nineteenth century ascendency of the Italian nation state with its unified civil and criminal codes played a significant role in shaping the perception of outlaws (Anderson 1965; Moss 1979). The result was that outlaws or bandits were glorified, or at least accepted, in their native districts while feared as raiders outside the area. These "Robin Hoods" walk an ambiguous line between the poverty of their neighbors and the wealth of others. Successful bandits stand out as men who evolved from poverty to relative wealth and acquired power in spite of existing government. The more successful they are as bandits, the more extensive the protection granted them, and the more they make themselves respected (Blok 1972; Hobsbawm 1972). In regard to the creation of Robin Hood-like myth, Eric Hobsbawm points out:

> The myth-making or otherwise distorting capacities of the human memory are well-known, and not confined to bandits. The significance of such information is, that it shows (a) the selectivity of the bandit myth (some bandits are "good" whereas others are not), (b) the bandit myth (high moral status, "good" actions) actually formulated by the policeman who fought the bandit, and therefore also (c) the myth of the "good" bandit as compatible with a close and critical acquaintance with the actual behavior of the "other." It seems simplest to assume that there is some relation between a bandit's real behavior and his subsequent myth. There is, of course,

also some evidence that certain bandits have genuinely attempted to play the Robin Hood role. (Hobsbawm 1972:505)

When the place of pirates in the imagination of America is cast against these observations we are better able to understand and separate fact from fiction. After nearly three hundred years of terror, piracy virtually ceased to exist in American and Caribbean waters and piracy began to enter the world of legend (Botting et al. 1978:182; Konstam 1999:156–57, 162–65; Saxon 1999).

As a result of the American Civil War the civil and criminal code of the federal government of the United States became omnipresent across the nation and especially in the former Confederacy. By 1875 Samuel Clemens (aka Mark Twain) began expressing the binary opposition of lovable, high-minded saviors vs. fearsome cutthroats, thieves, and killers. *Tom Sawyer* was published fifty years after Commodore David Porter of the United States Navy and his "special squadron of pirate killers" had cleared Galveston, Texas (in the Republic of Mexico), the Florida Keys, Spanish Puerto Rico and Cuba, and the rest of the Caribbean of the likes of Jean Lafitte and other pirates. The story was situated in the decades preceding the Civil War and thus was a nostalgic look at a freer time of both youth and the world. Tom knew:

> He would be a pirate! That was it! Now his future lay plain before him, and glowing with unimaginable splendor. How his name would fill the world, and make people shudder! How gloriously he would go plowing the dancing seas, in his long, low, black-hulled racer, the *Spirit of the Storm*, with his grisly flag flying at the fore! And at the zenith of his fame, how he would suddenly appear at the old village and stalk into church, brown and weather-beaten, in his black velvet doublet and trunks, his great jack boots, his crimson sash, his belt bristling with horse pistols, his crime-rusted cutlass at his side, his slouch hat with waving plumes, his black flag unfurled, with the skull and crossbones on it, and hear with swelling ecstasy the whisperings, "It's Tom Sawyer the Pirate!—the Black Avenger of the Spanish Main!" (Twain 1946:80)

Later, Huck Finn asked:

> "What does a pirate have to do?"
> Tom said:
> "Oh, they have just a bully time—take ships and burn them, and get the money and bury it in awful places in their island where there's ghosts and things to watch it and kill everybody in the ships—make 'em walk a plank."
> "And they carry the women to the island," said Joe; "they don't kill the women."
> "No," assented Tom, "they don't kill the women—they're too noble. And the women's always beautiful, too."

"And don't they wear the bulliest clothes! Oh, no! All gold and silver and di'monds," said Joe, with enthusiasm.

"Who?" said Huck.

"Why the pirates." (Twain 1946:127)

Twain's masterpiece propelled the people of the last third of the nineteenth century back in time to the freedom of their youth and to a world that was at once frightening and unregulated and exciting and full of potential. Pirates would be forever changed in the popular imagination as a result of his story.

Pirate Fact Today

During the past two and a quarter centuries the United States was engaged in several campaigns to eradicate pirates and protect its economic and political "interests." At the beginning of the nineteenth century it successfully fought the Tripolitan War with the so-called Barbary Pirate States of North Africa. A decade later, following the Monroe Doctrine, the Caribbean was swept of pirates. And at the beginning of the twentieth century the newly imperial United States fought a prolonged and bloody conflict with the Muslim Moros of the southern Philippines that led to the temporary suppression of these "pirates." In the nineteenth and twentieth-centuries the other imperial powers of Europe largely suppressed piracy throughout the globe in order to protect their far-flung colonies. Even as these colonial possessions were granted independence, Cold War alignments continued to hold piracy in check.

By the late 1970s acts of piracy were again becoming increasingly common. Like their forebears in the eighteenth century many are poverty-stricken people seeking easy pickings. Others are employed by transnational crime organizations, warlords, corrupt government officials, and terrorist cells (Burnett 2002:10). In 1983 armed attacks on merchant vessels had increased to the extent that concern was expressed by both governments and shipping interests. The United Nation's International Maritime Organization asked the International Chamber of Commerce's International Maritime Bureau to report on these armed attacks. Between 1981 and 1987, 733 incidents of piracy were reported. This number is very low, because many attacks are not reported and because dead men tell no tales. Some have estimated that this number may represent only 10–50 percent of the attacks actually committed (Hyslop 1989:5).

Since 1992 the International Maritime Bureau in conjunction with the International Chamber of Commerce's Commercial Crime Services has issued a "Weekly Piracy Report" from its reporting center in Kuala Lumpur, Malaysia. In the eleven years from 1992 to 2003, 2,993 attacks or attempted attacks were reported worldwide (table 14.1). By far the largest number of these incidents take place in Southeast Asia along the Malacca Straits and in the South China Sea. The International Maritime Bureau defines piracy and armed robbery as: "An act of boarding or attempting to board any ship with the apparent intent to commit theft or any other crime and with the apparent intent or capability to use force in the furtherance of that act." This definition covers actual or attempted attacks whether the ship is berthed, at anchor, or at sea. Jayant Abhyankar, the deputy director of the ICC International Maritime Bureau, estimates that the average annual monetary loss is $40 million (personal communication to Russell Skowronek, January 8, 2003). In international commerce this is not a significant amount of money; but the hijackings, hostage-taking, violent acts of robbery, and murder are very real and do make local, regional, and international newspapers, probably because the "P-word" is used (for example, Associated Press 2001; Lehman 2001; Wray 2001).

As John Burnett (2002:284–85) points out, it is hard to distinguish between piracy and terrorism. The Palestine Liberation Front's 1985 seizure of the *Achille Lauro* and the attack on the USS *Cole* in Aden have been termed acts of piracy. There was a policy that was universally accepted: if pirates get aboard a vessel, give them anything they want. This policy was in place in airplane hijackings until September 11, 2001. Clearly acts of piracy that turn into acts of terrorism are a very clear and present danger in today's world.

Assessing the Impact of Popular Culture in the Current Population

At the dawn of the twenty-first century hardly a week passes without a discussion in the media about the topic of "pirates" and "piracy." Perhaps in this age of instant information that is not surprising: simply typing in the words "pirate," "piracy," and "pirates" in the Google Internet search engine results in millions of "hits." But do these represent the kind of piracy that is the topic of this book? Many of these discussions have focused on the illegal acquisition of computer software, music, cable television, and film. In Silicon Valley headlines such as "Software Piracy Sweep Was 2 Years in the Making" (Stites 2002), "Turbo Tax Will Drop Anti-Piracy Feature" (Liedtke 2003), "Business Software Piracy Falls Slightly" (Jesdanun 2003), "Alleged Software Pirate Arrested" (Staff 2003), "The Hunt for Music Pirates" (Editorial 2003), "Music Stars Make Plea for Piracy Controls" (Associated Press 2002), "Fighting Music Piracy" (Chmielewski 2002), "Music Piracy Facing New Weapons" (Chmielewski 2003b), "Sales of Pirated Music Up 50%" (Reuters 2002), and "Cable Companies Crack Down on Service Pirates" (Kelly 2003) are regularly found in the pages of the *San Jose Mercury News*. Perhaps the most telling headline was "Colleges on Spot over Piracy" (Chmielewski 2003a) in terms of what it says about college-aged people. Not unlike the accounts from the early eighteenth century, these articles discuss how such acts of piracy hurt legitimate corporations. Newspapers came into being to report news that might positively or adversely affect business, so such articles are not surprising. What is surprising are the editorials that question some of the antipiracy laws (Editorial 2002) that infringe upon "fair use" rights

Table 14.1. Locations of Actual and Attempted Attacks, 1992–2003

Locations	1992	1993	1994	1995	1996	1997	1998	1999	2000	2001	2002	2003
SE Asia												
Cambodia	—	1	1	1	1	1	—	—	—	—	—	—
Indonesia	49	10	22	33	57	47	60	115	119	91	103	121
Malacca Straits	7	5	3	2	3	4	1	2	75	17	16	28
Malaysia	2	—	4	5	5	2	10	18	21	19	14	5
Myanmar (Burma)	—	—	—	—	1	2	—	1	5	3	—	—
Philippines	5	—	5	24	39	16	15	6	9	8	10	12
Singapore Straits	—	—	3	2	2	5	1	14	5	7	5	2
Thailand	—	—	—	4	16	17	2	5	8	8	5	2
Far East												
China/Hong Kong/ Macau	1	1	6	31	9	5	2	—	2	—	—	1
East China Sea	—	10	6	—	1	1	—	—	1	2	1	—
Hong Kong/Luzon/ Hainan (HLH) Area	—	27	12	7	4	1	—	—	—	—	—	—
Papua New Guinea	—	—	—	—	1	1	3	1	—	1	1	—
Solomon islands	—	—	—	—	—	—	—	—	2	—	2	—
South China Sea	6	31	6	3	2	6	5	3	9	4	—	2
Taiwan	—	—	—	2	—	—	—	—	—	2	1	1
Vietnam	—	—	2	4	—	4	—	2	6	8	12	15
Indian Subcontinent												
Bangladesh	—	—	2	2	4	9	9	25	55	25	32	58
India	5	1	1	8	11	15	12	14	35	27	18	27
Sri Lanka	—	2	1	6	9	13	1	6	3	1	2	2
Americas												
Brazil	—	4	7	17	16	15	10	8	8	3	6	7
Caribbean	—	—	1	—	—	—	—	—	—	—	—	4
Colombia	—	1	—	1	3	—	4	4	1	1	7	10
Costa Rica	—	—	—	—	—	—	—	—	—	—	1	—
Cuba	—	—	—	—	1	—	—	—	—	—	—	—
Dominican Republic	—	—	—	—	—	3	4	2	4	5	7	4
Ecuador	—	—	3	—	3	10	10	2	13	8	12	6
Guatemala	—	—	—	—	—	—	—	—	1	—	—	2

(continued)

Table 14.1—*Continued*

Locations	1992	1993	1994	1995	1996	1997	1998	1999	2000	2001	2002	2003
Guyana	—	1	—	—	2	—	2	—	1	—	12	6
Haiti	—	—	—	—	—	—	—	1	1	—	1	1
Honduras	—	—	—	—	1	—	—	—	1	—	—	1
Jamaica	—	—	—	—	1	3	2	2	—	—	2	5
Martinique	—	—	—	—	—	—	—	1	—	1	—	1
Mexico	—	—	—	1	—	—	—	—	—	1	—	—
Nicaragua	—	—	—	1	1	1	1	2	1	—	2	2
Panama	—	—	—	1	2	1	—	—	4	1	6	7
Peru	—	—	—	1	1	1	—	—	—	—	—	—
Salvador	—	—	—	—	—	—	—	—	—	1	—	2
Trinidad & Tobago	—	—	—	—	1	—	—	—	—	—	—	—
Uruguay	—	—	—	—	1	1	1	—	1	—	1	1
USA	—	—	—	—	1	3	1	6	3	1	8	13
Venezuela	—	—	—	—	—	—	—	—	—	—	—	—
Africa												
Algeria	—	—	1	—	—	1	1	1	—	1	—	3
Angola	—	3	—	1	—	1	1	1	3	1	—	1
Benin	—	—	—	—	—	—	—	—	—	—	—	2
Cameroon	—	—	—	—	—	3	5	3	2	7	5	—
Congo	—	—	—	—	—	—	—	—	1	1	—	—
Egypt	—	—	1	—	—	—	2	1	1	2	—	—
Equatorial Guinea	—	—	—	1	—	—	2	3	2	3	7	—
Gabon	—	—	—	—	—	—	—	—	—	—	1	3
Gambia	—	—	—	1	2	2	4	2	2	5	5	3
Ghana	—	—	1	1	2	3	2	6	6	3	2	4
Guinea	—	—	1	1	2	—	—	1	—	1	2	—
Guinea Bissau	—	—	1	—	4	4	1	5	5	9	5	2
Ivory Coast	—	—	—	—	—	—	7	—	5	—	2	1
Kenya	—	—	—	—	—	1	—	—	—	—	—	—
Liberia	—	—	—	—	—	—	—	—	—	1	3	1
Madagascar	—	—	—	—	—	—	—	1	1	1	—	—
Mauritania	—	—	1	—	—	—	—	—	1	1	—	—
Morocco	—	—	—	—	—	—	—	1	2	1	—	—
Mozambique	—	—	—	—	—	—	—	—	2	—	1	1

Location												
Nigeria	—	2	—	1	4	9	3	12	9	19	14	39
Oman	—	—	—	—	—	—	—	—	—	—	1	—
Red Sea/Gulf of Aden	—	—	—	—	—	6	2	1	13	11	11	18
Senegal	—	—	—	—	2	3	—	—	—	1	3	8
Sierra Leone	—	—	—	—	3	3	—	—	3	3	1	—
Somalia/Djibouti	—	—	1	14	4	5	9	14	9	8	6	3
South Africa	—	2	1	2	3	4	3	3	1	1	6	1
Tanzania	—	1	—	—	—	—	3	—	2	7	3	5
Togo	—	—	—	—	1	5	—	—	1	—	1	1
Yemen	—	—	—	—	—	—	—	2	1	1	5	—
Zaire	—	—	—	—	—	—	—	2	—	—	—	—
Rest of the World												
Albania	—	—	—	—	—	5	1	—	—	—	—	—
Arabian Sea	—	—	—	—	—	—	—	—	2	—	—	1
Arabian Gulf	—	—	—	—	—	—	—	—	1	—	—	—
Australia	—	—	—	—	—	—	—	—	—	—	—	1
Bulgaria	—	—	—	1	—	1	—	—	—	—	1	—
Denmark	—	—	—	—	—	1	—	—	—	—	1	1
France	—	—	—	—	—	—	1	—	—	—	—	—
Georgia	—	—	—	—	—	—	—	—	—	—	1	—
Greece	—	—	—	—	1	2	—	—	1	1	—	—
Indian Ocean	—	—	—	—	2	3	1	3	1	1	—	2
Iran	—	—	—	8	—	—	—	—	1	1	—	—
Iraq	—	—	—	1	2	—	1	2	—	2	1	—
Italy	—	—	—	—	—	—	—	—	—	—	—	—
Malta	—	—	—	—	1	1	1	—	—	—	—	—
Netherlands	—	—	—	1	1	—	—	—	—	—	1	—
Portugal	—	—	—	1	1	—	1	—	—	—	—	—
Russia	—	—	—	1	2	2	1	—	—	—	—	—
Turkey	—	—	—	1	2	—	1	—	—	—	—	—
UAE	—	—	—	—	—	—	—	—	1	—	2	—
United Kingdom	—	—	—	—	—	—	—	—	—	—	—	—
Location Not Available	31	2	—	1	—	1	1	—	1	1	—	1
Total for the year	106	103	90	188	228	247	202	300	469	335	370	445

of consumers. How these "acts of piracy" are seen in contemporary society is important when considering piracy in the past. Many in today's world see software and music piracy as noncrimes or victimless crimes. The people who are involved in such acts are invisible in society. Unlike the corporate executive officers or rock and film stars whose material is taken, the pirates are your neighbors or children or enterprising Third World entrepreneurs.

Pirates and piracy are very much a part of today's world whether in hi-tech, on the high seas, or in popular culture. Two questions arise from this reality. Just where are these competing views in the consciousness of the West? And how might those images influence the questions asked by anthropologists studying piracy in the archaeological record?

In order to gain insights into this issue, combination interviews/surveys were conducted with 302 individuals from the Philippines and the United States ranging from eighteen to eighty-seven years of age. The United States and the Philippines were chosen because of their differing colonial heritages—English and Spanish—and their intertwined history and cultures during the past century. Also, the educated people of both countries use English, which means that there is nearly equal access to print and film in that language. The following information was collected for all respondents: age, sex, place of birth, where they grew up, and ethnic identity. They then were asked to write down or state during interviews the first things that came to mind with the words "pirate" and "piracy."

The octogenarians were born and grew up in Los Angeles, Chicago, and New York. They shared similar images of English pirates operating in the Caribbean, adorned with eye patches, skulls and cross bones, head scarves, peg legs, and hooks (figure 14.1). The men, who were both officers in the U.S. Navy and veterans of World War II, used words like "adventuresome" and "glamorous," whereas the women used terms like "stealing," "robbery," "murder," and "violence" to describe the pirate lifestyle. One man tellingly said that pirates had "no structure, no restrictions, and did what they wanted, when they wanted, and where they wanted." He went on to reminisce about "Errol Flynn dashing about and rescuing women." The other man mentioned buried treasure. Both men and women specifically mentioned the book *Treasure Island* and the illustrations of N. C. Wyeth and Howard Pyle. Films about pirates starring Errol Flynn, Douglas Fairbanks, and Charles Laughton were mentioned by the men, and one of the women said that she "did not like pirates in the movies because of the violence, and she wished her parents had left her at home." The only pirate mentioned by name was Captain Kidd (and that was because he was a New Yorker), and the only sports team mentioned was the Pittsburgh Pirates.

Baby boomers paint a very different shared image of pirates. Five respondents were born in the United States. They grew up in Indianapolis, El Paso, San Fran-

Figure 14.1. The World War II generation had its stereotypes reinforced through paperback novels of the era.

cisco, and suburban New York City. Four mentioned the Disney film *Peter Pan*, and one recalled Mary Martin "flying" on the Ed Sullivan Show. The two men specifically mentioned the film *The Buccaneer*, about Jean Lafitte's role in the Battle of New Orleans. One of the men said that pirates were "cool" and had a "great flag," but most of all "they fought the same guys we fought—the British." He went on to discuss recollections from his youth, including reading the *Classics Illustrated Treasure Island* and more general associations of pirates with "buried treasure" and "maps with X-marks the spot." Interestingly, he noted that his college fraternity used the skull and cross bones as the symbol for their secret brotherhood—a covenant that he imagined to be as strong as that of the pirates. In the fraternity a pirate skull and cross bones flag was prominently displayed and used to intimidate pledges and other fraternities on the intramural fields of Indiana University. Finally, while associating "pirate" rum and grog with Jimmy Buffett, he recalled that on a recent trip to Disney World in Florida his five-year-old sons referred to the "Pirates of the Caribbean" adventure as "Daddy's ride."

Another male born in 1950 thought of *The Buccaneer* but also named Maureen O'Hara in the 1945 RKO Radio Picture *The Spanish Main* and others as *the* prototype for beautiful strong women in the swashbucklers of earlier years. He recalled dressing up like a pirate for Halloween and thinking of pirates not as "serial killers" but usually as good guys with a heart of gold who protect women. He also remembered the Pirates' House Restaurant in Savannah, Georgia, as the place where he had the "best pecan chicken in his life!" As a life-long resident of the Bay Area he noted that the Oakland Raiders were seen as "nasty and tough." Finally, as the father of a college-aged son, he stated: "I don't know but I wonder if they [his son's age-grade] have any point of reference for pirates and if they do it is probably not as powerful an image."

The two women mentioned the stereotypes of peg legs, eye patches, and pirate flags. One recalled playing with a plastic pirate ship and pretending to be a pirate with a rubber knife, and the other mentioned a pirate coloring book she had as a child. There was one mention of Marlon Brando in *Mutiny on the Bounty*, another of Pittsburgh Pirates baseball, and from both of them a discussion of illegally obtained computer software, music, and videos. One of Latina descent who was born and reared in El Paso noted that "pirates were English" and attacked the Spanish Armada and other Spanish ships.

Two individuals born and reared in Colombia and the Philippines also responded. The Colombian associates the term "pirate" with the English and secondarily with the French and Dutch in the Golden Age. For him it was the image of Blas de Leso, memorialized with a statue in Cartagena, who stood up to "el pirata el Draque" (Sir Francis Drake). He recalled being admonished by his parents to be good or "El Draque" would get him. When he reflected on his nieces and nephews and other children, he concluded that their image of "pirates" was less fearsome and more along the lines of the image created by Disney, a caricature. The Filipino also associated the term "pirate" with the images of the Golden Age; but unlike his fellow baby boomers, he noted the very real issue of the Abu Sayaf Islamic pirates in the southern Philippines and their connection to the "Moro Pirates" of the early twentieth century.

Last are the images of college-aged students. During the 2002/2003 academic year, 182 female and 109 male students at the Ateneo de Manila University in the Philippines, East Carolina University in North Carolina, and Santa Clara University in California were surveyed before the debut of the Disney film *Pirates of the Caribbean.*

From east to west the surveys were nearly identical. Recurring images included treasure, treasure maps, the skull and cross bones, eye patches, parrots, hooks, and peg legs. The most permeating "pirate" association is that of Disney's *Peter Pan* and his nemesis Captain Hook. Even in the Philippines the Disneyland/ World "Pirates of the Caribbean" adventure was noted. A few mentioned recent films such as Geena Davis in *Cutthroat Island* and Disney's *Treasure Planet*, but the classic *Treasure Island* was noted fewer than ten times. Blackbeard was the only named pirate, mentioned seventeen times; it is not surprising that thirteen of those were in North Carolina, while the other three were in Manila. A lone respondent listed Jimmy Buffett.

Sports images were never mentioned as the primary association with "pirates." No one in the Philippines and only five California students associated "pirates" with Pittsburgh, Oakland, or Tampa Bay. It is worth noting that the survey was conducted when Oakland and Tampa Bay played each other in the Super Bowl. Eleven East Carolina students did associate "pirate" with their mascot.

Finally, there is the issue of contemporary piracy. In all cases it was secondary to the "real" pirate images of the Golden Age. Fewer than 15 percent of the students surveyed in the United States mentioned music, video, and software piracy, whereas 80 percent of the Filipinos did. In fact, Ateneo's students mentioned the Green Hills/Quiapo section of Manila as a hotbed for "pirated" goods and named Bong Revilla as the Philippine government representative empowered with enforcing the law. Perhaps most surprising is that fewer than 5 percent of the Filipino respondents mentioned the Abu Sayaf pirates that plague the southern Philippines and the more generalized piracy of the South China Sea as being an issue.

In summary it is evident that the shift started a century and a quarter ago by Mark Twain is firmly entrenched in today's Western-educated populace. Pirates are a thing of the past. Stereotypically they are one-legged, one-handed, one-eyed, parrot-toting, treasure-burying, "arrrggghh"-saying, jolly English rogues who can be scary but usually are misunderstood, with a heart of gold. How do these pervasive images affect the historical archaeology of piracy?

Ramifications of Fiction and Fact in the Historical Archaeology of Piracy

> There comes a time in every rightly constructed boy's life when he has a raging desire to go somewhere and dig for hidden treasure . . . "Where'll we dig?" said Huck. "Oh, most anywhere." "Why, is it hid all around?" "No, indeed it ain't. It's hid in mighty particular places, Huck—sometimes on islands, sometimes in rotten chests under the end of a limb of an old dead tree, just where the shadow falls at midnight . . ." (Twain 1946:212–13)

Since the days of Howard Carter, archaeology has been likened to a treasure hunt by the general public. We need only look to our students to recall our own first discoveries and the excitement they engender. It is the hook that drives archaeologists and pot hunters alike. It is also the reason that the United States has had antiquities laws for a century. The confrontation between collectors and scientists is a replaying of the confrontation between the pirates of the past and governmental representatives who are enforcing the laws and as a result are perceived as keeping the "little guys" from striking it rich.

Making the case that archaeology "preserves, protects, and interprets" the past plays well in the classroom, but it may not be understood by the general public and by elected lawmakers who control funding for archaeology. The past for most is history, and history is a particularizing discipline whose documentary record can provide the details of who, when, where, how, and what transpired in the past. Anthropology, in contrast, is a generalizing social science that draws on oral histories, ethnohistory, documents, and material culture both synchronically and diachronically. Archaeology as part of anthropology can only provide particulars when activities occur. That is when specific events result in the creation of *de facto* archaeological sites that are associable with particular people or places. Examples would be the earthquake that sank the pirate lairs of Port Royal, Jamaica, and the storm that sank the *Whydah*. While both examples are thought to represent a moment in time, they also contain diachronic evidence for an English colonial town and an English-built and operated vessel used in the African slave trade. The result is that anthropological archaeology adds little new specific information to what is already known about particular "historical" people or events in the past beyond examples of material culture. That is not to say that historical archaeology is not important; but its strength lies in pattern identification and comparison in the examination of cultural continuity and change. Within this dimension lies the promise of maritime archaeology as the provenance for understanding piracy (Muckelroy 1978). Ships can be seen as closed hierarchical communities and as part of an economic system. Ports are seen as the nexus between the floating communities and the political system of which they were a part. A nonpirate pattern must be identified in order to identify a pirate pattern.

In this volume archaeologists have studied shipwrecks, port towns, and purported lairs in order to discern a pirate pattern. Have they been successful? As anthropologists we need to ask if the cherished preconceived notions that have been created over the past century are correct. For instance, was the pirate lifestyle noticeably different from the lifestyle of merchants or naval seamen? Did they have distinctive food preferences, clothing, or vessels? Was the alleged democratic or egalitarian lifestyle a reality or a fiction created in the nineteenth century? Were port towns such as Port Royal supplied with exotica that were significantly different from those of such contemporary English colonial communities as New York, Providence, or Boston? According to Donny Hamilton (this volume), no. Daniel Finamore, however, when viewing Barcadares from the perspective of conspicuous consumption, thinks that difference might be apparent.

When work is carried out in Bath, North Carolina, home to Blackbeard, will his short association with the community result in patterns that are demonstrably different from those of other English colonial towns in the Carolinas or Tidewater? From the evidence presented for Port Royal, this seems unlikely. Perhaps first we need to look at such staging communities as Lafitte's Grande Terre, Tortuga Island off of Haiti, Barcadares, Belize, St. Mary's Island, or other anchorages on Madagascar's east coast that can be solely linked to pirates. Documents tell us that illicit trade was rampant in the Spanish colonial world. Does the surviving material evidence support these allegations? In backwater communities such as St. Augustine house sites associated with the elites demonstrated a lower frequency of items that were demonstrably "non–Spanish empire" in origin than those associated with commoners (Skowronek 1984, 1992). Is this evidence of illegal trade making a mockery of the empire?

What of the effects of piracy in general on the citizenry of the Spanish Caribbean? We can point to the expense of constructing, maintaining, and garrisoning fortifications throughout the region. This leads, however, to the gray zone: where does privateering end and piracy begin? There is often a fine line between state-sponsored terrorism with troops or auxiliaries and pirate attacks. Were Drake and Sir Walter Raleigh pirates? Spain and England were not at war, yet there was no peace beyond the line. For the Spanish, they were pirates; for the English, heroes who would be tolerated if the Crown got their share. Captain Kidd did not reach the same hallowed halls, because his superiors felt they did not receive their share of his booty. As a result he is infamous rather than famous.

Others have suggested that a mixture of coins might be indicative of piracy. In the Golden Age of Piracy and beyond it was specie and not whose picture appeared on coinage that mattered. In the United States Spanish *reales* were legal tender until the 1850s, and coins from the Netherlands have been found in mission-era California. Certainly, no one suggests that Dutch pirates were at work in the region. Similarly, it has been suggested that a mixture of different calibers and types of guns and small arms might suggest a pirate vessel. Yet studies of the Spanish *flota* lost in the Florida Keys in 1733 show a mixture of armaments (Skowronek 1984). Perhaps it is more realistic to associate a lack of consistency with non-naval vessels in general, where there were two key issues. The first is the cost of outfitting a vessel; and the second, for merchant ships, is the cost associated with cargo space lost to shot, powder, and weapons. Thus, could the alleged *Queen Anne's Revenge* simply be an armed merchant ship? Unfortunately, since it lacked a name-embossed bell like the *Whydah*, it just might be (see Lusardi, this volume). Similarly, except for the documentary record, is there anything from the *Speaker* that says "this is a pirate ship"? No, and that is why the work will continue.

Another avenue of inquiry might involve the study of piracy by examining its victims. Perhaps the response of their prey may give us insights into the predators themselves. Although the flatboat *America* is popularly associated with river pirates, it has been interpreted as the victim of a river snag (see Wagner and McCorvie, this volume). Yet, looking at the evolution of Spanish settlement in the Caribbean, there is no denying that aggression by foreign pirates had a profound effect on their settlement patterns.

Our image of pirates during the Golden Age is one of violence and danger. Few died wealthy and aged. Blackbeard and Thomas Tew died in battle, Samuel Bellamy was lost at sea, and William Kidd and Stede Bonnet died at the end of a rope. Their bodies and those of thousands more were suspended from gibbets as a lesson to others about the cost of piracy. Merchantmen, naval seamen, and the shore-bound general public tended to live short, violent lives. Transportation and corporal and capital punishment were a very real part of everyday life onshore for thieves, debtors, and highwaymen, while floggings and hangings were part of life at sea. Ships' crews and members of the public watched the meting out of these punishments with the same rank fascination and horror evoked by the O. J. Simpson trial and the executions of Ted Bundy and Timothy McVeigh. Whether they are seen as the point of genesis for capitalism or the hypermasculine homo-erotic antihero (Rediker 1987; Turley 1999), pirates in the Golden Age were part of this society. The excavation of a ship, a community, or a gallows (Jones and Downing 1992) will not reveal a pirate way of life unless there is a larger scale against which it may be measured.

Conclusions

A recent television commercial in the United States depicted "pirates" attacking a suburban male who, while (ironically) barbecuing, defends himself from the buccaneers with the lid to his grill and a spatula. He is attacked because he does not carry a Capital One Bank Card. The imagery and meaning of raiders taking what is not theirs is not lost. Almost daily, people can open their newspapers and see comic strips featuring pirates that make them laugh. Children dress like pirates for Halloween and birthdays and receive "pirate gold coins." Few think about modern pirate/terrorists or computer/video/music piracy, and fewer still are exposed to how archaeologists might go about identifying a pirate ship (e.g., Hanks and Howell 2000).

Archaeologists are faced with a conundrum when asked to find the real pirates expected by the general public, whose images are firmly ingrained. Who were these people? Were they earlier versions of the Mob or drug cartels? They ask questions: How would you recognize them? Do they have specialized clothing, or technology that is different from that of their peers? Do they eat different foods or sail different ships? The short answer seems to be no; and that is why the analogy to modern gangs works. Pirates could be as invisible in their world as gangsters are in ours: a brotherhood at once fearsome to outside authorities and friendly to its neighbors. One final popularized view of pirates makes this point. Disney was behind the 1996 Jim Henson Production of the *Muppet Treasure Island*. This musical version of the Stevenson classic starring Tim Curry as Long John Silver earned an Academy Award for best musical score. The song "Professional Pirate" by Larry Mann and Cynthia Wehl, sung by Curry, sums up the argument made here: Curry notes that for the British, Drake was a hero; and for the Spanish, he was the devil. It was how you viewed them that made them bad or good, but members of a brotherhood.

As Western anthropologists we carry as much of our culture as the rest of the populace does. It is up to us to ask the questions that count when attempting to discern the subculture of piracy. These must be questions that can be tested in the archaeological record and not in childhood fantasy. With the baseline presented in this volume, pirate fact may begin to supplant fiction.

Acknowledgments

This chapter could never have been written without the aid of many people. Robert Swieringa of Grand Valley State University, Michigan, Charles Ewen of East Carolina University, and Jayant Abhyankar of the ICC International Maritime Bureau freely shared their insights into pirates in film and literature, childhood images, and the contemporary world. I am especially indebted to the students of Ateneo de Manila University, East Carolina University, and Santa Clara University for their insightful responses to the "pirate/piracy" questionnaire, and to the following individuals for their interviews: Luis Calero, S.J., of Santa Clara University, Alma Garcia of Santa Clara University, Dorothy E. Graham and Dennis M. Graham of Indianapolis, Indiana, Arthur Hauschild of Medford, Oregon, Lester Skowronek, Helen Wyszpolski Skowronek, and Leslie Skowronek of Hendersonville, North Carolina, Henry Totanes of Ateneo de Manila University, and George Westermark of Santa Clara Universtiy. Lisa Kealhofer of Santa Clara

University provided information on the archaeology of "capital punishment" in colonial Virginia.

I am especially grateful to my parents, Helen and Lester, for never having thrown out any of the toys, books, comic books, or record albums from my childhood. As I fondled, re-read, or listened to them again after a 35-year hiatus, every image of pirates came back into clear focus for me.

References Cited

Addis, John. 1979. *Southeast Asian and Chinese Trade Pottery.* Hong Kong, China: Oriental Ceramic Society.

Algemeen Rijksarchief, La Haye, Hollande. 1702a. VOC 4048 fol 344 a 359: copie missive door het opperhooft Roeloff Diodati en raed opt eylant Mauritius a den gouverneur en raed voornoemt van 5 September 1702.

———. 1702b. VOC 4048 fol. 364 a 369: copie resolutien genomen in raden op Mauritius van 9, 11 en 20 Januari en 20 Maen 1702 raackende de Engelse zeerovers op dat eylant haer schip verlooren hebbende.

Allen, Michael. 1990. *Western Rivermen, 1763–1861.* Baton Rouge: Louisiana State University Press.

———. 1991. The Ohio River: Artery of Movement. In *Always a River*, edited by Robert L. Reid, pp. 105–29. Bloomington: Indiana University Press.

Alvord, Clarence W. 1909. *Kaskaskia Records, 1778–1790.* Collections of the Illinois State Historical Library, Volume 5. Springfield, Ill.: Illinois State Historical Society.

Anderson, Dean L. 1994. The Flow of European Trade Goods into the Western Great Lakes Region, 1715–1760. In *The Fur Trade Revisited: Selected Papers of the Sixth North American Fur Trade Conference, Mackinac Island, Michigan, 1991*, edited by Jennifer S. Brown, W. J. Eccles, and David P. Heldman, pp. 93–116. East Lansing: Michigan State University Press.

Anderson, Robert T. 1965. From Mafia to Cosa Nostra. *American Journal of Sociology* 71:302–10.

Angley, F. Wilson. 1977. North Carolina shipwreck references from the *Boston Gazette*, 1719–1798, and the *Pennsylvania Gazette*, 1728–1812. Microfilm. Raleigh: North Carolina Division of Archives and History.

Anonymous. 1806. The Journal of a Trip from Champaign County, Ohio, and Down the Mississippi River to New Orleans with a Cargo of Flour, 25 Nov. 1805–26 July 1806. Manuscript Collection SC2148. Illinois State Historical Society, Springfield.

———. 1817. Journal of a Voyage Down the Ohio and Mississippi in the Spring of 1817. Manuscript Collections. Newberry Library, Chicago.

———. 1943. News and Comment. *Journal of the Illinois State Historical Society* 36(3):422–24.

Archives de la Bibliothèque Municipale de Genève.

Archives Nationales, Paris. $F^{2C}11$ Colonies: Mémoire du sieur Boucher sur Bourbon.

———. $C^{3}2$ Colonies, piece 11: Journal des diferents vents . . . par Jean Feuilley, avec l'acte de deces de J. Bowen.

———. 1702. $C^{2}66$ et 67 Colonies: correspondance générale de l'Inde, copies de lettres écrites par M. du Livier et les marchand des comptoirs d'Ougly relatives à la prise du *Speaker* (12–1–1702; fol. 232 et seq.).

Archives of the Diodati family.

Arnold, J. Barto, III, and Robert Weddle. 1978. *The Nautical Archaeology of Padre Island.* New York: Academic Press.

Ashe, Thomas. 1808. *Travels in America*. London: E. M. Blunt.

Associated Press. 2001. Indonesians Walk Plank, But It's All for Safer Seas. *New York Times*, November 11.

———. 2002. Music Stars Make Plea for Piracy Controls. *San Jose (California) Mercury News*, October 4.

Audubon, Maria. 1897. *Audubon and His Journals*. New York: Charles Scribners and Sons.

Augelli, John P., ed. 1965. *Caribbean Lands*. Grand Rapids, Mich.: Fideler Co.

Babits, L. E. 2001. Pirates. *Tributaries* 11 (October):7–13.

Babits, Lawrence E., and Waldemar Ossowski. 1999. 1785 Common Sailors' Clothing and a Ship's Camboose from the *General Carleton of Whitby*. In *Underwater Archaeology Proceedings from the Society for Historical Archaeology Conference, Richmond, Virginia*, edited by Adrian Askins Neidinger and Matthew A. Russell, pp. 115–22. Society for Historical Archaeology.

Bailey, De Witt. 1997. *Pattern Dates for British Ordnance Small Arms 1718–1783*. Gettysburg, Pa.: Thomas Publications.

Bailey, Jane Stubbs, Allen Hart Norris, and John H. Oden III. 2002. Legends of Black Beard and His Ties to Bath Town: A Study of Historical Events Using Genealogical Methodology. *North Carolina Genealogical Society Journal* 28(3) (August):247–306.

Baird, Donald. 1973. His Highness Prince Rupert's Way of Making Shot, 1665. *Canadian Journal of Arms Collecting* 11(3):83–85.

Baldwin, Leland. 1941. *The Keelboat Age on Western Waters*. Pittsburgh: University of Pittsburgh Press.

Bancroft, Edward. 1813. *Experimental Researches Concerning the Philosophy of Permanent Colours*. 2 vols. London: T. Cadell and W. Davies.

Bancroft, Mark. 1835. Mark Lee's Narrative. *Casket* 7:301–10.

Banta, R. E. 1949. *The Ohio*. New York: Rinehart and Company.

Barassin, Jean. 1955. *Naissance d'une chrétienté: Bourbon des origines jusqu'en 1714*. St. Denis, Réunion: Cazal.

Barbot, John. 1746. An Abstract of a Voyage to *New Calabar* River, or *Rio Real*, in the Year 1699. In *Collection of Voyages and Travels, Some Now First Printed from Original Manuscripts, Others Now First Published in English, in Six Volumes, with a General Preface, Giving an Account of the Progress of Navigation, from Its First Beginning*, edited by Awnsham Churchill and John Churchill, vol. 5, pp. 455–66. 3rd edition. 6 vols. London: Henry Lintot and John Osborn.

Barnard, John. 1976. *Ashton's Memorial*. Salem, Mass.: Peabody Museum of Salem.

Barnsley, Henry. 1742. The Island of Rattan. Library of Congress MS, Howe Collection No. 28.

Barrett, Richard A. 1984. *Culture and Conduct*. New York: Wadsworth Publishing Co.

Barrie, James Mathew. 1904. *Peter Pan* (play). London.

———. 1928. *Peter Pan*. New York: Scribner Publishers.

———. 1987. *Peter Pan*. Mahwah, N.J.: Watermill Press.

Barry, Dave. 2002. Pirate Talk Could Shiver Your Timbers. *San Jose (California) Mercury News*, September 8.

Bassett, John Spenser, ed. 1926–35. *The Correspondence of Andrew Jackson*. 6 vols. Washington, D.C.

Baum, Adolph, and Arthur C. Troncoso (translators). 1935. *Records and Deliberations of the Cabildo, Book No. 5, from July 19, 1802 to November 18, 1803*. New Orleans: New Orleans Public Library.

Baumgarten, Linda. 1986. *Eighteenth-Century Clothing at Williamsburg*. Williamsburg, Va.: Colonial Williamsburg.

Beer, Captain. 1717. Rhode Island Dispatch of May 3, 1717. *Boston News Letter*, May 6.

Benchley, Peter. 1980. *Island*. New York: Doubleday.

Bendix, William, 1959. *Famous Pirate Stories*. CR 30. Cricket Records, Pickwick Sales Corp. Recording.

Bibliothèque Nationale, Paris, France. Manuscrit Naf 9346: Mémoire pour servir à la connaissance particulière . . . d'Antoine Boucher.

Binford, Lewis R. 1978. New Method of Calculating Dates from Kaolin Pipe Stem Samples. In *Historical Archaeology: A Guide to Substantive and Theoretical Contributions*, edited by Robert L. Schuyler, pp. 66–67. Farmingdale, N.Y.: Baywood Publishing Co.

Bingeman, John M. 1985. Interim Report on Artefacts Recovered from *Invincible*. *International Journal of Nautical Archaeology* 14(3):203.

Black, Clinton V. 1983. *History of Jamaica*. Kingston, Jamaica: Longman Caribbean.

———. 1989. *Pirates of the West Indies*. London: Cambridge University Press.

Blackman, W. Haden. 1998. *The Field Guide to North American Hauntings*. New York: Three Rivers Press.

Blackmore, Howard L. 1976. *The Armouries of the Tower of London: Volume I, Ordnance*. London: Her Majesty's Stationery Office.

Blair, Claude. 1962. *European and American Arms c. 1100–1850*. New York: Bonanza Books.

Blair, Walter, and Franklin J. Meine, eds. 1956. *Half Horse, Half Alligator*. Chicago: University of Chicago Press.

Blanch, H. J., and Martin Rywell. 1956. *English Guns and Gun Makers*. Harriman, Tenn.: Pioneer Press.

Blok, Anton. 1972. The Peasant and the Brigand: Social Banditry Reconsidered. *Comparative Studies in Society and History* 14 (4):494–503.

Blowe, Daniel. 1820. *View of the United States of America*. London: n.p.

Bolland, O. Nigel. 1977. *The Formation of a Colonial Society: Belize, from Conquest to Crown Colony*. Baltimore: Johns Hopkins University Press.

Bond, Beverly W., ed. 1922. Memoirs of Benjamin Van Cleve. *Quarterly Publication of the Historical and Philosophical Society of Ohio* 17(1 and 2):3–71.

Bonnet, Stede. 1719. *The Tryals of Major Stede Bonnet, and Other Pirates*. London: Benjamin Cowse.

Bostock, Henry. 1717. The Deposition of Henry Bostock Mariner, before the Honorable William Mathew Lieutenant General of His Majesty's and Lieutenant Governor of This Island [December 19, 1717]. British Public Records Office, Colonial Office 152/12.

Botkin, B. A. 1955. *A Treasury of Mississippi River Folklore*. New York: Crown Publishers.

Botting, Douglas, and the editors of Time-Life Books. 1978. *The Pirates*. The Seafarers Series. Alexandria, Va.: Time-Life Books.

Boyette, Pat. 1991. Adaptation of Robert Louis Stevenson's *Treasure Island* (comic book). Classics Illustrated, no. 17. Chicago: Berkley Publishing Group and First Publishing, Inc.

Boy Scouts of America, 1954. *Bear Cub Scout Book*. New Brunswick, N.J.: Boy Scouts of America.

———. 1967. *Bear Cub Scout Book*. New Brunswick, N.J.: Boy Scouts of America.

Brand, Ellis. 1718. Letter of Captain Ellis Brand to the Board of Admiralty [July 12, 1718]. National Maritime Museum, Greenwich, ADM 1/1472.

Braudel, Fernand. 1973. *Capitalism and Material Life, 1400–1800*. New York: Harper and Row Publishers.

British Museum Catalogue (BMC). *Oriental Coins* III: 131, no. 358. London: British Museum.

Brooks, George E., ed. 1968. *Timothy Flint's Recollections of the Last Ten Years in the Valley of the Mississippi*. Carbondale and Edwardsville: Southern Illinois University Press.

Brown, John. 1717. Examination of John Brown, May 6, 1717. In *The Trials of Eight Persons Indicted for Piracy . . .* Early American Imprint Series No. 2003, Worcester, Mass.: American Antiquarian Society.

Brown, M. L. 1980. *Firearms in Colonial America: The Impact on History and Technology, 1492–1792*. Washington, D.C.: Smithsonian Institution Press.

Brown, Ruth R. 1997. Arms and Armour from Wrecks: an Introduction. In *Artefacts from Wrecks: Dated Assemblages from the Late Middle Ages to the Industrial Revolution*, edited by Mark Redknap, pp. 101–9. Monograph 84. Oxford: Oxbow.

Brown, Vera Lee. 1928. Contraband Trade: A Factor in the Decline of Spain's Empire in America. *Hispanic American Historical Review* 8:178–89.

Brown, Wilbert S. 1969. *The Amphibious Campaign for West Florida and Louisiana: A Critical Review of Strategy and Tactics at New Orleans*. University: University of Alabama Press.

Bryant, William Cullen. 1874. *Picturesque America*. New York: D. Appleton.

Buckley, Roger Norman. 1998. *The British Army in the West Indies: Society and the Military in the Revolutionary Age*. Gainesville: University of Florida Press.

Buffett, Jimmy. 1998. *A Pirate Looks at Fifty*. New York: Fawcett Crest. Recording.

Bulloch, Ivan, and Diane James. 1997. *I Wish I Were . . . a Pirate*. London: Two-Can Publishing, Ltd.

Burdon, Sir John Alder. 1931–35. *Archives of British Honduras*. 3 vols. London: Sifton Praed.

Burgess, Robert F., and Carl J. Clausen. 1982. *Florida's Golden Galleons: The Search for the 1715 Spanish Treasure Fleet*. Port Salerno: Florida Classics Library.

Burnett, John S. 2002. *Dangerous Waters, Modern Piracy and Terror on the High Seas*. New York: Dutton.

Burns, Alan Cuthbert. 1954. *History of the British West Indies*. London: George Allen and Unwin Ltd.

Butler, Lindley S. 2000. *Pirates, Privateers, and Rebel Raiders of the Carolina Coast*. Chapel Hill: University of North Carolina Press.

Cain, Robert J., ed. 1984. *Records of the Executive Council, 1664–1734*. The Colonial Records of North Carolina, vol. 7. Raleigh: North Carolina Division of Archives and History.

Caldwell, Norman. 1949. Cantonment Wilkinson. *Mid-America* 20(1):28.

Callahan, John E., J. William Miller, and James R. Craig. 2001. Ballast Stones from North Carolina Shipwreck 0003 BUI, the *Queen Anne's Revenge*: Hand Specimen, X-Ray,

Petrographic, Chemical, Paramagnetic and 40K-40Ar Age Results. *Southeastern Geology* 40(1):49–57.

Carter, John Henton. 1890. *Thomas Rutherton*. New York: H. C. Nixon.

Case, Bernard. 1999. Illustrations of the Sinking of *Queen Anne's Revenge*. On file, North Carolina Underwater Archaeology Branch, Kure Beach, N.C.

Ceramics Research Institute. 1959. *A Draft History of Ceramics at Ching-te Chen*. Beijing, China: Ceramics Research Institute.

Cervantes, Gonzalo López. 1977. *Porcelana Oriental en la Nueva España*. Anales de Antropología e Historia, Epoca 8a, vol. 1. Mexico City: Instituto Nacional de Antropología e Historia.

Chapuiset Le Merle, André de. 1950. *Précis d'histoire de l'Ile Maurice*. Port-Louis.

Chmielewski, Dawn C. 2002. Fighting Music Piracy. *San Jose (California) Mercury News*, September 15.

———. 2003a. Colleges on Spot over Piracy. *San Jose (California) Mercury News*, February 17.

———. 2003b. Music Piracy Facing New Weapons. *San Jose (California) Mercury News*, January 21.

Claiborne, J. F. H. 1880. *Mississippi as a Province, Territory, and State*. Jackson, Miss.: Power and Barksdale.

Claypole, William A. 1972. The Merchants of Port Royal, 1655–1700. Doctoral dissertation, Department of History, University of the West Indies.

Clifford, Barry. 1993. *The Pirate Prince: Discovering the Priceless Treasures of the Sunken Ship Whydah*. New York: Simon and Schuster.

Clifford, Barry, and Paul Perry. 1999a. *The Black Ship: The Quest to Recover an English Pirate Ship and Its Lost Treasure*. London: Headline Book Publishing.

———. 1999b. *Expedition Whydah: The Story of the First Excavation of a Pirate Treasure Ship and the Man Who Found Her*. New York: HarperCollins Publishers.

Clifford, Sheila A. 1991. A Preliminary Report on a Possible 17th-Century Shipwreck at Port Royal, Jamaica. In *Underwater Archaeology Proceedings from the Society for Historical Archaeology Conference, Richmond, Virginia*, edited by John D. Broadwater, pp. 80–83. Society for Historical Archaeology.

———. 1993. An Analysis of the Port Royal Shipwreck and Its Role in the Maritime History of Seventeenth-Century Port Royal, Jamaica. Master's thesis, Department of Anthropology, Texas A&M University, College Station.

Coates, Robert M. 1930. *The Outlaw Years*. New York: Literary Guild of America.

Collot, Georges-Henri-Victor. 1826. *Voyage dans l'Amérique Septentrionale*. Paris: A. Bertrand.

Cordingly, David, 1995. *Under the Black Flag: The Romance and the Reality of Life among the Pirates*. New York: Harcourt Brace.

Cordingly, David, and John Falconer. 1992. *Pirates, Fact & Fiction*. New York: ARTABRAS, a Division of Abbeville Publishing Group.

Corning, Howard, ed. 1929. *Journal of John James Audubon during His Trip to New Orleans in 1820–1821*. Cambridge, Mass.: Business Historical Society.

Corpus Nummorum Austriacorum. 1975. Wein, Vienna: Bundessammlung von Medaillen, Münzen und Geldzetchen, Kunsthist Museum.

Corpus Nummorum Italicorum. VIII.

Cotterell, Howard H. 1972. European Continental Pewter, Part 1. In *National Types of Old Pewter*, pp. 45–52, Princeton: Pyne Press.

———. 1985. *Old Pewter: Its Makers and Marks in England, Scotland and Ireland, an Account of the Old Pewterer and His Craft*. Rutland, Vt.: Charles E. Tuttle Company.

Council, Robert Bruce. 1975. Archaeology of the Convento de San Francisco. Master's thesis, Department of Anthropology, University of Florida, Gainesville.

Craig, Alan K. 1969. Logwood as a Factor in the Settlement of British Honduras. *Caribbean Studies* 9:53–62.

Craig, James R., John E. Callahan, J. William Miller, and Wayne R. Lusardi. 2001. Preliminary Studies of Some Base and Precious Metals from the *Queen Anne's Revenge*. *Southeastern Geology* 40(1):41–48.

Cramer, Zadok. 1811. *The Navigator*. Pittsburgh: Cramer, Spear, and Eichbaum.

Croft, Pauline. 1983. English Mariners Trading to Spain and Portugal 1558–1625. *The Mariner's Mirror: The Journal of the Society for Nautical Research* 69(3):251–66.

Crosby, Alfred W. 1972. *The Columbian Exchange: Biological and Cultural Consequences of 1492*. Westport, Conn.: Greenwood Press.

———. 1986. *Ecological Imperialism: The Biological Expansion of Europe, 900–1900*. Cambridge: Cambridge University Press.

Cuming, Fortescue. 1810. *Sketch of a Tour to the Western Country*. Pittsburgh: Cramer, Spear and Eichbaum.

Curryer, Betty Nelson. *Anchors: An Illustrated History*. Annapolis, Md: Naval Institute Press.

Curtin, Philip D. 1984. *Cross-Cultural Trade in World History*. Cambridge: Cambridge University Press.

Curtis, Julia B. 1988. Perceptions of an Artifact: Chinese Porcelain in Colonial Tidewater Virginia. In *Documentary Archaeology in the New World*, edited by Mary C. Beaudry, pp. 20–31. Cambridge: Cambridge University Press.

Cussler, Clive. 2003. *Trojan Odyssey*. New York: G. P. Putnam's Sons.

Dampier, William (Captain). 1906a. *Dampier's Voyages*. 2 vols. New York: E. P. Dutton.

———. 1906b. *Dampier's Voyages: Two Voyages to Campeachy*. 2 vols. Edited by John Masefield. London: E. Grant Richards. (Reprint of 1717 edition.)

Darroch, Alison C. 1986. The Visionary Shadow: A Description and Analysis of the Armaments Aboard the Santo Antonio de Tanna. M.A. thesis, Department of Anthropology, Texas A&M University, College Station.

Das, H. 1959. *The Norris Embassy to Aurengzeb, 1699–1702*. Calcutta: K. L. Mukhopadhyay.

Das Gupta, A. 1979. *Indian Merchants and the Decline of Surat: c. 1700–50*. Wiesbaden: Steiner.

Davidson, William V. 1974. *Historical Geography of the Bay Islands, Honduras*. Birmingham, Ala.: Southern University Press.

Davis, Ralph. 1973. *The Rise of the Atlantic Economies*. London: Weidenfeld and Nicolson.

Davis, Stephen. 1997. Piecing Together the Past: Footwear and Other Artefacts from the Wreck of a 16th-Century Spanish Basque Galleon. In *Artefacts from Wrecks*, edited by Mark Redknap, pp 110–20. Oxbow Monograph 84. Oxford:.Short Run Press.

Deagan, Kathleen. 1980. Spanish St. Augustine: America's First "Melting Pot." *Archaeology* 33(5):22–30.

———. 1983. *Spanish St. Augustine*. New York: Academic Press.

———. 1985. The Archaeology of 16th-Century St. Augustine. *Florida Anthropologist* 28(1–2, part 1):6–33.

———. 1987. *Artifacts of the Spanish Colonies of Florida and the Caribbean 1500–1800*. Washington, D.C.: Smithsonian Institution Press.

———. 1995. *Puerto Real: The Archaeology of a Sixteenth-Century Spanish Town in Hispaniola*. Gainesville: University Press of Florida.

de Bry, John. 1999. Report on Archival Research Pertaining to the Concorde of Nantes and Its Capture by Pirates in 1717. Contract Report furnished to the North Carolina Department of Cultural Resources, Raleigh, N.C.

Deetz, James. 1977. *In Small Things Forgotten: Archaeology of Early American Life*. Garden City, N.Y.: Anchor Books.

Defoe, Daniel. [Charles Johnson, pseud.]. 1972. *A General History of the Pyrates*. Edited by Manuel Schonhorn. London: Dent.

———. 1999. *A General History of the Pyrates*. Edited by Manuel Schonhorn. Mineola, N.Y.: Dover.

DeGrummond, Jane Lucas. 1961. *Baratarians and the Battle of New Orleans*. Baton Rouge: Louisiana State University Press.

Delmonte, A. 1967. *Le Benelux d'argent*. Amsterdam: J. Schulman.

De Maisonneuve, B. 1992. Excavation of the *Maidstone*, a British Man-of-War Lost Off Noirmoutier in 1747. *International Journal of Nautical Archaeology* 21(1):15–26.

Desroches, Jean-Paul, Gabriel Casal, and Franck Goddio. 1997. *Treasures of the San Diego*. Manila, Philippines: National Museum of the Philippines.

Dethlefson, Edwin. 1984. *Whidah: Cape Cod's Mystery Ship*. Woodstock, Vt.: Seafarers Heritage Library.

Disney, Walt. 1968. *Pirates of the Caribbean*. Sound Track of the Fabulous Disneyland Adventure (ST 3937). Walt Disney Productions. Recording.

Dosset, Pierre. 1718. Verification and Addendum to the Deposition of Ernaut, Lieutenant on the *Concorde*, Plundered and Taken by the Pirates [October 13, 1718]. Archives de Loire-Atlantique, Nantes, B4578, folio 90 v.

Douglas, Mary. 1991. A Distinctive Anthropological Perspective. In *Constructive Drinking*, edited by Mary Douglas, pp. 16–69. New York: Cambridge University Press.

Draper, Lyman. n.d.a. Notes, Series S, Volume 30. Draper Manuscripts. Wisconsin Historical Society, Madison.

———. n.d.b. Series CC, Kentucky Papers, Volume 2. Draper Manuscripts. Wisconsin Historical Society, Madison.

Ducoin, Jacques. 2001. Historical Research in the French Archives on the *Concorde* of Nantes: A French Slave Ship Captured by Pirates in November 1717. Contract Report furnished to the North Carolina Department of Cultural Resources, Raleigh.

Dunbar, Seymour. 1915. *A History of Travel in America*. Vol. 1. New York: Bobbs-Merrill Company.

Dunkle, Stacie E., James R. Craig, and Wayne R. Lusardi. 2001. Romarchite and the Corrosion of Pewter Artifacts. Paper presented at the Geological Society of America annual meeting and exposition, "Boston 2001: A Geo-Odyssey," A128.

Dunn, Richard S. 1973. *Sugar and Slaves: The Rise of the Planter Class in the English West Indies 1624–1713*. New York: W. W. Norton and Company.

Editorial. 2002. Jurors See through Unjust Anti-Piracy Law. *San Jose (California) Mercury News*, December 23.

———. 2003. The Hunt for Music Pirates. *San Jose (California) Mercury News*, January 27.

Ehrlich, Martha J. 1992. Akan Gold from the Wreck of the *Whydah*, Site WLF-HA-1. Appendix 1 in *Final Report of Archaeological Data Recovery, Text, The Whydah Shipwreck Site, WLF-HA-1, 1982–1992*. The Whydah Joint Venture, submitted to U.S. Army Corps of Engineers, Waltham, Mass., and the Massachusetts Historical Commission, Boston, Mass.

Einarsson, Lars. 1997. Artefacts from the *Kronan* (1676): Categories, Preservation and Social Structure. In *Artefacts from Wrecks*, edited by Mark Redknap, pp 209–18. Oxbow Monograph 84. Oxford: Short Run Press.

Elia, Ricardo. 1992. The Ethics of Collaboration: Archaeologists and the *Whydah* Project. *Historical Archaeology* 26(4):105–17.

Elliott, J. H. 1963. *Imperial Spain 1469–1716*. New York: New American Library.

Ellms, Charles. 1993. *The Pirates Own Book: Authentic Narratives of the Most Celebrated Sea Robbers*. Mineola, N.Y.: Dover Publications.

———. 1996. *The Pirates* (1837). New York: Gramercy Books.

Epstein, Jeremiah F. 1959. Dating the Ulua Polychrome Complex. *American Antiquity* 25:125–29.

Eras, Vincent J. M. 1974. *Locks and Keys throughout the Ages*. Folkestone: Bailey and Swinfen.

Ernaut, François. 1718. *La Concord de Nantes* Plundered and Taken by Pirates. Series B 4578, fols. 56v–57v. Nantes, France, Archives Départementales de Loire-Atlantique.

Eslinger, Kimberly L., and Mark Wilde-Ramsing. 2001. Live from Morehead City, It's *Queen Anne's Revenge*. A paper presented at the 35th Annual Conference on Historical and Underwater Archaeology. Mobile, Ala.

Evans, Sally K., Frederick Stielow, and Betsy Swanson. 1979. *Grand Isle on the Gulf: An Early History*. Jefferson Parish, La.: Jefferson Parish Historical Commission.

Ewen, Charles R. 1991. *From Spaniard to Creole: The Archaeology of Hispanic American Cultural Formation at Puerto Real, Haiti*. Tuscaloosa: University of Alabama Press.

Executive Journals, Council of Colonial Virginia. May 5, 1720. Accounts of Charges Exhibited for Apprehending the Pyrates Lately Tryed Here. Vol. 2, 22382, p. 525.

Fairbanks, Charles H. 1973. The Cultural Significance of Spanish Ceramics. In *Ceramics in America*, edited by Ian M. G. Quimby, pp. 141–74. Charlottesville: University Press of Virginia.

Falconer, William. 1870. *An Universal Dictionary of the Marine: or, A Copious Explanation of the Technical Terms and Phrases Employed in the Construction, Equipment, Furniture, Machinery, Movements, and Military Operations of a Ship*. New York: Augustus M. Kelley. (Reprint of 1789 edition.)

Faye, Stanley. 1940. The Great Stroke of Pierre Laffite. *Louisiana Historical Quarterly* 23(3):733–827.

Finamore, Daniel. 1994. Sailors and Slaves on the Woodcutting Frontier: Archaeology of the British Bay Settlement, Belize. Unpublished dissertation, Boston University.

———. 2004. "Pirate Water": Sailing to Belize in the Mahogany Trade. In *Maritime Empires: British Imperial Maritime Trade in the Nineteenth Century*, edited by David Killingray, Margarette Lincoln, and Nigel Rigby. Suffolk, U.K.: Boydell and Brewer.

Fisher, J. J. 1962. Geomorphic Expression of Former Inlets along the Outer Banks of North Carolina. Master's thesis. University of North Carolina, Chapel Hill.

Flagg, Edmund. 1838. *The Far West*. New York: Harper and Brothers.

Flint, Timothy. 1830a. The Boat-Wreckers, or Banditti of the West. *Casket* 3:103–6.

———. 1830b. Col. Plug. *Western Monthly Magazine*: 354–59.

Floyd, Troy S. 1967. *The Anglo-Spanish Struggle for Mosquitia*. Albuquerque: University of New Mexico Press.

———. 1973. *The Columbus Dynasty in the Caribbean, 1492–1526*. Albuquerque: University of New Mexico Press.

Forman, Major Samuel. 1888. *Narrative of a Journey Down the Ohio and Mississippi Rivers in 1789–1790*. Compiled for publication by Lyman Draper. Cincinnati: Robert Clarke and Company.

Foster, George M. 1960. *Culture and Conquest: America's Spanish Heritage*. Viking Fund Publications in Anthropology 27. New York: Wenner-Gren Foundation for Anthropological Research, Inc.

Franzen, Anders. 1966. *The Warship Vasa: Deep Diving and Marine Archaeology in Stockholm*. Stockholm: Norstedts Bonniers, P. A. Norstedt and Soners Forlag.

———. 1974. *The Warship Vasa*. Stockholm, Sweden: P. A. Norstedt and Soners Forlag.

Frazier, Charles. 1997 *Cold Mountain*. New York: Atlantic Monthly Press.

Gagliano, S., R. A. Weinstein, Eileen K. Burden, K. L. Brooks, and W. P. Glander. 1979. *Cultural Resources Survey of the Barataria, Segnetter and Rigaud Waterways, Jefferson Parish, Louisiana*. Submitted to the New Orleans District, U.S. Army Corps of Engineers, New Orleans.

Galvin, Peter R. 1999. *Patterns of Pillage: A Geography of Caribbean-Based Piracy in Spanish America, 1536–1718*. New York: Peter Lang Publishing.

Gerhard, Dietrich. 1981. *Old Europe: A Study of Continuity, 1000–1800*. New York: Academic Press.

Gibbs, Archibald Robertson. 1883. *British Honduras: An Historical and Descriptive Account of the Colony from Its Settlement, 1670*. London: Sampson Low.

Gibson, Charles. 1968. *The Spanish Tradition in America*. New York: Harper and Row.

Gibson, Kelly. Examination of Sub-Bottom Survey Data and Sediment Cores at the *Queen Anne's Revenge* Wreck Site. Senior Thesis, Department of Physical Sciences, Virginia Institute of Marine Sciences, College of William and Mary, Gloucester Point, Va.

Gilkerson, William. 1993. *Boarders Away with Fire: The Small Firearms and Combustibles of the Classical Age of Fighting Sail, 1626–1826, Tracing their Development in the Navies of England and Northern Europe through That of the United States*. Lincoln, R.I.: Andrew Mowbray.

Godzinski, Michael, B. D. Maygarden, A. Saltus, P. Heirich, R. Gray, E. Poitevent, J. Clary, J.-K. Yakubik, B. South, and R. Smith. 2001. Cultural Resource Investigations on Grand Terre Island, Jefferson Parish, Louisiana. Draft. Submitted to the New Orleans District, U.S. Army Corps of Engineers, New Orleans.

Goggin, John M. 1968. *Spanish Majolica in the New World*. Publications in Anthropology 72. New Haven: Yale University Press.

Gooding, S. James. 1986. *An Introduction to British Artillery in North America*. Alexandria Bay, N.Y.: Museum Restoration Service.

Goodman, Steve, 1973. Lincoln Park Pirates. Song on the album *Somebody Else's Troubles*. Buddah Records. Recording.

Goodwin, Peter. 1988. *The 20–Gun Ship Blandford*. Annapolis, Md.: Naval Institute Press.

Gordon, Lewis H. 1967. The British Military Blunderbuss and Musketoon. *Canadian Journal of Arms Collecting* 5(3):75–84.

Gould, E. W. 1859. *Fifty Years on the Mississippi*. St. Louis: Nixon-Jones Printing Company.

Gray, Harriet, 1956. *Gold for the Gay Masters*. New York: Avon Publications.

Grey, Charles. 1933. *Pirates of the Eastern Seas, 1618–1725*, edited by George MacMunn. London: S. Low, Marston.

Guye, S., and H. Michel Fribourg. 1970. *Mesures du temps et de l'espace*. London: Pall Mall Press.

Gwynn-Jones, Peter. 2001. Personal communication. Garter Principal King of Arms, the College of Arms, London.

Hakluyt, Richard. 1927. *The Principal Navigations, Voyages, Traffiques and Discoveries of the English Nation*. 8 vols. London: J. M. Dent.

Haldane, Cheryl W. 1995. *Sadana Island Shipwreck*. College Station, Tex.: Institute of Nautical Archaeology.

Hall, James. 1828. *Letters from the West*. London: Henry Colburn.

Hall, Martin. 1992 Small Things and the Mobile, Conflictual Fusion of Power, Fear, and Desire. In *The Art and Mystery of Historical Archaeology: Essays in Honor of James Deetz*, edited by Anne Elizabeth Yentsch and Mary C. Beaudry, pp. 373–99. Boca Raton, Fla.: CRC Press.

Hamilton, Christopher E., Regina Binder, and Garreth McNair-Lewis. 1992. *Final Report of Archaeological Data Recovery: Catalog/Inventory, The* Whydah *Shipwreck Site WLF-HA-1*. Report Submitted to U.S. Army Corps of Engineers, Waltham, Mass., and the Massachusetts Historical Commission, Boston. *Whydah* Joint Venture Laboratory. South Chatham, Mass.: Maritime Underwater Surveys, Inc.

Hamilton, Christopher E., and Michel Cembrola. 1991. *Underwater Archaeological Reconnaissance Survey of the Proposed Effluent Outfall Site, Boston, Massachusetts*. Report to Cashman/Interbeton: A Joint Venture. Quincy, Mass.: Maritime Underwater Surveys, Inc.

Hamilton, Christopher E., James R. Reedy Jr., and Kenneth Kinkor. 1988. *Final Report of Archaeological Testing: The* Whydah *Shipwreck, Site WLF-HA-1*. Report Submitted to the Massachusetts Board of Underwater Archaeological Resources, the U.S. Army Corps of Engineers, and the Advisory Council on Historic Preservation. South Chatham, Mass.: Maritime Underwater Surveys, Inc.

————. 1990. *The 1989 Annual Report of Archaeological Data Recovery: The* Whydah *Shipwreck, Site WLF-HA-1*. Report Submitted to the Massachusetts Board of Underwater Archaeological Resources, the U.S. Army Corps of Engineers, and the Advisory Council on Historic Preservation. South Chatham, Mass.: Maritime Underwater Surveys, Inc.

Hamilton, D. L. 1991. A Decade of Excavations at Port Royal, Jamaica. In *Underwater Archaeology Proceedings from the Society for Historical Archaeology Conference, Richmond, Virginia*, edited by John D. Broadwater, pp. 90–94. Society for Historical Archaeology.

————. 1992. Simon Benning, Pewterer of Port Royal. In *Text-Aided Archaeology*, edited by Barbara J. Little, pp. 39–53. New York: CRC Press.

Hamilton, D. L., and Robyn Woodward. 1984. A Sunken 17th-Century City: Port Royal, Jamaica. *Archaeology* 37(1):38–45.

Hamilton, Earl J. 1934. *American Treasure and the Price Revolution in Spain, 1503–1660.* Cambridge, Mass.: Harvard University Press.

Hamilton, T. M. 1968. *Early Indian Trade Guns: 1625–1775.* Lawton, Okla.: Museum of the Great Plains.

———. 1976. *Firearms on the Frontier: Guns at Fort Michilimackinac 1715–1781.* Midland, Mich.: Pendell Printing.

———. 1987. *Colonial Frontier Guns.* Union City, Tenn.: Pioneer Press.

Hamilton, Walter. n.d. Extract of a Letter from Genl Hamilton Governor of the Leeward Islands, without date [January 6, 1717/18]. British Public Records Office, Colonial Office 152/12.

Hamilton, William B. 1953. *Anglo-American Law on the Frontier: Thomas Rodney and His Territorial Cases.* Durham, N.C.: Duke University Press.

Hanks, Stephen, and Richard Howell. 2000. Blackbeard the Pirate (comic book). *Archaeology's Dig* 2(1):37–39.

Haring, Clarence H. 1910. *The Buccaneers in the West Indies in the XVII Century.* London: Methuen.

———. 1918. *Trade and Navigation between Spain and the Indies in the Time of the Habsburgs.* Cambridge, Mass.: Harvard University Press.

———. 1947. *The Spanish Empire in America.* New York: Harcourt, Brace and Jovanovich.

Harman, Joyce Elizabeth. 1969. *Trade and Privateering in Spanish Florida, 1732– 1763.* St. Augustine, Fla.: St. Augustine Historical Society.

Harrington, J. C. 1954. Dating Stem Fragments of Seventeenth and Eighteenth Century Clay Tobacco Pipes. *Quarterly Bulletin of the Archaeological Society of Virginia* 9:9–13.

Hatcher, John, and T. C. Barker. 1974. *A History of British Pewter.* London: Longman Group Limited.

Hatfield, Joseph. 1965. Governor William Charles Cole Claiborne, Indians, and Outlaws in Frontier Mississippi. *Journal of Mississippi History* 27(2):323–49.

———. 1976. *William Claiborne: American Centurion in the American Southwest.* Lafayette: University of Southwest Louisiana.

Hawkins, Colin, 1994. *Pirate Ship: A Pop-Up Adventure.* New York: Cobblehill Books.

Hawtrey Gyngell, Dudley S. 1959. *Armourers Marks: Being a Compilation of the Known Marks of Armourers, Swordsmiths, and Gunsmiths.* London: Thorsons Publishers.

Heath, Dwight. 1987 A Decade of Development in the Anthropological Study of Alcohol Use, 1970–1980. In *Constructive Drinking,* edited by Mary Douglas, pp. 16–69. New York: Cambridge University Press.

Henderson, Captain George. 1811. *An Account of the British Settlement of Honduras.* London: C. and R. Baldwin.

Hernandez, Greg. 2003. Disney's "Pirates" Hoists Victory Flag. *San Francisco Chronicle,* July 12.

Herrick, Francis H. 1926. Thomas Ashe and the Authenticity of His Travels in America. *Mississippi Valley Historical Review* 13:50–57.

Herriot, David. 1719. The Information of David Herriot and Ignatius Pell. In *The Tryals of Major Stede Bonnet and Other Pirates*, pp. 44–48. London: Benjamin Cowse Publisher.

Hildreth, Samuel P. 1843. Extracts from B. Van Cleve's Memoranda. *American Pioneer* 2:42.

Hill, E. 1995. Thimbles and Thimble Rings from the Circum-Caribbean region, 1500–1800: Chronology and Identification. *Historical Archaeology* 29(1):84–92.

Hills, S. C. 1919–20. Episodes of Piracy in Eastern Waters 1519–1851. *Indian Antiquary* 48/49.

———. 1926–19. Notes on the Piracy in Eastern Waters. *Indian Antiquary* 55/56.

Hinds, James R., and Edmund Fitzgerald. 1998. *Bulwark and Bastion: A Look at Musket Era Fortifications with a Glance at Period Siegecraft*. Union City, Tenn.: Pioneer Press.

Hobsbawm, E. J. 1972. Social Bandits: Reply. *Comparative Studies in Society and History* 14(4):503–5.

Hodges, William, and Eugene Lyon. 1995. A General History of Puerto Real. In *Puerto Real: The Archaeology of a Sixteenth-Century Spanish Town in Hispaniola*, edited by Kathleen Deagan, pp. 83–112. Gainesville: University Press of Florida.

Hoffman, Paul. 1980. *The Spanish Crown and the Defense of the Caribbean, 1535–1585*. Baton Rouge: Louisiana State University Press.

Howard, Frank. 1979. *Sailing Ships of War 1400–1860*. New York: Mayflower Books.

Hurst, J. G. 1977. Spanish Pottery Imported in Medieval Britain. *Medieval Archaeology* 21:68–109.

Hyslop, I. R. 1989. Contemporary Piracy. In *Piracy at Sea*, edited by Eric Ellen, pp. 3–40. Publication No. 455. Paris: ICC International Maritime Bureau and Woods Hole Oceanographic Institution.

Indiana Jones and the Last Crusade. 1989. Screenplay by Jeff Boam. Story by George Lucas and Menno Meyje.

India Office Library and Records. London. E-3-70, no. 8567. Capture *Speaker*, Captain Eastlake.

———. E-3-65, no. 8057. Déclaration de Thomas Towsey, charpentier du *Speaker*. Liste des Pirates qui capturent le *Speaker*.

Ingraham, Joseph Holt. 1841. Rapin of the Rock; or, the Outlaw of the Ohio, A Tale of the Cave-in-Rock. *Ladies' Companion* 15:15–21.

Jamaica Public Archives. 1689. Henry Morgan's Probate Inventory, Inventories vol. 3, folio 258–61. Spanish Town, Jamaica.

Jamborsky, William Eric. 1989. Davy Crockett and the Tradition of the Westerner in American Cinema. In *Crockett at Two Hundred: New Perspectives on the Man and the Myth*, edited by Michael A. Lofaro and Joe Cummings, pp. 97–113. Knoxville: University of Tennessee Press.

Jesdanun, Anick. 2003. Business Software Piracy Falls Slightly. *San Jose (California) Mercury News*, June 3.

Johnson, Charles [Daniel Defoe]. 1724. *A General History of the Robberies and Murders of the Most Notorious Pyrates*. London: C. Rivington, J. Lacy.

———. 1972. *A General History of the Pyrates*. Edited by Manuel Schonhorn. Columbia: University of South Carolina Press.

———. 1998. *A General History of the Robberies and Murders of the Most Notorious Pirates*. With introduction by David Cordingly. New York: Lyons Press.

Johnson, Robert. 1733. Letter of Affidavit of John Calcok on the Loss of the 1733 Spanish

Flota. MS on file, Florida Collection of the Monroe County Public Library, Islamorada, Fla.

Jones, Joseph B., and Charles M. Downing. 1992. *Capital Punishment in Colonial Virginia*. Phase III Data Recovery for Mitigation of Adverse Effects to Site 44WB66. Technical Report Series 18, William and Mary Center for Archaeological Research. Williamsburg, Va.: Department of Anthropology, College of William and Mary.

Jordan, William B. 1985. *Spanish Still Life in the Golden Age 1600–1650*. Fort Worth: Kimbell Art Museum.

Joseph, Gilbert M. 1980. John Coxon and the Role of Buccaneering in the Settlement of the Yucatán Colonial Frontier. *Terrae Incognitae* 12:65–84.

———. 1989. John Coxon and the Role of Buccaneering in the Settlement of the Yucatán Colonial Frontier. *Belizean Studies* 17(3):2–21.

Journal du Gouverneur de l'Isle Bourbon, de Villers. 1909. Isle Bourbon, documents, 1701–10. *Bulletin of the New York Public Library* 13 (January):7–63.

Judkins, Mary Palmer. n.d. 1845–1859 Journal. Manuscript Collection. Springfield, Illinois State Historic Society.

Kaijser, Ingrid, Ernst Nathort-Boos, and Inga-Lill Persson. 1982. *Ur Sjomannens Kista och Tunna*. Wasastudier 10. Stockholm: Statens Sjohistoriska Museum.

Karraker, Cyrus H. 1953. *Piracy Was a Business*. Rindge, N.H.: Richard R. Smith.

Katsev, Michael 1980. A Cargo from the Age of Alexander the Great. In *Archaeology under Water: An Atlas of the World's Submerged Sites*, edited by Keith Muckleroy, pp. 42–43. New York: McGraw-Hill.

———. 1987. The Kyrenia Ship Restored. In *The Sea Remembers, Shipwrecks and Archaeology*, edited by Peter Throckmorton, pp. 55–59. New York: Weidenfield and Nicolson.

Kelly, John F. 2003. Cable Companies Crack Down on Service Pirates. *San Jose (California) Mercury News*, February 11.

Kemble, Stephen. 1884. *The Kemble Papers*. Vol. 2. Collections of the New York Historical Society, 17. New York: New York Historical Society.

Kennard, A. N. 1986. *Gunfounding and Gunfounders: A Directory of Cannon Founders from Earliest Times to 1850*. London: Arms and Armour Press.

Kerfoot, John Barrett. 1924. *American Pewter*. New York: Bonanza Books.

Kilburn, Richard S. 1981. *Transitional Wares and their Forerunners*. Hong Kong, China: Oriental Ceramic Society.

King, Henry T. 1911. *Sketches of Pitt County, a Brief History of the County, 1704–1910*. Raleigh, N.C.: Edwards Publishing Company.

Kinkor, Kenneth J. 1991. Grenades Recovered from the *Whydah* Site. Appendix IV in *The 1990–1991 Annual Report of Archaeological Recovery: The* Whydah *Shipwreck Site WLF-HA-1*, edited by Christopher E. Hamilton. South Chatham, Mass.: *Whydah* Joint Venture Laboratory.

———. 1992a. *Final Report of Archaeological Data Recovery, Primary Source Bibliography, The* Whydah *Shipwreck Site, WLF-HA-1, October 1992*. Edited by Christopher E. Hamilton et al. Submitted to U.S. Army Corps of Engineers, Waltham, Mass., and the Massachusetts Historical Commission, Boston. South Chatham, Mass.: *Whydah* Joint Venture Laboratory.

———. 1992b. Freemasons, Jacobites and the Brethren of the Black Flag: The Iconography of 18th-Century European Piracy. Appendix IV in *Final Report of Archaeological*

Data Recovery, Text, The Whydah *Shipwreck Site, WLF-HA-1, 1982–1992*. Submitted to U.S. Army Corps of Engineers, Waltham, Mass., and the Massachusetts Historical Commission, Boston. South Chatham, Mass.: *Whydah* Joint Venture Laboratory.

Knight, Russell W., ed. 1976. *Ashton's Memorial: A History of the Strange Adventures and Signal Deliverances of Philip Ashton, Jr. of Marblehead*, by John Barnard. Salem, Mass.: Peabody Museum of Salem. (Reprint of 1725 edition.)

Konstam, Angus. 1999. *The History of Pirates*. New York: Lyons Press.

———. 2000. Personal communication. Former Curator of Arms, Tower of London.

Labat, R. P. 1730. *Voyage du Chevalier Des Marais*. Paris.

Lane, Arthur. 1947. *Early Islamic Pottery*. London: Faber and Faber.

Lavery, Brian. 1987. *The Arming and Fitting of English Ships of War 1600–1815*. Annapolis, Md.: Naval Institute Press.

———. 1989. *Nelson's Navy*. Anapolis, Md.: Naval Institute Press.

Lawrence, Richard W., and Mark Wilde-Ramsing. 2001. In Search of Blackbeard: Historical and Archaeological Research at Shipwreck Site 0003BUI. *Southeastern Geology* 40(1) (February):1–9.

Le Bris, Michel. 2001. *Pirates and Flibustiers des Caraïbes*. Daoulas, France: Hoëbeke.

Lee, Robert E. 1997. *Blackbeard the Pirate: A Reappraisal of His Life and Time*. Winston-Salem, N.C.: John F. Blair.

Lehman, Stan. 2001. New Zealand Yachtsman Peter Blake Killed by River Pirates in Brazil. *San Jose (California) Mercury News*, December 6.

L'Hour, Michel, Luc Long, and Eric Rieth. 1989. *Le Mauritius*. Grenoble, France: Caterman. D.C.

Liedtke, Michael. 2003. Turbo Tax Will Drop Anti-Piracy Feature. *San Jose (California) Mercury News*. May 15.

Lincoln, Abraham. 1953. Biographical Sketch Written for John L. Scripps. In *The Collected Works of Abraham Lincoln, Volume 4*, edited by Roy P. Basler, pp. 60–63. New York: H. Wolff Book Manufacturing Company.

Lindquist, Neils. 1998. Personal communication. Institute of Marine Sciences, University of North Carolina at Chapel Hill. Morehead City, N.C.

Link, Marian Clayton. 1960. Exploring the Drowned City of Port Royal. *National Geographic* 117(2):151–82.

Lister, Florence C., and Robert H. Lister. 1982. *Sixteenth Century Majolica Pottery in the Valley of Mexico*. Anthropological Papers of the University of Arizona No. 3. Tucson: University of Arizona Press.

Lockhart, James, and Stuart B. Schwartz. 1983. *Early Latin America: A History of Colonial Spanish America and Brazil*. Cambridge: Cambridge University Press.

Lofaro, Michael. 1987. *The Tall Tales of Davy Crockett*. Knoxville: University of Tennessee Press.

Lougnon, Albert. 1956. *L'Ile Bourbon pendant la Régence*. Paris: LaRose.

Lowick, N. 1983. In *Sans: An Arabian Islamic City*, edited by R. B. Serjeant and Ronald Lewcock. London: Festival of Islam Trust.

Ludlum, David M. *Early American Hurricanes, 1492–1870*. Boston: American Meteorological Society.

Lusardi, Wayne R. 1999. Do the Artifacts Identify the Beaufort Inlet Shipwreck as the Pirate Blackbeard's Flagship *Queen Anne's Revenge*? In *Underwater Archaeology Proceedings from the Society for Historical Archaeology Conference, Salt Lake City, Utah,* edited by Adriane Askins Neidinger and Matthew A. Russell, pp. 123–32. Society for Historical Archaeology.

———. 2000. The Beaufort Inlet Shipwreck Project. *International Journal of Nautical Archaeology* 29(1):57–68.

———. 2002. Damnation Seize My Soul If I Give You Quarter or Take Any from You: Cannon, Munitions and Small Arms from the Wreck of the Pirate Vessel *Queen Anne's Revenge* (1718). *Man at Arms* 24(2):32–39.

Lydon, James G. 1970. *Pirates, Privateers, and Profits*. Upper Saddle River, N.J.: Gregg Press, Inc.

Lynch, John. 1984. *Spain under the Habsburgs, Volume One: Empire and Absolutism 1516–1598*. New York: New York University Press.

Lyon, Eugene. 1977. St. Augustine 1580: The Living Community. *El Escribano* 14:20–33.

———. 1984. *Santa Elena: A Brief History of the Colony, 1566–1587*. Research Manuscript Series No. 193. Columbia: South Carolina Institute of Archaeology and Anthropology, University of South Carolina.

MacNeill, Ben Dixon, 1958. *The Hatterasman*. Winston-Salem, N.C.: John F. Blair, Publisher.

Manucy, Albert. 1949. *Artillery through the Ages: A Short Illustrated History of Cannon, Emphasizing Types Used in America*. Washington, D.C.: U.S. Government Printing Office.

———. 1985. The Physical Setting of Sixteenth Century St. Augustine. *Florida Anthropologist* 38(1–2):34–53.

Maritime Research Society. 1924. *Pirate's Own Book*. Publication No. 4. Salem, Mass.: Maritime Research Society.

Marsden, Peter, and David Lyon. 1977. A Wreck Believed to Be the Warship *Anne*, Lost in 1690. *International Journal of Nautical Archaeology and Underwater Exploration* 6(1):9–20.

Marx, Jenifer. 1992. *Pirates and Privateers of the Caribbean*. Malabar, Fla.: Krieger Publishing.

Marx, Robert F. 1973. *Port Royal Rediscovered*. New York: Doubleday.

Mason, F. Van Wyck. 1951. *Cutlass Empire*. New York: Pocket Books.

———. 1957. *Captain Nemesis*. New York: Pocket Books.

Mason, Richard Lee. 1915. *Narrative of Richard Lee Mason in the Pioneer West*. New York: Charles Fred Heartman.

Mason Trial Transcript. 1803. Samuel Mason Trial, 1803. Accession Number Z273. Jackson: Mississippi Department of Archives and History.

Massachusetts Historical Society. 1914–15. *Commerce of Rhode Island, 1726–1800*. Collections of the Massachusetts Historical Society, series 7:9–10. Boston: Massachusetts Historical Society.

Masters, Phillip. 2001. Vessels Reported as Lost at Beaufort Inlet in the Eighteenth Century, with Observations and Conclusions. Intersal, Inc., Research Report, Beaufort, N.C.

Masters, Phillip, and John Levin. 2004. Annual Reports of Activities in Beaufort Inlet from 1986 to 2003 by Intersal, Inc. as Required by UAB Permits 584 and 585. On file North Carolina Underwater Archaeology Branch, Kure Beach, N.C.

Mattern, David, J.C.A. Stagg, Ellen J. Barber, Anne Mandeville Colony, and Bradey J.

Daigle. 1986. *The Papers of James Madison, Volume 5.* Charlottesville and London: University Press of Virginia.

Mayes, Philip. 1972. *Port Royal, Jamaica: Excavations 1969–70.* Kingston, Jamaica: National Heritage Trust.

McAlister, Lyle N. 1984. *Spain and Portugal in the New World, 1492–1700.* Minneapolis: University of Minnesota Press.

McEwan, Bonnie G. 1983. Spanish Colonial Adaptation on Hispaniola: The Archaeology of Area 35 Puerto Real, Haiti. Master's thesis, Department of Anthropology, University of Florida, Gainesville.

———. 1986. The Historical Archaeology of Seville. Paper presented at the Sixteenth-Century Studies Conference, Concordia Seminary and Center for Reformation Research, St. Louis, Missouri, October 24, 1986.

———. 1988. An Archaeological Perspective of Sixteenth Century Spanish Life in the Old World and the Americas. Ph.D. dissertation, Department of Anthropology, University of Florida, Gainesville.

McIver, Edward. 1733. Letter of Affidavit of Edward McIver on the Loss of the 1733 Spanish *flota.* MS on file, Florida Collection of the Monroe County Public Library, Islamorada, Fla.

McKee, Alexander. 1972. *King Henry VIII's Mary Rose.* London: Souvenir Press.

McNair-Lewis, Garreth. 1992. Pewter Artifacts Aboard the *Whydah* Galley Site WLF-HA-1. Appendix III in *The 1990–1991 Annual Report of Archaeological Data Recovery: The* Whydah *Shipwreck Site WLF-HA-1,* edited by Christopher E. Hamilton, Kenneth J. Kinkor, and David A. Muncher. South Chatham, Mass.: *Whydah* Joint Venture Laboratory.

McNinch, Jesse E., John T. Wells, and Thomas G. Drake. 2001. Fate of Artifacts in an Energetic, Shallow-Water Environment: Scour and Burial at the Wreck Site of *Queen Anne's Revenge. Southeastern Geology* 40(1):19–27.

Mel Fisher Maritime Heritage Society (MFMHS). 1995. *A Slave Ship Speaks: The Wreck of the Henrietta Marie.* Key West, Fla.: Mel Fisher Maritime Heritage Society.

Melville, Herman. 1984. *Billy Budd, Sailor and Other Stories* (originally published in *The Piazza Tales,* 1856). New York: Bantam.

Mendizábal, Tomas. 1999. Current Archaeological Research in Panama Viejo, Panama. *Papers from the Institute of Archaeology* 10:25–36.

Merry, Ralph, and Samuel Roberts. 1717. Deposition of Ralph Merry and Samuel Roberts. Massachusetts Archives, Suffolk Court Files, May 11–16, 1717.

Mettas, Jean de. 1978. *Répertoire des expéditions négrières françaises au XVIIIe siècles.* Nantes, France: Société Française d'Histoire d'Outre-Mer.

Michener, James A. 1952. *Return to Paradise.* New York: Bantam Books.

Michener, James A., and A. Grove Day, 1958. *Rascals in Paradise.* New York: Bantam Books.

Millás, José Carlos. 1968. *Hurricanes of the Caribbean and Adjacent Regions, 1492–1800.* Miami: Academy of the Arts and Sciences of the Americas.

Miller, J. Jefferson, II, and Lyle M. Stone. 1970. *Eighteenth-Century Ceramics from Fort Michilimackinac: A Study in Historical Archaeology.* Smithsonian Studies in History and Technology, No. 4. Washington, D.C.: Smithsonian Institution Press.

Miller, Regis. 2003. Personal communication. USDA Forest Service, Forest Products Laboratory, Center for Wood Anatomy Research, Madison, Wis.

Mitford, John, Esq., R.N. 1819. *Adventures of Johnny Newcome in the Navy: A Poem in Four Cantos*. London: Sherwood, Neely, and Jones.

Moller, George D. 1993. *American Military Shoulder Arms*. Vol. 1. Niwot: University Press of Colorado.

Moore, David. 1989. Anatomy of a 17th-Century Slave Ship: Historical and Archaeological Investigations of the *Henrietta Marie*. M.A. thesis, Depart of History, East Carolina University, Greenville, N.C.

————. 1997a. Blackbeard Shipwreck Project, Old Topsail Inlet, North Carolina: Preliminary Research Design. MS on file, North Carolina Maritime Museum, Beaufort.

————. 1997b. A General History of Blackbeard the Pirate, the *Queen Anne's Revenge* and *Adventure*. *Tributaries* 7:31–38.

————. 2001. Blackbeard's *Queen Anne's Revenge*: Archaeological Interpretation and Research Focused on the Hull Remains and Ship-Related Accoutrements Associated with Site 31–CR-314. *Tributaries* 11:49–64.

Moore, David D., and Mike Daniel. 2001. Blackbeard's Capture of the Nantaise Slave Ship *La Concorde*: A Brief Analysis of the Documentary Evidence. *Tributaries* 11:14–31.

Moore, Simon. 1987. *Spoons, 1650–1930*. Princes Risborough, Buckinghamshire: Shire Publications.

Morange, Jean. Deposition upon Returning to Martinique. Série Colonies C8A 24 fol. 125. Archives Nationales, Paris.

Moreau, Roger. 1999. *Lost Treasure Mazes*. New York: Sterling Publishing Co.

Morison, Samuel Eliot. 1942. *Admiral of the Ocean Sea: A Life of Christopher Columbus*. Boston: Little, Brown.

Moss, David. 1979. Bandits and Boundaries in Sardinia. *Man* 14(3):477–96.

Moya Pons, Frank. 1976. *Historia Colonial de Santo Domingo*. Santiago R.D.: Universidad Católica Madre y Maestra.

Muckelroy, Keith. 1978. *Maritime Archaeology*. Cambridge: Cambridge University Press.

Muller, Jon. 1986. *Archaeology of the Lower Ohio River Valley*. Orlando, Fla.: Academic Press.

Munday, John. 1998. *Naval Cannon*. Princes Risborough, Buckinghamshire: Shire Publications.

Nash, Abner. 1777. Letter from Abner Nash to ?, dated 19 April 1777. *State Records of North Carolina* 11:719–20.

Newsom, Lee A. 1999. Wood Identifications, NCUAU #0003BUI (*Queen Anne's Revenge*). MS on file, Center for Archaeological Investigations, Southern Illinois University, Carbondale.

————. 2001. Grenades /Tompion! MS on file, Center for Archaeological Investigations, Southern Illinois University, Carbondale (dated July 6, 2001).

Newton, Arthur P. 1914. *The Colonising Activities of the English Puritans*. New Haven: Yale University Press.

————. 1933. *The European Nations in the West Indies, 1493–1688*. London: A and C Black.

Nickell, Joe. 2000. The Secrets of Oak Island. *Skeptical Inquirer* (March/April). 24(2): 14–19.

Noël Hume, Ivor. 1967. Rhenish Gray Stonewares in Colonial America. *Magazine Antiques* 92(3):349–53.

————. 1978. *A Guide to Artifacts of Colonial America*. New York: Alfred A. Knopf.

————. 1982. *A Guide to Artifacts of Colonial America*. New York: Vintage Books.

Nuttall, Thomas. 1819. *A Journal of Travels in the Arkansas Territory*. Philadelphia: Thos. W. Palmer.

O'Connor, D'Arcy. 1987. Treasure Hunt, Adventurers Still Try to Get to the Bottom of Fabled Money Pit. *Wall Street Journal*, July 20, p. 1.

Oertling, Thomas J. 1996. *Ships' Bilge Pumps: A History of Their Development, 1500–1900*. College Station: Texas A&M University Press.

Offen, Karl H. 2000. British Logwood Extraction from the Mosquitia: The Origin of a Myth. *Hispanic American Historical Review* 80:113–35.

Oldmixon, John. 1969. *The British Empire in America*. New York: Augustus M. Kelley Publishers.

Olds, Dorris L. 1976. *Texas Legacy from the Gulf: A Report on 16th-Century Shipwreck Materials Recovered from the Texas Tidelands*. Publication No. 2. Austin: Texas Antiquities Committee.

Pares, Richard. 1936. *War and Trade in the West Indies*. Oxford: Clarendon Press.

Parish, James Robert, 1995. *Pirates and Seafaring Swashbucklers on the Hollywood Screen*. Jefferson, N.C.: McFarland and Company, Publishers,

Parry, J. H., and Philip Sherlock. 1971. *A Short History of the West Indies*. 3rd ed. New York: St. Martin's Press.

Parsons, James J. 1956. *San Andres and Providencia: English-Speaking Islands in the Western Caribbean*. University of California Publications in Geography, 12(1). Berkeley: University of California Press.

Patten, David. 2000. Guns against the French: Late Short Land and India Pattern Muskets for the Ordnance. *Man at Arms* 21(1):18–28.

Pawson, Michael, and David Buisseret. 2000. *Port Royal, Jamaica*. Kingston, Jamaica: University of the West Indies Press.

Peal, Christopher A. 1971. *British Pewter and Britannia Metal for Pleasure and Investment*. New York and London: Peebles Press.

Pearson, Charles E., and Paul E. Hoffman. 1995. *The Last Voyage of Nuevo Constante: The Wreck and Recovery of an Eighteenth-Century Spanish Ship Off the Louisiana Coast*. Baton Rouge and London: Louisiana State University Press.

Peck, John Mason. 1823. *A Gazetteer of Illinois*. Philadelphia: Grigg and Elliot.

Pennell, C. R., ed. 2001. *Bandits at Sea*. New York: New York University Press.

Pennsylvania. 1718. Pirate Vessel Inventory. *Minutes of the Provincial Council of Pennsylvania* vol. 3, p. 53. Philadelphia, 1852. Reprint, New York: AMS Press, 1968.

————. 1840. *Minutes of the Provincial Council of Pennsylvania, May 31, 1717–January 23, 1735–36*. Vol. 3. Harrisburg. Pa.: Theophilus Fenn.

Pere, Nuri. 1968. *Coins of the Ottoman Empire*. Istanbul, no. 429.

Peterson, Harold L. 1969. *Round Shot and Rammers: An Introduction to Muzzle-Loading Land Artillery in the United States*. South Bend, Ind.: South Bend Replicas.

Peterson, Mendel. 1973. *History under the Sea: A Handbook for Underwater Exploration*. Washington, D.C.: Mendel Peterson.

Peterson, M. J. 1989. An Historical Perspective on the Incidence of Piracy. In *Piracy at Sea*, edited by Eric Ellen, pp. 41–60. Publication No. 455. Paris: ICC International Maritime Bureau and Woods Hole Oceanographic Institution.

Petruccio, Steven James. 1995. *Create Your Own Pirate Adventure Sticker Picture*. Toronto: General Publishing Company.

Petsche, Jerome E. 1974. *The Steamboat Bertrand*. Washington, D.C.: Government Printing Office.

Phillips, Carla Rahn. 1986. *Six Galleons for the King of Spain: Imperial Defense in the Early Seventeenth Century*. Baltimore: Johns Hopkins University Press.

Pidgeon, William. 1858. *Translations of De-Coo-Dah and Antiquarian Researches*. New York: Horace Thayer.

Pilkey, Orrin H., and Brian D. Bornhold. 1970. Gold Distribution on the Carolina Continental Margin: A Preliminary Report. In *U.S. Geological Survey Professional Paper 700–C*, pp. C30–C34. Durham, N.C.: U.S. Geological Survey.

Pirate and Traveler: A World Geography Game. 1953. Milton Bradley, Co., Springfield, Mass. Game.

Pitot, Albert. 1905. *T'Eylandt Mauritius, Port-Louis, Ile Maurice*. Port Louis: Esclapon, 19.

Pope, Peter. 1989. Historical Archaeology and the Demand for Alcohol in 17th-Century Newfoundland. *Acadiensis* 19(1):72–90.

Price, R., and Keith Muckelroy. 1974, The Second Season of Work on the *Kennemerland* Site, 1973: An Interim Report. *International Journal of Nautical Archaeology* 3:257–68.

Priddy, Antony. 1975. The 17th- and 18th-Century Settlement Pattern of Port Royal. *Jamaica Journal* 9(2 and 3):8–10.

Priest, Josiah. 1838. *American Antiquities and Discoveries in the West*. Albany: Hoffman and White.

Prigge, Daniel. 1973. *History of the Mouth of the Cache River*. Prepared for Mound City, Illinois, through Funding Provided by the Department of Local Government Affairs.

Public Records of Bermuda. Par-la-Ville, Hamilton, Bermuda. Arbre généalogique de J. Bowen.

Public Records Office Chancery Lane, London. High Court of Admiralty (H.C.A.) I-16, part 1, piece 41 et 42: Déposition de John Oneley, un marin du "*Speaker*."

Public Records Office, National Archives, Colonial Office, London. 1699. CO 5:860, no. 64xxv. Narrative of William Kidd, July 7, 1699.

———. 1742a. CO 700/British Honduras 2. A Map of Ruatan or Rattan. Surveyed by Lieutenant Henry Barnsley.

———. 1742b. Jamaica Board of Trade, Trelawny to Duke of Newcastle, December 19, 1742. 137/24.

———. 1745. Caulfield to Trelawney, September 30, 1745. 137/48.

———. 1749. Reports in Regard to Evacuating Rattan, and Leaving a Detachment on the Mosquito Shore. 137/48.

———. 1775. CO 700/British Honduras 8. A Map of Ruatan or Roatan. Surveyed by Lieutenant Henry Barnsley with improvements by Thomas Jefferys.

Purchas, Samuel. 1905–7. *Hakluytus Postumus or Purchas His Pilgrims* (1625). 20 vols. New York: Macmillan.

Pyle, Howard, 1921. *The Book of Pirates*. New York: Harper and Brothers.

Raban, Avner. 1971. *The Shipwreck of Sharm-el-Sheikh*. Long Island City, N.Y.: Archaeology Magazine.

Rankin, Hugh F. 1960. *The Pirates of Colonial North Carolina*. Raleigh: Division of Archives and History, North Carolina Department of Cultural Resources.

———. 1969. *The Golden Age of Piracy*. Williamsburg, Va.: Colonial Williamsburg, Inc.

Rediker, Marcus. 1987. *Between the Devil and the Deep Blue Sea: Merchant Seamen, Pirates, and the Anglo-American World, 1700–1750*. New York: Cambridge University Press.

Reiss, Warren, William A. Baryreuther, and Robert Cembrola. 1985. The Widdah Investigation: Satisfying Both Archaeological and Salvage Interests. In *Proceedings of the Sixteenth Conference on Underwater Archaeology*, edited by Paul F. Johnston, p. 96. Special Publication Series No. 4. Society for Historical Archaeology.

Reitz, Elizabeth J., and Margaret Scarry. 1985. *Reconstructing Historic Subsistence, with an Example from Sixteenth-Century Spanish Florida*. Special Publication Series No. 3. Tucson, Ariz.: Society for Historical Archaeology.

Reuters. 2002. Sales of Pirated Music Up 50%. *San Jose (California) Mercury News*, June 12.

Riff, Adolphe. 1972. European Continental Pewter, Part VI: The Pewter of France from the Sixteenth to the Nineteenth Century. In *National Types of Old Pewter*, pp. 76–78. Princeton: Pyne Press.

Ritchie, Robert C. 1986a. *Captain Kidd and the War against the Pirates*. Cambridge, Mass.: Harvard University Press,

———. 1986b. *Pirates: Myths and Realities*. James Ford Bell Lectures, No. 23. Minneapolis: University of Minnesota.

Robert, Sieur. 1730. Description en Général et en Détail de l'Isle de Madagascar. [SH 196 No. 3755.] Manuscript book in the Service Historique de la Marine, Paris.

Robinson Crusoe. 1962. Tale Spinners for Children UAC 11015. New York: United Artists Records, Inc. Recording.

Rocca, Mo. 1995. *Salty Dog* (teleplay). The Adventures of Wishbone. Richardson, Tex.: Big Feats! Entertainment. Recording.

Rodger, N.A.M. 1986. *The Wooden World*. Glasgow, Scotland: Fontana Press, William Collins Sons and Company.

Rogozinski, Jan. 2000. *Honor among Thieves*. Mechanicsburg, Pa.: Stackpole Books.

Rothert, Otto. 1924. *The Outlaws of Cave-in-Rock*. Cleveland, Ohio: A. H. Clark Co.

Rowland, Dunbar. 1917. *Official Letter Books of W.C.C. Claiborne, 1801–1816, Volume I*. Jackson, Miss.: State Department of Archives and History.

Rule, Margaret H. 1982. *The Mary Rose: The Excavation and Raising of Henry VIII's Flagship*. Annapolis, Md.: Naval Institute Press.

Russell, Carl P. 1980. *Guns on the Early Frontiers: A History of Firearms from Colonial Times through the Years of the Western Fur Trade*. Lincoln: University of Nebraska Press.

Sabatini, Rafael. 1915. *The Sea Hawk*. Philadelphia: Lippincott.

———. 1922. *Captain Blood: His Odyssey*. New York: Houghton Mifflin.

———. 1932. *The Black Swan*. New York: Houghton Mifflin.

Saint-Rémy, Pierre Surirey de. 1702. *Memoires d'artillerie*. Amsterdam: P. Mortier. Reprint, New York: Mt. Vernon, 1939.

Saltus, Allen R., and Charles E. Pearson. 1990. *Remote Sensing Survey of Two Borrow Areas for the Grand Isle and Vicinity Project, Jefferson Parish, Louisiana*. Submitted to the New Orleans District, U.S. Army Corps of Engineers, New Orleans.

Sands, A. L. 1818. Inventory of Pirates Property. A. L. Sands Papers, Yale University, New Haven, Conn.

Sauer, Carl Ortwin. 1966. *The Early Spanish Main*. Berkeley: University of California Press.

———. 1971. *Sixteenth Century North America*. Berkeley: University of California Press.

Savannah. 1814. *Republican Savannah (Georgia) and Evening Ledger*, August 20.

Sawyer, A. 1849. Journal of a Trip on a Flatboat from Evansville. Manuscripts Department, Lilly Library, Indiana University, Bloomington.

Saxon, Lyle. 1930. *The Buccaneer* (comic book). Classics Illustrated, no. 148. New York: Gilberton Company, Inc.

———. 1930. *Lafitte the Pirate*. New Orleans: Century Company.

———. 1999. *Lafitte the Pirate*. Gretna: Pelican Publishing Company.

Scheiber, Harry N. 1969. The Ohio-Mississippi Flatboat Trade: Some Reconsiderations. In *The Frontier in American Development*, edited by David M. Ellis, pp. 277–98. Ithaca and New York: Cornell University Press.

Schultz, Christian. 1810. *Travels on an Inland Voyage*. New York: Isaac Riley.

Schuyler, Robert L. 1977. The Spoken Word, the Written Word, Observed Behavior and Preserved Behavior: The Contexts Available to the Archaeologist. *The Conference on Historical Site Archaeology Papers* 10(2):99–120.

Schwegman, John. 2000. Ohio River Flatboat. *Springhouse* 2:23–25.

Scott Cummings, Linda. 1999. Analysis of Hair/Fiber Samples from Shipwreck Site 0003BUI, *Queen Anne's Revenge*. Ms. on file, Paleo Research Labs Technical Report 99–44, Golden, Colo.

Shaughnessy, Carol. 1995. The Archaeology of the *Henrietta Marie*. In *A Slave Ship Speaks: The Wreck of the Henrietta Marie*. Key West, Fla.: Mel Fisher Maritime Heritage Society.

Shepherd, James F., and Gary M. Walton. 1966. *Shipping, Maritime Trade, and the Economic Development of Colonial North America*. Cambridge: Cambridge University Press.

Ships and Boats Stand Up Lotto. 1955. New York: Samuel Gabriel Sons and Co. Game.

Shute, Nancy. 2002. Kidding about the Captain, He Rarely Buried Gold. Still, We Look. *U.S. News and World Report* (August 26–September 2):52.

Skenback, Urban. 1983. *Sjofolk ock Knektar pa Wasa*. Wasastudier 11. Stockholm: Statens Sjohistoriska Museum.

Skowronek, Russell K. 1984. Trade Patterns of 18th-Century Frontier New Spain: The 1733 *Flota* and St. Augustine. In *Volumes in Historical Archaeology*, edited by S. South. Conference on Historic Sites Archaeology. Columbia: South Carolina Institute of Archaeology and Anthropology.

———. 1987. Ceramics and Commerce: The 1554 *Flota* Revisited. *Historical Archaeology* 21(2):101–11.

———. 1989. A New Europe in the New World: Hierarchy: Continuity and Change in the Spanish Sixteenth-Century Colonization of Hispaniola and Florida. Ph.D. dissertation, Department of Anthropology, Michigan State University, East Lansing.

———. 1992. Empire and Ceramics: The Changing Role of Illicit Trade in Spanish America. *Historical Archaeology* 26(1):109–18.

———. 2002. Global Economics in the Creation and Maintenance of the Spanish Colonial Empire. In *Social Dimensions in the Economic Process*, edited by Norbert Dannhaeuser and Cynthia Werner, pp. 295–310. Research in Economic Anthropology, vol. 21. Orlando: Elsevier.

Skowronek, Russell K., Richard Johnson, Richard Vernon, and George Fischer. 1987. The Legare Anchorage Shipwreck Site—Grave of HMS *Fowey*. *International Journal of Nautical Archaeology* 16(4):313–24.

Smith, Alice C. 1997. Personal communication. Audubon subdivision resident, Wilmington, N.C.

Smith, Greg C. 1995. Indians and Africans at Puerto Real: The Ceramic Evidence. In *Puerto Real: The Archaeology of a Sixteenth-Century Spanish Town in Hispaniola*, edited by Kathleen Deagan, pp. 335–76. Gainesville: University Press of Florida.

Smith, Hale G. 1949. *Two Archaeological Sites in Brevard County, Florida*. Florida Anthropological Society Publication No. 1. Gainesville.

Smith, Roger C. 1988. Treasure Ships of the Spanish Main: The Iberian-American Maritime Empires. In *Ships and Shipwrecks of the Americas: A History Based on Underwater Archaeology*, edited by George F. Bass, pp. 85–90. London: Thames and Hudson.

South, Stanley. 1977. *Method and Theory in Historical Archaeology*. New York: Academic Press.

———. 1979. *The Search for Santa Elena on Parris Island, South Carolina*. Research Manuscript Series 150. Columbia: University of South Carolina, South Carolina Institute of Archaeology and Anthropology.

———. 1980. *The Discovery of Santa Elena*. Research Manuscript Series 165. Columbia: University of South Carolina, Institute of Archaeology and Anthropology.

———. 1982. *Exploring Santa Elena 1981*. Research Manuscript Series 184. Columbia: University of South Carolina, South Carolina Institute of Archaeology and Anthropology.

———. 1983. *Revealing Santa Elena 1982*. Research Manuscript Series 188. Columbia: University of South Carolina, South Carolina Institute of Archaeology and Anthropology.

———. 1984. *Testing Archaeological Sampling Methods at Fort San Felipe 1983*. Research Manuscript Series 190. Columbia: University of South Carolina, South Carolina Institute of Archaeology and Anthropology.

———. 1985. *Excavation of the Casa Fuerte and Wells at Fort San Felipe 1984*. Research Manuscript Series 196. Columbia: University of South Carolina, South Carolina Institute of Archaeology and Anthropology.

South, Stanley, Russell K. Skowronek, and R. E. Johnson. 1988. *Spanish Artifacts from Santa Elena*. Anthropological Studies 7, Occasional Papers of the South Carolina Institute of Archaeology and Anthropology, Columbia: University of South Carolina.

Southack, Cyprian. 1717. Journal of Cyprian Southack at Cape Cod, May 1–May 13, 1717. Massachusetts Archives, vol. 38, Journals 1695–1767.

South Carolina Historical (and Genealogical) Magazine. 1983. *South Carolina Genealogies: Articles from the South Carolina Historical (and Genealogical) Magazine, vol. IV (Rhett–Wragg)*. Spartanburg, S.C.: Reprint Company, Publishers.

Staff. 2003. Alleged Software Pirate Arrested. *San Jose (California) Mercury News*, May 22.

Stará, Dagmar. 1977. *Pewter Marks of the World*. London: Hamlyn.

Starling, Edmund L. 1887. *History of Henderson County, Kentucky*. Henderson, Ky.: n.p.

Stedman, Captain J. G. 1796. *Narrative of a Five Years' Expedition, against the Revolted Negroes of Surinam, in Guiana*. 2 vols. London: J. Johnson.

Steffy, J. Richard. 1994. *Wooden Ship Building and the Interpretation of Shipwrecks*. College Station: Texas A&M University Press.

Stenuit, Robert. 1974. Early Relics of the VOC Trade from Shetland: The Wreck of the Flute *Lastdrager* Lost off Yell, 1653. *International Journal of Nautical Archaeology* 3:213–56.

Stevenson, Robert Louis. 1949a. *Treasure Island* (1883). New York: Random House.

———. 1949b. *Treasure Island* (comic book). Classics Illustrated, no. 64. New York: Gilberton.

———. 1965. *Treasure Island*. New York: Signet, New American Library.

Stewart, Tamara. 2000. Evidence Mounts for Blackbeard's *Queen Anne's Revenge*: Artifacts Recovered from the Shipwreck Have Early 18th-Century Date. *American Archaeology* 4(4):11.

Stites, Roxanne. 2002. Software Piracy Sweep Was 2 Years in the Making. *San Jose (California) Mercury News*, April 20.

Stone, Edmund. 1723. *The Construction and Principal Uses of Mathematical Instruments. Translated from the French of M. Bion, Chief Instrument-Maker to the French King, to Which Is Added, The Construction and Uses of Such Instruments as Are Omitted by M. Bion; Particularly Those Invented or Improved by the English*. London. Reprint, Mendham, N.J.: Astragal Press, 1995.

Stone, Lyle M. 1970. Formal Classification and the Analysis of Historic Artifacts. *Historical Archaeology* 4:90–102.

———. 1974. *Fort Michilimackinac 1715–1781: An Archaeological Perspective on the Revolutionary Frontier*. East Lansing: Michigan State University.

Strickland, Brad. 1997. *Salty Dog*. The Adventures of Wishbone. Allen, Tex.: Big Red Chair Books.

Strong, W. D. 1933. Archaeological Investigation in Bay Islands, Honduras. *The Smithsonian Miscellaneous Collections* 92 (14). Washington, D.C.

Sugden, John. 1979. Jean Lafitte and the British Offer of 1814. *Louisiana History* 22(2): 159–67.

Suggs, Allison. 2004. Channel Movements over Wreckage Site 31CR314. Final Project for Youth Advocacy and Involvement Internship, Morehead City, N.C.

Sullivan, George. 1994. *Slave Ship: The Story of the Henrietta Marie*. New York: Cobblehill Books, Dutton.

Sunken Treasure Game. 1948. Salem, Mass.: Parker Brothers, Inc. Game.

Tanguy, Jean. 1956. *Le Commerce du Port de Nantes au milieu du XVIe siècle*. Paris: Ecole Pratique des Hautes-Etudes.

Tannehill, Ivan Ray. *Hurricanes: Their Nature and History—Particularly Those of the West Indies and the Southern Coasts of the United States*. 8th ed. Princeton: Princeton University Press.

Tannenbaum, Edward R. 1965. *European Civilization since the Middle Ages*. New York: John Wiley and Sons.

Taylor, John. 1688. Present State of the Island of Jamaica (1686–87). Unpublished manuscript at the National Library of Jamaica, Kingston, Jamaica.

Temperley, Harold W. V. 1909. The Causes of the War of Jenkins' Ear, 1939. *Transactions of the Royal Historical Society*, 3rd series, 3:197–236.

Tepaske, John. 1964. *The Governorship of Spanish Florida*. Durham, N.C.: Duke University Press.

Thomas, Isaac. 1714. Deposition by Captain Isaac Thomas of the *Concorde of Nantes* [July 19, 1714]. Marine B 4576.

Thompson, J. Eric S. 1988. *The Maya of Belize: Historical Chapters since Columbus.* Benque Viejo del Carmen, Belize: Cubola Productions.

Thompson, Julie, and Browsicnie Macintosh. 1996. *A Pirate's Life for Me!* Watertown, Mass.: Charlesbridge Publishing.

Thwaites, Reuben Gold, ed. 1895. *Chronicles of Border Warfare, by Alexander Scott Withers.* Cincinnati: Robert Clarke Company.

Thwaites, Reuben, and Louise Phelps Kellogg. 1912. *Frontier Defense on the Upper Ohio, 1777–1778.* Madison: Wisconsin Historical Society.

Tidewater Atlantic Research. 1998. *Underwater Archaeological Remote Sensing Survey and Site Investigation Adjacent to Radio Island, Morehead City, North Carolina.* Washington, N.C.: Tidewater Atlantic Research.

Toussaint, Auguste, 1956. *Bibliography of Mauritius.* Port Louis: Esclapon.

Trade Winds: Caribbean Sea Game. 1960. Salem, Mass.: Parker Brothers, Inc. Game.

Treasure Island. 1961. Tale Spinners for Children UAC 11013. New York: United Artists Records, Inc. Recording.

Trembanis, Arthur C., and Jesse E. McNinch. 2003. Predicting Scour and Maximum Settling Depths of Shipwrecks: A Numeric Simulation of the Fate of *Queen Anne's Revenge.* In *Proceedings of Coastal Sediments '03.* Clearwater Beach, Fla.: ASCE Press.

Tuck, James A. l985. Excavations at Red Bay, Labrador 1977–1984. In *Proceedings of the 16th Conference on Underwater Archaeology,* pp. 102–4. Special Publication Series No. 4. Tucson, Ariz.: Society for Historical Archaeology.

Tudor, Silke, 2003. All Things Piratical, Pirates Be Cool (Yarrrgh!). *SF Weekly,* March 12–18, pp. 23–30.

Turley, Hans. 1999. *Rum, Sodomy and the Lash.* New York: New York University Press.

Twain, Mark, 1946. *The Adventures of Tom Sawyer* (1875). New York: Grosset and Dunlap, Publishers.

Uring, Captain Nathaniel. 1726. *A History of the Voyages and Travels of Captain Nathaniel Uring.* London: W. Wilkins.

Virginia Gazette. 1779. *Virginia Gazette* (Williamsburg), October 2.

Vogel, Robert C. 1990. Jean Laffite, the Baratarians, and the Historical Geography of Piracy in the Gulf of Mexico. *Gulf Coast Historical Review* 5(2):64–77.

———. 2000. Jean Lafitte, the Baratarians, and the Battle of New Orleans: A Reappraisal. *Louisiana History* 61(3):261–76.

Wagner, Mark J. 2001. *The Windrose Site: An Early Nineteenth Century Potawatomi Village in the Kankakee River Valley of Illinois.* Reports of Investigations No. 56. Springfield: Illinois State Museum.

———. 2003. *The Flatboat* America *(11Pu280): An Early Nineteenth Century Ohio River Flatboat Wreck in Pulaski, Illinois.* Technical Report 03-1. Carbondale: Center for Archaeological Investigations, Southern Illinois University Carbondale.

Wagner, Mark J., and Mary R. McCorvie. 1992. *The Archaeology of the Old Landmark.* Kampsville, Ill.: Center for American Archaeology.

———. 2003. The Clarida Hollow Site: An Early Historic Period Pictograph Site in Southern Illinois. Paper Presented at the Eastern States Rock Art Research Association Meetings, March 20–23, Huntsville, Ala.

Walker, Iain. 1977. *Clay Tobacco Pipes with Particular Reference to the Bristol Industry.* 4 vols. Studies in Archaeology, Architecture, and History. Ottawa: Parks Canada.

Wallerstein, Immanuel. 1974. *The Modern World-System I: Capitalist Agriculture and the Origins of the European World-Economy in the Sixteenth Century*. New York: Academic Press.

———. 1980. *The Modern World-System II: Mercantilism and the Consolidation of the European World-Economy, 1600–1750*. New York: Academic Press.

Ward, Cheryl. 2000. *The Sadana Island Shipwreck*. Houston, Tex.: Saudi Aramco World.

Waters, David W. 1958. *The Art of Navigation in England in Elizabethan and Early Stuart Times*. New Haven: Yale University Press.

Waters, Gifford. 1997. Exploratory Excavations at Florida's First Spanish Fort: SJ-34. M.A. paper, Anthropology, Gainesville, University of Florida.

Watts, Gordon P., Jr. n.d. A Remote Sensing Survey and Reconnaissance Investigations to Identify and Assess Targets Located along Range A, a Bar Channel Widener, a Channel Extension, and Two Spoil Deposits at Beaufort Inlet, North Carolina. Contract Report DACW54-91-D-0011 submitted to the U.S. Army Corps of Engineers, Wilmington, N.C.

———. 1997. Underwater Remote Sensing Survey and Diver Inspection near Beaufort Inlet, North Carolina. Contract Report DACW54-96-D-0001 submitted to the U.S. Army Corps of Engineers, Wilmington, N.C.

Webster, Donovan. 1999. Pirates of the *Whydah*. *National Geographic* (May): 64–77.

Wede, Karl. 1972. *The Ship's Bell: Its History and Romance*. New York: South Street Seaport Museum.

Weibust, Knut. 1969. *Deep Sea Sailors: A Study in Maritime Ethnology*. Stockholm: Kungl. Boktryckeriet P. A. Norstedt and Söner.

Wellmann, Paul I. 1964. *Spawn of Evil*. Garden City, N.Y.: Doubleday and Company.

Wells, John T., and Jesse E. McNinch. 2001. Reconstructing Shoal and Channel Configuration in Beaufort Inlet: 300 Years of Change at the Site of *Queen Anne's Revenge*. *Southeastern Geology* 40(1):11–18.

West, Robert C., and John P. Augelli. 1976. *Middle America, Its Land and Peoples*. Englewood Cliffs, N.J.: Prentice Hall.

White, Karli. 1999. Analysis of Animal Bones Recovered from Beaufort Inlet Shipwreck 31CR314. MS on file, Department of Zooarchaeology, Illinois State Museum, Springfield.

White, Richard. 1991. *The Middle Ground: Indians, Empires, and Republics in the Great Lakes Region, 1650–1815*. Cambridge: Cambridge University Press.

Wilcoxen, Charlotte. 1987. *Dutch Trade and Ceramics in America in the Seventeenth Century*. Albany: Albany Institute of History and Art.

Wilde-Ramsing, Mark. 1998. A Report on the 1997 Archaeological Investigations at North Carolina Shipwreck Site 0003BUI. In *Underwater Archaeology Proceedings of the Society for Historical Archaeology, Atlanta, Georgia*, edited by Lawrence Babits, Catherine Fach, and Ryan Harris. pp. 54–60. Society for Historical Archaeology.

Williams, Eric, ed. 1963. *Documents of West Indian History, 1492–1655*. Vol. 1. Port-of-Spain, Trinidad: PNM Publishing Co., Ltd.

Willis, Raymond F. 1976. The Archaeology of 16th-Century Nueva Cadiz. M.A. thesis, Department of Anthropology, University of Florida, Gainesville.

———. 1995. Empire and Architecture at Puerto Real: The Archaeology of Public Space. In *Puerto Real: The Archaeology of a Sixteenth-Century Spanish Town in Hispaniola*, edited by Kathleen Deagan, pp. 141–66. Gainesville: University Press of Florida.

Wilmington News. 1929. *Wilmington News,* December 30. From the William M. Reaves Collection, New Hanover County Library, Wilmington, N.C.

Wolf, Eric R. 1982. *Europe and the People without History.* Berkeley: University of California Press.

Works Progress Administration of Louisiana. 1940. Survey of Federal Archives in Louisiana. Typescript, Louisiana Collection, Howard-Tilton Memorial Library, Tulane University, New Orleans.

Wray, Ed. 2001. Anti-Piracy Drills Help Battle Threat. *Lansing (Michigan) State Journal,* November 11.

Wright, Irene A. 1932. *Spanish Documents Concerning English Voyages to the Spanish Main, 1569–1580.* Series 11. London: Hakluyt Society.

Zacks, Richard. 2002. *The Pirate Hunter.* New York: Theia.

Zahedieh, Nuala. 1986a. The Merchants of Port Royal, Jamaica, and the Spanish Contraband Trade, 1655–1692. *William and Mary Quarterly,* 3rd series, 43(4) (October 1986):570–93.

———. 1986b. Trade, Plunder, and Development in Jamaica 1655–1689. *Economic History Review,* 2nd series, 39 (2):205–22.

Contributors

Lawrence E. Babits is professor in the Maritime Studies Program of the Department of History at East Carolina University.

Matthew Brenckle is a graduate student in the Maritime Studies Program of the Department of History at East Carolina University.

John de Bry is director of the Center for Historical Archaeology in Melbourne, Florida.

Charles R. Ewen is professor in the Department of Anthropology at East Carolina University.

Joan M. Exnicios is staff archaeologist for the Planning, Programs and Project Management, Division of the U.S. Army Corps of Engineers in New Orleans, Louisiana.

Daniel Finamore is Russell W. Knight Curator at the Peabody Essex Museum in Salem, Massachusetts, and arts editor of the *American Neptune*.

Christopher E. Hamilton is cultural resource manager/coordinator for Native American Affairs for the U.S. Army Infantry Center Directorate of Public Works at Fort Benning, Georgia.

Donny L. Hamilton is professor in the Nautical Archaeology Program of the Department of Anthropology at Texas A&M University.

Joshua B. Howard is a graduate student in the Maritime Studies Program of the Department of History at East Carolina University.

Patrick Lizé is a fellow of the Centro Nacional de Arqueologia Náutica e Subaquática in Lisbon, Portugal.

Wayne R. Lusardi is staff archaeologist for the Thunder Bay National Marine Sanctuary and Underwater Preserve in Alpena, Michigan.

J. David McBride is a consulting archaeologist for the Kentucky Archaeological Survey.

Mary R. McCorvie is staff archaeologist for the Shawnee National Forest, USDA Forest Service.

Russell K. Skowronek is associate professor in the Department of Anthropology and Sociology at Santa Clara University.

Mark J. Wagner is staff archaeologist for the Center for Archaeological Investigations at Southern Illinois University, Carbondale.

Mark U. Wilde-Ramsing is director of the *Queen Anne's Revenge* Project in the Underwater Archaeology Unit of the North Carolina Division of Archives and History.

Index

Page numbers in *italics* refer to figures and tables.

This book was set in 9.5/12.5 Sabon with Gill Sans display.